THE
CHRIST

Humbly he came,
Veiling his horrible Godhead in the shape
Of man, scorned by the world, his name unheard
Save by the rabble of his native town,
Even as a parish demagogue. He led
The crowd; he taught them justice, truth, and peace,
In semblance; but he lit within their souls
The quenchless flames of zeal, and blessed the sword
He brought on earth to satiate with the blood
Of truth and freedom his malignant soul.
At length his mortal frame was led to death.
I stood beside him; on the torturing cross
No pain assailed his unterrestrial sense;
And yet he groaned. Indignantly I summed
The massacres and miseries which his name
Had sanctioned in my country, and I cried
"Go! Go!" in mockery.

—*Shelley.*

THE
CHRIST

*A Critical Review
and Analysis of
the Evidence
of His Existence*

JOHN E. REMSBERG

 Prometheus Books

59 John Glenn Drive
Amherst, NewYork 14228-2197

Published 1994 by Prometheus Books
59 John Glenn Drive, Amherst, New York 14228-2197,
716-691-0133, FAX: 716-691-0137.

Library of Congress Cataloging-in-Publication Data

Remsburg, John E. (John Eleazer), 1846–1919.
    The Christ : a critical review and analysis of the evidence of his existence /
John E. Remsburg.
        p.   cm.
    Originally published: New York : The Truth Seeker Company, 1909.
    Includes bibliographical references and index.
    ISBN 0-87975-924-0 (alk. paper)
    1. Jesus Christ—Rationalistic interpretations. 2. Jesus Christ—
Historicity—Controversial literature. I. Title.
BT304.95.R46   1994
232.9′08—dc20   94-32833
                                                                            CIP

Printed in the United States of America on acid-free paper.

Contents

Preface 7

1. Christ's Real Existence Impossible 11

2. Silence of Contemporary Writers 18

3. Christian Evidence 35

4. The Infancy of Christ 44

5. The Ministry of Christ 85

6. The Crucifixion of Christ 161

7. The Resurrection of Christ 223

8. His Character and Teachings 257

9. The Christ a Myth 327

10. Sources of the Christ Myth—Ancient Religions 334

11. Sources of the Christ Myth—Pagan Divinities 367

12. Sources of the Christ Myth—Conclusion 410

Index 421

Preface

"We must get rid of that Christ, we must get rid of that Christ!" So spake one of the wisest, one of the most lovable of men, Ralph Waldo Emerson. "If I had my way," said Thomas Carlyle, "the world would hear a pretty stern command—Exit Christ." Since Emerson and Carlyle spoke a revolution has taken place in the thoughts of men. The more enlightened of them are now rid of Christ. From their minds he has made his exit. To quote the words of Prof. Goldwin Smith, "The mighty and supreme Jesus, who was to transfigure all humanity by his divine wit and grace—this Jesus has flown." The supernatural Christ of the New Testament, the god of orthodox Christianity, is dead. But priestcraft lives and conjures up the ghost of this dead god to frighten and enslave the masses of mankind. The name of Christ has caused more persecutions, wars, and miseries than any other name has caused. The darkest wrongs are still inspired by it. The wails of anguish that went up from Kishenev, Odessa, and Bialystok still vibrate in our ears.

Two notable works controverting the divinity of Christ appeared in the last century, the *Leben Jesu* of Strauss, and the *Vie de Jesus* of Renan. Strauss in his work, one of the masterpieces of Freethought literature, endeavors to prove, and proves to the satisfaction of a majority of his readers, that Jesus Christ is a historical myth. This work possesses permanent value, but it was written for the scholar and not for the general reader. In the German and Latin versions, and in the admirable

7

English translation of Marian Evans (George Eliot), the citations from the Gospels—and they are many—are in Greek.

Renan's "Life of Jesus," written in Palestine, has had, especially in its abridged form, an immense circulation, and has been a potent factor in the dethronement of Christ. It is a charming book and displays great learning. But it is a romance, not a biography. The Jesus of Renan, like the Satan of Milton, while suggested by the Bible, is a modern creation. The warp is to be found in the Four Gospels, but the woof was spun in the brain of the brilliant Frenchman. Of this book Renan's fellow-countryman, Dr. Jules Soury, thus writes:

"It is to be feared that the beautiful, the 'divine,' dream, as he would say, which the eminent scholar experienced in the very country of the Gospel, will have the fate of the 'Joconda' of Da Vinci, and many of the religious pictures of Raphael and Michaelangelo. Such dreams are admirable, but they are bound to fade. . . . The Jesus who rises up and comes out from those old Judaizing writings (Synoptics) is truly no idyllic personage, no meek dreamer, no mild and amiable moralist; on the contrary, he is very much more of a Jew fanatic, attacking without measure the society of his time, a narrow and obstinate visionary, a half-lucid thaumaturge, subject to fits of passion, which caused him to be looked upon as crazy by his own people. In the eyes of his contemporaries and fellow-countrymen he was all that, and he is the same in ours."

Renan himself repudiated to a considerable extent his earlier views regarding Jesus. When he wrote his work he accepted as authentic the Gospel of John, and to this Gospel he was indebted largely for the more admirable traits of his hero. John he subsequently rejected. Mark he accepted as the oldest and most authentic of the Gospels. Alluding to Mark he says:

"It cannot be denied that Jesus is portrayed in this gospel not as a meek moralist worthy of our affection, but as a dreadful magician."

This volume on "The Christ" was written by one who recognizes in the Jesus of Strauss and Renan a transitional step, but not the ultimate step, between orthodox Christianity and radical Freethought. By the Christ is understood the Jesus of the New Testament. The Jesus of the New Testament is the Christ of Christianity. The Jesus of the New

Testament is a supernatural being. He is, like the Christ, a myth. He is the Christ myth. Originally the word *Christ,* the Greek for the Jewish *Messiah,* "the anointed," meant the office or title of a person, while Jesus was the name of the person on whom his followers had bestowed this title. Gradually the title took the place of the name, so that *Jesus, Jesus Christ,* and *Christ* became interchangeable terms—synonyms. Such they are to the Christian world, and such, by the law of common usage, they are to the secular world.

It may be conceded as possible, and even probable, that a religious enthusiast of Galilee, named Jesus, was the germ of this mythical Jesus Christ. But this is an assumption rather than a demonstrated fact. Certain it is, this person, if he existed, was not a realization of the Perfect Man, as his admirers claim. There are passages in the Gospels which ascribe to him a lofty and noble character, but these, for the most part, betray too well their Pagan origin. The dedication of temples to him and the worship of him by those who deny his divinity is as irrational as it will prove ephemeral. One of the most philosophic and one of the most far-seeing minds of Germany, Dr. Edward von Hartmann, says:

"When liberal Protestantism demands religious reverence for the *man* Jesus, it is disgusting and shocking. They cannot themselves believe that the respect in which Jesus is held by the people, and which they have made use of in such an unprotestant manner, can be maintained for any length of time after the nimbus of divinity has been destroyed, and they may reflect on the insufficiency of the momentary subterfuge. The Protestant principle, in its last consequences, disposes of all kinds of dogmatic authority in a remorseless manner, and its supporters must, whether they like it or not, dispense with the authority of Christ."

1

Christ's Real Existence Impossible

The reader who accepts as divine the prevailing religion of our land may consider this criticism on "The Christ" irreverent and unjust. And yet for man's true saviors I have no lack of reverence. For him who lives and labors to uplift his fellow men I have the deepest reverence and respect, and at the grave of him who upon the altar of immortal truth has sacrificed his life I would gladly pay the sincere tribute of a mourner's tears. It is not against the man Jesus that I write, but against the Christ Jesus of theology; a being in whose name an Atlantic of innocent blood has been shed; a being in whose name the whole black catalogue of crime has been exhausted; a being in whose name five hundred thousand priests are now enlisted to keep

> "Truth forever on the scaffold,
> Wrong forever on the throne."

Jesus of Nazareth, the Jesus of humanity, the pathetic story of whose humble life and tragic death has awakened the sympathies of millions, is a possible character and may have existed; but the Jesus of Bethlehem, the Christ of Christianity, is an impossible character and does not exist.

From the beginning to the end of this Christ's earthly career he is represented by his alleged biographers as a supernatural being endowed with superhuman powers. He is conceived without a natural father: "Now the birth of Jesus Christ was on this wise: When, as his mother Mary was espoused to Joseph, before they came together, she was found with child of the Holy Ghost" (Matt. i, 18).

His ministry is a succession of miracles. With a few loaves and fishes he feeds a multitude: "And when he had taken the five loaves and the two fishes, he looked up to heaven, and blessed and brake the loaves, and gave them to his disciples to set before them; and the two fishes divided he among them all. And they did all eat, and were filled. And they took up twelve baskets full of the fragments, and of the fishes. And they that did eat of the loaves were about five thousand men" (Mark vi, 41–44).

He walks for miles upon the waters of the sea: "And straightway Jesus constrained his disciples to get into a ship, and to go before him unto the other side, while he sent the multitudes away. And when he had sent the multitudes away, he went up into a mountain apart to pray; and when the evening was come, he was there alone. But the ship was now in the midst of the sea, tossed with waves; for the wind was contrary. And in the fourth watch of the night Jesus went unto them, walking on the sea" (Matt. xiv, 22–25).

He bids a raging tempest cease and it obeys him: "And there arose a great storm of wind, and the waves beat into the ship, so that it was now full. . . . And he arose, and rebuked the wind, and said unto the sea, Peace, be still. And the wind ceased, and there was a great calm" (Mark iv, 37 39).

He withers with a curse the barren fig tree: "And when he saw a fig tree in the way, he came to it, and found nothing thereon, but leaves only, and said unto it, Let no fruit grow on thee, henceforth, forever. And presently the fig tree withered away" (Matt. xxi, 19).

He casts out devils: "And in the synagogue there was a man, which had a spirit of an unclean devil. . . . And Jesus rebuked him, saying, Hold thy peace, and come out of him. And when the devil had thrown him in the midst, he came out of him and hurt him not" (Luke iv, 33, 35).

He cures the incurable: "And as he entered into a certain village, there met him ten men that were lepers, which stood afar off; and they lifted up their voices, and said, Jesus, Master, have mercy on us. And when he saw them, he said unto them, Go show yourselves unto the priests. And it came to pass, that, as they went, they were cleansed" (Luke xvii, 12–14).

He restores to life a widow's only son: "And when he came nigh to the gate of the city, behold, there was a dead man carried out, the only son of his mother, and she was a widow; and much people of the city were with her. And when the Lord saw her, he had compassion on her, and said unto her, Weep not. And he came and touched the bier; and they that bore him stood still. And he said, Young man, I say unto thee, Arise. And he that was dead sat up, and began to speak. And he delivered him to his mother" (Luke vii, 12–15).

He revivifies the decaying corpse of Lazarus: "Then said Jesus unto them plainly, Lazarus is dead. . . . Then when Jesus came, he found that he had lain in the grave four days already. . . . And when he had thus spoken, he cried with a loud voice, Lazarus, come forth. And he that was dead came forth" (John xi, 14–44).

At his crucifixion nature is convulsed, and the inanimate dust of the grave is transformed into living beings who walk the streets of Jerusalem: "Jesus, when he had cried again with a loud voice, yielded up the ghost. And, behold, the veil of the temple was rent in twain from the top to the bottom; and the earth did quake, and the rocks rent; and the graves were opened; and many bodies of the saints, which slept, arose, and came out of the graves after his resurrection, and went into the holy city, and appeared unto many" (Matt. xxvii, 50–53).

He rises from the dead: "And when Joseph had taken the body, he wrapped it in a clean linen cloth, and laid it in his own new tomb, which he had hewn out in the rock; and he rolled a great stone to the door of the sepulchre, and departed. . . . And, behold, there was a great earthquake; for the angel of the Lord descended from heaven, and came and rolled back the stone from the door. . . . And as they went to tell his disciples, behold, Jesus met them, saying, All hail" (Matt. xxvii, 59, 60; xxviii, 2, 9).

He ascends bodily into heaven: "And he led them out as far as to Bethany, and he lifted up his hands and blessed them. And it came to pass, while he blessed them, he was parted from them, and carried up into heaven" (Luke xxiv, 50, 51).

These and a hundred other miracles make up to a great extent this so-called Gospel History of Christ. To disprove the existence of these miracles is to disprove the existence of this Christ.

Canon Farrar makes this frank admission: "If miracles be incredible, Christianity is false. If Christ wrought no miracles, then the Gospels are untrustworthy" (*Witness of History to Christ,* p. 25).

Dean Mansel thus acknowledges the consequences of the successful denial of miracles: "The whole system of Christian belief with its evidences, . . . all Christianity in short, so far as it has any title to that name, so far as it has any special relation to the person or the teaching of Christ, is overthrown" (*Aids to Faith,* p. 3).

Dr. Westcott says: "The essence of Christianity lies in a miracle; and if it can be shown that a miracle is either impossible or incredible, all further inquiry into the details of its history is superfluous" (*Gospel of the Resurrection,* p. 34).

A miracle, in the orthodox sense of the term, is impossible and incredible. To accept a miracle is to reject a demonstrated truth. The world is governed, not by chance, not by caprice, not by special providences, but by the laws of nature; and if there be one truth which the scientist and the philosopher have established, it is this: THE LAWS OF NATURE ARE IMMUTABLE. If the laws of Nature are immutable, they cannot be suspended; for if they could be suspended, even by a god, they would not be immutable. A single suspension of these laws would prove their mutability. Now these alleged miracles of Christ required a suspension of Nature's laws; and the suspension of these laws being impossible the miracles were impossible, and not performed. If these miracles were not performed, then the existence of this supernatural and miracle-performing Christ, except as a creature of the human imagination, is incredible and impossible.

Hume's masterly argument against miracles has never been refuted: "A miracle is a violation of the laws of Nature; and as a firm and unalterable experience has established these laws, the proof against a miracle, from the very nature of the fact, is as entire as any argument from experience can possibly be imagined. Why is it more than probable that all men must die; that lead cannot of itself remain suspended in the air; that fire consumes wood, and is extinguished by water; unless it be that these events are found agreeable to the laws of Nature, and there is required a violation of these laws, or, in other words, a miracle, to prevent them? Nothing is esteemed a miracle if it ever happens in the common course of Nature. It is no miracle that a man, seemingly in good health, should die suddenly; because such a kind of death, though more unusual than any other, has yet been frequently observed to happen. But it is a miracle that a dead man should come to life; because that has never been observed in any age or country. There must, therefore, be a uniform experience against any miraculous event, otherwise the event would not merit the appellation. And as a uniform experience amounts to a proof, there is here a direct and full proof, from the nature of the fact, against the existence of any miracle" (*Essay on Miracles*).

Alluding to Christ's miracles, M. Renan, a reverential admirer of Jesus of Nazareth, says: "Observation, which has never been once falsified, teaches as that miracles never happen but in times and countries in which they are believed, and before persons disposed to believe them. No miracle ever occurred in the presence of men capable of testing its miraculous character. . . . It is not, then, in the name of this or that philosophy, but in the name of universal experience, that we banish miracles from history" (*Life of Jesus,* p. 29).

Christianity arose in what was preeminently a miracle-working age. Everything was attested by miracles, because nearly everybody believed in miracles and demanded them. Every religious teacher was a worker of miracles; and however trifling the miracle might be when wrought, in this atmosphere of unbounded credulity, the breath of exaggeration soon expanded it into marvelous proportions.

To show more clearly the character of the age which Christ illustrates, let us take another example, the Pythagorean teacher, Apollonius of Tyana, a contemporary of the Galilean. According to his biographers— and they are as worthy of credence as the Evangelists—his career, particularly in the miraculous events attending it, bore a remarkable resemblance to that of Christ. Like Christ, he was a divine incarnation; like Christ his miraculous conception was announced before his birth; like Christ he possessed in childhood the wisdom of a sage; like Christ he is said to have led a blameless life; like Christ his moral teachings were declared to be the best the world had known; like Christ he remained a celibate; like Christ he was averse to riches; like Christ he purified the religious temples; like Christ he predicted future events; like Christ he performed miracles, cast out devils, healed the sick, and restored the dead to life; like Christ he died, rose from the grave, ascended to heaven, and was worshiped as a god.

The Christian rejects the miraculous in Apollonius because it is incredible; the Rationalist rejects the miraculous in Christ for the same reason. In proof of the human character of the religion of Apollonius and the divine character of that of Christ it may be urged that the former has perished, while the latter has survived. But this, if it proves anything, proves too much. If the survival of Christianity proves its divinity, then the survival of the miracle-attested faiths of Buddhism and Mohammedanism, its powerful and flourishing rivals, must prove their divinity also. The religion of Apollonius languished and died because the conditions for its development were unfavorable; while the religions of Buddha, Christ, and Mohammed lived and thrived because of the propitious circumstances which favored their development.

With the advancement of knowledge the belief in the supernatural is disappearing. Those freed from Ignorance, and her dark sister, Superstition, know that miracles are myths. In the words of Matthew Arnold, "Miracles are doomed; they will drop out like fairies and witchcraft, from among the matter which serious people believe" (*Literature and Dogma*).

What proved the strength of Christianity in an age of ignorance is proving its weakness in an age of intelligence. Christian scholars themselves, recognizing the indefensibility and absurdity of miracles, endeavor to explain away the difficulties attending their acceptance by affirming that they are not real, but only apparent, violations of Nature's laws; thus putting the miracles of Christ in the same class with those performed by the jugglers of India and Japan. They resolve the supernatural into the natural, that the incredible may appear credible. With invincible logic and pitiless sarcasm Colonel Ingersoll exposes the lameness of this attempt to retain the shadow of the supernatural when the substance is gone:

"Believers in miracles should not try to explain them. There is but one way to explain anything, and that is to account for it by natural agencies. The moment you explain a miracle it disappears. You should not depend upon explanation, but assertion. You should not be driven from the field because the miracle is shown to be unreasonable. Neither should you be in the least disheartened if it is shown to be impossible. The possible is not miraculous."

Miracles must be dismissed from the domain of fact and relegated to the realm of fiction. A miracle, I repeat, is impossible. Above all this chief of miracles, The Christ, is impossible, and does not, and never did, exist.

2

Silence of Contemporary Writers

Another proof that the Christ of Christianity is a fabulous and not a historical character is the silence of the writers who lived during and immediately following the time he is said to have existed.

That a man named Jesus, an obscure religious teacher, the basis of this fabulous Christ, lived in Palestine about nineteen hundred years ago, may be true. But of this man we know nothing. His biography has not been written. A Renan and others have attempted to write it, but have failed—have failed because no materials for such a work exist. Contemporary writers have left us not one word concerning him. For generations afterward, outside of a few theological epistles, we find no mention of him.

The following is a list of writers who lived and wrote during the time, or within a century after the time, that Christ is said to have lived and performed his wonderful works:

Josephus	Arrian
Philo-Judaeus	Petronius
Seneca	Dion Pruseus
Pliny the Elder	Paterculus
Suetonius	Appian
Juvenal	Theon of Smyrna
Martial	Phlegon

18

Persius
Plutarch
Justus of Tiberius
Apollonius
Pliny the Younger
Tacitus
Quintilian
Lucanus
Epictetus
Silius Italicus
Statius
Ptolemy
Hermogones
Valerius Maximus

Pompon Mela
Quintius Curtius
Lucian
Pausanias
Valerius Flaccus
Florus Lucius
Favorinus
Phaedrus
Damis
Aulus Gellius
Columella
Dio Chrysostom
Lysias
Appion of Alexandria

Enough of the writings of the authors named in the foregoing list remains to form a library. Yet in this mass of Jewish and Pagan literature, aside from two forged passages in the works of a Jewish author, and two disputed passages in the works of Roman writers, there is to be found no mention of Jesus Christ.

Philo was born before the beginning of the Christian era, and lived until long after the reputed death of Christ. He wrote an account of the Jews covering the entire time that Christ is said to have existed on earth. He was living in or near Jerusalem when Christ's miraculous birth and the Herodian massacre occurred. He was there when Christ made his triumphal entry into Jerusalem. He was there when the crucifixion with its attendant earthquake, supernatural darkness, and resurrection of the dead took place—when Christ himself rose from the dead, and in the presence of many witnesses ascended into heaven. These marvelous events which must have filled the world with amazement, had they really occurred, were unknown to him. It was Philo who developed the doctrine of the Logos, or Word, and although this Word incarnate dwelt in that very land and in the presence of multitudes revealed himself and demonstrated his divine powers, Philo saw it not.

Josephus, the renowned Jewish historian, was a native of Judea. He was born in 37 A.D., and was a contemporary of the Apostles.

He was, for a time, Governor of Galilee, the province in which Christ lived and taught. He traversed every part of this province and visited the places where but a generation before Christ had performed his prodigies. He resided in Cana, the very city in which Christ is said to have wrought his first miracle. He mentions every noted personage of Palestine and describes every important event which occurred there during the first seventy years of the Christian era. But Christ was of too little consequence and his deeds too trivial to merit a line from this historian's pen.

Justus of Tiberius was a native of Christ's own country, Galilee. He wrote a history covering the time of Christ's reputed existence. This work has perished, but Photius, a Christian scholar and critic of the ninth century, who was acquainted with it, says: "He [Justus] makes not the least mention of the appearance of Christ, of what things happened to him, or of the wonderful works that he did" (Photius' *Bibliotheca,* code 33).

Judea, where occurred the miraculous beginning and marvelous ending of Christ's earthly career, was a Roman province, and all of Palestine is intimately associated with Roman history. But the Roman records of that age contain no mention of Christ and his works. The Greek writers of Greece and Alexandria, who lived not far from Palestine and who were familiar with its events, are silent also.

Josephus

Late in the first century Josephus wrote his celebrated work, *The Antiquities of the Jews,* giving a history of his race from the earliest ages down to his own time. Modern versions of this work contain the following passage:

"Now, there was about this time Jesus, a wise man, if it be lawful to call him a man, for he was a doer of wonderful works; a teacher of such men as receive the truth with pleasure. He drew over to him both many of the Jews, and many of the Gentiles. He was [the] Christ; and when Pilate, at the suggestion of the principal men amongst us, had condemned him to the cross, those that loved him at the first did not forsake him; for he appeared to them alive again the third day, as the divine prophets had foretold these and ten thousand other wonderful things concerning him; and the tribe of Christians, so named from him, are not extinct at this day" (Book XVIII, Chap. iii, sec. 3).

For nearly sixteen hundred years Christians have been citing this passage as a testimonial, not merely to the historical existence, but to the divine character of Jesus Christ. And yet a ranker forgery was never penned.

Its language is Christian. Every line proclaims it the work of a Christian writer. "If it be lawful to call him a man." "He was the Christ." "He appeared to them alive again the third day, as the divine prophets had foretold these and ten thousand other wonderful things concerning him." These are the words of a Christian, a believer in the divinity of Christ. Josephus was a Jew, a devout believer in the Jewish faith— the last man in the world to acknowledge the divinity of Christ. The inconsistency of this evidence was early recognized, and Ambrose, writing in the generation succeeding its first appearance (360 A.D.) offers the following explanation, which only a theologian could frame: "If the Jews do not believe us, let them, at least, believe their own writers. Josephus, whom they esteem a very great man, hath said this, and yet hath he spoken truth after such a manner; and so far was his mind wandered from the right way, that even he was not a believer as to what he himself said; but thus he spake, in order to deliver historical truth, because he thought it not lawful for him to deceive, while yet he was no believer, because of the hardness of his heart, and his perfidious intention."

Its brevity disproves its authenticity. Josephus' work is voluminous and exhaustive. It comprises twenty books. Whole pages are devoted to petty robbers and obscure seditious leaders. Nearly forty chapters are devoted to the life of a single king. Yet this remarkable being, the greatest product of his race, a being of whom the prophets foretold ten thousand wonderful things, a being greater than any earthly king, is dismissed with a dozen lines.

It interrupts the narrative. Section 2 of the chapter containing it gives an account of a Jewish sedition which was suppressed by Pilate with great slaughter. The account ends as follows: "There were a great number of them slain by this means, and others of them ran away wounded; and thus an end was put to this sedition." Section 4, as now numbered, begins with these words: "About the same time also another sad calamity put the Jews into disorder." The one section naturally and logically follows the other. Yet between these two closely connected paragraphs the one relating to Christ is placed; thus making the words, "another sad calamity," refer to the advent of this wise and wonderful being.

The early Christian fathers were not acquainted with it. Justin Martyr, Tertullian, Clement of Alexandria, and Origen all would have quoted this passage had it existed in their time. The failure of even one of these fathers to notice it would be sufficient to throw doubt upon its genuineness; the failure of all of them to notice it proves conclusively that it is spurious, that it was not in existence during the second and third centuries.

As this passage first appeared in the writings of the ecclesiastical historian, Eusebius, as this author openly advocated the use of fraud and deception in furthering the interests of the church, as he is known to have mutilated and perverted the text of Josephus in other instances, and as the manner of its presentation is calculated to excite suspicion, the forgery has generally been charged to him. In his *Evangelical Demonstration,* written early in the fourth century, after citing all the known evidences of Christianity, he thus introduces the Jewish historian: "Certainly the attestations I have already produced concerning our Savior may be sufficient. However, it may not be amiss, if, over and above, we make use of Josephus the Jew for a further witness" (Book III, p. 124).

Chrysostom and Photius both reject this passage. Chrysostom, a reader of Josephus, who preached and wrote in the latter part of the fourth century, in his defense of Christianity, needed this evidence, but was too honest or too wise to use it. Photius, who made a revision of Josephus, writing five hundred years after the time of Eusebius, ignores the passage, and admits that Josephus has made no mention of Christ.

Modern Christian scholars generally concede that the passage is a forgery. Dr. Lardner, one of the ablest defenders of Christianity, adduces the following arguments against its genuineness:

"I do not perceive that we at all want the suspected testimony to Jesus, which was never quoted by any of our Christian ancestors before Eusebius.

"Nor do I recollect that Josephus has anywhere mentioned the name or word Christ, in any of his works; except the testimony above mentioned, and the passage concerning James, the Lord's brother.

"It interrupts the narrative.

"The language is quite Christian.

"It is not quoted by Chrysostom, though he often refers to Josephus, and could not have omitted quoting it had it been then in the text.

"It is not quoted by Photius, though he has three articles concerning Josephus.

"Under the article Justus of Tiberias, this author (Photius) expressly states that the historian [Josephus], being a Jew, has not taken the least notice of Christ.

"Neither Justin in his dialogue with Trypho the Jew, nor Clemens Alexandrinus, who made so many extracts from ancient authors, nor Origen against Celsus, has ever mentioned this testimony.

"But, on the contrary, in chapter xxxv of the first book of that work, Origen openly affirms that Josephus, who had mentioned John the Baptist, did not acknowledge Christ" (*Answer to Dr. Chandler*).

Again Dr. Lardner says: "This passage is not quoted nor referred to by any Christian writer before Eusebius, who flourished at the beginning of the fourth century. If it had been originally in the works of Josephus it would have been highly proper to produce it in their disputes with Jews and Gentiles. But it is never quoted by Justin Martyr, or Clement of Alexandria, nor by Tertullian or Origen, men of great learning, and well acquainted with the works of Josephus. It was certainly very proper to urge it against the Jews. It might also have been fitly urged against the Gentiles. A testimony so favorable to Jesus in the works of Josephus, who lived so soon after our Savior, who was so well acquainted with the transactions of his own country, who had received so many favors from Vespasian and Titus, would not be overlooked or neglected by any Christian apologist" (Lardner's *Works,* Vol. I, chap. iv).

Bishop Warburton declares it to be a forgery: "If a Jew owned the truth of Christianity, he must needs embrace it. We, therefore, certainly conclude that the paragraph where Josephus, who was as much a Jew as the religion of Moses could make him, is made to acknowledge Jesus as the Christ, in terms as strong as words could do it, is a rank forgery, and a very stupid one, too" (Quoted by Lardner, *Works,* Vol. I, chap. iv).

The Rev. Dr. Giles, of the Established Church of England, says:

"Those who are best acquainted with the character of Josephus, and the style of his writings, have no hesitation in condemning this passage as a forgery, interpolated in the text during the third century by some pious Christian, who was scandalized that so famous a writer as Josephus should have taken no notice of the gospels, or of Christ, their subject. But the zeal of the interpolator has outrun his discretion, for we might as well expect to gather grapes from thorns, or figs from thistles, as to find this notice of Christ among the Judaizing writings of Josephus. It is well known that this author was a zealous Jew, devoted to the laws of Moses and the traditions of his countrymen. How, then, could he have written that Jesus was the Christ? Such an admission would have proved him to be a Christian himself, in which case the passage under consideration, too long for a Jew, would have been far too short for a believer in the new religion, and thus the passage stands forth, like an ill-set jewel, contrasting most inharmoniously with everything around it. If it had been genuine, we might be sure that Justin Martyr, Tertullian, and Chrysostom would have quoted it in their controversies with the Jews, and that Origen or Photius would have mentioned it. But Eusebius, the ecclesiastical historian (I, 11), is the first who quotes it, and our reliance on the judgment or even honesty of this writer is not so great as to allow our considering everything found in his works as undoubtedly genuine" (*Christian Records,* p. 30).

The Rev. S. Baring-Gould, in his *Lost and Hostile Gospels,* says:

"This passage is first quoted by Eusebius (fl. A.D. 315) in two places (*Hist. Eccl.,* lib. i, c. xi; *Demonst. Evang.,* lib. iii); but it was unknown to Justin Martyr (fl. A.D. 140), Clement of Alexandria (fl. A.D. 192), Tertullian (fl. A.D. 193), and Origen (fl. A.D. 230). Such a testimony would certainly have been produced by Justin in his apology or in his controversy with Trypho the Jew, had it existed in the copies of Josephus at his time. The silence of Origen is still more significant. Celsus, in his book against Christianity, introduces a Jew. Origen attacks the argument of Celsus and his Jew. He could not have failed to quote the words of Josephus, whose writings he knew, had the passage existed in the genuine text. He, indeed, distinctly affirms that Josephus did not believe in Christ (*Contr. Cels.* i)."

Dr. Chalmers ignores it, and admits that Josephus is silent regarding Christ. He says: "The entire silence of Josephus upon the subject of Christianity, though he wrote after the destruction of Jerusalem, and gives us the history of that period in which Christ and his Apostles lived, is certainly a very striking circumstance" (Kneeland's *Review,* p. 169).

Referring to this passage, Dean Milman, in his *Gibbon's Rome* (Vol. II, p. 285, note) says: "It is interpolated with many additional clauses."

Canon Farrar, who has written the ablest Christian life of Christ yet penned, repudiates it. He says: "The single passage in which he [Josephus] alludes to him is interpolated, if not wholly spurious" (*Life of Christ,* Vol. I, p. 46).

The following, from Dr. Farrar's pen, is to be found in the *Encyclopedia Britannica*: "That Josephus wrote the whole passage as it now stands no sane critic can believe."

"There are, however, two reasons which are alone sufficient to prove that the whole passage is spurious—one that it was unknown to Origen and the earlier fathers, and the other that its place in the text is uncertain" (ibid.).

Theodor Keim, a German-Christian writer on Jesus, says: "The passage cannot be maintained; it has first appeared in this form in the Catholic church of the Jews and Gentiles, and under the dominion of the Fourth Gospel, and hardly before the third century, probably before Eusebius, and after Origen, whose bitter criticisms of Josephus may have given cause for it" (*Jesus of Nazara,* p. 25).

Concerning this passage, Hausrath, another German writer, says it "must have been penned at a peculiarly shameless hour."

The Rev. Dr. Hooykaas, of Holland, says: "Flavius Josephus, the well known historian of the Jewish people, was born in A.D. 37, only two years after the death of Jesus; but though his work is of inestimable value as our chief authority for the circumstances of the times in which Jesus and his Apostles came forward, yet he does not seem to have mentioned Jesus himself. At any rate, the passage in his 'Jewish Antiquities' that refers to him is certainly spurious, and was inserted by a later and a Christian hand" (*Bible for Learners,* Vol. III, p. 27). This conclusion of Dr. Hooykaas is endorsed by the eminent Dutch critic, Dr. Kuenen.

Dr. Alexander Campbell, one of America's ablest Christian apologists, says: "Josephus, the Jewish historian, was contemporary with the Apostles, having been born in the year 37. From his situation and habits, he had every access to know all that took place at the rise of the Christian religion.

"Respecting the founder of this religion, Josephus has thought fit to be silent in history. The present copies of his work contain one passage which speaks very respectfully of Jesus Christ, and ascribes to him the character of the Messiah. But as Josephus did not embrace Christianity, and as this passage is not quoted or referred to until the beginning of the fourth century, it is, for these and other reasons, generally accounted spurious" (*Evidences of Christianity,* from Campbell-Owen Debate, p. 312).

Another passage in Josephus, relating to the younger Ananus, who was high priest of the Jews in 62 A.D., reads as follows:

"But this younger Ananus, who, as we have told you already, took the high priesthood, was a bold man in his temper and very insolent; he was also of the sect of Sadducees, who are very rigid in judging offenders, above all of the rest of the Jews, as we have already observed; when, therefore, Ananus was of this disposition, he thought he had now a proper opportunity. Festus was dead, and Albinus was but upon the road; so he assembled the Sanhedrim of judges and brought before them the brother of Jesus, who was called Christ, whose name was James, and some others; and when he had formed an accusation against them as breakers of the law, he delivered them to be stoned" (*Antiquities,* Book XX, chap. ix, sec. I).

This passage is probably genuine with the exception of the clause "who was called Christ," which is undoubtedly an interpolation, and is generally regarded as such. Nearly all the authorities that I have quoted reject it. It was originally probably a marginal note. Some Christian reader of Josephus believing that the James mentioned was the brother of Jesus made a note of his belief in the manuscript before him, and this a transcriber afterward incorporated with the text, a very common practice in that age when purity of text was a matter of secondary importance.

The fact that the early fathers, who were acquainted with Josephus, and who would have hailed with joy even this evidence of Christ's existence, do not cite it, while Origen expressly declares that Josephus has not mentioned Christ, is conclusive proof that it did not exist until the middle of the third century or later.

Those who affirm the genuineness of this clause argue that the James mentioned by Josephus was a person of less prominence than the Jesus mentioned by him, which would be true of James, the brother of Jesus Christ. Now some of the most prominent Jews living at this time were named Jesus. Jesus, the son of Damneus, succeeded Ananus as high priest that very year; and Jesus, the son of Gamaliel, a little later succeeded to the same office.

To identify the James of Josephus with James the Just, the brother of Jesus, is to reject the accepted history of the primitive church which declares that James the Just died in 69 A.D., seven years after the James of Josephus was condemned to death by the Sanhedrim.

Whiston himself, the translator of Josephus, referring to the event narrated by the Jewish historian, admits that James, the brother of Jesus Christ, "did not die till long afterward."

The brief "Discourse Concerning Hades," appended to the writings of Josephus, is universally concerned to be the product of some other writer —"obviously of Christian origin"—says the *Encyclopedia Britannica.*

Tacitus

In July, 64 A.D., a great conflagration occurred in Rome. There is a tradition to the effect that this conflagration was the work of an incendiary and that the Emperor Nero himself was believed to be the incendiary. Modern editions of the *Annals* of Tacitus contain the following passage in reference to this:

"Nero, in order to stifle the rumor, ascribed it to those people who were abhorred for their crimes and commonly called Christians: These he punished exquisitely. *The founder of that name was Christus, who, in the reign of Tiberius, was punished as a criminal by the procurator, Pontius Pilate.* This pernicious superstition, thus checked for a while, broke out again; and spread not only over Judea, the source of this evil, but reached the city also: whither flow from all quarters all things vile and shameful, and where they find shelter and encouragement. At first, only those were apprehended who confessed themselves of that sect; afterwards, a vast multitude were detected by them, all of whom were condemned, not so much for the crime of burning the city, as their hatred of mankind. Their executions were so contrived as to expose them to derision and contempt. Some were covered over with the skins of wild beasts, and torn to pieces by dogs; some were crucified. Others, having been daubed over with combustible materials, were set up as lights in the night time, and thus burned to death. Nero made use of his own gardens as a theatre on this occasion, and also exhibited the diversions of the circus, sometimes standing in the crowd as a spectator, in the habit of a charioteer; at other times driving a chariot himself, till at length those men, though really criminal, and deserving exemplary punishment, began to be commiserated as people who were destroyed, not out of regard to the public welfare, but only to gratify the cruelty of one man" (*Annals,* Book XV, sec. 44).

This passage, accepted as authentic by many, must be declared doubtful, if not spurious, for the following reasons:

1. It is not quoted by the Christian fathers.

2. Tertullian was familiar with the writings of Tacitus, and his arguments demanded the citation of this evidence had it existed.

3. Clement of Alexandria, at the beginning of the third century, made a compilation of all the recognitions of Christ and Christianity that had been made by Pagan writers up to his time. The writings of Tacitus furnished no recognition of them.

4. Origen, in his controversy with Celsus, would undoubtedly have used it had it existed.

5. The ecclesiastical historian Eusebius, in the fourth century, cites all the evidences of Christianity obtainable from Jewish and Pagan sources, but makes no mention of Tacitus.

6. It is not quoted by any Christian writer prior to the fifteenth century.

7. At this time but one copy of the *Annals* existed, and this copy, it is claimed, was made in the eighth century—600 years after the time of Tacitus.

8. As this single copy was in the possession of a Christian the insertion of a forgery was easy.

9. Its severe criticisms of Christianity do not necessarily disprove its Christian origin. No ancient witness was more desirable than Tacitus, but his introduction at so late a period would make rejection certain unless Christian forgery could be made to appear improbable.

10. It is admitted by Christian writers that the works of Tacitus have not been preserved with any considerable degree of fidelity. In the writings ascribed to him are believed to be some of the writings of Quintilian.

11. The blood-curdling story about the frightful orgies of Nero reads like some Christian romance of the dark ages, and not like Tacitus.

12. In fact, this story, in nearly the same words, omitting the reference to Christ, is to be found in the writings of Sulpicius Severus, a Christian of the fifth century.

13. Suetonius, while mercilessly condemning the reign of Nero, says that in his public entertainments he took particular care that no human lives should be sacrificed, "not even those of condemned criminals."

14. At the time that the conflagration occurred, Tacitus himself declares that Nero was not in Rome, but at Antium.

Many who accept the authenticity of this section of the *Annals* believe that the sentence which declares that Christ was punished in the reign of Pontius Pilate, and which I have italicized, is an interpolation. Whatever may be said of the remainder of this passage, this sentence bears the unmistakable stamp of Christian forgery. It interrupts the narrative; it disconnects two closely related statements. Eliminate this sentence, and there is no break in the narrative. In all the Roman records there was to be found no evidence that Christ was put to death by

Pontius Pilate. This sentence, if genuine, is the most important evidence in Pagan literature. That it existed in the works of the greatest and best known of Roman historians, and was ignored or overlooked by Christian apologists for 1,360 years, no intelligent critic can believe. Tacitus did not write this sentence.

Pliny the Younger

This Roman author, early in the second century while serving as a pro-consul under Trajan in Bithynia, is reputed to have written a letter to his Emperor concerning his treatment of Christians. This letter contains the following:

"I have laid down this rule in dealing with those who were brought before me for being Christians. I asked whether they were Christians; if they confessed, I asked them a second and a third time, threatening them with punishment; if they persevered, I ordered them to be executed. . . . They assured me that their only crime or error was this, that they were wont to come together on a certain day before it was light, and to sing in turn, among themselves, a hymn to Christ, as to a god, and to bind themselves by an oath—not to do anything that was wicked, that they would commit no theft, robbery, or adultery, nor break their word, nor deny that anything had been entrusted to them when called upon to restore it. . . . I therefore deemed it the more necessary to enquire of two servant maids, who were said to be attendants, what was the real truth, and to apply the torture. But I found it was nothing but a bad and excessive superstition."

Notwithstanding an alleged reply to this letter from Trajan, cited by Tertullian and Eusebius, its genuineness may well be questioned, and for the following reasons:

1. The Roman laws accorded religious liberty to all, and the Roman government tolerated and protected every religious belief. Renan says: "Among the Roman laws, anterior to Constantine, there was not a single ordinance directed against freedom of thought; in the history of the Pagan emperors not a single persecution on account of mere doctrines or creeds" (*The Apostles*). Gibbon says: "The religious tenets of the

Galileans, or Christians, were never made a subject of punishment, or even of inquiry" (*Rome,* Vol. II, p. 215).

2. Trajan was one of the most tolerant and benevolent of Roman emperors.

3. Pliny, the reputed author of the letter, is universally conceded to have been one of the most humane and philanthropic of men.

4. It represents the distant province of Bithynia as containing, at this time, a large Christian population, which is improbable.

5. It assumes that the Emperor Trajan was little acquainted with Christian beliefs and customs, which cannot be harmonized with the supposed historical fact that the most powerful of primitive churches flourished in Trajan's capital and had existed for fifty years.

6. Pliny represents the Christians as declaring that they were in the habit of meeting and singing hymns "to Christ as to a god." The early Christians did not recognize Christ as a god, and it was not until after the time of Pliny that he was worshiped as such.

7. "I asked whether they were Christians; if they confessed, I asked them a second and a third time, threatening them with punishment; if they persevered I ordered them to be executed." That this wise and good man rewarded lying with liberty and truthfulness with death is difficult to believe.

8. "I therefore deemed it more necessary to inquire of two servant maids, who were said to be attendants, what was the real truth, and to apply the torture." Never have the person and character of woman been held more sacred than they were in Pagan Rome. That one of the noblest of Romans should have put to torture young women guiltless of crime is incredible.

9. The declaration of the Christians that they took a solemn obligation "not to do anything that was wicked; that they would commit no theft, robbery, or adultery, nor break their word," etc., looks like an ingenious attempt to parade the virtues of primitive Christians.

10. This letter, it is claimed, is to be found in but one ancient copy of Pliny.

11. It was first quoted by Tertullian, and the age immediately preceding Tertullian was notorious for Christian forgeries.

12. Some of the best German critics reject it. Gibbon, while not

denying its authenticity, pronounces it a "very curious epistle"; and Dr. Whiston, who considers it too valuable to discard, applies to its contents such epithets as "amazing doctrine!", "amazing stupidity!"

Josephus, Tacitus, Pliny—these are the disinterested witnesses adduced by the church to prove the historical existence of Jesus Christ; the one writing nearly one hundred years, the others one hundred and ten years after his alleged birth; the testimony of two of them self-evident forgeries, and that of the third a probable forgery.

But even if the doubtful and hostile letter of Pliny be genuine, it was not written until the second century, so that there is not to be found in all the records of profane history prior to the second century a single allusion to the reputed founder of Christianity.

To these witnesses is sometimes, though rarely, added a fourth, Suetonius, a Roman historian who, like Tacitus and Pliny, wrote in the second century. In his *Life of Nero,* Suetonius says: "The Christians, a race of men of a new and villainous superstition, were punished." In his *Life of Claudius,* he says. "He [Claudius] drove the Jews, who at the instigation of Chrestus were constantly rioting, out of Rome." Of course no candid Christian will contend that Christ was inciting Jewish riots at Rome fifteen years after he was crucified at Jerusalem.

Significant is the silence of the forty Jewish and Pagan writers named in this chapter. This silence alone disproves Christ's existence. Had this wonderful being really existed the earth would have resounded with his fame. His mighty deeds would have engrossed every historian's pen. The pages of other writers would have abounded with references to him. Think of going through the literature of the nineteenth century and searching in vain for the name of Napoleon Bonaparte! Yet Napoleon was a pigmy and his deeds trifles compared with this Christ and the deeds he is said to have performed.

With withering irony Gibbon notes this ominous silence: "But how shall we excuse the supine inattention of the Pagan and philosophic world, to those evidences which were represented by the hand of Omnipotence, not to their reason, but to their senses? During the age of Christ, of his apostles, and of their first disciples, the doctrine which they preached was confirmed by innumerable prodigies. The lame walked, the blind saw, the sick were healed, the dead were raised, demons were expelled, and the laws of Nature were frequently suspended for the benefit of the church. But the sages of Greece and Rome turned aside from the awful spectacle, and, pursuing the ordinary occupations of life and study, appeared unconscious of any alterations in the moral or physical government of the world. Under the reign of Tiberius, the whole earth, or at least a celebrated province of the Roman empire, was involved in a preternatural darkness of three hours. Even this miraculous event, which ought to have excited the wonder, the curiosity, and the devotion of mankind, passed without notice in an age of science and history. It happened during the lifetime of Seneca and the elder Pliny, who must have experienced the immediate effects, or received the earliest intelligence of the prodigy. Each of these philosophers, in a laborious work, has recorded all the great phenomena of Nature, earthquakes, meteors, comets, and eclipses, which his indefatigable curiosity could collect. Both the one and the other have omitted to mention the greatest phenomenon to which the mortal eye has been witness since the creation of the globe" (*Rome,* Vol. I, pp. 588–590).

Even conceding, for the sake of argument, both the authenticity and the credibility of these passages attributed to the Roman historians, what do they prove? Do they prove that Christ was divine—that he was a supernatural being, as claimed? No more than do the writings of Paine and Voltaire, which also contain his name. This evidence is favorable not to the adherents, but to the opponents, of Christianity. If these passages be genuine, and their authors have penned historical truths, it simply confirms what most Rationalists admit, that a religious sect called Christians, who recognized Christ as their founder, existed as early as the first century; and confirms what some have charged, but what the church is loath to admit, that primitive Christians, who have been declared the highest exemplars of human virtue, were the most depraved of villains.

An unlettered and credulous enthusiast, named Jones, imagines that he has had a revelation, and proceeds to found a new religious sect. He gathers about him a band of "disciples" as ignorant and credulous as himself. He soon gets into trouble and is killed. But the Jonesists increase—increase in numbers and in meanness—until at length they become sufficiently notorious to receive a paragraph from an annalist who, after holding them up to ridicule and scorn, accounts for their origin by stating that they take their name from one Jones who, during the administration of President Roosevelt, was hanged as a criminal. The world contains two billions of inhabitants—mostly fools, as Carlyle would say—and as the religion of this sect is a little more foolish than that of any other sect, it continues to spread until at the end of two thousand years it covers the globe. Then think of the adherents of this religion citing the uncomplimentary allusion of this annalist to prove that Jones was a god!

3

Christian Evidence

The Four Gospels

Farrar, in his *Life of Christ,* concedes and deplores the dearth of evidence concerning the subject of his work. He says: "It is little short of amazing that neither history nor tradition should have embalmed for us one certain or precious saying or circumstance in the life of the Savior of Mankind, except the comparatively few events recorded in four very brief biographies."

With these four brief biographies, the Four Gospels, Christianity must stand or fall. These four documents, it is admitted, contain practically all the evidence which can be adduced in proof of the existence and divinity of Jesus Christ. Profane history, as we have seen, affords no proof of this. The so-called apocryphal literature of the early church has been discarded by the church itself. Even the remaining canonical books of the New Testament are of little consequence if the testimony of the Four Evangelists be successfully impeached. Disprove the authenticity and credibility of these documents and this Christian deity is removed to the mythical realm of Apollo, Odin, and Osiris.

In a previous work, *The Bible,* I have shown that the books of the New Testament, with a few exceptions, are not authentic. This evidence cannot be reproduced here in full. A brief summary of it must suffice.

The Four Gospels, it is claimed, were written by Matthew, Mark,

Luke, and John, two of them apostles, and two companions of the apostles of Christ. If this claim be true the other writings of the apostles, the writings of the Apostolic Fathers, and the writings of the early Christian Fathers, ought to contain some evidences of the fact.

Twenty books—nearly all of the remaining books of the New Testament—are said to have been written by the three apostles, Peter, John, and Paul, a portion of them after the first three Gospels were written; but it is admitted that they contain no evidence whatever of the existence of these Gospels.

There are extant writings accredited to the Apostolic Fathers, Clement of Rome, Barnabas, Hermas, Ignatius, and Polycarp; written, for the most part, early in the second century. These writings contain no mention of the Four Gospels. This also is admitted by Christian scholars. Dr. Dodwell says: "We have at this day certain most authentic ecclesiastical writers of the times, as Clemens Romanus, Barnabas, Hermas, Ignatius, and Polycarp, who wrote in the order wherein I have named them, and after all the writers of the New Testament. But in Hermas you will not find one passage or any mention of the New Testament, nor in all the rest is any one of the Evangelists named" (*Dissertations upon Irenaeus*).

The Four Gospels were unknown to the early Christian Fathers. Justin Martyr, the most eminent of the early Fathers, wrote about the middle of the second century. His writings in proof of the divinity of Christ demanded the use of these Gospels had they existed in his time. He makes more than three hundred quotations from the books of the Old Testament, and nearly one hundred from the Apocryphal books of the New Testament; but none from the Four Gospels. The Rev. Dr. Giles says: "The very names of the Evangelists, Matthew, Mark, Luke, and John, are never mentioned by him [Justin]—do not occur once in all his writings" (*Christian Records,* p. 71).

Papias, another noted Father, was a contemporary of Justin. He refers to writings of Matthew and Mark, but his allusions to them clearly indicate that they were not the Gospels of Matthew and Mark. Dr. Davidson, the highest English authority on the canon, says: "He [Papias] neither felt the want nor knew the existence of inspired Gospels" (*Canon of the Bible,* p. 123).

Theophilus, who wrote after the middle of the latter half of the second century, mentions the Gospel of John, and Irenaeus, who wrote a little later, mentions all of the Gospels, and makes numerous quotations from them. In the latter half of the second century, then, between the time of Justin and Papias, and the time of Theophilus and Irenaeus, the Four Gospels were undoubtedly written or compiled.

These books are anonymous. They do not purport to have been written by Matthew, Mark, Luke and John. Their titles do not affirm it. They simply imply that they are "according" to the supposed teachings of these Evangelists. As Renan says, "They merely signify that these were the traditions proceeding from each of these Apostles, and claiming their authority." Concerning their authorship the Rev. Dr. Hooykaas says: "They appeared anonymously. The titles placed above them in our Bibles owe their origin to a later ecclesiastical tradition which deserves no confidence whatever" (*Bible for Learners,* Vol. III, p. 24).

It is claimed that the Gospel of Matthew originally appeared in Hebrew. Our version is a translation of a Greek work. Regarding this St. Jerome says: "Who afterwards translated it into Greek is not suf-ficiently certain." The consequences of this admission are thus expressed by Michaelis: "If the original text of Matthew is lost, and we have nothing but a Greek translation; then, frankly, we cannot ascribe any divine inspiration to the words."

The contents of these books refute the claim that they were written by the Evangelists named. They narrate events and contain doctrinal teachings which belong to a later age. Matthew ascribes to Christ the following language. "Thou art Peter, and upon this rock I will build my church" (xvi, 18). This Gospel is a Roman Catholic Gospel, and was written after the beginning of the establishment of this hierarchy to uphold the supremacy of the Petrine Church of Rome. Of this Gospel Dr. Davidson says: "The author, indeed, must ever remain unknown" (*Introduction to New Testament,* p. 72).

The Gospel of Luke is addressed to Theophilus. Theophilus, Bishop of Antioch, who is believed to be the person addressed, flourished in the latter half of the second century.

Dr. Schleiermacher, one of Germany's greatest theologians, after a critical analysis of Luke, concludes that it is merely a compilation, made up of thirty-three preexisting manuscripts. Bishop Thirlwall's Schleiermacher says: "He [Luke] is from beginning to end no more than the compiler and arranger of documents which he found in existence" (p. 313).

The basis of this Gospel is generally believed to be the Gospel of Marcion, a Pauline compilation, made about the middle of the second century. Concerning this Gospel, the Rev. S. Baring-Gould, in his *Lost and Hostile Gospels,* says: "The arrangement is so similar that we are forced to the conclusion that it was either used by St. Luke or that it was his original composition. If he used it then his right to the title of author of the Third Gospel falls to the ground, as what he added was of small amount."

Mark, according to Renan, is the oldest of the Gospels; but Mark, according to Strauss, was written after the Gospels of Matthew and Luke were written. He says: "It is evidently a compilation, whether made from memory or otherwise, from the first and third Gospels" (*Leben Jesu,* p. 51). Judge Waite, in his *History of Christianity,* says that all but twenty-four verses of this Gospel have their parallels in Matthew and Luke. Davidson declares it to be an anonymous work. "The author," he says, "is unknown."

Omitting the last twelve verses of Mark, which all Christian critics pronounce spurious, the book contains no mention of the two great miracles which mark the limits of Christ's earthly career, his miraculous birth and his ascension.

Concerning the first three Gospels, the *Encyclopedia Britannica* says: "It is certain that the Synoptic Gospels took their present form only by degrees." Of these books Dr. Westcott says: "Their substance is evidently much older than their form." Professor Robertson Smith pronounces them "unapostolic digests of the second century."

The internal evidence against the authenticity of the Fourth Gospel is conclusive. The Apostle John did not write it. John, the apostle, was a Jew; the author of the Fourth Gospel was not a Jew. John was born at Bethsaida; the author of the Fourth Gospel did not know where Bethsaida was located. John was an uneducated fisherman; the author of this Gospel was an accomplished scholar. Some of the most important events in the life of Jesus, the Synoptics declare, were witnessed by

John; the author of this knows nothing of these events. The Apostle John witnessed the crucifixion; the author of this Gospel did not. The Apostles, including John, believed Jesus to be a man; the author of the Fourth Gospel believed him to be a god.

Regarding the authorship of the Fourth Gospel, Dr. Davidson says: "The Johannine authorship has receded before the tide of modern criticism, and though this tide is arbitrary at times, it is here irresistible" (*Canon of the Bible,* p. 127).

That the authenticity of the Four Gospels cannot be maintained is conceded by every impartial critic. The author of *Supernatural Religion,* in one of the most profound and exhaustive works on this subject ever written, expresses the result of his labors in the following words: "After having exhausted the literature and the testimony bearing on the point, we have not found a single distinct trace of any of those Gospels during the first century and a half after the death of Jesus" (*Supernatural Religion,* Vol. II, p. 248).

Fifteen hundred years ago, Bishop Faustus, a heretical Christian theologian, referring to this so-called Gospel history, wrote: "It is allowed not to have been written by the son himself nor by his apostles, but long after by some unknown men who, lest they should be suspected of writing things they knew nothing of, gave to their books the names of the Apostles."

The following is the verdict of the world's greatest Bible critic, Baur: "These Gospels are spurious, and were written in the second century."

Acts, Catholic Epistles, and Revelation

The Acts of the Apostles is supposed to have been written by the author of the Third Gospel. Like this book it is anonymous and of late origin. It contains historical inaccuracies, contradicts the Gospel of Matthew, and conflicts with the writings of Paul. Concerning the last, the *Bible for Learners* (Vol. III, p. 25) says: "In the first two chapters of the Epistle to the Galatians, he [Paul] gives us several details of his own past life; and no sooner do we place his story side by side with that of the Acts than we clearly perceive that this book contains an incorrect account, and that its inaccuracy is not the result of accident or ignorance, but of a deliberate design."

This book purports to be the product chiefly of three minds: that of the author who gives a historical sketch of the early church, and those of Peter and Paul whose discourses are reported. And yet the three compositions are clearly the products of one mind—that of the author. The evident purpose of the work is to heal the bitter dissensions which existed between the Petrine and Pauline churches, and this points unmistakably to the latter part of the second century as the date of its appearance, when the work of uniting the various Christian sects into the Catholic church began. Renan considers this the most faulty book of the New Testament.

The seven Catholic Epistles, James, First and Second Peter, First, Second and Third John, and Jude, have never been held in very high esteem by the church. Many of the Christian Fathers rejected them, while modern Christian scholars have generally considered them of doubtful authenticity. The first and last of these were rejected by Martin Luther. "St. James' Epistle," says Luther, "is truly an epistle of straw" (Preface to Luther's New Testament, ed. 1524). Jude, he says, "is an abstract or copy of St. Peter's Second, and allegeth stories and sayings which have no place in Scripture" (Standing Preface).

The First Epistle of Peter and the First Epistle of John have generally been accorded a higher degree of authority than the others; but even these were not written by apostles, nor in the first century. Dr. Soury says that First Peter "dates, in all probability, from the year 130 A.D., at the earliest" (*Jesus and the Gospels,* p. 32). Irenaeus, the founder of the New Testament canon, rejected it. The Dutch critics, who deny the Johannine authorship of the Fourth Gospel, and assign its composition to the second century, say: "The First Epistle of John soon issued from the same school in imitation of the Gospel" (*Bible for Learners,* Vol. III, p. 692).

Second Peter is a forgery. Westcott says there is no proof of its existence prior to 170 A.D. Smith's *Bible Dictionary* says, "Many reject the epistle as altogether spurious." The brief epistles of Second and Third John are anonymous and of very late origin. They do not purport to be the writings of John. The superscriptions declare them to be from an elder, and this precludes the claim that they are from an apostle. The early Fathers ignored them.

Revelation is the only book in the Bible which claims to be the word of God. At the same time it is the book of which Christians have always been the most suspicious. It is addressed to the seven churches of Asia, but the seven churches of Asia rejected it. Concerning the attitude of ancient churchmen toward it, Dionysius, Bishop of Alexandria, says: "Divers of our predecessors have wholly refused and rejected this book, and by discussing the several parts thereof have found it obscure and void of reason and the title forged."

"The most learned and intelligent of Protestant divines," says the *Edinburgh Review,* "almost all doubted or denied the canonicity of the book of Revelation." It is a book which, Dr. South said, "either found a man mad or left him so." Calvin and Beza both forbade their clergy to attempt an explanation of its contents. Luther says: "In the Revelation of John much is wanting to let me deem it either prophetic or apostolical" (Preface to N.T., 1524).

Considered as evidences of Christ's historical existence and divinity these nine books are of no value. They are all anonymous writings or forgeries, and, with the possible exception of Revelation, of very late origin. While they affirm Christ's existence they are almost entirely silent regarding his life and miracles.

The Epistles of Paul

Of the fourteen epistles ascribed to Paul, seven—Ephesians, Colossians, Second Thessalonians, First and Second Timothy, Titus, and Hebrews—are conceded by nearly all critics to be spurious, while three others—Philippians, First Thessalonians, and Philemon—are generally classed as doubtful.

The general verdict concerning the first seven is thus expressed by the Rev. Dr. Hooykaas: "Fourteen epistles are said to be Paul's; but we must at once strike off one, namely, that to the Hebrews, which does not bear his name at all. . . . The two letters to Timothy and the letter to Titus were certainly composed long after the death of Paul. . . . It is more than possible that the letters to the Ephesians and Colossians are also unauthentic, and the same suspicion rests, perhaps, on the first, but certainly on the second of the Epistles to the Thessalonians" (*Bible for Learners,* Vol. III, p. 23).

The author of Second Thessalonians, whose epistle is a self-evident forgery, declares First Thessalonians to be a forgery. Baur and the Tübingen school reject both Epistles. Baur also rejects Philippians: "The Epistles to the Colossians and to the Philippians . . . are spurious, and were written by the Catholic school near the end of the second century, to heal the strife between the Jew and the Gentile factions" (*Paulus*). Dr. Kuenen and the other Dutch critics admit that Philippians and Philemon, as well as First Thessalonians, are doubtful.

That the Pastoral Epistles are forgeries is now conceded by all critics. According to the German critics they belong to the second century. Hebrews does not purport to be a Pauline document. Luther says: "The Epistle to the Hebrews is not by St. Paul, nor, indeed, by any apostle" (Standing Preface to Luther's N.T.).

Four Epistles—Romans, First and Second Corinthians, and Galatians—while rejected by a few critics, are generally admitted to be the genuine writings of Paul. These books were written, it is claimed, about a quarter of a century after the death of Christ. They are the only books of the New Testament whose authenticity can be maintained.

Admitting the authenticity of these books, however, is not admitting the historical existence of Christ and the divine origin of Christianity. Paul was not a witness of the alleged events upon which Christianity rests. He did not become a convert to Christianity until many years after the death of Christ. He did not see Christ (save in a vision); he did not listen to his teachings; he did not learn from his disciples. "The Gospel which was preached of me is not after man, for I neither received it of man, neither was I taught it" (Gal. i, 11, 12). Paul accepted only to a very small extent the religion of Christ's disciples. He professed to derive his knowledge from supernatural sources—from trances and visions. Regarding the value of such testimony the author of *Supernatural Religion* (p. 970) says: "No one can deny, and medical and psychological annals prove, that many men have been subject to visions and hallucinations which have never been seriously attributed to supernatural causes. There is not one single valid reason removing the ecstatic visions and trances of the Apostle Paul from this class."

The corporeal existence of the Christ of the Evangelists receives slight confirmation in the writings of Paul. His Christ was not the incarnate Word of John, nor the demi-god of Matthew and Luke. Of the immaculate conception of Jesus he knew nothing. To him Christ was the son of God in a spiritual rather than in a physical sense. "His son Jesus Christ our Lord, which was made of the seed of David according to the flesh; and declared to be the son of God with power, according to the spirit of holiness, by the resurrection from the dead" (Rom. i, 3, 4). "God sent forth his son, made of a woman [but not of a virgin], made under the law" (Gal. iv, 4).

With the Evangelists the proofs of Christ's divinity are his miracles. Their books teem with accounts of these. But Paul evidently knows nothing of these miracles. With him the evidences of Christ's divine mission are his resurrection and the spiritual gifts conferred on those who accept him.

The Evangelists teach a material resurrection. When the women visited his tomb "they entered in and found not the body of Jesus" (Luke xxiv, 3). The divine messengers said to them, "He is not here, but is risen" (6). "He sat at meat" with his disciples; "he took bread, and blessed it, and brake, and gave to them" (30). "Then he said to Thomas, Reach hither thy finger, and behold my hands; and reach hither thy hand, and thrust it into my side" (John xx, 27). This is entirely at variance with the teachings of Paul. "But now is Christ risen from the dead, and become the first fruits of them that slept. For since by man came death, by man came also the resurrection of the dead" (I Cor. xv, 20, 21). "But some man will say, How are the dead raised up? and with what body do they come? Thou fool, that which thou sowest is not quickened, except it die; and that which thou sowest, thou sowest not that body that shall be" (35–37). "It is sown a natural body; it is raised a spiritual body. There is a natural body, and there is a spiritual body" (44). "Now this I say brethren, that flesh and blood cannot inherit the kingdom of God" (50).

The Christ that Paul saw in a vision was a spiritual being—an apparition; and this appearance he considers of exactly the same character as the post mortem appearances of Christ to his disciples. "He was seen of Cephas, then of the twelve; after that he was seen of above five hundred brethren at once; . . . after that, he was seen of James; then of all the Apostles. And last of all, he was seen of me also" (I Cor. xv, 5–8).

4

The Infancy of Christ

We have seen that the Four Gospels are not authentic, that they are anonymous writings which appeared late in the second century. If their contents seemed credible and their statements harmonized with each other this want of authenticity would invalidate their authority, because the testimony of an unknown witness cannot be accepted as authoritative. On the other hand, if their authenticity could be established, if it could be shown that they were written by the authors claimed, the incredible and contradictory character of their contents would destroy their authority.

As historical documents these books are hardly worthy of credit. The *Arabian Nights* is almost as worthy of credit as the Four Gospels. In both are to be found accounts of things possible and of things impossible. To believe the impossible is gross superstition; to believe the possible, simply because it is possible, is blind credulity. These books are adduced as the credentials of Christ. A critical analysis of these credentials reveals hundreds of errors. A presentation of these errors will occupy the five succeeding chapters of this work. If it can be shown that they contain errors, however trivial some of them may appear, this refutes the claim of inerrancy and divinity. If it can be shown that they abound with errors, this destroys their credibility as historical documents. Destroy the credibility of the Four Gospels and you destroy all proofs of Christ's divinity—all proofs of his existence.

1

When was Jesus born?

Matthew: "In the days of Herod" (ii, 1).

Luke: "When Cyrenius was governor of Syria" (ii, 1–7).

Nearly every biographer gives the date of his subject's birth. Yet not one of the Evangelists gives the date of Jesus' birth. Two, Matthew and Luke, attempt to give the time approximately. But between these two attempts there is a discrepancy of at least ten years; for Herod died 4 B.C., while Cyrenius did not become governor of Syria until 7 A.D.

A reconciliation of these statements is impossible. Matthew clearly states that Jesus was born during the reign of Herod. Luke states that Augustus Caesar issued a decree that the world should be taxed, that "this taxing was first made when Cyrenius was governor of Syria," and that Jesus was born at the time of this taxing.

The following extracts from Josephus, the renowned historian of the race and country to which Jesus belonged, give the date of this taxing and the time that elapsed between the death of Herod and the taxing, and which reckoned backward from this gives the date of Herod's death:

"And now Herod altered his testament upon the alteration of his mind; for he appointed Antipas, to whom he had before left his kingdom, to be tetrarch of Galilee and Berea, and granted the kingdom to Archelaus. . . . When he had done these things he died" (*Antiquities,* B. xvii, ch. 8, sec. 1).

"But in the tenth year of Archelaus's government, both his brethren, and the principal men of Judea and Samaria, not being able to bear his barbarous and tyrannical usage of them, accused him before Caesar. . . . And when he was come [to Rome], Caesar, upon hearing what certain accusers of his had to say, and what reply he could make, both banished him, and appointed Vienna, a city of Gaul, to be the place of his habitation, and took his money away from him" (ibid., ch. 13, sec. 2).

"Archelaus's country was laid to the province of Syria; and Cyrenius, one that had been consul, was sent by Caesar to take account of people's effects in Syria, and to sell the house of Archelaus" (ibid., sec. 5).

"When Cyrenius had now disposed of Archelaus's money, and when the taxings were come to a conclusion, which were made in the thirty-seventh of Caesar's victory over Antony at Actium," etc. (ibid., B. xviii, ch. 2, sec. 1).

The battle of Actium was fought September 2, B.C. 31. The thirty-seventh year from this battle comprehended the time elapsing between September 2, A.D. 6, and September 2, A.D. 7, the mean of which was March 2, A.D. 7. The mean of the tenth year preceding this—the year in which Herod died—was September 2, B.C. 4.

It has been suggested by some unacquainted with Roman history that Cyrenius [Quirinus] may have been twice governor of Syria. Cyrenius was but once governor of Syria, and this not until 7 A.D. During the last years of Herod's reign, and during all the years of Archelaus's reign, Sentius Saturninus and Quintilius Varus held this office. Even if Cyrenius had previously held the office the events related by Luke could not have occurred then because Judea prior to 7 A.D. was not a part of Syria.

The second chapter of Luke which narrates the birth and infancy of Jesus, conflicts with the first chapter of this book. In this chapter it is expressly stated that Zacharias, the priest, lived in the time of Herod and, inferentially, that the conceptions of John and Jesus occurred at this time.

Christian chronology, by which events are supposed to be reckoned from the birth of Christ, agrees with neither Matthew nor Luke, but dates from a point nearly intermediate between the two. According to Matthew, Christ was born at least five years before the beginning of the Christian era; according to Luke he was born at least six years after the beginning of the Christian era. This is 1907: but according to Matthew Christ was born not later than 1912 years ago; while according to Luke he was born not earlier than 1901 years ago.

At least ten different opinions regarding the year of Christ's birth have been advanced by Christian scholars. Dodwell places it in 6 B.C., Chrysostom 5 B.C., Usher, whose opinion is most commonly received, 4 B.C., Irenaeus 3 B.C., Jerome 2 B.C., Tertullian 1 B.C. Some modern authorities place it in 1 A.D., others in 2 A.D., and still others in 3 A.D.; while those who accept Luke as infallible authority must place it as late as 7 A.D.

2

It is generally assumed that Jesus was born in the last year of Herod's reign. How long before the close of Herod's reign was he born?

Matthew: At least two years (ii, 1–16).

Matthew says that when the wise men visited Herod he diligently inquired of them the time when the star which announced the birth of Jesus first appeared. When he determined to destroy Jesus and massacred the infants of Bethlehem and the surrounding country, he slew those "from two years old and under, according to the time which he had diligently inquired of the wise men," clearly indicating that Jesus was nearly or quite two years old at this time.

In attempting to reconcile Matthew's visit of the wise men to Jesus at Bethlehem with the narrative of Luke, which makes his stay there less than six weeks, it has been assumed that this visit occurred immediately after his birth, whereas, according to Matthew, it did not occur until about two years after his birth.

3

In what month and on what day of the month was he born?

Not one of his biographers is prepared to tell; primitive Christians did not know; the church has never been able to determine this. A hundred different opinions regarding it have been expressed by Christian scholars. Wagenseil places it in February, Paulius in March, Greswell in April, Lichtenstein in June, Strong in August, Lightfoot in September, and Newcome in October. Clinton says that he was born in the spring; Larchur says that he was born in the fall. Some early Christians believed that it occurred on the 5th of January; others the 19th of April; others still on the 20th of May. The Eastern church believed that he was born on the 7th of January. The church of Rome, in the fourth century, selected the 25th of December on which to celebrate the anniversary of his birth; and this date has been accepted by the greater portion of the Christian world.

4

What determined the selection of this date?

"There was a double reason for selecting this day. In the first place it had been observed from a hoary antiquity as a heathen festival, following the longest night of the winter solstice, and was called "the Birthday of the Unconquerable Sun." It was a fine thought to celebrate on that day the birth of him whom the Gospel called "the light of the world." . . . The second reason was, that at Rome the days from the 17th to the 23rd of December were devoted to unbridled merrymaking. These days were called the Saturnalia. . . . Now the church was always anxious to meet the heathen, whom she had converted or was beginning to convert, half-way, by allowing them to retain the feasts they were accustomed to, only giving them a Christian dress, or attaching a new and Christian signification to them" (*Bible for Learners,* Vol. III, pp. 66, 67).

Gibbon says: "The Roman Christians, ignorant of the real time of the birth of Jesus, fixed the solemn festival on the 25th of December, the winter solstice when the Pagans annually celebrated the birth of the sun."

5

What precludes the acceptance of this date?

Luke: At the time of his birth "there were in the same country shepherds abiding in the field, keeping watch over their flocks by night" (ii, 8).

Shepherds did not abide in the field with their flocks at night in mid-winter. The Rev. Cunningham Geikie, D.D., a leading English orthodox authority on Christ, says:

"One knows how wretched even Rome is in winter and Palestine is much worse during hard weather. Nor is it likely that shepherds would lie out through the night, except during unseasonably fine weather" ("Christmas at Bethlehem," in Deems' *Holydays and Holidays,* p. 405).

"The nativity of Jesus in December should be given up."—Dr. Adam Clarke.

In regard to the date of Christ's birth Dr. Farrar says: "It must be admitted that we cannot demonstrate the exact year of the nativity. . . . As to the day and month of the nativity it is certain that they can never be recovered; they were absolutely unknown to the early fathers, and there is scarcely one month of the year which has not been fixed upon as probable by modern critics."

The inability of Christians to determine the date of Christ's birth is one of the strongest proofs of his nonexistence as a historical character. Were the story of his miraculous birth and marvelous life true the date of his birth would have been preserved and would be today, the best authenticated fact in history.

6

Where was Jesus born?

Matthew and Luke: In Bethlehem of Judea (Matt. ii, 1; Luke ii, 1–7).

Aside from these stories in Matthew and Luke concerning the nativity, which are clearly of later origin than the remaining documents composing the books and which many Christian scholars reject, there is not a word in the Four Gospels to confirm the claim that Jesus was born in Bethlehem. Every statement in Matthew, Mark, Luke, and John, as well as Acts, concerning his nativity, is to the effect that he was born in Nazareth of Galilee. He is never called "Jesus of Bethlehem," but always "Jesus of Nazareth." According to modern usage "Jesus of Nazareth" might merely signify that Nazareth was the place of his residence and not necessarily the place of his birth. But this usage was unknown to the Jews. Had he been born at Bethlehem, he would, according to the Jewish custom, have been called "Jesus of Bethlehem," because the place of birth always determined this distinguishing adjunct, and the fact of his having removed to another place would not have changed it.

Peter (Acts ii, 22; iii, 6), Paul (Acts xxvi, 9), Philip (John i, 45), Cleopas and his companion (Luke xxiv, 19), Pilate (John xix, 19), Judas and the band sent to arrest Jesus (John xviii, 5, 7), the High Priest's maid (Mark xiv, 67), blind Bartimaeus (Mark x, 47), the unclean spirits (Mark i, 24; Luke iv, 34), the multitudes that attended his meetings (Matt. xxi, 11; Luke xviii, 37), all declared him to be a native of Nazareth.

To the foregoing may be added the testimony of Jesus himself. When Paul asked him who he was he answered: "I am Jesus of Nazareth" (Acts xxii, 8).

Many of the Jews rejected Christ because he was born in Galilee and not in Bethlehem. "Others said, This is the Christ. But some said, Shall Christ come out of Galilee? Hath not the scriptures said, That Christ cometh out of the seed of David, and out of the town of Bethlehem, where David was?" (John vii, 41, 42).

Concerning this subject the *Bible for Learners* says: "The primitive tradition declared emphatically that Nazareth was the place from which Jesus came. We may still see this distinctly enough in our Gospels. Jesus is constantly called the Nazarene, or Jesus of Nazareth. This was certainly the name by which he was known in his own time; and of course such local names were given to men from the place of their birth, and not from the place in which they lived, which might constantly be changing. Nazareth is called in so many words his own, that is his native city, and he himself declares it so" (Vol. III, pp. 39, 40).

That Jesus the man, if such a being existed, was not born at Bethlehem is affirmed by all critics. That he could not have been born at Nazareth is urged by many. Nazareth, it is asserted, did not exist at this time. Christian scholars admit that there is no proof of its existence at the beginning of the Christian era outside of the New Testament. The *Encyclopedia Biblica,* a leading Christian authority, says: "We cannot perhaps venture to assert positively that there was a city called Nazareth in Jesus' time."

7

His reputed birth at Bethlehem was in fulfillment of what prophecy?

"And thou Bethlehem, in the land of Juda, art not the least among the princes of Juda; for out of thee shall come a governor that shall rule my people Israel" (Matthew ii, 6).

The Infancy of Christ   51

This is a misquotation of Micah v, 2. The passage as it appears in our version of the Old Testament is itself a mistranslation. Correctly rendered it does not mean that this ruler shall come from Bethlehem, but simply that he shall be a descendant of David whose family belonged to Bethlehem.

Concerning this prophecy it may be said, 1. That Jesus never became governor or ruler of Israel; 2. That the ruler referred to was to be a military leader who should deliver Israel from the Assyrians. "And this man shall be the peace, when the Assyrian shall come into the land . . . thus shall he deliver us from the Assyrian" (Micah v, 5, 6).

8

Jesus is called the Son of David. Why?

Matthew and Luke: Because Joseph, who was not his father, but merely his guardian or foster father, was descended from David.

The Jews expected a Messiah. This expectation was realized, it is claimed, in Jesus Christ. His Messianic marks, however, were not discernible and the Jews, for the most part, rejected him. This Messiah must be a son of David. Before Jesus' claims could even be considered his Davidic descent must be established. This Matthew and Luke attempt to do. Each gives what purports to be a genealogy of him. If these genealogies agree they may be false; if they do not agree one must be false.

9

How many generations were there from David to Jesus?

Matthew: Twenty-eight (i, 6–16).

Luke: Forty-three (iii, 23–31).

Luke makes two more generations from David to Jesus in a period of one thousand years than Matthew does from Abraham to Jesus in a period of two thousand years.

10

How many generations were there from Abraham to Jesus?

Matthew: "From Abraham to David are fourteen generations; and from David until the carrying away into Babylon are fourteen generations; and from the carrying away into Babylon unto Christ are fourteen generations"—in all, forty-two generations (i, 17).

Here Matthew contradicts his own record given in the preceding sixteen verses; for, including both Abraham and Jesus, he names but forty-one generations: 1. Abraham, 2. Isaac, 3. Jacob, 4. Judas, 5. Phares, 6. Ezrom, 7. Aram, 8. Aminadab, 9. Naason, 10. Salmon, 11. Booz, 12. Obed, 13. Jesse, 14. David, 15. Solomon, 16. Roboam, 17. Abia, 18. Asa, 19. Josaphat, 20. Joram, 21. Ozias, 22. Joatham, 23. Achaz, 24. Ezekias, 25. Manasses, 26. Amon, 27. Josias, 28. Jechonias, 29. Salathiel, 30. Zorobabel, 31. Abiud, 32. Eliakim, 33. Azor, 34. Sadoc, 35. Achim, 36. Eliud, 37. Eleazer, 38. Matthan, 39. Jacob, 40. Joseph, 41. Jesus Christ.

11

Does Luke's genealogy agree with the Old Testament?

It does not. Luke gives twenty generations from Adam to Abraham, while Genesis (v, 3–32; xi, 10–26) and Chronicles (1 Ch. i, 1–4; 24–27) each gives but nineteen.

12

How many generations were there from Abraham to David?

Matthew: "From Abraham to David are fourteen generations" (i, 17).

From Abraham to David are not fourteen, but thirteen generations; for David does not belong to this period. The genealogical table of Matthew naturally and logically comprises three divisions which he recognizes. The first division comprises the generations preceding the establishment of the Kingdom of David, beginning with Abraham; the second comprises the kings of Judah, beginning with David the first and ending with Jechonias the last; the third comprises the generations following the kings of Judah, from the Captivity to Christ.

13

How many generations were there from David to the Captivity?

Matthew: "From David until the carrying away into Babylon are fourteen generations" (i, 17).

In order to obtain a uniformity of numbers—three periods of double seven (seven was the sacred number of the Jews) each—Matthew purposely falsifies the records of the Old Testament. A reference to the Davidic genealogy (1 Chronicles iii) shows that he omits the generations of Ahaziah, Joash, Amaziah, and Jehoiakim, four Jewish kings, lineal descendants of David, whose combined reigns amount to over eighty years.

Matthew	Chronicles
David	David
Solomon	Solomon
Reboam	Rehoboam
Abia	Abia
Asa	Asa
Josaphat	Jehoshaphat
Joram	Joram
	Ahaziah
	Joash
	Amaziah
Ozias	Azariah
Joatham	Jotham
Achaz	Ahaz
Ezekias	Hezekiah
Manasses	Manasseh
Amon	Amon

Josias	Josiah
	Jehoiakim
Jechonias	Jechoniah

The first three omissions are thus explained by Augustine: "Ochozias [Ahaziah], Joash, and Amazias were excluded from the number, because their wickedness was continuous and without interval."

As if the exclusion of their names from a genealogical list would expunge their records from history and drain their blood from the veins of their descendants. But aside from the absurdity of this explanation, the premises are false. Those whose names are excluded from the list were not men whose "wickedness was continuous and without interval," while some whose names are not excluded were. Ahaziah reigned but one year. Joash reigned forty years and both Kings and Chronicles affirm that "He did that which was right in the sight of the Lord" (2 Kings xii, 2; 2 Chron. xxiv, 2). Amaziah reigned twenty-nine years, and he, too, "did that which was right in the sight of the Lord" (2 Kings xiv, 3). On the other hand, Rehoboam, Joram and Jechonias, whose names are retained in Matthew's table, are represented as monsters of wickedness.

14

Name the generations from David to the Captivity.

Matthew	Luke
David	David
Solomon	Nathan
Roboam	Mattatha
Abia	Menan
Asa	Melea
Josaphat	Eliakim
Joram	Jonan
Ozias	Joseph
Joatham	Juda

Achas	Simeon
Ezekias	Levi
Manasses	Matthat
Amon	Jorim
Josias	Eliezer
Jechonias	Jose
	Er
	Elmodam
	Cosam
	Addi
	Melchi
	Neri

15

How many generations were there from the Captivity to Christ?

Matthew: "From the carrying away into Babylon unto Christ are fourteen generations" (i, 17).

Matthew is again guilty of deception. A reference to his table shows that there were but thirteen generations. In order to carry out his numerical system of fourteen generations to each period he counts the generation of Jechonias in this period which he has already counted in the preceding period; thus performing the mathematical feat of dividing 27 by 2 and obtaining 14 for a quotient.

Had Matthew given a true summary of this genealogy, assuming the generations from the close of the Old Testament record to Christ to be correct, instead of these periods of double seven each, we would have the following: "So all the generations from Abraham to David are thirteen generations; and from David until the carrying away into Babylon are nineteen generations; and from the carrying away into Babylon unto Christ are thirteen generations."

16

Name the generations from the Captivity to Christ.

Matthew	Luke	Chronicles
Salathiel	Salathiel	Pediah
Zorobabel	Zorobabel	Zerubabel
Abiud	Rhesa	Hananiah
Eliakim	Joanna	Schecania
Azor	Juda	Shemaiah
Sadoc	Joseph	Neariah
Achim	Semei	Elioenai
Eliud	Mattathias	Hodaiah
Eleazer	Maath	(Here the genealogy of
Matthan	Nagge	Chronicles ends.)
Jacob	Esli	
Joseph	Naum	
Jesus	Amos	
	Mattathias	
	Joseph	
	Janna	
	Melchi	
	Levi	
	Heli	
	Matthat	
	Joseph	
	Jesus	

17

According to the accepted chronology, what was the average age of each generation from David to Jesus?

Luke: Twenty-five years.

Matthew: Forty years.

18

What was the average age from David to the Captivity?

Matthew: Thirty-seven years.

According to Chronicles the average age of the same line for the same period was but twenty-six years.

19

What was the average age from the Captivity to Jesus?

Luke: Twenty-eight years.

Matthew: Fifty years.

While the average age from David to the Captivity by way of Solomon was but twenty-six years the average age from the Captivity to Jesus by the same line, according to Matthew, was fifty years. This proves the falsity of Matthew's genealogy from the Captivity to Jesus.

20

What was the average length of each generation from Abraham to David?

Matthew and Luke: Seventy years.

Seventy years is said to constitute the natural life of man. According to these Evangelists Christ's Pre-Davidic ancestors only reached maturity at seventy. How slow was man's development then—a babe in his mother's arms at twenty; a playful child at forty; at sixty an ardent youth wooing a blushing maiden of half a hundred years; at three score years and ten a fond young father rejoicing at the birth of his first-born!

21

What was the average length of each generation from Adam to Abraham?

Luke: One hundred years.

22

How many generations were there from Adam to Abraham?

Luke: Twenty (iii, 34–38).

Luke makes less than half as many generations from Adam to Abraham in a period of two thousand years as he does from David to Jesus in a period of one thousand years.

23

How many generations were there between Rachab, the mother of Booz, and David?

Matthew: Three—Booz, Obed, and Jesse (i, 5, 6).

Rachab lived at Jericho when it was taken by the Israelites. Jericho was taken in 1451 B.C., the year that Moses died. David was born in 1085 B.C.—nearly four centuries later.

24

Assuming the generations following the Captivity in Matthew and Chronicles to run parallel, how many generations were there between the last generation named in Chronicles and Jesus?

Matthew: Four.

Yet Chronicles was written, it is claimed, from 458 to 604 years before Christ.

"If the Chronicles were written by Ezra, the date of their composition was not far from B.C. 458, the year of the return from the Captivity. If by Daniel, the earlier period of from 604 to 534 must be adopted."— Rev. Dr. Hitchcock.

25

Name the first ten ancestors of Jesus.

Luke: Adam, Seth, Enos, Cainan, Maleleel, Jared, Enoch, Mathusala, Lamech, Noe (iii, 36–38).

Archeological researches have shown these to be ten Babylonian kings.*

26

Who was Sala?

Luke: "Sala, which was the son of Cainan, which was the son of Arphaxad" (iii, 35, 36).

"And Arphaxad lived five and thirty years and begat Salah" (Genesis xi, 12).

According to Luke Sala was the grand-son of Arphaxad; according to Genesis he was the son of Arphaxad.

27

Who begat Ozias?

Matthew: "Joram begat Ozias" (i, 8).

"Ahaziah his [Joram's] son, Joash his son, Amaziah his son, Azariah [Ozias] his son" (1 Chronicles iii, 11, 12).

According to the New Testament Ozias was the son of Joram; according to the Old Testament he was the great great-grandson of Joram.

28

Who was Josiah's successor?

Matthew: Jechonias (i, 11).

---

*Based on current research, this statement is now incorrect—ed.

"Then the people of the land took Jehoahaz, the son of Josiah, and made him king in his father's stead" (2 Chronicles xxxvi, 1).

"For thus saith the Lord touching Shallum, the son of Josiah, king of Judah, which reigned instead of Josiah, his father" (Jeremiah xxii, 11).

"And Pharaoh-nechoh made Eliakim the son of Josiah king in the room of Josiah, his father, and turned his name to Jehoiakim" (2 Kings xxiii, 34).

According to Matthew, Josiah's successor was Jechonias; according to Chronicles, Jehoahaz; according to Jeremiah, Shallum; according to Kings, Jehoiakim.

29

Who was the father of Jechonias?

Matthew: "Josias begat Jechonias" (i, 11).

Josias was not the father but the grandfather of Jechonias. "And the sons of Josiah were, . . . the second Jehoiakim. . . . And the sons of Jehoiakim: Jechoniah, his son" (1 Chron. iii, 15, 16).

30

When did Josias beget Jechonias?

Matthew: "And Josias begat Jechonias and his brethren, about the time they were carried away into Babylon" (i, 11).

Josiah became king in 641 B.C. and died in 610 B.C. Jechonias was carried to Babylon in 588 B.C., 22 years after Josiah died.

31

Did Jechonias have a son?

Matthew: "And after they were brought to Babylon, Jechonias begat Salathiel" (i, 12).

"As I live, saith the Lord, though Coniah [Jechonias], the son of Jehoiakim, king of Judah, were the signet upon my right hand, yet would I pluck thee thence. . . . O earth, earth, earth, hear the word of the Lord. Thus saith the Lord, Write ye this man childless, a man that shall not prosper in his days: for no man of his seed shall prosper, sitting upon the throne of David, and ruling no more in Judah" (Jeremiah xxii, 24–30).

This curse was pronounced upon Jechonias before he was taken to Babylon. By this divine oath Jesus is precluded from becoming an heir to the throne of David. God swears that Jechonias shall be childless, and that no descendant of his shall ever sit upon the throne. Yet Matthew, in the face of this oath, declares that Jechonias did not remain childless, that he begat a son, Salathiel, the progenitor of Jesus. In attempting to make Jesus an heir to David's throne Matthew makes God a liar and perjurer.

32

Matthew says that Salathiel was the son of Jechonias. Who does Luke declare him to be?

"The son of Neri" (iii, 27).

33

Who was the father of Zorobabel?

Matthew: "And Salathiel begat Zorobabel" (i, 12).

Luke: "Zorobabel, which was the son of Salathiel" (iii, 27).

Here both Evangelists agree—agree to disagree with Chronicles which says that Zorobabel was the son of Pedaiah, the brother of Salathiel. "And the sons of Pedaiah were Zerubbabel and Shimei" (1 Chron. iii, 19).

34

Who was the son of Zorobabel?
   Matthew: "And Zorobabel begat Abiud" (i, 13).
   Luke: "Rhesa, which was the son of Zorobabel" (iii, 27).
   Each contradicts the other, and both contradict the Old Testament (1 Chron. iii, 19, 20).

35

Who was the father of Joseph?
   Matthew: "And Jacob begat Joseph" (i, 16).
   Luke: "Joseph, which was the son of Heli" (iii, 23).

36

If Jesus was descended from David, the descent was through one of David's sons. Which one?
   Matthew: Solomon (i, 6–16).
   Luke: Nathan (iii, 23-31).
   Luke reaches the same person by way of one brother that Matthew does by way of the other.

37

Many commentators attempt to reconcile these discordant genealogies by assuming that Matthew gives the genealogy of Joseph, while Luke gives the genealogy of Mary. What do the Evangelists themselves declare?
   Matthew: "And Jacob begat Joseph the husband of Mary, of whom was born Jesus, who is called Christ," etc. (i, 16).
   Luke: "And Jesus himself began to be about thirty years of age, being (as was supposed) the son of Joseph, which was the son of Heli," etc. (iii, 23).

Dr. Geikie, in his *Life of Christ* (Vol. I, p. 531, note), says: "The genealogies given by both Matthew and Luke seem unquestionably to refer to Joseph."

Regarding this the Rev. Dr. McNaught says: "Let the reader bear in mind how Matthew states that 'Jacob begat Joseph, the husband of Mary,' and how Luke's words are 'Joseph which was the son of Heli,' and then let him say whether it is truthful to allege that these different genealogies belong to different individuals. Is it not plain that each of them professes to trace the lineal descent of one and the same man, Joseph?"

William Rathbone Greg says: "The circumstance that any man could suppose that Matthew when he said, 'Jacob begat Joseph,' or Luke, when he said, 'Joseph was the son of Heli,' could refer to the wife of the one, or the daughter-in-law of the other, shows to what desperate stratagems polemical orthodoxy will resort in order to defend an untenable position."

Smith's Bible Dictionary offers the following explanation: "They are both the genealogies of Joseph, i.e., of Jesus Christ, as the reputed and legal son of Joseph and Mary. The genealogy of St. Matthew is Joseph's genealogy as legal successor to the throne of David. St. Luke's is Joseph's private genealogy, exhibiting his real birth, as David's son, and thus showing why he was heir to Solomon's crown. The simple principle that one Evangelist exhibits that genealogy which contained the successive heirs to David's and Solomon's throne, while the other exhibits the paternal stem of him who was the heir, explains all the anomalies of the two pedigrees."

This "simple principle" necessitates three disagreeable postulates. 1. That the lineage of Nathan, who is not the recorded possessor of even one wife, survived, while that of Solomon who had seven hundred wives became extinct. 2. That Joseph was legal successor to the throne of David, when Heli, his father, was not. 3. That the first chapter of Matthew contains more than a score of errors. That little word "begat" is fatal to the above theory. Matthew declares that Jacob begat Joseph. If Jacob begat Joseph, then Jacob, and not Heli, was the father of Joseph. According to Matthew, the royal line descends from David to Joseph unbroken; each heir begetting the succeeding one, thus precluding the possibility of a collateral branch inheriting the throne.

The hypothesis that Jesus was merely the adopted son and legal heir of Joseph and yet fulfilled the Messianic requirements is untenable. Strauss says: "Adoption might indeed suffice to secure to the adopted son the reversion of certain external family rights and inheritances; but such a relationship could in no wise lend a claim to the Messianic dignity, which was attached to the true blood and lineage of David" (*Leben Jesu*, p. 122).

The Messiah must be a natural and lineal descendant of David, which Peter expressly declares Jesus to be: "God had sworn with an oath to him [David], that of the fruit of his loins, according to the flesh, he would raise up Christ to sit on his throne" (Acts ii, 30).

It is assumed by some that a Levirate marriage had taken place between the parents of Joseph, and that the one genealogy belonged to the natural, the others to the legal father of Joseph. By a Levirate marriage if a man died without heirs his remaining brother married his widow and raised up heirs to him. But in this case the brothers would have the same father, and the genealogies would differ only in the father of Joseph. It is only by a succession of Levirate marriages and a juggling of words, which no intelligent critic can seriously entertain, that such a hypothesis can be considered possible, even waiving the Old Testament writers, and the Evangelists themselves, whose language forbids it.

Eusebius advances an explanation characteristic of this ecclesiastical historian and of the early church whose history he professes to record. The Jews, it is said, were divided in their opinions regarding the descent of the Messiah. While some contended that his descent must be through the royal line, others believed that because of the excessive wickedness of the kings the descent would be through another line. Eusebius says: "Matthew gives his opinion, Luke repeats the common opinion of many, not his own. . . . This last view Luke takes, though conscious that Matthew gives the real truth of the genealogy."

Matthew's genealogy is self-evidently false; while Luke's, according to the admission of the historian of the primitive church, is merely a fabrication of early Christians, designed to influence those who rejected Matthew's genealogy of the Messiah.

38

If the miraculous conception be true the Davidic descent could only be through Mary. Was Mary descended from David?

"We are wholly ignorant of the name and occupation of St. Mary's parents. She was, like Joseph, of the tribe of Judah, and of the lineage of David (Ps. cxxxii, 11; Luke i, 32; Rom. i, 3)."—*Smith's Bible Dictionary.*

Three passages are cited in support of this claim:

1. "The Lord hath sworn in truth unto David; he will not turn from it. Of the fruit of thy body will I sit upon thy throne. If thy children will keep my covenant and my testimony that I shall teach them, their children shall also sit upon thy throne forevermore" (Ps. cxxxii, 11, 12).

2. "He shall be great, and shall be called the son of the Highest; and the Lord God shall give unto him the throne of his father David" (Luke i, 32).

3. "Concerning his son Jesus Christ our Lord, which was made of the seed of David according to the flesh" (Rom. i, 3).

The second and third passages do not refer to Mary; the first passage refers neither to Jesus nor Mary. There is no evidence to prove that Mary was descended from David. On the contrary there is evidence to prove that she was not descended from him.

1. "The angel Gabriel was sent from God unto a city in Galilee, called Nazareth, to a virgin espoused to a man whose name was Joseph, of the house of David; and the virgin's name was Mary" (Luke i, 27). Joseph, and not Mary, is declared to be of the house of David.

2. It is stated that Joseph went to Bethlehem "to be taxed with Mary," not because they, but "because he was of the house and lineage of David" (Luke ii, 4, 5).

3. Mary was the cousin of Elizabeth (Luke i, 3), and Elizabeth "was of the daughters of Aaron" (i, 5), i.e., descended from Levi, while the house of David was descended from Judah.

This desperate, yet ineffectual, effort to establish the Davidic descent of Mary is virtually an abandonment of the genealogical tables of Matthew and Luke, and a falling back upon this pitiable *argumentum* in circulo: Mary was descended from David because the Messiah was to be descended from David, and Jesus was the Messiah because Mary was descended from David.

These genealogies do not give the lineage of Mary who is said to have been his only earthly parent, but the lineage of Joseph who, it is claimed, was not his father. But if Joseph was not the father of Jesus, what is the use of giving his pedigree? If Joseph was not the father of Jesus how does proving that he was descended from David prove that Jesus was descended from David? If these genealogies run through Joseph to Jesus, as stated by Matthew and Luke, then Joseph must have been the father of Jesus; and if he was the father of Jesus the story of the miraculous conception is false.

The Synoptics, as we have seen, are for the most part, mere compilations, made up of preexisting documents. These documents belonged to different ages of the primitive church. In the first ages of the church Christians believed that Jesus was simply a man—the son of Joseph and Mary. The genealogies of Matthew and Luke, which trace his descent from David through Joseph, belonged to this age. The story of the miraculous conception was the product of a later age.

If the dogma of the miraculous conception be true, if God, and not Joseph, was the father of Jesus as taught, these genealogies, being genealogies of Joseph, fail to prove what they are intended to prove, the royal descent of Jesus from David. The genealogies of Matthew and Luke and their accounts of the miraculous conception mutually exclude each other.

39

Did Jesus believe himself to be descended from David?

Synoptics: He did not (Matt. xxii, 41–46; Mark xii, 35–37; Luke xx, 41–44).

A principal objection to accepting Jesus as the Messiah by the Jews was the fact that he was not descended from David. He tacitly admitted that he was not, and the whole burden of his argument was to convince them that it was not necessary that he should be.

40

The miraculous conception was in fulfillment of what prophecy?

Matthew: "Now all this was done, that it might be fulfilled which was spoken of the Lord by the prophet, saying, Behold, a virgin shall be with child, and shall bring forth a son and they shall call his name Emmanuel" (i, 22, 23).

This is esteemed the "Gem of the Prophecies," and may be found in the seventh chapter of Isaiah. The facts are these: Rezin, king of Syria, and Pekah, king of Israel, had declared war against Ahaz, king of Judah. God assured Ahaz that they should not succeed, but that their own kingdoms should be destroyed by the Assyrians. To convince him of the truth of this he requested Ahaz to demand a sign. "But Ahaz said, I will not ask, neither will I tempt the Lord. . . . Therefore the Lord himself shall give you a sign; Behold, a virgin shall conceive, and bear a son, and shall call his name Emmanuel. . . . Before the child shall know to refuse the evil, and choose the good, the land that thou abhorrest shall be forsaken of both her kings."

In the succeeding chapter the fulfillment of this prophecy is recorded: "And I went unto the prophetess; and she conceived, and bare a son. Then said the Lord to me, Call his name Mahershalal-hash-baz. For before the child shall have knowledge to cry, My father, and my mother, the riches of Damascus [the capital of Rezin's kingdom] and the spoils of Samaria [the capital of Pekah's kingdom] shall be taken away before the king of Assyria." Rezin and Pekah were overthrown by the Assyrians about 720 B.C.

One of the most convincing proofs of Christ's divinity, with many, is the supposed fact that he was born of a virgin and that his miraculous birth was foretold by a prophet seven hundred years before the event occurred. Now, there is not a passage in the Jewish Scriptures declaring that a child should be born of a virgin. The word translated "virgin" does not mean a virgin in the accepted sense of the term, but simply a young woman, either married or single. The whole passage is a mistranslation. The words rendered "a virgin shall conceive and bear a son" should read, "a young woman is with child and beareth a son." In this so-called prophecy there is not the remotest reference to a miraculous conception and a virgin-born child. The Jews themselves did not regard this passage as a Messianic prophecy; neither did they believe that the Messiah was to be born of a virgin.

Next to the preceding the following is most frequently cited as a Messianic prophecy: "The sceptre shall not depart from Judah, . . . until Shiloh come" (Genesis xlix, 10).

If Shiloh refers to Christ the prophecy was not fulfilled, for the sceptre did depart from Judah 600 years before Christ came. But Shiloh does not refer to a Messiah, nor to any man. Shiloh was the seat of the national sanctuary before it was removed to Jerusalem. This so-called prophecy, like the preceding, is a mistranslation. The correct reading is as follows: "The preeminence shall not depart from Judah so long as the people resort to Shiloh."

"For unto us a child is born, unto us a son is given; and the government shall be upon his shoulder; and his name shall be declared Wonderful, Counsellor, The Mighty God, the everlasting Father, the Prince of Peace" (Isaiah ix, 6).

Prof. Cheyne, the highest authority on Isaiah, pronounces this a forgery. Every honest Christian scholar must admit this. It is a self-evident forgery. No Jewish writer could have written it. To have declared even the Messiah to be "The mighty God, the everlasting Father" would have been the rankest blasphemy, a crime the punishment of which was death.

These alleged Messianic prophecies are, in their present form, Christian rather than Jewish. Christian translators and exegetists have altered their language and perverted their meaning to make them appear to refer to Christ. The following is an example:

"I will raise unto David a righteous Branch, and a King shall reign and prosper, and shall execute judgment and justice in the earth. In his days Judah shall be saved, and Israel shall dwell safely; and this is his name whereby he shall be called, THE LORD OUR RIGHTEOUSNESS" (Jeremiah xxiii, 5, 6).

The correct rendering of this passage is as follows:

"I will raise unto David a righteous branch, and a king shall reign and prosper, and shall execute judgment and justice in the land. In his days Judah shall be saved and Israel shall dwell safely; and this is the name whereby they shall call themselves: The Eternal is our righteousness."

To make a Messianic prophecy of this passage and give it effect no less than eight pieces of deception were employed by the editors of our Authorized Version:

1. The word "branch" is made to begin with a capital letter.
2. The word "king" also begins with a capital.
3. "The name" is rendered "his name."
4. The pronoun "they," relating to the people of Judah and Israel, is changed to "he."
5. The word "Eternal" is translated "Lord."
6. "The Lord our righteousness" is printed in capitals.
7. In the table of contents, at the head of the chapter, are the words "Christ shall rule and save them."
8. At the top of the page are the words "Christ promised."

Another example of this Messianic prophecy making is the following:

"Know therefore and understand that from the going forth of the commandment to restore and to build Jerusalem, unto Messiah the Prince, shall be seven weeks, and three score and two weeks" (Daniel ix, 25).

The term "week," it is claimed, means a period of seven years, and assumed that by Messiah is meant Christ. Seven weeks and three score and two weeks are sixty-nine weeks, or 483 years, the time that was to elapse from the command to rebuild Jerusalem to the coming of Christ, if the prophecy was fulfilled. The decree of Cyrus to rebuild Jerusalem and the temple was made 536 B.C. According to the accepted chronology Christ was born 4 B.C. From the decree of Cyrus, then, to the coming of Christ was 532 years instead of 483 years, a period of seven weeks, or forty-nine years, longer than that named by Daniel. Ezra, the priest, went to Jerusalem in 457 B.C. This event, however, had nothing whatever to do with the decree for rebuilding Jerusalem and the temple. It occurred 79 years after the decree was issued, and 58 years after the temple was finished. But a searcher for Messianic prophecies found that from the time of Ezra to the beginning of Christ's ministry was about 483 years, or 69 prophetic weeks; and notwithstanding there was a deficiency of 79 years at one end of the period, and an excess of 30 years at the other, it was declared to fit exactly.

Christian theologians pretend to recognize in the Old Testament two kinds of Messianic prophecies: 1. Specific predictions concerning Christ which were literally fulfilled; 2. Passages in which the writer refers to other persons or events, but which God, without the writer's knowledge, designed as types of Christ. The fallaciousness of the former having been exposed—it having been shown that there is not a text in the Jewish Scriptures predicting the coming of Christ—they now rely chiefly upon the latter to support their claims. These "prophecies" are almost limitless; for a firm believer in prophecy can, with a vivid imagination, take almost any passage and point out a fancied resemblance between the thing it refers to and the thing he wants confirmed; apparently oblivious to the fact that the passage is equally applicable to a thousand other things. Had the Mormons accepted Joe Smith as a Messiah instead of a prophet they would have no lack of prophecies to support their claims; and by translating and revising the Scriptures to suit their views, as Christians did, these prophecies would fit him as well as they do the Christ.

41

What name was to be given the child mentioned in Isaiah's prophecy?

"They shall call his name Emmanuel" (Matthew i, 23).

What name was to be given Mary's son?

"Thou shalt call his name Jesus" (Matt. i, 21). In the naming of the Christian Messiah Isaiah's prophecy was not fulfilled. He was never called Emmanuel, but Jesus.

42

To whom did the angel announcing the miraculous conception appear?

Matthew: To Joseph (i, 20, 21).

Luke: To Mary (i, 26–38).

"An angel did not appear, first to Mary, and also afterwards to

Joseph; he can only have appeared either to the one or to the other. Consequently, it is only the one or the other relation which can be regarded as historical. And here different considerations would conduct to opposite decisions. . . . Every criticism which might determine the adoption of the one, and the rejection of the other, disappears; and we find ourselves, in reference to both accounts, driven back by necessity to the mythical view."—Strauss.

43

For what purpose was the Annunciation made?

Luke: Simply to acquaint Mary with the heavenly decree that she had been chosen to become the mother of the coming Messiah (i, 26–33).

Matthew: To allay the suspicions of Joseph respecting Mary's chastity and prevent him from putting her away (i, 18–20).

44

Did the Annunciation take place before or after Mary's conception?

Luke: Before (i, 26–31).

Matthew: After (i, 18–20).

45

Who was declared to be the father of Jesus?

Matthew: The Holy Ghost (i, 18, 20).

With the Jews the Holy Ghost (Spirit) was of feminine gender; with the Greeks, of masculine gender. The belief that the Holy Ghost was the father of Jesus originated, not with the Jewish Christians of Palestine, as claimed, but with the Greek Christians of Alexandria.

46

What prediction did the angel Gabriel make to Mary concerning Jesus?

"The Lord shall give unto him the throne of his father David" (Luke i, 32).

Respecting this prediction the Rev. Dr. Hooykaas, of Holland, says: "If a messenger from Heaven had really come to bring a divine revelation to Mary, the result must have confirmed his prediction; and since Jesus never fulfilled these expectations it is obvious that the revelation was never made."

47

When Mary visited Elizabeth what did she do?

Luke: She uttered a hymn of praise (i, 46–55).

Had Mary uttered such a hymn we would suppose that it would have been original and inspired by the Almighty Father of her unborn child. Yet the hymn which Luke puts into her mouth was borrowed from the song of Hannah.

Hannah	Mary
"My heart rejoiceth in the Lord" (1 Sam. ii, 1).	"My spirit hath rejoiced in God" (Luke i, 47).
"If thou wilt indeed look on the affliction of thine handmaid" (i, 11).	"For he hath regarded the low estate of his handmaiden" (48).
"Talk no more so exceeding proudly" (ii, 3).	"He hath scattered the proud" (51).
"The bows of the mighty men are broken, and they that stumbled are girded with strength (4).	"He hath put down the mighty from their seats and exalted them of low degree" (52).
"They that were full hath hired out themselves for bread; and they that were hungry ceased" (5).	"He hath filled the hungry with good things; and the rich he hath sent empty away" (53).

48

What decree is said to have been issued by Caesar Augustus immediately preceding the birth of Christ?

Luke: "That all the world should be taxed" (ii, 1).

No such decree was issued by Augustus, nor even one that the Roman world should be taxed. The taxation of different provinces of the empire was made at various times, no general decree ever having been issued and no uniform assessment ever having been attempted by Augustus. An enrollment of Roman citizens for the purpose of taxation was made in Syria in 7 A.D.

49

Of what king was Joseph a subject when Jesus was born?

Matthew: Of Herod.

If Jesus was born during the reign of Herod, Joseph, whether a resident of Judea or of Galilee, could not have been taxed by Augustus, for neither province was then a part of Syria. Both provinces belonged to Herod's kingdom and Herod's subjects were not taxed by the Roman government.

50

Of what province was Joseph a resident?

Matthew: Of Judea.

Luke: Of Galilee.

If he was a resident of Galilee he could not have been taxed by Augustus, even in the time of Cyrenius, for Galilee was not a Roman province, but an independent state, and had no political connection with Syria.

Again, this decree could not have applied to Judea prior to the banishment of Archelaus, ten years after the time of Herod; for Judea did not become a Roman province until that time; and while Archelaus had paid tribute to Rome the assessments of the people were made by him and not by Augustus.

51

Why was Joseph with his wife obliged to leave Galilee and go to Bethlehem of Judea to be enrolled?

Luke: "Because he was of the house and lineage of David," and Bethlehem was the "city of David" (ii, 4).

Even if he had been subject to taxation there was no law or custom requiring him to leave his own country and go to that of his ancestors to be enrolled. The assessment, according to the Roman custom, was made at the residence of the person taxed. Nothing surpasses in absurdity this story of Luke, that a woman, on the eve of confinement, and the subject of another ruler, was dragged across two provinces to be enrolled for taxation.

In regard to this taxation Dr. Hooykaas says: "But here again we are met by overwhelming difficulties. In itself, the Evangelist's account of the manner in which the census was carried out is entirely incredible. Only fancy the indescribable confusion that would have arisen if every one, through the length and breadth of the land of the Jews, had left his abode to go and enroll himself in the city or village from which his family originally came, even supposing he knew where it was. The census under David was conducted after a very different fashion. But it is still more important to note that the Evangelist falls into the most extraordinary mistakes throughout. In the first place history is silent as to a census of the whole (Roman) world ever having been made at all. In the next place, though Quirinus [Cyrenius] certainly did make such a register in Judea and Samaria, it did not extend to Galilee; so that Joseph's household was not affected by it. Besides it did not take place till ten years after the death of Herod, when his son Archelaus was deposed by the Emperor, and the districts of Judea and Samaria were thrown into a Roman province. Under the reign of Herod nothing of the kind took place, nor was there any occasion for it. Finally, at the time of the birth of Jesus the governor of Syria was not Quirinus, but Quintus Sentius Saturninus" (*Bible for Learners,* Vol. III, pp. 55, 56).

52

Was Jesus born in a house or in a stable?

Matthew: "And when they were come into the house, they saw the young child with Mary his mother" (ii, 11).

Luke: "And she brought forth her first born son, and wrapped him in swaddling clothes, and laid him in a manger" (ii, 7).

Nothing can be clearer than that the author of Matthew supposes that Jesus was born in a house. The author of Luke, on the other hand, expressly declares that he was born in a stable. Luke's story concerning the place of Mary's accouchement has been received, while that of Matthew has been ignored.

Christ's birth in a manger and death on the cross are the lodestones that have attracted the sympathies of the world, and kept him on the throne of Christendom; for sentiment rather than reason dominates mankind. Referring to Luke's story, the *Bible for Learners* says: "Such is the well-known story of the birth of Jesus, one of the sweetest and most deeply significant of all the legends of the Bible. That it is a legend, without even the smallest historical foundation, we must, of course, admit" (Vol. III, p. 54).

Justin Martyr states that Jesus was born in a cave, and this statement Farrar is disposed to accept: "Justin Martyr, the Apologist, who, from his birth at Shechem, was familiar with Palestine, and who lived less than a century after the time of our Lord, places the scene of the nativity in a cave. This is, indeed, the ancient and constant tradition both of the Eastern and the Western churches, and it is one of the few to which, though unrecorded in the Gospel history, we may attach a reasonable probability" (*Life of Christ,* p. 3).

53

Why did Joseph and his wife take shelter in a stable?

Luke: "Because there was no room for them in the inn" (ii, 7).

Luke states that there was an inn at Bethlehem. There was no inn in the place. Dr. Geikie says: "We must not moreover think of Joseph seeking an inn at Bethlehem, for inns were unknown among the Jews" (*Christmas at Bethlehem*).

54

What celestial phenomenon attended Christ's birth?

Matthew: A new star appeared and stood in the heavens above him (ii, 1–9).

Luke: An angelic choir appeared and sang praises to God (ii, 13, 14).

Matthew's story of the star and the Magi, even to the language itself, was borrowed from the writings of the Persians; Luke's story of the celestial visitants was taken from Pagan mythology.

55

Who visited him after his birth?

Matthew: Wise men from the East (ii, 1–11).

Luke: Shepherds from a neighboring field (ii, 8–20).

Matthew makes no mention of the shepherds' visit; Luke is evidently ignorant of the visit of the wise men.

56

From where did the wise men come?

Matthew: "Now when Jesus was born in Bethlehem of Judea in the days of Herod the king, behold, there came wise men from the

East to Jerusalem, saying: Where is he that is born King of the Jews? for we have seen his star in the East, and are come to worship him" (ii, 1, 2).

By the "East" was meant Persia or India, and from one of these countries the Magi are popularly supposed to have come.

Justin Martyr says: "When a star rose in heaven at the time of his birth, as is recorded in the 'Memoirs' of his Apostles, the Magi from Arabia, recognizing the sign by this, came and worshiped him" (*Dialogues,* cvi).

If they came from Arabia, as this Christian father declares, they came not from the East, but from the South.

57

What announcement did the angel make to the shepherds?

"For behold I bring you good tidings of great joy, which shall be to all people" (Luke ii, 10).

According to Luke the visit of the angels is to proclaim to the world the birth of the newborn Messiah. Had the celestial phenomenon reported by this Evangelist really occurred the news of it would have quickly spread over Palestine. Yet the people of Jerusalem, only a few miles away, learn nothing of it; for, according to Matthew, the first intimation that Herod has of Christ's birth, is from the wise men who visit him at a much later period. The inhabitants of Bethlehem themselves are ignorant of it. Could they have discovered to Herod this wonderful babe, or the place where his parents abode while there if they had departed, it would have saved their own children from the wrath of this monarch. But they knew nothing of him.

58

What effect had the announcement of Christ's birth upon Herod and the people of Jerusalem?

Matthew: "When Herod the king had heard these things, he was troubled, and all Jerusalem with him" (ii, 3).

According to Matthew the announcement filled with alarm the entire populace, and the most diligent efforts were made to discover and destroy the babe. In strange contrast to this statement of Matthew is Luke's narrative (ii, 22–27), which declares that Jesus, when forty days old, was brought to Jerusalem and publicly exhibited in Herod's own temple, without exciting any alarm or provoking any hostility.

59

What did his parents do with him?

Matthew: They fled with him into Egypt (ii, 13, 15).

Luke: They remained with him in Palestine (ii, 22–52).

"All attempts to reconcile these two contradictory statements, seem only elaborate efforts of art."—Dr. Schleiermacher.

60

When unable to discover Jesus what did Herod do?

Matthew: "Then Herod, when he saw that he was mocked of the wise men, was exceeding wroth, and sent forth, and slew all the children that were in Bethlehem, and in all the coasts thereof, from two years old and under" (ii, 16).

If this statement be true hundreds of innocent babes (the Greek Calendar says fourteen thousand) must have perished, a crime the enormity of which is almost without a parallel in the annals of history. It is strange that Mark, Luke, and John make no mention of this frightful tragedy. Luke's silence is especially significant. It is passing strange that the Roman historians and Rabbinical writers of that age, who wrote of Herod, should be silent regarding it. Josephus devotes nearly forty chapters to the life of Herod. He narrates with much particularity every important event in his life. He detested this monarch and dwells upon his crimes and errors. Yet Josephus knew nothing of this massacre.

In this silence of Josephus Dr. Farrar recognizes a difficulty too damaging to ignore. He says: "Why then, it has been asked, does Josephus make no mention of so infamous an atrocity? Perhaps because it was performed so secretly that he did not even know of it. Perhaps because, in those terrible days, the murder of a score of children, in consequence of a transient suspicion, would have been regarded as an item utterly insignificant in the list of Herod's murders. Perhaps because it was passed over in silence by Nikolaus of Damascus, who, writing in the true spirit of those Hellenizing courtiers, who wanted to make a political Messiah out of a corrupt and blood-stained usurper, magnified all his patron's achievements, and concealed or palliated all his crimes. But the more probable reason is that Josephus, whom, in spite of all the immense literary debt which we owe to him, we can only regard as a renegade and a sycophant, did not choose to make any allusion to facts which were even remotely connected with the life of Christ" (*Life of Christ,* pp. 22, 23).

A more absurd reason than the first advanced by Farrar it is difficult to conceive. The second, that it was a matter of too little consequence to record, an explanation which other Christian apologists have assigned, is as unreasonable as it is heartless. The silence of Nikolaus, who wrote of Herod after his death, is also significant, and the excuse offered by Farrar that he omitted it because he was the friend of Herod, even if admitted, cannot apply to Josephus, who abhorred the memory of this monarch. The contention that Josephus purposely ignored the existence of Christ because he saw in him a menace to his faith is childish. Jesus Christ, admitting his existence, had made no history to record. His birth was attended by no prodigies, and there was nothing in his advent to excite the fear or envy of a king. Josephus mentions no Herodian massacre at Bethlehem because none occurred. Had Herod slain a single child in the manner stated the fact would be attested by a score of authors whose writings are extant. Herod did not slay one babe. This story is false.

Herod's massacre of the infants of Bethlehem and the escape of Jesus was probably suggested by Kansa's massacre of the infants of Matura and the escape of Krishna. Pharaoh's slaughter of the first born in Egypt may also have suggested it.

61

What was the real cause of Herod's massacre?

Matthew: The visit of the wise men and the disclosures made by them (ii, 1–16).

These wise men, it is claimed, were under divine guidance. In view of this terrible slaughter their visit must be regarded as a divine blunder.

62

In the massacre of the innocents what prophecy was fulfilled?

Matthew: "Then was fulfilled that which was spoken by Jeremy the prophet, saying, In Rama was there a voice heard, lamentation, and weeping, and great mourning, Rachel weeping for her children, and would not be comforted, because they are not" (ii, 17, 18).

This so-called prophecy is in Jeremiah xxxi, 15. It was written at the time of the Babylonian captivity and refers to the captive Jews. In the next verse Jeremiah says: "They shall come again from the land of the enemy."

63

When Herod died what did the Lord command Joseph to do?

"Arise, and take the young child and his mother and go into the land of Israel, for they are dead which sought the young child's life" (Matthew ii, 20)

"And the Lord said unto Moses in Midian, Go, return to Egypt: for all the men are dead which sought thy life" (Exodus iv, 19).

64

The sojourn of Joseph and Mary with Jesus in Egypt was in fulfillment of what prophecy?

Matthew: That "spoken of the Lord by the prophet, saying, Out of Egypt have I called my son" (ii, 15).

This may be found in Hosea xi, 1, and clearly refers to the exodus of the Israelites from Egypt.

65

Jesus was subsequently taken to Nazareth. Why?

Matthew: "That it might be fulfilled which was spoken by the prophet, He shall be called a Nazarene" (ii, 23).

The Bible contains no such prophecy. Fleetwood admits that "the words are not to be found" in "the prophetical writings," and Farrar says, "It is well known that no such passage occurs in any extant prophecy" (*Life of Christ,* p. 33). The only passage to which the above can refer is Judges xiii, 5. Here the child referred to was not to be called a Nazarene, but a Nazarite, and Matthew knew that "Nazarene" and "Nazarite" were no more synonymous than "Jew" and "priest." A Nazarene was a native of Nazareth; a Nazarite was one consecrated to the service of the Lord. Matthew likewise knew that this Nazarite referred to in Judges was Samson.

66

Had Joseph and Mary lived in Nazareth previous to the birth of Jesus?

Luke: They had.

Matthew: They had not.

"And Joseph also went up from Galilee, out of the city of Nazareth, unto the city of David, which is called Bethlehem, . . . to be taxed with Mary his espoused wife. . . . And when they had performed all things according to the law of the Lord, they returned into Galilee, to their own city Nazareth" (Luke ii, 4, 5, 39).

"When he [Joseph] arose, he took the young child and his mother by night, and departed into Egypt: and was there until the death of Herod. . . . But when Herod was dead, . . . he arose, and took the young child and his mother, and came into the land of Israel. And when he heard that Archelaus did reign in the room of his father Herod, he was afraid to go thither; notwithstanding, being warned of God in a dream, he turned aside into the parts of Galilee: and he came and dwelt in a city called Nazareth" (Matthew ii, 14–23).

According to Luke their home was in Nazareth of Galilee; according to Matthew their home was in Bethlehem of Judea. Luke states that they merely visited Bethlehem to be enrolled for taxation and fulfill a certain Messianic prophecy. Matthew states that after the flight into Egypt and the death of Herod they were returning to Judea when fearing Archelaus they turned aside into Galilee to avoid this ruler and fulfill another Messianic prophecy.

67

How did the parents of Jesus receive the predictions of Simeon concerning him?

Luke: "And Joseph and his mother marvelled at those things which were spoken of him" (ii, 33).

Why should they marvel at the predictions of Simeon when long before they had been apprised of the same thing by the angel Gabriel?

68

Does the name "Joseph" belong in the text quoted above?

It does not. The correct reading is: "And his father and his mother were marvelling at the things which were spoken concerning him." It declares Joseph to be the father of Jesus, and as this did not harmonize with the story of the miraculous conception the makers of our version substituted "Joseph" for "father."

69

What does Luke say regarding the infancy of John and Jesus?

"And the child [John] grew and waxed strong in spirit" (i, 80).

"And the child [Jesus] grew and waxed strong in spirit" (ii, 40).

Between the growth of the man John and the growth of the God Jesus there is, according to the Evangelist, no difference, and the growth of each is identical with that of the demi-god Samson.

70

What custom did Jesus's parents observe?

Luke: "His parents went to Jerusalem every year at the feast of the passover" (ii, 41).

The preceding verse (40) shows that Luke means every year following the birth of Jesus. In the succeeding verse (42) it is clearly implied that Jesus always accompanied them. It is impossible to reconcile this statement of Luke, who evidently knows nothing of the enmity of Herod and Archelaus, with the statements of Matthew who declares them to have been his mortal enemies.

71

On one of these occasions where did they find him?

Luke: "They found him in the temple, sitting in the midst of the doctors, both hearing them, and asking them questions" (ii, 46).

Not until the time of Gamaliel, who lived as late as the middle of the first century, was a child allowed to sit in the presence of the rabbis. He was always required to stand, and those acquainted with the Jewish history of that age know that the rabbis were the most rigid sticklers for ecclesiastical formalities, the slightest breach of which was never tolerated. The author of the third Gospel is familiar with the later, but not with the earlier custom.

72

What was the medium of communication through which the will of Heaven was revealed to the participants in this drama?

Matthew: A dream (i, 20; ii, 12, 13, 19, 22).

Luke: An angel (i, 11, 26; ii, 9).

In Matthew every message respecting the child Jesus is communicated by means of a dream; in Luke every announcement is made through the agency of an angel. Yet, after all, these Evangelists differ only in terms; for Luke's angels are created out of the same stuff that Matthew's dreams are made of, and the world is fast coming to a realization of the fact that this whole theological structure, founded on sleepers' dreams and angels' tales, is but "The baseless fabric of a vision."

5

The Ministry of Christ

73

When, and at what age, did Jesus begin his ministry?

Luke: "In the fifteenth year of the reign of Tiberius Caesar" (iii, 1). "Jesus himself began to be about thirty years of age" (23).

In the fifteenth year of Tiberius, who began his reign in August, 14 A.D., Jesus, according to Matthew, was at least thirty-three years of age; according to Luke, about twenty-two.

Regarding this subject, Dr. Geikie writes as follows: "The age of Jesus at his entrance on his public work has been variously estimated. Ewald supposes that he was about thirty-four, fixing his birth three years before the death of Herod. Wieseler, on the contrary, believes him to have been in his thirty-first year, setting his birth a few months before Herod's death. Bunsen, Anger, Winer, Schurer, and Renan agree with this. Lichtenstein makes him thirty-two. Hausrath and Keim, on the other hand, think that he began his ministry in the year A.D. 34, but they do not give any supposed date for his birth, though if that of Ewald be taken as a medium he must have been forty years old, while, if Wieseler's date be preferred, he would only have been thirty-seven. . . . Amidst such difference, exactness is impossible" (*Life of Christ,* Vol. I, pp. 455, 456).

74

John the Baptist is said to have been the person sent to announce the mission of Christ. Who was John the Baptist?

Jesus: "This is Elias, which was for to come" (Matthew xi, 14).

John: "And they asked him [John], what then? Art thou Elias? And he saith, I am not" (i, 21).

A question of veracity between Jesus and John.

75

The advent of John was in fulfillment of what prophecy?

Mark: "As it is written in the prophets, Behold I send my messenger before thy face, which shall prepare the way before thee" (i, 2).

This passage is quoted from Malachi (iii, 1): God threatens to destroy the world, and says (iv, 5), "Behold I will send you Elijah the prophet before the coming of the great and dreadful day of the Lord." John expressly declared that he was not Elijah (Elias), and the destruction of the world did not follow his appearance.

76

What was predicted concerning John?

"He shall be great in the sight of the Lord, and shall drink neither wine nor strong drink; and he shall be filled with the Holy Ghost, even from his mother's womb" (Luke i, 15).

For the above Luke was indebted to the biographer of Samson. "Both [Samson and John] were to be consecrated to God from the womb, and the same diet was prescribed for both."—Strauss.

77

When the conception of John was announced what punishment was inflicted upon Zacharias for his doubt?

Luke: "And the angel answering said unto him, I am Gabriel, that stand in the presence of God; . . . And behold, thou shalt be dumb, and not able to speak, until the day that these things be performed" (i, 19, 20).

This was evidently suggested by a passage in Daniel: "And when he [Gabriel] had spoken such words unto me, I set my face toward the ground, and I became dumb" (x, 15).

78

Where was John baptizing when he announced his mission to the Jews?

John (New Ver.): "In Bethany beyond Jordan" (i, 28).

Bethany was a suburb of Jerusalem and was not beyond Jordan.

The Authorized Version reads "Bethabara," conceded to be an interpolation, regarding which Geikie says: "The most ancient MSS. read Bethany instead of Bethabara, but no site of that name is now known on the Jordan. Bethabara was introduced into the text by Origen" (*Life of Christ*, Vol. I, p. 566).

79

How old was Jesus when John began his ministry?

Luke: "About thirty years of age" (iii, 2, 3, 23).

Matthew: "In those days [when Jesus' parents brought him out of Egypt and settled in Nazareth, he being then about two years of age] came John the Baptist, preaching in the wilderness of Judea" (ii, 19–23; iii, 1).

Matthew, it is claimed, was written only ten or twenty years after Jesus' baptism. If so, the phrase "in those days" clearly implies that he was but a child when John began his ministry. If the phrase was intended to comprehend a period of thirty years this gospel, it must be admitted, was written at least one hundred years after the event described.

80

Were Jesus and John related?

Luke: They were, their mothers being cousins (i, 36).

Mary had visited the mother of John, and each was acquainted with the character of the other's child. John before his birth is declared to have recognized and acknowledged the divinity of the unborn Jesus (Luke i, 41–44). Yet, according to the Fourth Gospel, at the beginning of Jesus' ministry John said, "I know him not" (i, 33).

81

When Jesus desired John to baptize him, what did the latter do?

Matthew: "John forbade him saying, I have need to be baptized of thee" (iii, 14).

According to Matthew, John was not only acquainted with Jesus, but cognizant of his divine mission, which cannot be harmonized with his statement in the Fourth Gospel.

Dr. Geikie admits that John and Jesus were strangers to each other. He says: "Though cousins, the Baptist and the Son of Mary had never seen each other" (*Life of Christ,* Vol. i, p. 389).

This is not only a rejection of Matthew's statement, but a repudiation of the first chapter of Luke, one of the most important chapters of the New Testament; for it is utterly impossible for reason to harmonize these alleged revelations concerning the miraculous conceptions and divine missions of John and Jesus to their parents and the fact that John remained for thirty years in absolute ignorance of Jesus' existence.

82

What did John say regarding Jesus?

"He that cometh after me is mightier than I, whose shoes I am not worthy to bear" (Matthew iii, 11).

"There cometh one mightier than I after me, the latchet of whose shoes I am not worthy to stoop down and unloose" (Mark i, 7).

83

What other testimony did he bear concerning Jesus?

"And of his fulness have all we received" (John i, 16).

This was uttered prior to the beginning of Jesus' ministry, and before he had been baptized with the Holy Ghost. At this time "his fulness" had not been received, and the words are an anachronism.

84

At Jesus' baptism there came a voice from heaven. To whom were its words addressed?

Matthew: To those who stood by. "This is my beloved Son, in whom I am well pleased" (iii, 22).

Luke: To Jesus himself. "Thou art my beloved Son; in thee I am well pleased" (iii, 22).

85

John heard this voice from heaven; did he believe it?

Matthew: He evidently did not; for he afterwards sent two of his disciples to ascertain if Jesus were the Christ. "Now when John had heard in prison the words of Christ, he sent two of his disciples, and said unto him, Art thou he that should come or do we look for another?" (xi, 2, 3).

86

Do all the Evangelists record Jesus' baptism by John?

They do not. According to the Synoptics, John's baptism of Jesus was the initial act in his ministry, and one of the most important events in his career. But of this baptism the author of the Fourth Gospel knows nothing. In regard to this omission the author of *Supernatural Religion* says: "According to the Synoptics, Jesus is baptized by John, and as he goes out of the water the Holy Ghost descends upon him like a dove. The Fourth Gospel knows nothing of the baptism, and makes John the Baptist narrate vaguely that he saw the Holy Ghost descend like a dove and rest upon Jesus, as a sign previously indicated to him by God by which to recognize the Lamb of God" (p. 681).

87

With what did John say Jesus would baptize?

Mark and John: "He shall baptize you with the Holy Ghost" (Mark i, 8; John i, 33).

Matthew and Luke: "He shall baptize you with the Holy Ghost, and with fire" (Matt. iii, 11; Luke iii, 16).

88

How many were baptized by John?

Matthew and Mark: "Jerusalem and all Judea" (Matt. iii, 5; Mark i, 5).

John, if the account in Josephus is to be credited, made some converts; but all the inhabitants of Judea were not baptized by him.

Is John the Baptist a historical character? Aside from the anonymous and apocryphal writings of the church, which appeared in the second century, the only evidence of his existence is a passage in Josephus (*Antiquities*, B. xviii, ch. v, sec. 2). The language of this passage, while not avowedly Christian like the passage pertaining to Christ, is yet of such a character as to excite suspicion regarding its genuineness. Its position strongly suggests an interpolation. Josephus gives an account of the troubles that arose between Herod Antipas, tetrarch of Galilee, and Aretas, king of Arabia Petrea. Herod had married the daughter of Aretas; but becoming infatuated with Herodias, his sister-in-law, he resolved to put her away and marry Herodias. Discovering his intentions his wife obtained permission to visit her father, who when he had been informed of Herod's perfidy, made war upon him and defeated him in battle. Herod appealed to the Emperor Tiberius, who was his friend, and who ordered Vitellius, governor of Syria, to invade the dominions of Aretas and capture or slay him. I quote the concluding portion of section 1 and the opening sentence of section 3 of the chapter containing this history, separating the two with an ellipsis:

"So Herod wrote about these affairs to Tiberius, who, being very angry at the attempt made by Aretas, wrote to Vitellius to make war upon him, and either to take him alive, and bring him in bonds, or to kill him, and send him his head. This was the charge that Tiberius gave to the president of Syria. . . . So Vitellius prepared to make war with Aretas, having with him two legions of armed men."

It will be readily observed that the two sections are closely connected, the one naturally and logically following the other. Yet between these two closely connected sections, the section containing the account of John the Baptist is inserted.

89

Who held the office of high priest at the time Jesus began his ministry?

Luke: "Annas and Caiaphas" (iii, 2).

If the writer were to declare that Washington and Monroe were presidents of the United States at the same time it would be no more erroneous than the declaration of Luke that Annas and Caiaphas were high priests at the same time. Two priests never held this office jointly. Caiaphas was high priest at this time, and three others had held the office previous to him and subsequent to Annas. Referring to Pontius Pilate's predecessor, Gratus, who was procurator of Judea from 15 to

26 A.D., Josephus says:

"This man deprived Ananus [Annas] of the high priesthood, and appointed Ishmael, the son of Phabi, to be high priest. He also deprived him in a little time, and ordained Eleazer, the son of Ananus, who had been high priest before, to be high priest; which office, when he had held for a year, Gratus deprived him of it, and gave the high priesthood to Simon, the son of Camithus, and, when he had possessed the dignity no longer than a year, Joseph Caiaphas was made his successor" (*Antiquities* B. xviii, ch. ii, sec. 2).

90

Who was tetrarch of Abilene at this time?

Luke: Lysanias (iii, 1).

Lysanias was put to death at the instigation of Cleopatra sixty years before Jesus began his ministry. "She [Cleopatra] hurried Antony on perpetually to deprive others of their dominions, and give them to her; and as she went over Syria with him, she contrived to get it into her possession; so he slew Lysanias" (Josephus, *Antiq.,* B. xv, ch. iv, sec. 1).

At the time mentioned by Luke the territory of Abila, or Abilene, was no longer a tetrarchy.

91

Where was Jesus three days after he began his ministry?

Synoptics: In the wilderness fasting (Matt. iv, 1; Mark i, 9–13; Luke iv, 1).

John: At a wedding in Cana, feasting (ii, ii).

92

Was he led, or driven by the spirit into the wilderness?

Matthew and Luke: "Then was Jesus led up of the spirit into the wilderness" (Matt. iv, 1; Luke iv, 1).

Mark: "And immediately the spirit driveth him into the wilderness" (i, 12).

93

When did the temptation take place?

Mark: During the forty days' fast. "And he was there in the wilderness forty days tempted of Satan" (i, 13).

Matthew: After the fast. "And when he had fasted forty days and forty nights . . . the tempter came to him" (iv, 2, 3).

94

During the temptation the devil is said to have set him on the temple. On what part of the temple did he set him?

Matthew and Luke: "On a pinnacle" (Matt. iv, 5; Luke iv, 9).

The indefinite article "a" clearly implies that the temple had several pinnacles, whereas it had but one. After eighteen hundred years the Holy Ghost discovered his mistake and moved the Oxford revisers to substitute "the" for "a."

95

What did the devil next do?

Matthew: "The devil taketh him up into an exceeding high mountain, and sheweth him all the kingdoms of the world" (iv, 8). It must have been "an exceedingly high mountain" to have enabled him to see the kingdoms of the opposite hemisphere.

96

What did the devil propose?

"All these things will I give thee [Jesus], if thou wilt fall down and worship me" (Matthew iv, 9).

If Jesus was the Christ, and Christ was God, as claimed, who owned "these things," he or the devil? Think of a tramp offering you a quit-claim deed to your home for a meal.

97

Where did the devil take him first, to the temple, or to the mountain?

Matthew: To the temple (iv, 5–8).

Luke: To the mountain (iv, 5–9).

Concerning this discrepancy, Farrar says: "The order of the temptation is given differently by St. Matthew and St. Luke, St. Matthew placing second the scene on the pinnacle of the temple, and St. Luke the vision of the kingdoms of the world. Both orders cannot be right" (*Life of Christ,* p. 70).

Some of the ablest Christian scholars have refused to accept the Temptation as historical. Farrar says: "From Origen down to Schleiermacher some have regarded it as a vision or allegory—the symbolic description of a purely inward struggle; and even so literal a commentator as Calvin has embraced this view" (ibid., p. 65).

98

Had John been cast into prison when Jesus began his ministry?

Matthew: He had.

John: He had not.

Matthew says that immediately after his temptation, and before he began his ministry, "Jesus had heard that John was cast into prison" (iv, 12). Then "he departed into Galilee; and leaving Nazareth, he came and dwelt in Capernaum" (12, 13). "From that time Jesus began to preach" (17). This was the beginning of his ministry.

According to the Fourth Gospel, Jesus had called his disciples; had traveled over Galilee and Judea; had baptized (iii, 22); had performed miracles (ii, 1–11; 23; iii, 2); had held controversies with the Jews (ii, 18–21; iii, 1–21); had attended the Passover (ii, 13–23); had purged the temple (ii, 13–16); and after all these things "John was not yet cast into prison" (iii, 24).

99

Name the Twelve Apostles.

Matthew	Mark	Luke
Simon Peter	Simon Peter	Simon Peter
Andrew	Andrew	Andrew
James	James	James
John	John	John
Philip	Philip	Philip
Bartholomew	Bartholomew	Bartholomew
Thomas	Thomas	Thomas
Matthew	Matthew	Matthew
James Less	James Less	James Less
LEBBEUS	THADDEUS	JUDAS
Simon	Simon	Simon
Judas Iscariot	Judas Iscariot	Judas Iscariot

John does not name the Twelve Apostles and this important omission is admitted to be a grave defect in the Fourth Gospel.

100

Relate the circumstances attending the calling of Peter.

Matthew: "And Jesus, walking by the sea of Galilee, saw two brethren, Simon called Peter, and Andrew his brother, casting a net into the sea: for they were fishers. And he saith unto them, Follow me, and I will make you fishers of men. And they straightway left their nets, and followed him" (iv, 18–20).

Luke: "He [Jesus] stood by the lake of Gennesaret, and saw two ships standing by the lake; but the fishermen were gone out of them and were washing their nets. And he entered into one of the ships, which was Simon's, and prayed him that he would thrust out a little from the land. And he sat down and taught the people out of the ship. Now when he had left speaking, he said unto Simon, Launch out into the deep, and let down your nets for a draught" (v, 1–4).

"And when they had this done they inclosed a great multitude of fishes" (6).

"And Jesus said unto Simon, Fear not; from henceforth thou shalt catch men. And when they [Peter, James and John] had brought their ships to land, they forsook all, and followed him" (10, 11).

John: "Again the next day after John stood, and two of his disciples; and looking upon Jesus as he walked, he saith, Behold the Lamb of God! And the two disciples heard him speak, and they followed Jesus" (i, 35–37).

"They came and saw where he [Jesus] dwelt, and abode with him that day. . . . One of the two which heard John speak, and followed him, was Andrew, Simon Peter's brother. He first findeth his own brother Simon, and saith unto him, We have found the Messias. . . . And he brought him to Jesus" (40–42).

Here are three accounts of the calling of Peter, each entirely at variance with the others.

101

In what country were they when Peter was called?
Synoptics: In Galilee.
John (Old Ver.): In Perea (i, 28–42).
Bethabara and the territory beyond Jordan were in Perea.
John (New Ver.): In Judea.
Bethany and all the country surrounding it were in Judea.

102

Who did Jesus declare Peter to be?

"Thou art Simon the son of Jona" (John i, 42).

"Simon, son of Jonas" (John xxi, 15).

"Thou art Simon the son of John" (John, New Ver., i, 42; xxi, 15).

There is no relation whatever between "Jona," or "Jonas," and "John." Jona (Jonah), or Jonas, means a dove; John means the grace of God.

103

Jesus gave Simon (Peter) the name of Cephas. What meaning did he attach to the word Cephas?

"Thou shalt be called Cephas, which is by interpretation, A stone" (John i, 42).

"Thou shalt be called Cephas (which is by interpretation, Peter)" (ibid., New Ver.).

Here Jesus is represented as interpreting the meaning of an Aramaic word, with which his hearers were familiar, by the use of a Greek word of whose meaning they were ignorant, the incongruity of which must be apparent to every reader.

104

When were James and John called?

Matthew: After Peter was called.

After giving an account of the calling of Peter and Andrew, Matthew says: "And going on from thence, he saw other two brethren, James the son of Zebedee, and John his brother, in a ship with Zebedee their father, mending their nets: and he called them. And they immediately left the ship and their father, and followed him" (iv, 21, 22).

Luke: At the time that Peter was called.

Luke states that James and John were partners of Peter, and with him on the lake, in another boat, when the miraculous draught of fishes was made, that both boats were filled with the fish, "And when they [Peter, James and John] had brought their ships to land, they forsook all, and followed him" (v, 1–11).

105

Where was Jesus when he called Peter, James and John?
    Matthew: "Walking by the sea of Galilee" (iv, 18–21).
    Luke: On the lake in a ship (v, 1–11).
    In regard to Matthew's and Luke's accounts of the calling of Peter, James and John, Strauss says: "Neither will bear the other to precede, or to follow it—in short, they exclude each other" (*Leben Jesu,* p. 337).

106

Was Andrew called when Peter was called?
    Matthew and Mark: He was (Matt. iv, 18–20; Mark i, 16–18).
    According to Luke, Andrew was not called when Peter was called, but after he was called. According to John (i, 35–42) Andrew was the first to follow Jesus.

107

Who was called from the receipt of custom?
    Matthew: "A man named Matthew" (ix, 9).
    Luke: "A publican named Levi" (v, 27).
    Orthodox scholars claim that Matthew and Levi are the same person. Dr. Hooykaas does not believe that they are the same, and does not believe that any one of the Apostles was called from the receipt of custom. He says: "It is in reality very unlikely that Levi and Matthew are the same man, or that one of the Twelve was a tax-gatherer" (*Bible for Learners,* Vol. III, p. 201).

108

Who was the mother of James the Less and Joses?

In the earlier parts of their narratives, Matthew (xiii, 55) and Mark (vi, 3) declare them to be sons of the Virgin Mary and brothers of Jesus. Paul (Gal. i, 19) affirms that James was the brother of Jesus. Later Matthew (xxvii, 56) and Mark (xv, 40) state that James and Joses were sons of Mary, the sister of the Virgin.

109

Who was their father?

If they were sons of the Virgin Mary, Joseph must have been their father. But Matthew (x, 3) and Mark (iii, 18) state that James the Less was "the son of Alpheus." According to John (compare John xix, 25 with Matthew xxvii, 56) Cleophas was their father.

Referring to this and the preceding discrepancy, *Smith's Bible Dictionary* says: "This is one of the most difficult questions in the Gospel history."

110

Were Matthew and James the Less brothers?

It is not admitted that they were. Yet it is claimed that Matthew and Levi were the same; Mark (ii, 14) declares that Levi was "the son of Alpheus"; while both Matthew and Mark (Matt. x, 3; Mark iii, 18) declare that James was "the son of Alpheus."

111

To what city did John belong, and where was it located?

John: "Bethsaida of Galilee" (xii, 21).

John states that Peter was a resident of Bethsaida (i, 44), and as

John and Peter were partners (Luke v, 10), they must have belonged to the same city. But Bethsaida was not in Galilee, but in Gaulonitis. Hence if John wrote the Gospel ascribed to him, he did not know the location of his own city.

It is remarkable with what ease theologians harmonize the most discordant statements. In this case the only thing required was, in drawing the map of Palestine, to make two dots instead of one and write the word Bethsaida twice.

112

Who was the tenth apostle?
Mark: Thaddeus (iii, 18).
Matthew: "Lebbeus, whose surname was Thaddeus" (x, 3).

In the earlier manuscripts of Matthew, the words, "whose surname was Thaddeus," are not to be found. Subsequent transcribers added them to reconcile his Gospel with Mark.

113

How many of the apostles bore the name of Judas?
Matthew and Mark: But one (Matt. x, 1-4; Mark iii, 14-19).
Luke: Two (vi, 16).

114

One of these was Judas Iscariot. Who was the other?
Luke (Old Ver.): "The brother of James" (vi, 16).
Luke (New Ver.): "The son of James."

115

Name the chief apostles.

Synoptics: Peter, James and John.

John: Peter and John.

In the Synoptics, Peter, James and John constitute an inner circle or group who are with their master on every important occasion. In John this group is limited to Peter and John.

116

Who was Jesus's favorite apostle?

Synoptics: Peter.

John: John.

From the Synoptics the conclusion is inevitable that if there was one disciple whom Jesus esteemed higher than the others it was Peter whom he is declared to have chosen for the head of his church. John, on the other hand, assuming that he wrote the Fourth Gospel, as claimed, takes frequent occasion to impress us with the idea that he was the bright particular star in the Apostolic galaxy. Four times (xiii, 23; xix, 26; xx, 2; xxi, 20) he declares himself to be "the disciple whom Jesus loved."

If John wrote the Fourth Gospel this self-glorification proves him to have been a despicable egotist; if he did not write it the book is a forgery. The first assumption, if correct, impairs its credibility; the latter destroys its authenticity.

117

Is the Apostle James mentioned in John?

He is not. This omission is the more remarkable when we remember that James was not only one of the chief apostles, but the brother of John.

Respecting this omission, Strauss says: "Is it at all probable that the real John would so unbecomingly neglect the well-founded claims of his brother James to special notice? and is not such an omission rather indicative of a late Hellenistic author, who scarcely had heard the name of the brother so early martyred?" (*Leben Jesu,* p. 353.)

118

What other disciples besides the Twelve did Jesus send out?

Luke: "After these things the Lord appointed other seventy also, and sent them two and two before his face into every city and place, whither he himself would come" (x, 1).

In not one of the other twenty-six books of the New Testament is this important feature of Christ's ministry mentioned. The seventy elders of Moses doubtless suggested it. "And the Lord came down in a cloud, and spoke unto him [Moses], and took of the spirit that was upon him, and gave it unto the seventy elders" (Num. xi, 25).

Seventy was a sacred number with the Jews and is of frequent occurrence in their writings. "And all the souls that came out of the loins of Jacob were seventy souls" (Ex. i, 5). Abimelech had "seventy brethren" (Jud. ix, 56). "Ahab had seventy sons" (2 K. x. 1). Isaiah prophesied that "Tyre shall be forgotten seventy years" (xxiii, 15). Jeremiah prophesied that the Jews were to "serve the king of Babylon seventy years" (xxv, 11). In Ezekiel's vision there stood before the idols of Israel "seventy men of the ancients of the house of Israel" (viii, 11). In Daniel's vision "seventy weeks are determined upon thy people and upon the holy city [Jerusalem]" (ix, 24).

119

What charge did Jesus make to his disciples?

"Go not into the way of the Gentiles, and into any city of the Samaritans enter ye not" (Matt. x, 5).

"Then cometh he [with his disciples] to a city of Samaria" (John iv, 5). "And he abode there two days" (40).

120

Did Jesus have a habitation of his own?

Matthew: "And leaving Nazareth he came and dwelt in Capernaum" (iv, 13).

Mark: "Jesus sat at meat in his [Jesus'] house" (ii, 15).

Luke: "And Jesus said unto him, Foxes have holes, and birds of the air have nests; but the Son of man hath not where to lay his head" (ix, 58).

121

His residence in Capernaum was in fulfillment of what prophecy?

Matthew: "The land of Zabulon, and the land of Nephthali, by way of the sea, beyond Jordan, Galilee of the Gentiles; the people which sat in darkness saw great light; and to them which sat in the region and shadow of death is light sprung up" (iv, 15, 16).

The "prophecy" which Matthew pretends to quote is in Isaiah (ix, 1, 2), and reads as follows: "Nevertheless the dimness shall not be such as was in her vexation, when at the first he lightly afflicted the land of Zebulon, and the land of Naphtali, and afterwards did more grievously afflict her by way of the sea, beyond Jordan, in Galilee of the nations. The people that walked in darkness have seen a great light; they that dwell in the land of the shadow of death, upon them hath the light shined."

Matthew both misquotes and misapplies this passage. He eliminates the facts and alters the language to make a Messianic prophecy. The words were not intended as a prophecy. The events mentioned by Isaiah had occurred when he wrote. The "great light," which they had already seen, referred to his own work in destroying witchcraft and idolatry.

122

Were Zebulon and Nephthali situated "beyond Jordan," as stated?

They were not. "Beyond Jordan" means east of the Jordan, which formed the eastern boundary of Palestine. Zebulon and Nephthali were both situated west of the Jordan.

123

Were Peter, Andrew, James and John with Jesus when he taught in the synagogue at Capernaum?

Mark: They were (i, 16–21).

Luke: They were not; for they had not yet been called (iv, 31; v, 1–11).

124

Did Jesus perform many miracles in Galilee at the beginning of his ministry?

Matthew: "And Jesus went about all Galilee, teaching in their synagogues, and preaching the gospel of the kingdom, and healing all manner of sickness and all manner of disease among the people. And his fame went throughout all Syria; and they brought unto him all sick people that were taken with divers diseases and torments, and those which were possessed with devils, and those which were lunatic, and those that had the palsy; and he healed them" (iv, 23, 24).

Mark: "He healed many that were sick with divers diseases, and cast out many devils" (i, 34).

Luke: "All they that had any sick with divers diseases brought them unto him; and he laid his hands on every one of them, and healed them. And devils also came out of many" (iv, 40, 41).

John declares that his curing the nobleman's son (iv, 46–54), which was not until the second mission in Galilee, was the second miracle he performed there, his miracle at Cana being the only one he performed during the first period of his ministry. According to this Evangelist (iv, 45) all the notoriety he had at this time in Galilee, had been achieved, not by any miracles he had performed in that country, but through the reports of some Galileans who had seen his works at Jerusalem in Judea.

In regard to these conflicting statements of the Evangelists, Farrar says: "At this point we are again met by difficulties in the chronology, which are not only serious, but to the certain solution of which there appears to be no clew" (*Life of Christ,* p. 124).

125

Did he perform any miracles before he called his disciples?

Luke: He did (iv, 40, 41; v, 1-11).

John: "And both Jesus was called, and his disciples, to the marriage [at Cana, where he turned the water into wine]. . . . This beginning of miracles did Jesus in Cana" (ii, 1-11).

Luke declares that he had performed many miracles before the first disciples were called; John declares that his disciples had been called and were with him when he performed his first miracle.

126

When was the miraculous draught of fishes made?

Luke: At the beginning of his ministry (v, 6).

John: Not until after his death and resurrection (xxi, 11).

127

What accident was caused by the enormous draught of fishes?

Luke: "Their net brake" (v, 6).

John: "For all there were so many, yet was not the net broken" (xxi, 11).

In Luke and John we have two different versions of a Pythagorian legend. After comparing and noting the agreements and variations of the three versions of the legend, Strauss says:

"If there be a mind that, not perceiving in the narratives we have compared the fingermarks of tradition, and hence the legendary character of these evangelical anecdotes, still leans to the historical interpretation, whether natural or supernatural; that mind must be alike ignorant of the true character both of legend and of history, of the natural and the supernatural" (*Leben Jesu,* p. 339).

128

How long did the Jews say it took to build the temple?

"Forty and six years was this temple in building" (John ii, 20).

One year and six months was this temple in building.

Josephus (B. xv, ch. xi) gives a full account of the building of the temple. Of its commencement, he says: "And now Herod, in the eighteenth year of his reign, and after the acts already mentioned, undertook a very great work—that is, to build of himself the temple of God" (sec. 1). Concerning its completion, he says: "But the temple itself was built by the priests in a year and six months—upon which all the people were full of joy; and presently they returned thanks, in the first place, to God; and in the next place, for the alacrity the king had shown. They feasted and celebrated this rebuilding of the temple" (sec. 6).

The building of the temple was begun in 19 B.C.; it was finished and dedicated in 17 B.C.

129

Where did Jesus deliver his so-called Sermon on the Mount?

Matthew: "He went up into a mountain" (v, 1).

Luke: "He came down with them, and stood in the plain" (vi, 17).

Both Matthew and Luke represent him as being on a mountain;

but while Matthew has him go up into the mountain to deliver his sermon, Luke has him come down out of the mountain to deliver it.

In regard to this discrepancy, the Dutch theologian, Dr. Hooykaas, says: "The Evangelist [Matthew] had a special motive for fixing upon a mountain for this purpose. He intended to represent Jesus laying down the fundamental laws of the kingdom of heaven as the counterpart of Moses who promulgated the constitution of the Old Covenant from Mount Sinai. Luke, on the other hand, not wishing Jesus to be regarded as a second Moses, or another lawgiver, just as deliberately makes the Master deliver this discourse on a plain" (*Bible for Learners,* Vol III, p. 141, 142).

130

Did he deliver his sermon sitting or standing?
    Matthew: "He was set" (v, 1).
    Luke: He "stood" (vi, 17).

131

Repeat the Beatitudes which are common to both Evangelists.
    "Blessed are the poor in spirit; for theirs is the kingdom of heaven" (Matthew v, 3).
    "Blessed be ye poor; for yours is the kingdom of God" (Luke vi, 20).
    "Blessed are they that mourn: for they shall be comforted" (Matthew).
    "Blessed are ye that weep now: for ye shall laugh" (Luke).
    "Blessed are they which do hunger and thirst after righteousness: for they shall be filled" (Matthew).
    "Blessed are ye which hunger now: for ye shall be filled" (Luke).
    "Blessed are ye, when men shall revile you, and persecute you, and shall say all manner of evil against you falsely, for my sake" (Matthew).
    "Blessed are ye, when men shall hate you, and when they shall separate you from their company, and shall reproach you, and cast

out your name as evil for the Son of man's sake" (Luke).

"Rejoice, and be exceeding glad: for great is your reward in heaven: for so persecuted they the prophets which were before you" (Matthew).

"Rejoice ye in that day, and leap for joy: for, behold, your reward is great in heaven: for in like manner did their fathers unto the prophets" (Luke).

The agreements between the two versions of this sermon, of which the foregoing are a part, are ample to prove them to be reports of the same discourse; while the variations are certainly sufficient to disprove the infallibility of the evangelistic reporters.

Whether it be historical or fabricated—whether Jesus delivered the sermon or not—Matthew and Luke have given merely different versions of the same composition. The exordiums are the same; the perorations are the same—both end with the illustration of the men, one of whom built his house on a frail, the other on a firm foundation; the doctrines enunciated are substantially the same; while the words in which they are clothed proclaim a common origin. Matthew's version is longer than Luke's; either Matthew has added to, or Luke has taken from the original report of the sermon.

132

Repeat the Golden Rule.

"All things whatsoever ye would that men should do to you, do ye even so to them: for this is the law and the prophets" (Matthew vii, 12; Luke vi, 31).

Seventy years before Christ, Hillel, the Jewish rabbi, said:

"Do not to others what you would not have them do to you. This is the substance of the law."

Rabbi Hirsch says: "Before Jesus, the Golden Rule was one of the household sayings of Israel."

133

Repeat the Lord's Prayer.

According to Matthew.

Old Version.   New Version.

"Our Father which art in heaven, Hallowed be thy name. Thy kingdom come. Thy will be done in earth, as it is in heaven. Give us this day our daily bread. And forgive us our debts as we forgive our debtors. And lead us not into temptation, but deliver us from evil: For thine is the kingdom, and the power, and the glory, for ever. Amen" (vi, 9–13).

"Our Father which art in heaven, Hallowed be thy name. Thy kingdom come. Thy will be done, as in heaven, so on earth. Give us this day our daily bread. And forgive us our debts, as we also have forgiven our debtors. And bring us not into temptation, but deliver us from the evil one."

According to Luke.

Old Version.   New Version.

"Our Father which art in heaven, Hallowed be thy name. Thy kingdom come. Thy will be done, as in heaven, so in earth. Give us day by day our daily bread. And forgive us our sins; for we also forgive every one that is indebted to us. And lead us not into temptation: but deliver us from evil" (xi, 2–4).

"Father, Hallowed be thy name. Thy kingdom come. Give us day by day our daily bread. And forgive us our sins; for we ourselves also forgive every one that is indebted to us. And bring us not into temptation."

The commonly accepted version of the Lord's Prayer is the Authorized Version of Matthew. This version is admitted to be grossly inaccurate. It contains sixty-six words. The Revised Version of Matthew contains but fifty-five. Twenty-four words either do not belong to the prayer, or have been misplaced; while words which do belong to it have been omitted. If the custodians of the Christian Scriptures have permitted the prayer of their Lord to be corrupted to this extent, what reliance can be placed upon the genuineness of the remainder of these writings?

The Lord's Prayer, like so many more of the precepts and discourses ascribed to Jesus, is borrowed. Dr. Hardwicke, of England, says: "The so-called 'Lord's Prayer' was learned by the Messiah as the 'Kadish' from the Talmud." The Kadish, as translated by a Christian scholar, Rev. John Gregorie, is as follows:

"Our Father which art in heaven, be gracious to us, O Lord, our God; hallowed be thy name, and let the remembrance of thee be glorified in heaven above and in the earth here below. Let thy kingdom reign over us now and forever. The holy men of old said, Remit and forgive unto all men whatsoever they have done against me. And lead us not into temptation, but deliver us from the evil thing. For thine is the kingdom, and thou shalt reign in glory for ever and for evermore."

The eminent Swiss theologian, Dr. Wetstein, says: "It is a curious fact that the Lord's Prayer may be constructed almost verbatim out of the Talmud."

The Sermon on the Mount is derived largely from the teachings of the Essenes, a Jewish sect to which Jesus is believed by many to have belonged.

134

When and where was the Lord's Prayer delivered?

Matthew: During his Sermon on the Mount, before the multitude.

Luke: At a later period, before the disciples alone (xi, 1).

135

Was the Sermon on the Mount delivered before Matthew (Levi in Mark and Luke) was called from the receipt of custom?

Matthew: It was (v, 7; ix, 9).

Luke: It was not (v, 27; vi, 20).

136

When did Jesus cleanse the leper?

Matthew: After the Sermon on the Mount (v, 1; viii, 1–4).

Luke: Before the Sermon on the Mount (v, 12–14; vi, 20–49).

137

When did he cure Peter's mother-in-law?

Matthew: After he cleansed the leper (viii, 2, 3; 14, 15).

Mark and Luke: Before he cleansed the leper (Mark i, 29–31; 40–42; Luke iv, 38, 39; v, 12, 13).

138

Was this before or after Peter was called to the ministry?

Luke: Before (iv, 38, 39; v, 10).

Matthew and Mark: After (Matt. iv, 18, 19; viii, 14, 15; Mark i, 16, 17; 30, 31).

139

Were James and John with Jesus when he performed this cure?

Mark: They were (i, 29).

‑

Luke: They were not. They had not yet been called (iv. 38, 39; v, 10, 11).

140

When was the centurion's servant healed?

Matthew: Between the cleansing of the leper and the curing of Peter's mother-in-law (viii. 2–14).

Luke: Not until after both these cures had been performed (iv, 38, 39; v, 12, 13; vii, 1–10).

141

Who came for Jesus?

Matthew: The centurion came himself (viii, 5).

Luke: The centurion did not come himself, but sent the Jewish elders for him (vii, 2–4).

142

Where was he when he performed this miracle?

Matthew and Luke: In Capernaum (Matt. viii, 5; Luke vii, 1).

John: In Cana (iv, 46).

According to Matthew and Luke, Jesus was in Capernaum while the patient lived elsewhere; according to John, Jesus was in Cana while the patient lived in Capernaum. John says he was a nobleman's son, but all critics (as well as the Archbishop of York, in his *Harmony of the Gospels*) agree that he refers to the same miracle.

143

When did he still the tempest?

Matthew: Before Matthew was called from the receipt of custom (viii, 23–27; ix, 9).

Mark: After Matthew (Levi) was called (ii, 14; iv, 35–41).

144

When did he cast out the devils that entered into the herd of swine?

Matthew: Before Matthew was called to the ministry (viii, 28, 33; ix, 9).

Mark and Luke: Not until after he was called (Mark ii, 14; v, 1–13; Luke v, 27; viii, 26–33).

145

How many were possessed with devils?

Matthew: "There met him two possessed with devils coming out of the tombs" (viii, 28).

Mark and Luke: "There met him out of the tombs a man with an unclean spirit" (Mark v, 2; Luke viii, 27).

146

When asked his name what did the demoniac answer?

"My name is Legion" (Mark v, 9).

Concerning this the Rev. Dr. Giles says: "The Four Gospels are written in Greek, and the word 'legion' is Latin; but in Galilee and Perea the people spoke neither Latin nor Greek, but Hebrew, or a dialect of it. The word 'legion' would be perfectly unintelligible to the disciples of Christ, and to almost everybody in the country" (*Christian Records,* p. 197).

147

How many swine were there?

Mark: "They were about two thousand" (v, 13).

If each hog received a devil there must have been two thousand devils. Legion must have been a very large man, or they were very little devils.

148

Where did this occur?

Matthew: In "the country of the Gergesenes" (viii, 28).

Mark and Luke: In "the country of the Gadarenes" (Mark v, 1; Luke viii, 26).

It is generally conceded by orthodox critics that it occurred neither in the country of the Gergesenes nor in the country of the Gadarenes, but in the country of the Gerasenes. It could not have occurred in the country of the Gadarenes because it is said to have occurred on the sea shore and Gadara was situated several miles from the sea.

Voltaire says the story is disproved by the fact that the event is alleged to have taken place in a country where no swine were kept.

149

Do the Evangelists all agree in regard to the expulsion of demons by Jesus?

The Synoptics abound with these miracles: Matthew viii, 28–34; ix, 32–34; xv, 22–28; xvii, 14–21; Mark i, 21–28; v, 1–20; vii, 24–30; ix, 20–29; Luke iv, 31–37; viii, 26–39; ix, 37–42. John never mentions them.

150

What great miracle did Jesus perform at Nain?

Luke: "Now when he came nigh to the gate of the city, behold, there was a dead man carried out, the only son of his mother, and she was a widow: and much people of the city was with her. And when the Lord saw her he had compassion on her, and said unto her, Weep not. And he came and touched the bier: and they that bare him stood still. And he said, Young man, I say unto thee, Arise. And he that was dead sat up, and began to speak. And he delivered him to his mother" (vii, 12–15).

The other Evangelists were certainly ignorant of this miracle; for if they had known of it they could not have omitted it, as it is the most important miracle related by a Synoptist, and, with one exception, the most important of all Christ's miracles.

A miracle almost identical with this is related of Apollonius. Referring to the two, Baur says: "As according to Luke, it was a young man, the only son of a widow, who was being carried out of the city; so, in Philostratus, it is a young maiden already betrothed, whose bier Apollonius meets. The command to set down the bier, the mere touch, and a few words, are sufficient here, as there, to bring the dead to life" (*Apollonius of Tyana and Christ,* p. 145).

151

In their accounts of his curing the paralytic what parenthetical clause is to be found in each of the Synoptics?

"(Then saith he to the sick of the palsy)" (Matthew ix, 6; Mark ii, 10; Luke v, 24).

As the clause is superfluous, this agreement, instead of furnishing proof of divine inspiration, tends to prove what has already been affirmed, that these books are not original, but copied, for the most part, from older documents.

152

What effect had the teachings of Jesus upon the people?

Matthew: "They were astonished at his doctrine" (xxii, 33).

Mark: "They were astonished at his doctrine" (i, 22).

Luke: "They were astonished at his doctrine" (iv, 32).

153

What did he say to the people in regard to letting their light shine?

"No man, when he hath lighted a candle, putteth it in a secret place, neither under a bushel, but on a candle stick" (Luke, Old Ver., xi, 33).

"No man, when he hath lighted a lamp, putteth it in a cellar, neither under the bushel, but on the stand" (New Ver.).

154

What did he say concerning the way that leads to life?

"Strait is the gate, and narrow is the way, which leadeth unto life" (Matthew, Old Ver., vii, 14).

"Narrow is the gate, and straitened the way, that leadeth unto life" (New Ver.).

The Old Version has a strait gate and a narrow way; the New Version a narrow gate and a strait way.

155

Quote the words which relate the calling of Peter.

John: "He [Andrew] first findeth his own brother Simon, and saith unto him, We have found the Messias, which is being interpreted the Christ.

"And he brought him to Jesus. And when Jesus beheld him, he

said, Thou art Simon the son of Jona: thou shalt be called Cephas, which is by interpretation, A stone" (i, 41, 42).

The last clause of each is an interpolation.

156

Where was John baptizing when Jesus and his disciples came into Judea?

John: "In Aenon near to Salim" (iii, 22, 23).

This is declared by nearly all critics to be a geographical error. No place corresponding to this existed in Judea.

157

What city of Samaria did Jesus visit?

John: "Then cometh he to a city of Samaria which is called Sychar" (iv, 5).

Samaria contained no city of this name. Bible commentators believe that Shechem is intended.

158

What did his disciples say to him when about to leave Bethany?

"Master, the Jews of late sought to stone thee" (John xi, 8).

The disciples were themselves Jews, and the above is not the language of a Jew speaking of his own people, but of a foreigner.

159

Where was he when he dined with publicans and sinners?

Mark: At his own house. "As Jesus sat at meat in his house, many publicans and sinners sat also together with Jesus and his disciples" (ii, 15).

Luke: At the house of Levi. "And Levi made him a great feast in his own house; and there was a great company of publicans and of others that sat down with them" (v, 29).

160

What did the Pharisees say to his disciples, because they, with Jesus, dined with publicans and sinners?

"Why do ye eat and drink with publicans and sinners?" (Luke v, 30.)

"Why eateth your master with publicans and sinners?" (Matthew ix, 11.)

161

Who inquired of Jesus the reason for his disciples not fasting?

Matthew: "Then came to him the disciples of John, saying, Why do we and the Pharisees fast oft, but thy disciples fast not?" (ix, 14.)

Luke: "And they [the scribes and Pharisees] said unto him, why do the disciples of John fast often, . . . and likewise the disciples of the Pharisees; but thine eat and drink?" (v, 33.)

162

What did he say when reproved for plucking the ears of corn on the Sabbath?

"Have ye never read what David did? . . . How he went into the house of God in the days of Abiathar, the high priest, and did eat the shew bread?" (Mark ii, 25, 26.)

David did not do this "in the days of Abiathar," but in the days of Ahimelech. "Then came David to Nob to Ahimelech the priest. . . . So the priest gave him hallowed bread; for there was no bread there but the shew bread" (1 Sam. xxi, 1, 6).

163

What did he claim regarding Moses?

"He [Moses] wrote of me" (John v, 46).

The passage referred to is quoted in Acts iii, 22, and may be found in Deuteronomy xviii, 15. It alludes to Joshua, the successor of Moses. "The Lord thy God will raise up unto thee a prophet from the midst of thee, of thy brethren like unto me; unto him ye shall hearken."

Had Jesus been omniscient he would have known that Moses did not write this; that it was not written until nearly 800 years after the time of Moses.

164

Jesus is credited with having raised the daughter of Jairus from the dead. Was she really dead?

Matthew: Jairus said, "My daughter is even now dead" (ix, 18).

Mark: He said, "My little daughter lieth at the point of death" (v, 23).

Luke: It was reported that "she lay a dying" (viii, 42).

According to Matthew, in this miracle he restored the dead to life; according to Mark and Luke, he merely healed the sick.

165

Who of Christ's disciples witnessed the raising of Jairus's daughter?

Mark and Luke: Peter, James and John (Mark v, 37–40; Luke viii, 51).

John, who alone of his alleged biographers is said to have witnessed this miracle, is the only one who fails to mention it.

"A proper witness is silent, while an improper witness testifies."— Bishop Faustus.

166

What did Jesus say when sending out his Twelve Apostles?

"He that receiveth you receiveth me, and he that receiveth me receiveth him that sent me" (Matthew x, 40; Luke x, 16).

According to John (xiii, 20) these words were uttered not at the beginning of his ministry as stated by Matthew and Luke, but at the Last Supper; regarding which *Supernatural Religion* says: "It is clear that its insertion here is a mistake."

167

What command did he give them respecting the provision of staves?

Matthew and Luke: They were not to provide themselves with staves. "Provide neither gold, nor silver, nor brass in your purses, nor scrip for your journey, neither two coats, neither shoes, nor yet staves" (Matt. x, 9, 10; Luke ix, 3).

Mark: "Commanded them that they should take nothing for their journey, save a staff only" (vi, 8).

168

When the Samaritans refused to receive him what was said?

Luke: "And when his disciples James and John saw this, they said, Lord, wilt thou that we command fire to come down from heaven, and consume them even as Elias did?

"But he turned and rebuked them, and said, Ye know not what manner of spirit ye are of.

"For the Son of man is not come to destroy men's lives, but to save them. And they went to another village" (ix, 54–56).

It is conceded by the best Christian scholars that the words "as Elias did" and all that follow, excepting "he turned and rebuked them," are spurious.

169

What did Jesus say to the multitude concerning John the Baptist?

"From the days of John the Baptist until now the kingdom of heaven suffereth violence" (Matthew xi, 12).

The words, "from the days of John the Baptist until now," signify that a long period of time had elapsed since the days of John. Yet, on the very day that Jesus is said to have uttered them, he received a visit from the disciples of John, who was still living (Matthew xi, 2, 3).

170

Whose rejection of him provoked the declaration, "A prophet is not without honor, save in his own country"?

Matthew: "And when he came into his own country [Galilee], he taught them in their synagogue, . . . and they were offended in him. But Jesus said unto them, A prophet is not without honor, save in his own country" (xiii, 54–57).

John: "He departed thence, [he had come from Judea and Samaria] and went into Galilee. For Jesus himself testified, that a prophet hath no honor in his own country. Then when he was come into Galilee, the Galileans received him" (iv, 43–45).

According to Matthew, he was without honor in Galilee; according to John, he went to Galilee because he was without honor in Judea. According to Matthew the Galileans rejected him; according to John "the Galileans received him." According to Matthew, Galilee was "his own country"; according to John, Judea was "his own country."

Regarding these contradictory statements, Scott, in his *English Life of Jesus* (p. 114), says: "The Synoptists in every case give a special reason for his leaving Galilee, while the fourth gospel is equally careful in specifying the reason for his leaving Jerusalem. According to the former, Jesus would not have left Galilee if he could have avoided it; according to the latter, he would have remained at Jerusalem if he could have done so with safety. The inconsistency is glaring."

171

When he came into his own country and taught in the synagogue what did the people say?

Mark: "Is not this the carpenter?" (vi, 3.)

Matthew: "Is not this the carpenter's son?" (xiii, 55.)

172

When Herod heard of his wonderful works, what did he say?

"This is John the Baptist; he is risen from the dead" (Matthew xiv, 2).

Here, early in Christ's ministry, the tetrarch of Galilee is represented as entertaining the Christian doctrine of a bodily resurrection.

173

When and for what reason was John beheaded?

Matthew and Mark: "But when Herod's birthday was kept, the daughter of Herodias [Salome] danced before them, and pleased Herod. Whereupon he promised with an oath to give her whatsoever she would ask. And she, being before instructed of her mother, said, Give me here John Baptist's head in a charger. And the king was sorry: nevertheless for the oath's sake, and them which sat with him at meat, he commanded it to be given her. And he sent, and beheaded John in the prison. And his head was brought in a charger, and given to the damsel: and she brought it to her mother" (Matt. xiv, 6–11; Mark vi, 21–28).

This account of the death of John is utterly at variance with that given in Josephus. This historian, assuming the passage relating to John to be genuine, says:

"Herod, who feared lest the great influence John had over the people might put it into his power and inclination to raise rebellion (for they seemed to do anything he should advise), thought it best by putting him to death, to prevent any mischief he might cause, and not bring himself into difficulties, by sparing a man who might make him repent of it when it should be too late. Accordingly he was sent a prisoner, out of Herod's suspicious temper, to Macherus, the castle I before mentioned, and was there put to death" (*Antiquities,* B. xviii, ch. v, sec. 2).

Macherus, where Josephus states that John was executed, was a place far removed from Herod's capital—was outside of his dominions—in Arabia Petrea.

Referring to the Evangelistic account of John's death, Dr. Hooykaas says: "This eminently dramatic story certainly cannot be accepted as it stands. It betrays too much art in its striking contrasts between the manners of the court and the person of the prophet. We have already seen that the occasion of John's imprisonment is not correctly given by the Gospels. That such a man as Herod 'delighted in hearing' John is, to say the least, an exaggeration. The ghastly scene in which the prophet's head is carried into the festive hall may not be quite impossible in such an age and at such a court, but it is hardly probable. It is easy to see that Herodias is drawn after the model of Ahab's wife, who hated and persecuted the first Elijah; and Salome is evidently copied from Esther, for she, too, visits the prince by surprise, captivates him by her beauty, obtains a promise of anything up to the half of his kingdom, and at the festive board demands the death of her enemy as the royal boon" (*Bible for Learners,* Vol. III, p. 272).

174

Who was Herodias?

Synoptics: "His [Herod's] brother Philip's wife" (Matt. xiv, 3; Mark vi, 17; Luke iii, 19).

Herodias was a granddaughter of Herod the Great, and married her uncle Herod, the disinherited son of Herod the Great. She subsequently married Antipas, the Herod who is said to have put John to death. Herod's brother Philip (Tetrarch of Trachonitis and Gaulonitis) was not the son of Marianne, as the first husband of Herodias was, but the son of Cleopatra. Philip's wife was Salome, the daughter of Herodias. The daughter of Herodias, instead of being a damsel dancing at the court of Herod, as the Synoptics declare, was at this time the wife of an aged ruler of a foreign province. According to Whiston, she became a widow in the very year in which John died. Herodias was not the wife, but the mother-in-law of Herod's brother Philip. Whiston, in his translation of Josephus, attempts to gloss over the Synoptics' error by inserting in brackets after Herod the word "Philip." *Scribners' Bible Dictionary* concedes the error and accounts for it "By supposing that there is a confusion between the first husband and the son-in-law of Herodias, for her daughter Salome married Philip the tetrarch."

175

What is said of the numbers baptized by Jesus and his disciples as compared with those baptized by John?

John: "The Pharisees had heard that Jesus made and baptized more disciples than John. (Though Jesus himself baptized not, but his disciples.)" (iv, 1, 2.)

Matthew (iii, 5) and Mark (i, 5) declare that John had baptized "Jerusalem and all Judea." It is admitted, both in the New Testament and by Christians, that Jesus made but few converts during his lifetime, and to assert or intimate that he and his disciples baptized more than John is preposterous.

176

Who furnished the loaves and fishes with which the multitude in the desert was fed?

Synoptics: The disciples (Matt. xiv, 15–17; Mark vi, 35–38; Luke ix, 12, 13).

John: "A lad" (vi, 9).

177

How many were fed?

Mark: "And they that did eat of the loaves were about five thousand men" (vi, 44).

Matthew: "And they that had eaten were about five thousand men, beside women and children" (xiv, 21).

178

Where did this miracle occur?

Luke: "In a desert place belonging to the city called Bethsaida" (ix, 10).

Mark says that after the miracle, "He constrained his disciples to get into a ship, and to go to the other side before unto Bethsaida" (vi, 45).

If the miracle was performed in a place belonging to the city of Bethsaida, as stated by Luke, they did not cross the sea to reach Bethsaida, as stated by Mark.

179

After feeding the five thousand what did Jesus do?

Matthew and Mark: "He sent the multitudes away" (Matt. xiv, 22; Mark vi, 45).

John: He did not send the multitude away, but withdrew himself into a mountain (vi, 15).

180

For what purpose did he go to the mountain?

Matthew and Mark: "And when he had sent the multitudes away, he went up into a mountain, apart to pray" (Matt. xiv, 23; Mark vi, 46).

John: "When Jesus therefore perceived that they [the multitude] would come and take him by force, to make him a king, he departed again into a mountain alone" (vi, 15).

Matthew and Mark say nothing about the attempt to make him king; John says nothing about his praying.

181

Were his disciples with him?

Matthew and Mark: "And straightway Jesus constrained his disciples to get into a ship, and to go before him unto the other side, while he sent the multitude away. And when he had sent the multitudes away, he went up into a mountain apart to pray; and when the evening was come, he was there alone. But the ship was now in the midst of the sea" (Matt. xiv, 22–24; Mark vi, 45–47).

Luke: "And it came to pass, as he was alone praying, his disciples were with him" (ix, 18).

Matthew and Mark send his disciples ahead in a ship to make room for his miracle of walking on the sea, a miracle that Luke knows nothing of.

182

To what port did he command his disciples to sail?
Mark: "Unto Bethsaida" (vi, 45).
Pursuant to this command toward what place did they steer?
John: "Toward Capernaum" (vi, 17).
Where did this bring them?
Matthew: "Into the land of Gennesaret" (xiv, 34).

183

Jesus himself is said to have followed them on foot. Where did he overtake them?

Matthew and Mark: "In the midst of the sea" (Matt. xiv, 24–26; Mark vi, 47, 48).

John: As they were nearing the land (vi, 19–21).

According to John, he walked entirely across the sea; according to Matthew and Mark, but half way across.

Christ's walking on the sea was probably suggested by Job (ix, 8), who says God "treadeth upon the waves of the sea," or, according to the Septuagint, "walking upon the sea as upon a pavement."

184

What remarkable feat was attempted on the trip?

Matthew: "And when Peter was come down out of the ship, he walked on the water, to go to Jesus. And when he saw the wind boisterous, he was afraid; and beginning to sink, he cried, saying, Lord save me. And immediately Jesus stretched forth his hand, and caught him" (Matt. xiv, 29–31).

Mark and John, who relate with much particularity the events of this voyage, do not mention Peter's adventure.

"Probably they had good reason for omitting it. A profane mind might make a jest of an apostle 'half seas over,' and ridicule an apostolic gate-keeper who couldn't keep his head above water."—Bradlaugh.

185

What did the Jews say to Jesus respecting his Messianic mission?

"Search and look: for out of Galilee ariseth no prophet" (John vii, 52).

Search and look; for out of Galilee arose some of their greatest prophets, Jonah, Hosea, Nahum and Elijah. It may be urged that it is the Jews who give expression to the error; but it is plain the Evangelist accepts the statement as true.

186

What notable incident occurred at Jerusalem?

John: The release by Jesus of the woman taken in adultery (vii, 53, viii, 1–11).

This is popularly regarded as one of the most admirable acts in Christ's ministry. In the New Version the twelve verses relating it are declared by the Oxford revisers to be an interpolation.

187

In the miracle of restoring the sight of the man born blind, what did he tell the man to do?

"Go wash in the pool of Siloam" (John ix, 7).

"The Lord sent the blind man to wash, not in, as our version has it, but at the pool of Siloam; for it was the clay from his eyes that was to be washed off."—*Smith's Bible Dictionary.*

188

What is the meaning of the word "Siloam"?

John: "Which is by interpretation, 'Sent' " (ix, 7).

Which is not by interpretation "sent," but "aqueduct."

189

Who provoked the displeasure of the Pharisees by eating with unwashed hands?

Matthew and Mark: The disciples of Jesus (Matt. xv, 1, 2; Mark vii, 1, 2).

Luke: Jesus himself (xi, 37, 38).

190

Of what nationality was the woman who desired Jesus to cast the devil out of her daughter?

Matthew: "A woman of Canaan" (xv, 22).

Mark: "The woman was a Greek" (vii, 26)

191

What did his disciples say when he expressed his intention of feeding the four thousand?

Mark: "And his disciples answered him, From whence can a man satisfy these men with bread here in the wilderness? And he asked them, How many loaves have ye? And they said, Seven" (viii, 4, 5).

Why should they be surprised at his intention of feeding four thousand with seven loaves when but a few weeks before he had fed five thousand with five loaves?

In regard to this miracle Rev. William Sanday, of England, author of "Jesus Christ," the most important article in *Scribners' Bible Dictionary,* says: "Are the two Feedings of Mark to be regarded as two events or one? Besides the general resemblance between the two narratives, a weighty argument in favor of the latter hypothesis is, that in the second narrative the disciples' question implies that the emergency was something new. They could hardly have put this question as they did if a similar event had happened only a few weeks before." This is also the opinion of Dr. Schleiermacher.

192

After feeding the four thousand where did he come?

Matthew (Old Ver.): "Came into the coasts of Magdala" (xv, 39).

Matthew (New Ver.): "Came into the borders of Magadan."

193

Where does Mark say he came?

"Came into the parts of Dalmanutha" (viii, 10).

Criticising this statement, the *Bible for Learners* says: "Mark makes him journey still farther north, through the district of Sidon, and then turn southeast to the lake of Galilee, pass some way down its eastern shore apparently, and finally take ship and cross in a southwesterly direction to Dalmanutha, where we meet him once again. But the Evangelist's geography is open to suspicion, and we are inclined to lay these apparently purposeless wanderings of Jesus to the account of Mark's want of accuracy" (Vol. III, p. 282).

194

What did he say to the Pharisees who asked for a sign?

"There shall no sign be given unto this generation" (Mark viii, 12).

"There shall no sign be given unto it, but the sign of the prophet Jonas" (Matthew xvi, 4).

195

On the way to Caesarea Philippi what remarkable discovery was made by Peter?

Matthew: "He [Jesus] asked his disciples, saying, Whom do men say that I the Son of Man am? And they said, Some say that thou art John the Baptist: some Elias; and others, Jeremias, or one of the prophets. He saith unto them, But whom say ye that I am? And Simon Peter answered and said, Thou art the Christ, the Son of the living God. And Jesus answered and said unto him, Blessed art thou, Simon Barjona; for flesh and blood hath not revealed it unto thee, but my Father which is in heaven" (xvi, 13–17).

According to Matthew Jesus is astonished at the discovery of Peter and attributes it to a revelation from Heaven. Yet previous to this, and in the presence of Peter, according to the same writer, the other disciples had declared him to be "the Son of God" (Matthew xiv, 33).

196

The Synoptics all declare that the Messiahship of Jesus was not revealed to his disciples until late in his ministry. Is this true?

John: It is not. It was known to them at the beginning of his ministry. Before Peter was called Andrew said, "We have found the Messias, which is, being interpreted, the Christ" (i, 41). On the following day Nathanael said to Jesus, "Thou art the Son of God; thou art the King of Israel" (49).

197

When did the Transfiguration take place?

Matthew and Mark: Six days after the discourse in which he announced his second coming (Matt. xvii, 1; Mark ix, 2).

Luke: "About eight days after these sayings" (ix, 28).

198

Was the countenance of Jesus changed?

Matthew and Luke: It was. "And his face did shine as the sun, and his raiment was white as the light" (Matt. xvii, 2). "The fashion of his countenance was altered, and his raiment was white and glistening" (Luke ix, 29).

Mark: The appearance of his raiment only was changed. "And his raiment became shining, exceeding white as snow" (ix, 3).

199

When did Peter propose building the three tabernacles to Jesus, Moses and Elias?

Matthew and Mark: While Moses and Elias were yet with them (Matt. xvii, 3, 4; Mark ix, 4–8).

Luke: After they had departed (ix, 33).

200

What did the voice from the clouds declare?

Mark and Luke: "This is my beloved Son; hear ye him" (Mark ix, 7; Luke ix, 35).

Matthew: "This is my beloved Son, in whom I am well pleased, hear ye him" (xvii, 5).

Luke's account of the Transfiguration differs in many respects from that of Matthew and Mark. Luke says that Jesus went up into the mountain to pray; Matthew and Mark make no mention of this. Luke says the disciples were asleep when Moses and Elias appeared. According to Matthew and Mark they were awake. Luke says that Moses and Elias "spake of his decease." Matthew and Mark do not know what they talked about.

201

Who witnessed the Transfiguration?

Synoptics: Peter, James and John (Matt. xvii, 1; Mark ix, 2; Luke ix, 28).

It is remarkable that Matthew, Mark and Luke, who did not witness the Transfiguration, are the only ones to report it; while John, who is declared to have witnessed it, knows nothing about it. Concerning this and other events which John is said to have witnessed, Greg says: "All the events said to have been witnessed by John alone are omitted by John alone. This fact seems fatal either to the reality of the events in question or to the genuineness of the Fourth Gospel."

Regarding this subject Scott says: "By some singular fatality the writer of the fourth gospel seems incapable of describing any one incident in the life of Jesus as the Synoptics have described it. . . . It is hard to believe that we are reading narratives which profess to relate the life of the same person. . . . If then in these particulars, the Synoptic Gospels are correct, the Johannine version of the events is pure fiction; and if the latter be taken as the true account, no dependence whatever can be placed upon the former" (*Life of Jesus,* pp. 259–263).

202

Compare the account of the Transfiguration of Jesus with the account of Moses at Mount Sinai.

Matthew	Exodus
"And after six days Jesus taketh Peter, James, and John his brother, and bringeth them up into a high mountain apart,	"Then went up Moses, and Aaron, Nadab and Abihu" (xxiv, 9).
"And was transfigured before them, and his face did shine as the sun, and his raiment was white as the light" (xvii, 1, 2).	"And Moses went up into the mount, and a cloud covered the mount.
"While he yet spake, behold, a bright cloud overshadowed them; and behold a voice out of the cloud," etc. (5).	"And the glory of the Lord abode upon Mount Sinai, and the cloud covered it six days; and the seventh day he called unto Moses out of the midst of the cloud.
	"And the sight of the glory of the Lord was like devouring fire" (15–17)

We have in each account a prophet and three companions; in each the persons mentioned go up into a mountain; in each there is a supernatural brightness; in each an overshadowing cloud; in each a celestial voice speaking out of the cloud; in each Moses is a prominent figure; in each a period of six days is mentioned.

203

What occurred immediately after the Transfiguration?

Matthew: "His disciples asked him, saying, Why then say the scribes that Elias must first come? And Jesus answered and said unto them, Elias truly shall first come, and restore all things. But I say unto you, that Elias is come already and they know him not. . . . Then the disciples understood that he spake unto them of John the Baptist" (xvii, 10–13).

It is quite natural that the writing of one story concerning Elias should suggest another; but reason forbids the acceptance of both as true. If Elias was seen and recognized at the mountain, as stated, the above conversation did not follow that appearance.

204

What ailed the man's son whom Jesus cured after the Transfiguration?

Matthew (Old Ver.): He was a lunatic (xxii, 15).

Matthew (New Ver.): He was an epileptic.

Mark: He had "a dumb spirit" (ix, 17).

205

When the authorities at Capernaum demanded tribute of Jesus what did he command Peter to do?

"Go thou to the sea, and cast an hook, and take up the fish that first cometh up; and when thou hast opened his mouth, thou shalt find a piece of money; that take, and give unto them for me and thee" (Matthew xvii, 27).

Matthew does not venture to say that Peter was successful, doubtless recognizing the fact that there ought to be limits even to a fish story.

Regarding this story Archbishop Trench says: "It is remarkable, and is a solitary instance of the kind, that the issue of this bidding is not told us." Dr. Farrar says: "I agree with the learned and thoughtful Olshausen in regarding this as the most difficult to comprehend of all the gospel miracles" (*Life of Christ*, p. 288).

206

What was the nature of the tribute demanded?

It was an annual tax, known as the temple service tax, a tax from which no Jew, rich or poor, was exempt. Regarding the time and manner of its collection, Farrar says: "On the 1st of Adar, the demand was made quietly and civilly; if, however, it had not been paid by the 25th, then it seems that the collectors of the contribution (*tobhin shekalim*) might take a security for it from the defaulter" (*Life of Christ*, p. 285).

The tax was always collected in the early spring. Yet according to Matthew it was collected from Jesus in the autumn, just before the feast of tabernacles. Either Matthew was ignorant of the time of its collection, or Jesus was a defaulter.

Nor is this the only difficulty needing explanation. It is assumed that Peter secured the coin in the manner directed. If so, how did it come into existence? Did Jesus miraculously create it? If so, he was a counterfeiter. Was it a lost coin? In this case, if he was omniscient, as claimed, he knew the owner and should have restored it.

207

After leaving Galilee where did Jesus go?

Matthew: "Into the coasts of Judea beyond Jordan" (xix, 1).

The Jordan being the eastern boundary of Judea, no "coasts of Judea" existed beyond it.

208

In going to Jerusalem to attend his last Passover, what route did he take?

Luke: "He passed through the midst of Samaria" (xvii, 11).

Mark: He "cometh into the coasts of Judea by the farther side of the Jordan" (x, 1).

Two entirely different routes. As the province of Samaria lay between those of Galilee and Judea, the direct route from Galilee to Jerusalem was "through the midst of Samaria." The orthodox Jews, however, in order to avoid the Samaritans, whom they thoroughly despised, usually crossed the Jordan, which formed the boundary of the three provinces, came down on the east side of the river through Perea, recrossed the river, and thus entered "into the coasts of Judea from the farther side of Jordan."

209

What city did he pass through on his way to Jerusalem?

Luke: "And Jesus entered and passed through Jericho" (xix, 1).

Luke here contradicts his previous statement that "he passed through the midst of Samaria," for Jericho was not on the route from Samaria, but on the route from Perea by way of "the farther side of Jordan," the route which Mark declares he took.

210

What miracle did he perform on the way?

Luke: "As he entered into a certain village, there met him ten men that were lepers, which stood afar off; and they lifted up their voices, and said, Jesus, Master, have mercy on us. And when he saw them, he said unto them, Go shew yourselves to the priests. And it came to pass, that, as they went, they were cleansed" (xvii, 12–14).

The other Evangelists do not mention this miracle. Concerning it the *Bible for Learners* says: "It is an unsuccessful imitation of the account we have already examined of the healing of a leper. It is absolutely unhistorical" (Vol. III, p. 310).

211

Was it one or two blind men that sat by the wayside beseeching him to heal them?

Mark: "Blind Bartimeus, the son of Timeus, sat by the highway side begging. And when he heard that it was Jesus of Nazareth, he began to cry out, and say, Jesus, thou son of David, have mercy on me" (x, 46, 47).

Luke: "A certain blind man sat by the wayside begging: . . . And he cried, saying, Jesus, thou son of David, have mercy on me" (xviii, 35, 38).

Matthew: "Two blind men sitting by the wayside, when they heard that Jesus passed by, cried out, saying, Have mercy on us, O Lord, thou son of David" (xx, 30).

212

What inquiry did the disciples make regarding the cause of the man's blindness?

"Master, who did sin, this man, or his parents, that he was born blind?" (John ix, 2).

· Regarding this, Mrs. Evans, in her *Christ Myth* (p. 55), says: "Such a suggestion has no meaning when uttered by a Jew, but to a believer in the transmigration of souls the query would be natural and pertinent, and the story appears to be a modification of a well-known Buddhistic parable."

213

When did this occur?

Luke: "As he was come nigh into Jericho" (xviii, 35).

Matthew: "As they separated from Jericho" (xx, 29).

Mark: "As he went out of Jericho" (x, 46).

Mark agrees with Luke and disagrees with Matthew as to the number of men, and agrees with Matthew and disagrees with Luke as to the time of its occurrence.

214

What did Jesus say regarding divorce?

Mark: "And he saith unto them, Whosoever shall put away his wife and marry another, committeth adultery against her. And if a woman shall put away her husband, and be married to another, she committeth adultery" (x, 11, 12).

This was written by one acquainted with the Roman, but not with the Jewish law. The Jewish law did not recognize the right of a wife to put away her husband for any cause whatever. Matthew (v, 31, 32) and Luke (xvi, 18) knew better.

215

According to Mark he said, "Whosoever shall put away his wife, and marry another, committeth adultery." What did he say according to Matthew?

"Whosoever shall put away his wife, except it be for fornication, and shall marry another, committeth adultery" (xix, 9).

This is a notable discrepancy. According to Mark if a husband divorce his wife for any cause whatever he cannot lawfully marry another. According to Matthew if he divorce his wife for fornication he can lawfully marry again.

216

In his conversation with the rich man what commandments did he prescribe?

"Do not commit adultery, Do not kill, Do not steal, Do not bear false witness, Honor thy father and thy mother" (Luke xviii, 20).

"Do not commit adultery, Do not kill, Do not steal, Do not bear false witness, Defraud not, Honor thy father and thy mother" (Mark x, 19).

"Thou shalt do no murder, Thou shalt not commit adultery, Thou shalt not steal, Thou shalt not bear false witness, Honor thy father and thy mother; and, Thou shalt love thy neighbor as thyself" (Matthew xix, 18, 19).

No two of the Synoptics agree. Mark and Matthew each give a commandment not given by either of the others.

217

What great miracle did he perform at Bethany?

John: The raising of Lazarus from the dead. "Then said Jesus unto them plainly, Lazarus is dead" (xi, 14). "Jesus therefore again groaning in himself cometh to the grave. It was a cave, and a stone lay upon it. Jesus said, Take ye away the stone. Martha, the sister of him that was dead, saith unto him, Lord, by this time he stinketh; for he hath been dead four days" (38, 39). "Then they took away the stone from the place where the dead was laid. And Jesus lifted up his eyes, and said, Father, I thank thee that thou hast heard me" (41). "And when he thus had spoken, he cried with a loud voice, Lazarus, come forth. And he that was dead came forth, bound hand and foot with grave clothes" (43, 44).

The Synoptics make no mention of this miracle; and as it is the greatest miracle ascribed to Jesus it was certainly unknown to them.

Commenting on the doubtful character of alleged events narrated by one Evangelist and omitted by the others, Strauss says: "But this ground of doubt falls with incomparably greater weight, on the narrative of the resurrection of Lazarus in the fourth gospel. If the authors or collectors of the three first gospels knew of this, they could not, for more than one reason, avoid introducing it into their writings. For, first, of all the resuscitations effected by Jesus, nay, of all his miracles, this resurrection of Lazarus, if not the most wonderful, is yet the one in which the marvelous presents itself the most obviously and strikingly, and which, therefore, if its historical reality can be established, is a preeminently strong proof of the extraordinary endowments of Jesus as a divine messenger; whence, the evangelists, although they had related one or two other instances of the kind, could not think it superfluous to add this also. But, secondly, the resurrection of Lazarus had, according to the representation of John, a direct influence in the development of the fate of Jesus; for we learn from xi, 47 ff., that the increased resort to Jesus, and the credit which this event procured him, led to that consultation of the Sanhedrim in which the sanguinary counsel of Caiaphas was given and approved. Thus the event had a double importance—pragmatical as well as dogmatical; consequently, the synoptical writers could not have failed to narrate it, had it been within their knowledge" (*Leben Jesu,* p. 548).

Referring to this miracle and the restoration of the sight of the man born blind, Prof. Newman says: "That the three first narrators should have been ignorant of them is simply impossible; that they should not have felt their preeminent value is incredible" (*Religion not History,* p. 27).

There are three alleged instances in the Gospels of Christ restoring the dead to life.

1. The raising of the daughter of Jairus from her death bed, related by Matthew.

2. The raising of the son of the widow of Nain from his bier as they were carrying him to the grave, related by Luke.

3. The raising of Lazarus from his grave after he had lain four days, related by John.

Even if these miracles were possible one fact disproves them: the silence of the other Evangelists. Of these three stories not one is confirmed by another Evangelist. His less important miracles, such as healing the sick, are, many of them, recorded in all of the gospels, or at least in all of the Synoptics; yet each of these, his greatest miracles, stands alone, unnoticed by the other writers. Mark and Luke mention the daughter of Jairus, but only to deny the miracle by declaring that she was not dead. Had these miracles really been performed, all of the Evangelists would have had a knowledge of them, and all would have recorded them. These writers do not complement each other, as claimed: they exclude each other. There are many Lives of Napoleon; but not one of his biographers has seen fit to omit his greatest victories because some other biographer has narrated them.

218

Who was it requested that James and John might sit, one on the right and the other on the left hand of Jesus in his kingdom?

Matthew: "She [their mother] said unto him, Grant that these my two sons may sit, the one on thy right hand, and the other on the left, in thy kingdom" (xx, 21).

Mark: "They [James and John] said unto him, Grant unto us that we may sit, one on thy right hand, and the other on thy left, in thy glory" (x, 37).

219

Who occupies a seat at the left hand of Jesus?

Mark: God (xvi, 19).

The modesty of the foregoing request is apparent. Zebedee's family were evidently trying to play a sharp game on Jesus, and get a first mortgage on his Father's throne.

220

What did Jesus affirm in regard to the mustard seed?

"Which indeed is the least of all seeds; but when it is grown is the greatest among the herbs" (Matthew xiii, 32).

A mustard seed is not "the least of all seeds;" neither is the plant "the greatest among herbs."

221

With faith as large as a grain of mustard seed, what did he say his disciples could do?

"If ye have faith as a grain of mustard seed, ye shall say unto this mountain, Remove hence to yonder place and it shall remove" (Matthew xvii, 20).

"If ye had faith as a grain of mustard seed, ye might say unto this sycamine tree, Be thou plucked up by the root, and be thou planted in the sea; and it should obey you" (Luke xvii, 6).

222

In the parable of the Great Feast what was the character of the feast?

Matthew: A wedding "dinner" (xxii, 4).

Luke: "A great supper" (xiv, 16).

223

Whom did the giver of the feast send to invite the guests?

Matthew: "His servants" (3).

Luke: "His servant" (17).

Such errors may be considered trivial and their notice captious; but infallible writings do not contain even trivial errors.

224

What befell the servants, or servant?

Matthew: "And the remnant took his servants, and entreated them spitefully, and slew them" (6).

Luke: The servant returned unharmed (21).

225

What did the giver of the feast declare respecting those who refused to attend?

"That none of those men which were bidden shall taste my supper" (xiv, 24).

As they had already declined to do so, the force of the interdiction is not apparent.

226

Relate the circumstances connected with the attendance of the guest who wore no wedding garment.

Matthew: "Then saith he to his servants, The wedding is ready, but they which were bidden were not worthy. Go ye therefore into the highways, and as many as ye shall find, bid to the marriage. . . . And when the king came in to see the guests, he saw there a man which had not on a wedding garment; and he saith unto him, Friend, how camest thou in hither not having a wedding garment? And he was speechless" (xxii, 8–12).

The relator of this incident, which is omitted by Luke, would have us suppose that the frequenters of the highways went clad in wedding garments.

The parables of Jesus are declared to be perfect models of literary composition, and filled with lessons of divine wisdom. A few of them possess some literary merit; but the most of them are faulty. They contain many questionable ethical teachings; they are illogically constructed; the imagery is unnatural, and the language crude.

227

In the parable of the Wicked Husbandmen did the owner of the vineyard send one servant, or more than one, each time to collect the rent?
> Mark and Luke: He sent but one (Mark xii, 2–5; Luke xx, 10–12).
> Matthew: He sent more than one (xxi, 33–36).

228

What happened to the servants?
> Matthew and Mark: Some of them were killed.
> Luke: They were beaten and sent away, but none was killed.

229

In the parable of the talents how did the master apportion his money?
> Matthew: He gave to the first servant five talents, to the second two, to the third, one (xxv, 15).
> Luke: He gave to each one pound (xix, 13).

230

What was their gain?
> Matthew: Each doubled his money (16, 17).
> Luke: The first increased his tenfold, the second fivefold (16, 18).

231

What did the unprofitable servant do with the money entrusted to him?

Matthew: He "digged in the earth, and hid his lord's money" (xxv, 18).

Luke: He said, "Lord, behold, here is thy pound, which I have kept laid up in a napkin" (xix, 20).

232

What are the concluding words of Jesus in this parable?

"For unto every one that hath shall be given: . . . but from him that hath not shall be taken away even that which he hath. And cast ye the unprofitable servant into outer darkness: there shall be weeping and gnashing of teeth" (Matthew xxv, 29, 30).

"That unto every one which hath shall be given; and from him that hath not, even that he hath shall be taken away from him. But those mine enemies, which would not that I should reign over them, bring hither, and slay them before me" (Luke xix, 26, 27).

233

In the lawyer's interview with Jesus, who was it, the lawyer, or Jesus, that stated the two great commandments?

Matthew and Mark: Jesus. "Then one of them, which was a lawyer, asked him a question, tempting him, saying, Master which is the great commandment in the law? Jesus said unto him, Thou shalt love the Lord thy God with all thy heart, and with all thy soul, and with all thy mind. This is the first and great commandment. And the second is like unto it, Thou shalt love thy neighbor as thyself" (xxii, 35–39).

Luke: The lawyer. "And, behold, a certain lawyer stood up, and tempted him, saying, Master, what shall I do to inherit eternal life? He said unto him, What is written in the law? how readest thou? And he [the lawyer] answering said, Thou shalt love the Lord thy God with all thy heart, and with all thy soul, and with all thy strength, and with all thy mind; and thy neighbor as thyself" (x, 25–27).

234

"And after that they durst not ask him any questions." After what?

Matthew: After his controversy with the Pharisees respecting David and Christ (xxii, 41–46).

Mark: After his conversation with the scribe regarding the commandments (xii, 28–37).

Luke: After confuting the Sadducees in regard to the resurrection (xx, 27–40).

235

Did his controversy concerning David and Christ take place with the Pharisees, as stated by Matthew?

Luke: It did not. It was with "certain of the scribes" (xx, 39).

236

Where was Jesus on the day preceding his triumphal entry into Jerusalem?

John: With Lazarus at Bethany (three miles from Jerusalem) (xii, 1–15).

Luke: With Zaccheus near Jericho (twenty miles from Jerusalem) (xix, 1–40).

237

Preparatory to his triumphal entry what command did he give his disciples?

"Go ye into the village over against you; in the which at your entering ye shall find a colt tied, whereon yet never man sat: loose him, and bring him hither" (Luke xix, 30).

"Go into the village over against you, and straightway ye shall find an ass tied, and a colt with her: loose them, and bring them unto me" (Matthew xxi, 2).

238

Did he ride both animals?

Matthew: He did. "And the disciples went, and did as Jesus commanded them, and brought the ass, and the colt, and put on them their clothes, and they set him thereon" (6, 7).

The equestrian feat of his riding two asses, a large one and a small one, at the same time, must have heightened the effect of this sublime pageant.

Matthew is continually seeing double. In the demoniac of Gadara he sees two demoniacs; in the blind man by the wayside he sees two men; and in other instances where the other Evangelists see but one person or thing he sees two.

239

The riding of two asses by Jesus was in fulfillment of what prophecy?

Matthew: "And this was done, that it might be fulfilled which was spoken by the prophet, saying, Tell ye the daughter of Sion, Behold, thy King cometh unto thee, meek, and sitting upon an ass, and a colt the foal of an ass" (xxi, 4, 5).

Matthew's rendering of this passage (Zechariah ix, 9) arises from a misunderstanding of the meaning of its words. The prophet, or poet, does not mean two asses, but one; the clause "a colt the foal of an ass," is merely a poetical repetition or qualification of the preceding clause.

This blunder of Matthew is significant. It exposes the fictitious character of this so-called Gospel history. It proves that Christ's triumphal entry into Jerusalem is not a historical event—that this story is a pure fabrication, suggested by this alleged prophecy.

240

When did Jesus purge the temple?

Synoptics: At the close of his ministry, a few days before his death (Matthew xxi, 12–16; Mark xi, 15–18; Luke xix, 45–48).

John: At the beginning of his ministry, three years before his death (ii, 13–22).

Origen doubted the occurrence of this event, believing it to be a mere allegory.

241

When did he curse the fig tree?

Matthew: After he purged the temple (xxi, 12–19).

Mark: Before he purged the temple (xi, 12–15).

242

When was the tree discovered by his disciples to be withered?

Matthew: As soon as cursed (19).

Mark: Not until the next morning (13–20).

243

Mark says that he visited the tree for the purpose of obtaining figs. Why did the tree contain no fruit?

Mark: "Because the time of figs was not yet" (13).

This was before the Passover which occurred in March or April. In that part of Palestine where the miracle is said to have been performed the bocore, or early fig, ripened its first crop during the latter part of June; while the kermus, or fig proper, ripened in August. What a spectacle! An omniscient God searching for figs in March, and disappointed at not finding them—creating a tree to bear fruit in the summer and cursing it for not bearing in the spring!

244

What did Jesus accuse the Jews of doing?

Matthew: Of having slain prophets and wise men, among them "Zacharias son of Barachias" (xxiii, 35).

The Zacharias mentioned was slain in Jerusalem, 69 A.D.; so that Matthew makes Jesus refer to an event that occurred forty years after his death.

Referring to this passage, the Catholic scholar Dr. Hug says: "There cannot be a doubt, if we attend to the name, the fact and its circumstances, and the object of Jesus in citing it, that it was the same Zacharias Barouchos, who, according to Josephus, a short time before the destruction of Jerusalem, was unjustly slain in the temple."

Commenting on this passage, Prof. Newman says: "There is no other man known in history to whom the verse can allude. If so, it shows how late, how ignorant, how rash is the composer of a text passed off on us as sacred truth" (*Religion not History,* p. 46).

245

Repeat his lamentation concerning Jerusalem's rejection of him.

"O Jerusalem, Jerusalem, thou that killest the prophets, and stonest them which are sent unto thee, how often would I have gathered thy children together, even as a hen gathereth her chickens under her wings, and ye would not!" (Matthew xxiii, 37; Luke xiii, 34.)

Where was he when he uttered this lamentation?

Matthew: During his visit at Jerusalem.

Luke: In Galilee before he went to Jerusalem.

Not only are these writers at variance with each other as to the time and place of utterance, but the lamentation itself, which declares that he had made repeated efforts to convert Jerusalem, is at variance with both of them. For according to Matthew he had just arrived on his first visit to Jerusalem, while according to Luke he had never yet, during his ministry, visited Jerusalem.

246

Who anointed Jesus?
Matthew and Mark: "A woman" (Matt. xxvi, 7; Mark xiv, 3).
Luke: "A sinful woman" (vii, 37).
John: Mary, the sister of Lazarus (xii, 3).

Luke's "sinful woman" is recognized as Mary Magdalene. Farrar says: "In the popular consciousness she will till the end of time be identified with the Magdalene." Matthew and Mark's "woman" may be harmonized with either Mary Magdalene or Mary the sister of Lazarus; but Luke and John are irreconcilable.

247

Where did she put the ointment?
Matthew and Mark: On his head (Matt. xxvi, 7; Mark xiv, 3).
Luke and John: On his feet (Luke vii, 38–46; John xii, 3).

248

Where did this occur?
Matthew, Mark and John: In Bethany (Matt. xxvi, 6; Mark xiv, 3; John xii, 1).
Luke: In Nain (vii, 11–37).

249

At whose house did it occur?

Synoptics: At the house of Simon (Matt. xxvi, 6, 7; Mark xiv, 3; Luke vii, 36–40).

John: At the house of Lazarus (xii, 1–3).

250

Who was Simon?

Matthew and Mark: A leper (Matt. xxvi, 6; Mark xiv, 3).

Luke: A Pharisee (vii, 39–40).

251

At what time during his ministry did this anointing occur?

Matthew, Mark and John: At the close of his ministry (Matt. xxvi, xxvii; Mark xiv; John xii).

Luke: Early in his ministry (vii, 36–50).

252

Did it occur before or after his triumphal entry?

Matthew and Mark: After (Matt. xxi, 1–11, xxvi, 6–13; Mark xi, 1–11, xiv, 3–9).

John: Before (xii, 1–15).

253

How many days before the Passover did it occur?

Mark: Two days (xiv, 1–3).

John: Six days (xii, 1–3).

"The prima facie view would certainly be that the anointing at Bethany was placed by Mark two days and by John six days before the Passover."—*Scribner's Bible Dictionary.*

254

Who objected to this apparent waste of the ointment?

Matthew: His disciples" (xxvi, 8, 9).

John: "Judas Iscariot" (xii, 4, 5).

These different versions of the anointing of Jesus present so many discrepancies that some have supposed that two or more anointings were made. The Archbishop of York, the most popular of Gospel harmonists, concedes that but one anointing was made.

After an exhaustive review of the case, Strauss says: "Without doubt, we have here but one history under three various forms; and this seems to have been the real conclusion of Origen, as well as recently of Schleiermacher."

255

While Jesus was at Jerusalem there came a voice from heaven. For what purpose was the voice sent?

John: For the sake of those who stood by. "Jesus answered and said, This voice came not because of me, but for your sakes" (xii, 30).

Of what benefit was the voice when those who heard it were unable to distinguish it from thunder? "The people therefore, that stood by and heard it, said that it thundered" (29).

The Evangelists relate several instances of celestial voices being heard. As there is, in nearly every instance, a disagreement in regard to the message conveyed, it is probable that an electrical disturbance inspired the voice, while a vivid imagination interpreted its meaning. Regarding these voices, the Duke of Somerset says: "A belief in these heavenly voices was a common superstition among the Jews."

256

When did the Last Supper take place?

Synoptics: On the Passover (Matt. xxvi, 18–20; Mark xiv, 16–18; Luke xxii, 13–15).

John: On the day preceding the Passover.

Luke says: "And they made ready the passover. And when the hour was come, he sat down, and the twelve apostles with him. And he said unto them, With desire I have desired to eat this passover with you before I suffer."

John, in his account of the Last Supper, says it was "before the feast of the passover" (xiii, 1). The Evangelists all agree that his trial and execution took place on the day following the Last Supper. John says the Jews "went not into the judgment hall, lest they should be defiled; but that they might eat the passover" (xviii, 28). After narrating the events of the trial, John says: "And it was the preparation of the passover" (xix, 14).

According to the Synoptics, the Last Supper was eaten on the 14th Nisan, and, by our mode of reckoning time, on Thursday evening; according to John, it was eaten on the 13th Nisan, and, by our mode of reckoning, on Wednesday evening. The Synoptics declare that this supper was the regular Paschal meal; according to John, it was an ordinary meal, the Paschal meal not being eaten until after Christ's death.

"The Synoptics represent most clearly that Jesus on the evening of the 14th Nisan, after the custom of the Jews, ate the Passover with his disciples, and that he was arrested in the first hours of the 15th Nisan, the day on which he was put to death. Nothing can be more distinct than the statement that the last supper was the Paschal feast. . . . The fourth Gospel, however, in accordance with the principle which is dominant throughout, represents the last repast which Jesus eats with his disciples as a common supper, which takes place, not on the 14th, but on the 13th Nisan, the day 'before the feast of the Pass-over.' "—*Supernatural Religion.*

Thousands of pages have been written in vain attempts to reconcile this grave discrepancy. *Scribner's Bible Dictionary,* which contains the best fruits of orthodox scholarship, both of England and America, concedes a contradiction. It says: "The Synoptics seem to identify the two [the Last Supper and the Paschal meal], whereas St. John expressly places the Last Supper before the Passover."

After an exhaustive review of the subject, Strauss voices the conclusion of German scholars in the following words: "Our only course is to acknowledge an irreconcilable contradiction between the respective accounts, without venturing a decision as to which is the correct one" (*Leben Jesu*, p. 702).

257

The Synoptics state that the Last Supper was the Paschal meal. Describe the Paschal meal.

"All leaning upon the cushions around the table, the first cup of wine was served, and grace pronounced over the same and the feast. This cup of wine being disposed of, vegetables and sauce were placed on the table, and the vegetables, dipped in the sauce, were blessed and eaten. Next the unleavened bread, the bitter herb, and a piquant sauce called Haroseth were served, and the bitter herb, dipped in the Haroseth, was blessed and eaten. Then the Paschal lamb was placed on the table with portions of another sacrifice. One of the company asked the question why all this was done, during which the second cup of wine was served. The head of the table explaining narrated the story of the Exodus, closed with a hymn, spoke the second time grace over the wine, and all disposed of the same. Now came the breaking of the bread and the eating and drinking. This finished, the third cup of wine was served, and grace after meal was pronounced. After which the fourth cup was served, and the ceremonies closed with hymns and psalms, and disposing of the fourth cup of wine" (Mishna).

This was the Paschal meal as it was observed in the reputed time of Christ and up to 70 A.D. After the fall of Jerusalem and the destruction of the temple the great Passover feast retained but the shadow of its former glory. The Paschal meal and the ceremonies attending it were generally shortened. The fact that the Evangelists were unacquainted with the regular Paschal meal, that the Synoptics were familiar only with the ceremonies of later times, shows that the Last Supper is a myth, and the Gospels the products of a later age.

Criticising the Synoptics' accounts of the Paschal meal, Dr. Isaac Wise, an able Jewish scholar, says:

"If any evidence is required that neither Mark nor Matthew had ever seen the Paschal meal, or described that of Jesus, it is furnished here. They do not mention any one point connected with the Paschal supper, the ceremonies of which were established. They mention only one ceremony, viz., the breaking of the bread, and the cup of wine after the meal, which is not only a mistake, but shows conclusively, that either of them had seen the Paschal supper, after the destruction of Jerusalem, in some Jewish house, and the ceremonies connected therewith, called the Seder. Therefore, no mention whatsoever is made of the main thing—the Paschal lamb—and the bread is broken after the meal, which was done by the Jews after closing the Paschal meal, outside of Jerusalem, when the altar had been destroyed; and no Paschal lamb was eaten" (*Martyrdom of Jesus,* pp. 36, 37).

"Luke begins correctly, but makes a mistake in having the bread broken right after the first cup of wine was handed round, which was done so at every festive meal, except at the one described, and has but two cups of wine instead of four. So we know that Luke did not describe what actually happened that evening. He had seen the Jewish custom of opening the festive meals with grace over the wine and bread, and made of it an introduction to the Last Supper, without knowing that just that evening the custom was changed" (ibid., p. 38).

258

What ceremony was instituted at the Last Supper?

Synoptics: The Eucharist (Matt. xxvi, 26–28; Mark xiv, 22–24; Luke xxii, 19, 20).

John: The washing of feet (xiii, 4–9).

John does not mention the former ceremony, and the Synoptics do not mention the latter; yet each is said to have been performed immediately after supper.

259

He told his disciples that he would no more drink of the fruit of the vine until he drank it in his Father's kingdom. When was this?

Matthew: After instituting the Eucharist.

"And as they were eating, Jesus took bread, and blessed it, and brake it, and gave it to the disciples, and said, Take, eat; this is my body. And he took the cup and gave thanks, and gave it to them, saying, Drink ye all of it; for this is my blood of the new testament, which is shed for many for the remission of sins.

"But I say unto you, I will not drink henceforth of this fruit of the vine, until that day when I drink it new with you in my Father's kingdom" (xxvi, 26–29).

Luke: Before instituting the Eucharist.

"For I say unto you, I will not drink of the fruit of the vine, until the kingdom of God shall come.

"And he took bread, and gave thanks, and brake it, and gave unto them, saying, This is my body which is given for you: this do in remembrance of me. Likewise also the cup after supper, saying, This cup is the new testament in my blood, which is shed for you" (xxii, 18–20).

260

At the Last Supper did Jesus pass the cup once, or twice?

Matthew and Mark: Once (Matt. xxvi, 26–30; Mark xiv, 16–26).

Luke: Twice (xxii, 13–20).

Regarding this discrepancy, *Scribner's Bible Dictionary* says: "The temptation to expand was much stronger than to contract; and the double mention of the cup raises real difficulties of the kind which suggest interpolation."

261

Where was Jesus when he uttered his last prayer?

Synoptics: In the garden of Gethsemane (Matt. xxvi, 36–39; Mark xiv, 32–36; Luke xxii, 39–42).

John: In Jerusalem before he retired to the garden (xvii, xviii, 1).

262

What is said of his agony at Gethsemane?

Luke: "His sweat was as it were great drops of blood falling down to the ground" (xxii, 44).

Whatever was the character of this so-called "bloody sweat," it may be remarked that Matthew, who was an apostle; Mark, who is claimed to be the interpreter of Peter, an apostle who was with Jesus at the time; and John who was not only an apostle, but present also, do not refer to it. Luke, who was not an eye-witness—who was not an apostle—is the only one who mentions it.

263

How many times did Jesus visit Jerusalem during his ministry?

John: At least four times (ii, 13; v, 1; x, 22, 23; xii, 12).

The Synoptics record but one visit.

264

To what country was his ministry chiefly confined?

Synoptics: To Galilee.

John: To Judea.

According to the Synoptics nearly his entire ministry was confined to Galilee. It was only at the close of his ministry, a few days before his death, that he visited Judea to attend the Passover. According to

John his ministry was confined chiefly to Judea. It requires but three or four of his twenty-one chapters to record his work in Galilee. Farrar says: "The Synoptists almost confine themselves to the Galilean, and St. John to the Judean ministry" (*Life of Christ,* p. 361).

265

How long did his ministry last?
  Synoptics: One year.
  John: At least three years.
  The Rev. Dr. Giles says: "According to the first three Gospels, Christ's public life lasted only one year" (*Christian Records,* p. 11).
  Referring to this and the preceding discrepancy, the author of *Supernatural Religion* says: "The Synoptics clearly represent the ministry of Jesus as having been limited to a single year, and his preaching is confined to Galilee and Jerusalem, where his career culminates at the fatal Passover. The fourth Gospel distributes the teaching of Jesus between Galilee, Samaria, and Jerusalem, makes it extend over at least three years, and refers to three Passovers spent by Jesus at Jerusalem" (p. 681).
  Irenaeus, the greatest of the early Christian Fathers, and who lived in the century following Jesus, declares that his ministry lasted twenty years. In his principal work, *Against Heresies,* he combats the heresy of a one-year ministry of Jesus. He says:
  "They however, that they may establish their false opinion regarding that which is written, 'To proclaim the acceptable year of the Lord,' maintain that he preached for one year only, and then suffered in the twelfth month. They are forgetful of their own disadvantage, destroying his whole work, and robbing him of that age which is both more necessary and more honorable than any other; that more advanced age, I mean, during which also, as a teacher, he excelled all others. For how could he have had disciples if he did not teach? And how could he have taught, unless he had reached the age of a master? For when he came to be baptized, he had not yet completed his thirtieth year, but was beginning to be about thirty years of age. . . . Now, that the first stage

of early life embraces thirty years, and that this extends onward to the fortieth year, every one will admit; but from the fortieth and fiftieth year, a man begins to decline toward old age; which our Lord possessed, while he still fulfilled the office of a teacher. . . . He did not therefore preach for only one year, nor did he suffer in the twelfth month of the year. For the period included between the thirtieth and fiftieth year can never be regarded as one year" (Book ii, ch. xxii, secs. 5, 6).

266

What is said regarding the extent of his works?

John: "If they should be written every one, I suppose that even the world itself could not contain the books" (xxi, 25).

In the very next verses of the Bible (Acts i, 1, 2) Luke declares that his brief Gospel contains a record "of all that Jesus began both to do and teach, until the day in which he was taken up."

267

Can the alleged teachings of Jesus be accepted as authentic?

Three facts disprove, for the most part, their authenticity.

1. The most important teachings ascribed to him by the Synoptics were borrowed, either by him or his biographers, from other teachers and writers.

2. His teachings as presented by the Synoptics, and as presented by John, exclude each other. No critic can seriously contend that the discourses and sayings of Jesus recorded in the Synoptics and those given in the Fourth Gospel emanated from the same mind. They are wholly dissimilar, both in doctrine and phraseology. Dr. Westcott says: "It is impossible to pass from the Synoptic Gospels to that of St. John without feeling that the transition involves the passage from one world of thought to another. No familiarity with the general teaching of the Gospels, no wide conception of the character of the Savior, is sufficient to destroy the contrast which exists in form and spirit between the earlier

and later narratives" (*Introduction to Study of Gospels,* p. 249).

3. The discourses attributed to Jesus in the Fourth Gospel were evidently composed by the author of that Gospel. This is apparent to every careful reader.

The teachings ascribed to Jesus in John, then, are spurious; while those ascribed to him in Matthew, Mark and Luke are of doubtful authenticity. If any of the teachings of Jesus have been preserved they exist in the first three Gospels, but the unauthentic character of the Gospels themselves renders it impossible to ascribe to him with certainty a single teaching.

6

The Crucifixion of Christ

268

When did Jesus first foretell his passion?

Synoptics: Not until late in his ministry (Matt. xvi, 21; Mark viii, 31; Luke ix, 21–27).

According to John (ii, 19–22) he referred to it at the beginning of his ministry.

269

When did he announce his betrayal?

Matthew and Mark: At the Last Supper, while they were eating. "Now when the even was come, he sat down with the twelve. And as they did eat, he said, Verily I say unto you, that one of you shall betray me" (Matt. xxvi, 20, 21; Mark xiv, 18).

Luke and John: Not until after supper (Luke xxii, 20, 21; John xiii, 2–21). John says that after supper he washed his disciples' feet and delivered a discourse to them, after which he said, "Verily, verily, I say unto you, that one of you shall betray me."

270

Did Jesus say who should betray him?

Matthew and John: He did (Matt. xxvi, 25; John xiii, 26).

Mark and Luke: He did not.

271

How did he disclose his betrayer?

Matthew: By an implied affirmative answer to Judas' question, "Is it I?" "Then Judas which betrayed him, answered and said, Master, is it I? He said unto him, Thou hast said" (xxvi, 25).

John: By giving Judas a sop. "Jesus answered, He it is to whom I shall give a sop, when I have dipped it. And when he had dipped the sop, he gave it to Judas Iscariot."

272

When did Satan enter into Judas?

Luke: Before the Last Supper (xxii, 3–7).

John: After the Last Supper (xiii, 1–27)

273

How did Judas betray Jesus?

Matthew and Mark: "Now he that betrayed him, gave them a sign, saying, Whomsoever I shall kiss, that same is he; hold him fast. And forthwith he came to Jesus, and said, Hail, Master, and kissed him" (Matt. xxvi, 48, 49; Mark xiv, 44, 45).

According to John, Judas did not betray him with a kiss.

274

What did Jesus say to Judas when he betrayed him?

"Friend, wherefore art thou come?" (Matthew xxvi, 50.)

"Judas, betrayest thou the Son of man with a kiss?" (Luke xxii, 48.)

275

What was Judas, and what office did he hold?

John: "He was a thief, and had the bag, and bare what was put therein" (xii, 6).

Judas was thus the first Christian treasurer. But why did Jesus, if omniscient, as claimed, select a thief for this office? Was he unable to conduct his ministry without the aid of one?

276

What did Judas receive for betraying his master?

Matthew: "And they covenanted with him for thirty pieces of silver" (xxvi, 15).

"It is strange that a man who kept the purse, and knew what he would lose by the death of his chief, should abandon the profits of his office for so small a sum."—Renan.

277

What did he do with the money?

Matthew: "Then Judas, which had betrayed him, when he saw that he was condemned, repented himself, and brought again the thirty pieces of silver to the chief priests and elders. . . . And he cast down the pieces of silver in the temple and departed" (xxvii, 3–5).

Peter: "Now this man [Judas] purchased a field with the reward of iniquity" (Acts i, 18).

278

The purchase of the potter's field was in fulfillment of what prophecy?

Matthew: "That which was spoken by Jeremy the prophet, saying, And they took the thirty pieces of silver, the price of him that was valued, . . . and gave them for the potter's field, as the Lord appointed me" (xxvii. 9, 10).

This was not spoken by Jeremiah, but by Zechariah. "And the Lord said unto me, Cast it unto the potter: a goodly price that I was prized at of them. And I took the thirty pieces of silver and cast them to the potter in the house of the Lord" (xi, 13).

It is evident that the account of the betrayal was inspired, not by a historical fact, but by a desire to "fulfill" a Messianic prophecy. Zechariah did not predict an event, but his words did suggest a fiction. This is the more probable from the fact that Matthew is the only Evangelist who mentions the thirty pieces of silver.

The story of Christ's last visit to Jerusalem and the story of his betrayal exclude each other. According to the Evangelists he was not arrested for any offense he had committed during this visit, but for offenses he had committed prior to this. Yet during this visit he is said to have appeared openly with his disciples, making a triumphal entry into the city, visiting the temple and teaching in public. In the face of this the story that the Jews were obliged to bribe one of his disciples in order to apprehend him is absurd. One of these stories must be false. Regarding them Lord Amberley observes: "The representation of the Gospels, that Jesus went on teaching in public to the very end of his career, and yet that Judas received a bribe for his betrayal, is self-contradictory" (*Life of Jesus*, p. 214).

To those who believe the accounts of the betrayal of Jesus to be historical, the ecclesiastical historian, Neander, in his *Life of Christ*, advances a suggestion that is worthy of consideration. The betrayal of Jesus by Judas, it is suggested, was intended as a test of his Messiaship.

If Jesus was the Messiah, Judas reasoned, he could save himself; if he was not the Messiah he was an impostor and deserved death.

279

What became of Judas?

Matthew: He "went and hanged himself" (xxvii, 5).

Peter: "Falling headlong he burst asunder in the midst, and all his bowels gushed out" (Acts i, 18).

Papias, bishop of Hierapolis, one of the chief Christian authorities of the second century, and who wrote before the books of Matthew and Acts were written, gives the following account of the fate of Judas:

"Judas walked about in the world a great example of impiety; for his body having swollen so that, on an occasion, when a wagon was moving on its way, he could not pass it, he was crushed by the chariot and his bowels gushed out."

The German commentator, Dr. Hase, attempts to reconcile his suicide, as related by Matthew, with his death by accident, as related by Peter, by supposing that he attempted to hang himself, but that the rope broke, causing him to fall with such force as to disembowel himself. This harmonist apparently forgets to note that Peter says he fell "headlong," which makes it necessary to suppose that he hung himself by the feet.

280

To whom did Peter deliver his speech describing the fate of Judas?

"Peter stood up in the midst of the disciples" (Acts i, 15).

Is it not reasonable to suppose that the alleged information conveyed in his speech was as familiar to the disciples whom he addressed as to himself? Regarding this De Wette aptly says: "In the composition of this speech the author has not considered historical decorum."

281

What did Peter say in regard to the name of the field?

"And it was known unto all the dwellers of Jerusalem; insomuch as that field is called in their proper tongue, Aceldama, that is to say, The field of blood" (Acts i, 19).

Here Peter is represented as interpreting in Greek a Jewish word to his Jewish brethren.

282

Were there more than one of Jesus' disciples concerned in his betrayal?

John: There were. "For Jesus knew from the beginning who they were [of his disciples] that believed not, and who should betray him" (vi, 64).

283

When the Jewish council met to plan the arrest of Jesus, to what conclusion did they come?

Matthew and Mark: Not to arrest him on the feast day (Matt. xxvi, 3–5; Mark xiv, 1, 2).

Yet this was the very day on which Matthew and Mark declare that he was arrested.

284

Who arrested him?

Matthew and Mark: "A great multitude . . . from the chief priests and elders of the people" (Matt. xxvi, 47; Mark xiv, 43).

Luke: "The chief priests, and captains of the temple, and the elders" themselves (xxii, 47–52).

285

Who does John say was sent to arrest him?

A "band of soldiers and officers" (xviii, 3, New Ver.).

This contradicts the Synoptics, who declare that it was a mob of civilians.

286

What is said regarding the multitude sent out to apprehend him?

Synoptics: They were armed "with swords and staves" (Matt. xxvi, 47; Mark xiv, 43; Luke xxii, 52).

Were the disciples armed?

All: They were, or one of them at least (Matt. xxvi, 51; Mark xiv, 47; Luke xxii, 38, 50; John xviii, 10).

This is incredible, for Jews were never allowed to carry arms on a holy day.

287

How did they go out to capture him?

John: "With lanterns and torches" (xviii, 3).

His enemies are represented as believing that his arrest could be secured only by strategy and stealth. Under these circumstances is it reasonable to suppose that the chief priests would send out a torchlight procession to apprehend him? Besides, as it was at the full of the moon, what need had they of lanterns and torches? Again, lanterns were unknown in Palestine.

288

When the band sent to capture him first came up to him what did they do?

Matthew and Mark: "They laid hands on him and took him" (Matt. xxvi, 47–50; Mark xiv, 43–46).

John: "They went backward and fell to the ground" (xviii, 3–6).

289

What did Peter do when Jesus was arrested?

John: "Then Simon Peter having a sword drew it, and smote the high priest's servant, and cut off his right ear" (xviii, 10).

Yet no efforts were made to arrest and punish Peter, notwithstanding he was recognized and pointed out by the kinsman of the wounded man. It may be urged that Jesus had healed the servant's ear. This, even if true, would not have removed the guilt of the militant disciple. Had Peter really committed the deed, it is not probable that he would have visited the house of the high priest and remained in the presence of his enemies.

290

When was Jesus bound?

John: When he was arrested (xviii, 12).

Matthew and Mark: Not until after his trial before the Sanhedrim when he was taken to Pilate (Matt. xxvii, 2; Mark xv, 1).

According to Luke he was not bound.

291

What did they do with Jesus when he was taken?

Matthew: "Led him away to Caiaphas" (xxvi, 57).

John: "Led him away to Annas first" (xviii, 13).

292

Did he have an examination before his trial?

John: He did (xviii, 13-23).

Our laws provide for what is known as a preliminary examination before a magistrate. This was forbidden by the Jewish law, and his alleged examination before a priest could not have taken place.

293

Before whom did his preliminary examination take place?

John: Before Annas (xviii, 13-23).

The Synoptics state that he was examined and tried before Caiaphas.

294

Repeat John xviii, 24.

"Now Annas had sent him bound unto Caiaphas the high priest" (Old Ver.).

"Annas therefore sent him bound unto Caiaphas the high priest" (New Ver.).

This verse follows the account of Jesus' preliminary examination and shows clearly that this examination took place before Annas, and that he was not sent to Caiaphas until its conclusion. The King James translators, in order to hide the discrepancy, prefixed the word "now" and changed the tense of the verb, substituting "had sent" for "sent," so that it might appear that Annas had sent him to Caiaphas before the examination commenced.

Concerning this corruption of the text, Scott says: "There is no conjunction 'now,' and an aorist cannot mark a definite time. If a hiatus is suspected, it may be indicated by an asterisk; but to insert words and alter the force of a tense in order to get over a grave historical difficulty is sheer dishonesty" (*Life of Jesus,* p. 289, note).

295

Matthew and John state that Caiaphas was high priest at this time. Who does the author of Acts state was high priest?

"And Annas the high priest, and Caiaphas, and John, and Alexander, and as many as were of the kindred of the high priest, were gathered together at Jerusalem" (iv, 6).

Luke (iii, 2), who is declared to be the author of Acts, says that Annas and Caiaphas were both high priests.

Criticizing John's account of the examination before Annas, the author of "Supernatural Religion" says: "The Synoptics know nothing of the preliminary examination before Annas, and the reason given by the writer of the fourth Gospel why the soldiers first took Jesus to Annas: 'for he was father-in-law to Caiaphas who was first high priest that year,' is inadmissible. The assertion is a clear mistake, and it probably originated in a stranger writing of facts and institutions with which he was not well acquainted, being misled by an error equally committed by the author of the third Gospel, and of the Acts of the Apostles. . . . Such statements, erroneous in themselves and not understood by the author of the fourth Gospel, may have led to the confusion in the narrative. Annas had previously been high priest, as we know from Josephus, but nothing is more certain than the fact that the title was not continued after the office was resigned; and Ishmael, Eleazar, and Simon, who succeeded Annas and separated his term of office from that of Caiaphas, did not subsequently bear the title. The narrative is a mistake, and such an error could not have been committed by a native of Palestine, and much less by an acquaintance of the high priest" (p. 660).

296

What is said regarding the tenure of Caiaphas' office?

John: He was "high priest that year" (xi, 49).

John's language implies that the high priest was appointed annually, whereas he held his office for life, or until removed. Caiaphas had been high priest for many years.

297

What had Caiaphas prophesied concerning Jesus?

John: "He prophesied that Jesus should die for that nation; and not for that nation only, but that also he should gather together in one the children of God that were scattered abroad" (xi, 51, 52).

A high priest did not assume the role of prophet, much less would he have given utterance to the prophecy ascribed to Caiaphas. The Roman procurator might have expressed such a sentiment, for according to Roman law and ethics an individual could be sacrificed for the welfare of the state. The high priest, on the other hand, could not have uttered such a sentiment, because it was abhorrent to the Jewish mind. If all Israel could have been saved, and could have been saved only by the death of one of its innocent members, that member could not have been put to death, because, according to Jewish law, it would have made of every Jew concerned in it a murderer. It was a fundamental principle of the Jewish code that, "No human life must be abandoned on account of any other life."

298

Did Jesus have a trial before the Sanhedrim?

Synoptics: He had (Matt. xxvi, 57–75; Mark xiv, 53–72; Luke xxii, 54–71).

It was about this time (30 A.D.), that the Sanhedrim ceased to have jurisdiction over capital offenses. After its jurisdiction ceased Jesus could not have been tried before it; and before its jurisdiction ceased he would not have had a subsequent trial before Pilate.

299

Where was his trial held?

Matthew and Mark: At the palace of the high priest.

No trial was ever held at the residence of the high priest. All meetings

of the Sanhedrim were held in the hall adjoining the temple. A trial
at any other place would have been illegal.

300

What was the charge preferred against him?

All: Blasphemy.

Jesus, it was charged, had declared himself to be the son of God.
This, if true, would not have constituted blasphemy. It was no offense
against the law for a man to claim that he was the son of God. All
men, and especially all good men, were recognized as the sons of God.
Referring to Christ's claim, a Jewish writer says: "No law, no precedent,
and no fictitious case in the Bible or the rabbinical literature, can be
cited to make of this expression a case of blasphemy." And even if
he had been proven guilty of blasphemy, he could not have been put
to death, for blasphemy, at this time, had ceased to be a capital offense.
And is it reasonable to suppose that the Romans would have condemned
a man to death for an offense against a religion in which they did
not themselves believe, but which they regarded as one of the vilest
of superstitions? It may be urged that in his trial before Pilate the charge
was changed to sedition. This charge was not sustained.

301

What is said regarding witnesses?

Matthew and Mark: "Now the chief priests, and elders, and all
the council, sought false witnesses against Jesus, to put him to death;
but found none; yea, though many false witnesses came, yet found they
none" (Matt. xxvi, 59, 60; Mark xiv, 55, 56).

When every step thus far taken by the council had been illegal,
why should it have been so particular in regard to the witnesses? The
fact is the Evangelists were ignorant of Jewish laws. They believed that
while the prosecution of Jesus was unjust it was yet conducted according
to the established rules of Jewish courts. Referring to Mark, Dr. Wise

says: "In his ignorance of Jewish law, he imagined the trial which he described was lawful among the Jews. He proves this, in the first place, by the very statement that witnesses were sought and produced. A court convoked and acting in rebellion to law and custom can be considered only a band of rebels. What use have such men of witnesses? Being lawless from the beginning, no legal restraint makes the presence of witnesses necessary. . . . He certainly thought of an honest, lawful trial, in the legal form; an honest and legal examination of witnesses, a fair consideration of the testimony, and after mature reflection the rejection thereof on account of insufficiency" (*Martyrdom of Jesus,* pp. 69, 70).

302

What did the so-called false witnesses that appeared against him testify that he had said?

"I am able to destroy the temple of God, and to build it in three days" (Matthew xxvi, 61).

"I will destroy this temple that is made with hands, and within three days I will build another made without hands" (Mark xiv, 58).

303

What had Jesus said?

"Destroy this temple and in three days I will raise it up" (John ii, 19).

Passing over the discrepancies of Matthew and Mark, if they have given the substance of these witnesses' testimony, then they were not false, but truthful witnesses; for Jesus, it is seen, had given utterance to such a declaration. If he referred to the temple of his body, as John affirms, and the Jews misunderstood him, the fault was his, not theirs.

Josephus gives an account of a so-called prophet who, a few years later, boasted of his supernatural powers in much the same manner that Jesus is said to have done:

"There came out of Egypt about this time to Jerusalem, one that said that he was a prophet, and advised the multitude of the common people to go along to the Mount of Olives, as it was called, which lay over against the city, and at the distance of five furlongs. He said further, that he would show them from hence, how, at his command, the walls of Jerusalem would fall down" (*Antiquities,* Book xx, chap. viii, sec. 6).

304

Was he questioned by the Sanhedrim?

Synoptics: He was. They tried to convict him by his own testimony (Matt. xxvi, 62–64; Mark xiv, 60–63; Luke xxii, 66–71).

A Jewish court did not question a prisoner. A prisoner could not even plead guilty.

305

To the priest's question, "Art thou the Christ?" what answer did he give?

Mark: "Jesus said, I am" (xiv, 61, 62).

Luke: "He said unto them, If I tell you, ye will not believe" (xxii, 67).

306

When did his trial before the Sanhedrim take place?

Matthew and Mark: During the night. After his arrest, which probably occurred not later than midnight, they at once "led him away to Caiaphas the high priest, where . . . the chief priests, and elders, and all the council [Sanhedrim]" had assembled, when his trial immediately began (Matt. xxvi, 57–68; Mark xiv, 58–65).

Luke: Not until the next morning. During the night he was held in custody at the house of the high priest. "As soon as it was day, the elders of the people and the chief priests and the scribes came together, and led him into the council" (xxii, 66).

This, according to Luke, was his first and only appearance before the Sanhedrim. Matthew and Mark, in addition to the night trial mentioned by them, also mention an adjourned session in the morning corresponding to the meeting of Luke.

307

Could this trial have been held in the night as stated by Matthew and Mark?

It could not. The Jewish law prohibited the opening of a trial at night. The Sanhedrim could not hold a session before 6 a.m. or after 3 p.m. Luke was seemingly acquainted with this law; Matthew and Mark were not.

308

During what religious festivities was his trial held?

Synoptics: During the feast of the Passover.

It could not have been held during the Passover, for no trials were held by the Jews during this feast.

309

On what day of the week was it held?

Synoptics: On Friday, the day preceding the Sabbath.

No trial for a capital offense was ever allowed to begin on the day preceding the Sabbath.

310

How long did this trial last?

All: But a few hours.

The Jewish law required at least two days for a capital trial—one for prosecution, and one for the defense.

311

Did he have a defender or counselor in the Sanhedrim?

Synoptics: He did not.

According to the Synoptics he had no counsel, and the Sanhedrim were unanimous in their condemnation of him. This was contrary to Jewish law. The Sanhedrim might be unanimous in their belief that he was guilty, but it was the duty of at least one of them to defend him. This was the law: "If none of the judges defend the culprit, i.e., all pronounce him guilty, having no defender in the court, the verdict of guilty was invalid and the sentence of death could not be executed" (Maimonides).

Dr. Geikie admits that the trial of Jesus before the Sanhedrim, as related in the Gospels, was in nearly every particular contrary to Jewish law. He says:

"The accused was in all cases to be held innocent, till proved guilty. It was an axiom, that 'the Sanhedrim was to save, not to destroy life.' No one could be tried and condemned in his absence, and when a person accused was brought before the court, it was the duty of the president, at the outset, to admonish the witnesses to remember the value of human life, and to take care that they forgot nothing that would tell in the prisoner's favor. Nor was he left undefended; a Baal-Rib, or counsel, was appointed, to see that all possible was done for his acquittal. Whatever evidence tended to aid him was to be freely admitted, and no member of the court who had once spoken in favor of acquittal could afterwards vote for condemnation. The votes of the youngest of the judges were taken first, that they might not be influenced by their seniors. In capital charges, it required a majority of at least two to condemn, and while the verdict of acquittal could be given at once, that of guilty could only be pronounced the next day. Hence, capital trials could not begin on the day preceding a Sabbath, or public feast. No criminal trial could be carried through in the night; the judges who condemned any one to death had to fast all the day before, and no one could be executed on the same day on which the sentence was pronounced." (*Life of Christ,* Vol. II, p. 487.)

312

Had Jesus been tried, convicted and executed by the Jews would he have been crucified?

He would not. Crucifixion was a mode of punishment never employed by the Jews. Had the Jews executed him he would have been stoned.

It is impliedly stated in the Synoptics, and expressly stated in John, that the Sanhedrim's jurisdiction over capital crimes had ceased. "It is not lawful for us to put any man to death" (xviii, 31). The Sanhedrim's authority ceased in 30 A.D., and it is generally claimed by Christians that the crucifixion occurred from one to five years after this time.

313

What does Peter say in regard to the mode of punishment employed in his execution?

"The God of our fathers raised up Jesus, whom ye slew and hanged on a tree" (Acts v, 30).

"And we are witnesses of all things which he did both in the land of the Jews, and in Jerusalem; whom ye slew and hanged on a tree" (x, 39).

Concerning this, Mrs. Evans says: "With regard to his death, it was said that the Jews slew him and hanged him on a tree; and again that he was taken down from the tree; expressions which do not imply crucifixion, but rather the legal execution for such crimes as the one alleged, that is, stoning to death and the exposure of the dead body upon a stake, or a tree" (*Christ Myth,* p. 79).

314

How was he treated by the Sanhedrim?

Matthew and Mark: "They spit in his face, and buffeted him; and others smote him with the palms of their hands" (Matt. xxvi, 67; Mark xiv, 65).

Every Jew, and every other person acquainted with the Jewish history of that age, knows that this is false. The Sanhedrim was composed of the wisest and the best men of that race. Superstitious, bigoted and fanatical some of them doubtless were, but in that august court law and dignity and decorum reigned.

These accounts of the trial of Christ before the Sanhedrim afford overwhelming proof that they were not written by apostles nor by residents of Palestine. They were written by Gentile Christians, or by Jewish converts living in foreign lands, and presumably the former, for even foreign Jews must have possessed a better knowledge of Jewish laws and customs than the Evangelists display.

315

During the trial Peter denied his master. What had Jesus predicted concerning his denial?

Matthew, Luke and John: "Jesus said unto him, Verily I say unto thee, that this night, before the cock crow, thou shalt deny me thrice" (Matt. xxvi, 34; Luke xxii, 34; John xiii, 38).

Mark: "And Jesus saith unto him, Verily I say unto thee, that this day, even in this night, before the cock crow twice, thou shalt deny me thrice" (xiv, 30).

316

Did Peter deny him three times before the cock crew?

Matthew, Luke and John: He did (Matt. xxvi, 69–75; Luke xxii, 54–62; John xviii, 15–27).

Mark: He did not; he had denied him but once when the cock crew (xiv, 66–68).

317

Where were they when Jesus foretold Peter's denial?

Matthew and Mark: At the Mount of Olives (Matt. xxvi, 30–35; Mark xiv, 26–30).

Luke: In Jerusalem, at supper, before they went out to the Mount of Olives (xxii, 7–39).

318

What did Peter do when he entered the palace?

Luke: "Peter sat down among them" (xxii, 55).

John: "Peter stood with them" (xviii, 18).

319

When was he first accused of being the friend of Jesus?

John: As he entered the room (xviii, 16, 17).

Mark and Luke: As he sat by the fire (Mark xiv, 66, 67; Luke xxii, 54–57).

320

When was he accused the second time?

John: In the house as he "stood and warmed himself" (xviii, 25).

Matthew: "When he was gone out into the porch" (xxvi, 71).

321

By whom was he accused the second time?

Matthew and Mark: By a "maid" (Matt. xxvi, 71; Mark xiv, 69).

Luke: By a "man" (xxii, 59, 60).

322

Who accused him the third time?

Matthew and Mark: "They that stood by" (Matt. xxvi, 73; Mark xiv, 70).

John: "One of the servants of the high priest" (xviii, 26).

323

Was Jesus present when Peter denied him?

Matthew and Mark: He was not.

Luke: He was. "The Lord turned and looked upon Peter" (xxii, 60, 61).

324

Where was Jesus next sent for trial?

Luke: To Herod, tetrarch of Galilee, who was attending the Passover at Jerusalem (xxiii, 6–11).

In the matter of trials the Evangelists, as in everything else, have overdone things. Notwithstanding no trial was ever held during the Passover they give him four trials in one day, and not finding courts enough in Judea for the purpose, they import one from Galilee.

There is nothing more improbable than this alleged examination of Jesus by Herod. Imagine the Governor General of Canada sitting in judgment on a criminal at Washington, because the criminal is a Canadian, or an Ohio court holding a session in New York because the prisoner arraigned once lived in Ohio. The offenses with which Jesus was charged were committed, not in Herod's province, Galilee, but in Pilate's province, Judea.

It is strange that John, who pretends to relate every important event connected with the trial of Jesus, should omit his trial before Herod. Concerning this Strauss says: "The conjecture, that it may probably have appeared to him [John] too unimportant, loses all foundation when it is considered that John does not scorn to mention the leading away to Annas, which nevertheless was equally indecisive; and in general, the narrative of these events in John is, as Schleiermacher himself confesses, so consecutive that it nowhere presents a break in which such an episode could be inserted. Hence even Schleiermacher at last takes refuge in the conjecture that possibly the sending to Herod may have escaped the notice of John, because it happened on an opposite side to that on which the disciple stood, through a back door; and that it came to the knowledge of Luke because his informant had an acquaintance in the household of Herod, as John had in that of Annas; the former conjecture, however, is figuratively as well as literally nothing more than a back door; the latter, a fiction which is but the effort of despair" (*Leben Jesu,* pp. 764, 765).

325

What was the result of Pilate's sending Jesus to Herod?

Luke: "And the same day Pilate and Herod were made friends together, for before they were at enmity between themselves" (xxiii, 12).

Pilate and Herod did not become friends. To the day of Pilate's recall they were enemies. Herod was continually plotting and striving to unite with his tetrarchy the province of Judea which belonged to his father's kingdom, and which his father had promised to give him.

326

Did Jesus's trial before Pilate take place in the presence of his accusers?
   Luke: It did (xviii, 1–4, 13, 14).
   John: It did not (xviii, 28).

327

Did Pilate go out of the judgment hall to consult with those who were prosecuting Jesus?
   Luke: He did not (xxiii, 1–25).
   John: He did. "Pilate then went out unto them [the Jews], and said, What accusation bring ye against this man? They answered and said unto him, If he were not a malefactor, we would not have delivered him up unto thee. . . . Then Pilate entered into the judgment hall again, and called Jesus, and said unto him, Art thou the King of the Jews? Jesus answered him, Sayest thou this thing of thyself, or did others tell it thee of me?" (xxiii, 29, 30, 33, 34.)
   The prosecution and the defense are both declared to have returned insolent answers to the questions of Pilate. The Jewish priests were too wise for this, and Christians will be loath to admit that their Savior was so indiscreet and so impolite as to indulge in such insolence.

328

What was the result of his trial before Pilate?
   All: Pilate declared him innocent and sentenced him to death.
   "And Pilate, when he had called together the chief priests and the rulers and the people, said unto them, Ye have brought this man unto me, as one that perverteth the people; and, behold, I, having examined

him before you, have found no fault in this man touching those things whereof ye accuse him. . . . And Pilate gave sentence that it should be as they required. . . . He delivered Jesus to their will" (Luke xxiii, 13, 14, 24, 25).

"Pilate saith unto them, Take ye him, and crucify him; for I find no fault in him" (John xix, 6).

It is impossible to believe that the highest court of a country would pronounce a prisoner innocent and then condemn him to death. Judicial murders are sometimes committed, but the murderers do not confess their guilt.

It is declared that Pilate desired to release Jesus but could not. Who ruled Judea, Pilate or the Sanhedrim? According to the Evangelists, the Romans ruled Judea, while the Jews ruled the Romans.

Between the Pilate of the New Testament and the Pilate of history there is nothing in common. The Pilate of the New Testament is subservient to the Jews, acceding to their every wish, even to murdering an innocent prisoner. The Pilate of history is noted for his hatred of the Jews and his cruelties to them. It was these which provoked his recall.

329

When Pilate could not prevail upon the Jews to allow him to release Jesus, what did he do?

Matthew: "He took water, and washed his hands before the multitude, saying, I am innocent of the blood of this just person" (xxvii, 24).

Matthew does not appear to realize the absurdity of supposing that a Roman official would adopt a custom peculiar to a people whom he held in contempt.

"And all the elders of that city, that are next unto the slain man, shall wash their hands . . . and they shall answer and say, Our hands have not shed this blood" (Deuteronomy xx, 6, 7).

330

What indignities were heaped upon Jesus during his trial before Pilate?

John: "Then Pilate therefore took Jesus, and scourged him. And the soldiers platted a crown of thorns, and put it on his head, and they put on him a purple robe, and said, Hail, King of the Jews! and they smote him with their hands. Pilate therefore went forth again, and saith unto them, Behold, I bring him forth to you, that ye may know that I find no fault in him. Then came Jesus forth, wearing the crown of thorns and the purple robe. And Pilate saith unto them, Behold the man!" (xix, 1–5.)

These indignities Jesus is said to have suffered, not at the hands of a Jewish mob, but at the hands of a Roman court, from which the Jews had absented themselves and whose proceedings they could not witness nor directly influence. Every lawyer knows that for more than two thousand years the Roman court has been the world's model for dignity and fairness. That an innocent and defenseless prisoner was subjected to these insults and brutalities in a Roman court, presided over by a Roman governor, none but a slave of superstition can believe.

331

When was he scourged?

Matthew and Mark: Before he was executed. "And when he [Pilate] had scourged Jesus, he delivered him to be crucified" (Matt. xxvii, 26; Mark xv, 15).

John: Before the termination of his trial (xix, 1–16).

Scourging was frequently inflicted by the Romans before execution, but never before the prisoner was convicted and sentenced. The *Bible Dictionary* concedes the illegal and unusual character of the scourging mentioned by John. "In our Lord's case, however, this infliction seems neither to have been the legal scourging after sentence nor yet the examination by torture" (Acts xxii, 24).

332

What custom is said to have been observed at the Passover?

All: The release of a prisoner by the Roman governor (Matt. xxvii, 15; Mark xv, 6; Luke xxiii, 17; John xviii, 39).

"Now at that feast the governor was wont to release unto the people a prisoner, whom they would."

There is no historical authority whatever for this alleged custom. It was a custom that the Roman government in Judea could not with safety adopt. The Jews were a subject people, waiting and hoping for an opportunity to throw off the Roman yoke. To release to them "whomsoever they desired" (Mark xv, 6) might be to release a political prisoner whose liberty would endanger the government itself. This story was probably suggested by a custom of the Roman emperors who released a prisoner at their birthday festivals.

333

They demanded and obtained the release of Barrabas. Who was Barrabas?

John: A robber. "Now Barrabas was a robber" (xviii, 40).

Mark and Luke: A murderer. "Barrabas (who for a certain sedition made in the city, and for murder, was cast into prison)" (Luke xxiii, 18, 19; Mark xv, 7).

334

By whom was Jesus clad in mockery?

Matthew, Mark and John: By Pilate's soldiers (Matt. xxvii, 27, 28; Mark xv, 16, 17; John xix, 1, 2).

Luke: By Herod and his soldiers. "And Herod with his men of war set him at nought, and mocked him, and arrayed him in a gorgeous robe" (xxiii, 11).

335

What was the color of the robe they put on him?

Matthew: "They stripped him, and put on him a scarlet robe" (xxvii, 28).

Mark and John: "They put on him a purple robe" (John xix, 2; Mark xv, 17).

336

When did this occur?

John: During his trial (xix, 1, 2, 12–16).

Matthew and Mark: After Pilate had delivered him to be crucified (Matt. xxvii, 26–28; Mark xv, 15–17).

337

Describe the mocking of Jesus.

Matthew: "Then released he Barrabas unto them; and when he had scourged Jesus, he delivered him to be crucified. Then the soldiers of the governor took Jesus into the common hall, and gathered unto him the whole band of soldiers. And they stripped him, and put on him a scarlet robe. And when they had platted a crown of thorns, they put it upon his head, and a reed in his right hand; and they bowed the knee before him, saying, Hail, King of the Jews!" (xxvii, 26–29.)

The original of this account of the mocking of Jesus is to be found in Philo's "Adversus Flaccum," written more than one hundred years before the Gospels made their appearance. Herod Agrippa was on his way from Rome to Palestine to assume the government of that country. When he stopped at Alexandria his enemies, to annoy him, instituted a mock coronation, which Philo relates as follows:

"There was a certain poor wretch named Carrabas, who spent all his days and nights in the roads, the sport of idle children and wanton youths; and the multitude, having driven him as far as the public gymnasium, and having set him up there on high, that he might be seen of everybody, flattening out a papyrus leaf, put it on his head instead of a crown, and clothed the rest of his body with a common mat in place of a robe, and in lieu of a sceptre thrust into his hand a reed, which they found lying by the wayside. And when he had received all the insignia of royalty, and had been dressed and adorned like a king, young men bearing sticks on their shoulders stood on each side of him in imitation of guards, while others came up, some as if to salute him, and others pretending to plead their causes before him" (*Philo's Works,* Vol. IV, pp. 68, 69).

338

Who smote Jesus after his trial?

Mark: "The servants did strike him with the palms of their hands" (xiv, 65).

John: "One of the officers which stood by struck Jesus with the palm of his hand" (xviii, 22).

The stories of these mockings, revilings, and brutal assaults cannot be accepted as historical. They are self-evidently false. Were they alleged to have been committed by an irresponsible Jewish or Roman mob they might be credited; but when they are declared to have been committed by, or while in the custody of the highest Jewish and Roman officials they must be rejected.

339

To whom did Pilate deliver him to be crucified?

Matthew and Mark: To the Roman soldiers. "And when he had scourged Jesus he delivered him to be crucified. Then the soldiers of the governor took Jesus. . . . And when they were come unto a place called Golgotha, that is to say, a place of a skull, . . . they crucified him" (Matt. xxvii, 26–35; Mark xv 15–24).

John: He delivered him to the Jews. "And he saith unto the Jews,

Behold your King! But they cried out, Away with him, crucify him. Pilate saith unto them, Shall I crucify your King? The chief priests answered, We have no king but Caesar. Then delivered he him therefore unto them to be crucified. And they took Jesus and led him away. And he bearing his cross went forth into a place called the place of the skulls, which is called in Hebrew Golgotha; where they crucified him" (xix, 14–18).

Matthew and Mark plainly state that Jesus was delivered to the Roman soldiers; John just as plainly states that he was delivered to the Jews. Matthew and Mark declare that he was crucified by the soldiers; John declares that he was crucified by the Jews. Were it not that John elsewhere (xix, 23) contradicts himself and states that the soldiers crucified him, the conclusion would be, after reading John, that he was crucified by the Jews.

Peter declares that the Jews executed him. Addressing the Sanhedrim, he says: "The God of our fathers raised up Jesus, whom ye slew and hanged on a tree" (Acts v, 30).

340

Who was compelled to carry the cross?

Synoptics: "And as they came out, they found a man of Cyrene, Simon by name; him they compelled to bear his cross" (Matt. xxvii, 32; Mark xv, 21; Luke xxiii, 26).

John: The cross was borne by Jesus himself (xix, 17).

341

Where was Simon when they compelled him to carry the cross?

Mark: "Coming out of the country" (xv, 21).

The correct reading of this is, "coming from the field," i.e., "coming from his work." This is improbable as they did not work on the Passover.

342

The Synoptics agree in stating that Simon was compelled to carry the cross. Is this probable?

It is not. In executions of this kind the criminal was always required to carry it himself as a mark of disgrace.

343

It is inferred from the Synoptics that the cross was too heavy for Jesus to bear, and Christian writings and paintings represent him bending with fatigue beneath the burden of the entire cross. What was the burden he was required to carry?

Simply the patibulum, or cross piece, which was not heavy. The upright portion of the cross was a permanent fixture.

344

On his way to execution he made a speech to the women of Jerusalem who bewailed his fate. Alluding, as is alleged, to the coming destruction of Jerusalem, what did he declare they would say?

"To the mountains, Fall on us; and to the hills, Cover us" (Luke xxiii, 30).

Luke attempts to put into the mouth of Jesus a quotation from Hosea, but his memory was defective. What the prophet said was as follows:

"To the mountains, Cover us; and to the hills, Fall on us" (Hosea x, 8).

Renan pronounces this speech spurious. He says: "The speech to the women of Jerusalem could scarcely have been conceived except after the siege of the year 70."

345

Where was he crucified?

Matthew and Mark: At "a place called Golgotha, that is to say, a place of a skull" (Matt. xxvii, 33; Mark xv, 22).

Luke: At Calvary (xxiii, 33).

Calvary, like Golgotha, means a place of skulls in the vicinity of Jerusalem. The explanation given by Christian commentators is that "it was a spot where executions ordinarily took place, and therefore abounded in skulls." Fleetwood says it "was called Golgotha, or Place of Skulls, from the criminals' bones which lay scattered there" (*Life of Christ,* p. 416). Where Jewish customs prevailed—and it is admitted that they did prevail in Jerusalem and Judea at this time, and had for hundreds of years—a human skull or bone was not allowed to be exposed for even a moment.

346

What was the inscription on the cross?

Mark: "The King of the Jews" (xv, 26).

Luke: "This is the King of the Jews" (xxiii, 38).

Matthew: "This is Jesus the King of the Jews" (xxvii, 37).

John: "Jesus of Nazareth, the King of the Jews" (xix, 19).

There was placed on the cross a certain inscription. According to Luke and John it appeared in Greek, Latin and Hebrew. Four divinely inspired historians attempt to report in Greek the exact words of this inscription. Yet no two of their reports agree.

347

Did the name of Jesus appear on the cross?

Matthew and John: It did.

Mark and Luke: It did not.

348

Did the word "Nazareth" appear in the inscription?
  John: It did.
  Synoptics: It did not.

349

What did they offer him to drink before crucifying him?
  Matthew: "Vinegar mingled with gall" (xxvii, 34).
  Mark: "Wine mingled with myrrh" (xv, 23).
  Luke: "Vinegar" alone (xxiii, 36).
  The draughts mentioned by Matthew and Mark refer to a Jewish mixture intended to produce stupefaction and lessen pain. Had the Romans crucified him it is not probable that they would have observed this Jewish custom.

350

How was he fastened on the cross?
  Luke and John: His hands and feet were nailed to it (Luke xxiv, 39; John xx, 25, 27).
  The Evangelists do not say that he was nailed to the cross; but it has been inferred from the texts mentioned in Luke and John that he was. In crucifixion the victim was usually bound to the cross. Nails were sometimes driven through the hands, but never through the feet. The allusions to the supposed wounds on his hands and feet were evidently inserted in the accounts for the purpose of establishing his identity after the resurrection. Great prominence has been given them by Christians in order to make Christ's crucifixion appear especially cruel and create sympathy for him.

351

At what hour of the day was he crucified?

Mark: "It was the third hour [nine o'clock in the morning]" (xv, 25).

Luke: "It was about the sixth hour [noon]" (xxiii, 44).

John: At the sixth hour he had not been sentenced and delivered to the executioners; hence he was not crucified until the afternoon (xix, 14–16).

Dr. Geikie admits that three hours may have elapsed between the termination of his trial and his crucifixion. Hence, according to John, the crucifixion may have occurred as late as three o'clock in the afternoon.

It has been attempted to explain the discrepancy between Mark and John by supposing that John used a different method of reckoning time. Concerning this, Prof. Sanday, one of England's highest orthodox authorities, says: "The writer of this was at one time inclined to look with favor on these attempts. If the premise could be proved, the data would work out satisfactorily. . . . But it must definitely be said that the major premise cannot be proved, and that the attempt to reconcile the two statements on this basis breaks down."

352

How did the soldiers divide the garments?

Matthew: "And they crucified him, and parted his garments, casting lots; that it might be fulfilled which was spoken by the prophet, They parted my garments among them, and upon my vesture did they cast lots" (xxvii, 35).

John: "Then the soldiers when they had crucified Jesus, took his garments, and made four parts, to every soldier a part; and also his coat: now the coat was without seam, woven from the top throughout. They said, therefore, among themselves, Let us not rend it, but cast lots for it, whose it shall be; that the scripture might be fulfilled, which saith, They parted my raiment among them, and for my vesture they did cast lots" (xix, 23, 24).

According to Matthew they cast lots for all the garments; according to John they cast lots for the coat alone. John here makes the same error in regard to the garments that Matthew does in regard to the ass on which Jesus made his triumphal entry. In the verse cited from Psalms garments and vesture are the same thing—the clothing of the writer. One of the chief characteristics of Hebrew poetry, or much of it at least, is that each successive thought is stated twice, but in different words.

353

Who were crucified with Jesus?

Mark and Matthew: "And with him they crucify two thieves" (Mark xv, 27; Matt. xxvii, 38).

Thieves were not crucified. Crucifixion, or death in any form, for theft was contrary to both Jewish and Roman law. Theft was not a capital offense.

354

His crucifixion between two thieves fulfilled what prophecy?

Mark: "And the scripture was fulfilled which saith, And he shall be numbered with the transgressors" (xv, 28).

"The same thing might be said of the thieves."—Paine.

This passage is not to be found in the earlier manuscripts of Mark, and Westcott declares it to be an interpolation.

355

How long did Jesus survive after being placed upon the cross?

Luke: About three hours (xxiii, 44).

A Jamaica negro slave, crucified in 1760, lived two hundred and ten hours.

Kitto says: "We may consider thirty-six hours to be the earliest period at which crucifixion would occasion death in a healthy adult" (*Biblical Cyclopedia*, Art. "Crucifixion").

356

What were his last words?

Matthew: "Eli, Eli, lama sabachthani, that is to say, My God, my God, why hast thou forsaken me?" (xxvii, 46).

Mark: "Eloi, Eloi, lama sabachthani, which is, being interpreted, My God, my God, why hast thou forsaken me?" (xv, 34.)

Luke: "Father, into thy hands I commend my spirit" (xxiii, 46).

John: "It is finished" (xix, 30).

With the Four Gospels before them, Christians do not know what his last words were. The two most popular English *Lives of Christ* are those of Dr. Farrar and Dr. Geikie. These writers were contemporaries and friends, and both were adherents of the same church. Both, with these Gospels for their authorities, attempt to portray the closing scene. I quote from each:

Dr. Farrar: "And now the end was come. Once more, in the words of the sweet Psalmist of Israel, but adding to them that title of trustful love which, through Him, is permitted to the use of all mankind, 'Father' he said, 'into Thy hands I commend my spirit.' Then with one more great effort he uttered the last cry—the one victorious word, 'IT IS FINISHED.' "

Dr. Geikie: "A moment more, and all was over. The cloud had passed as suddenly as it rose. Far and wide, over the vanquished throngs of his enemies, with a loud voice, as if uttering his shout of eternal victory before entering into his glory, he cried, 'It is finished!' Then, more gently, came the words, 'FATHER, INTO THY HANDS I COMMEND MY SPIRIT.' "

357

In what language were his last words uttered?
Matthew: In Hebrew.
Mark: In Aramaic and Hebrew.
The language spoken by Jesus and by the people of Palestine at this time was the Aramaic. Mark attempts to give the words of Jesus in this language. But while the first two words are Aramaic, the last two are Hebrew. The words Mark attempts to give are "Elohi, Elohi, metul mah shabaktani?" This Gospel was written by one ignorant of the language of Palestine.

358

Matthew interprets the Hebrew words quoted by him to mean, "My God, my God, why hast thou forsaken me?" Is this correct?
It is not. The words mean, "My God, my God, why hast thou sacrificed me?"
The Gospel of Matthew, it is claimed, originally appeared in Hebrew. But this shows that the author of Matthew did not understand the Hebrew language.

359

What are the words given by Matthew and Mark?
The first words of the 22d Psalm. In the words of Farrar, "He borrowed from David's utter agony the expression of his own."
Is it probable that a man in the agonies of a terrible death would devote his expiring breath to a recital of Hebrew poetry? When even the dying words of this Christ are borrowed, is it not evident that the whole story of his life is fabulous?
The accounts of the crucifixion given by the Evangelists are to a large extent reproductions of the 22d Psalm, even to the language itself, the poetical allusions of the psalmist being transformed into alleged

historical facts. The devout Christian who is familiar with this Passion Psalm sees in the Evangelists' account of the crucifixion a wonderful fulfillment of prophecy. But the critic sees merely the borrowed embellishments of a legend.

360

What expression did his words, "Eli, Eli, lama sabachthani," provoke?

Matthew: "Some of them that stood there, when they heard that, said, This man calleth for Elias" (xxvii, 47).

This is additional proof of Matthew's ignorance of Hebrew. He supposes a similarity of sound between the two words, whereas they were utterly unlike in pronunciation. Eli was pronounced Ali (long a), while Elias was pronounced Eleeyahu. But even had they been so much alike in sound that one might have been mistaken for the other, as Matthew supposes, the alleged incident is disproved by the fact that the Jews were not allowed to attend the execution, while to the Romans the words were meaningless.

361

Who was it bade them see whether Elias would come to his rescue?

Mark: The one who gave him the sponge filled with vinegar. "And one ran and filled a sponge full of vinegar, and put it on a reed, and gave him to drink, saying, Let alone, let us see whether Elias wiil come to take him down" (xv, 36).

Matthew: It was not this person, but those who were with him. "And straightway one of them ran, and took a sponge and filled it with vinegar, and put it on a reed, and gave him to drink. The rest said, Let be, let us see whether Elias will come to save him" (xxvii, 48, 49).

In regard to these alleged last words of Jesus, Dr, Hooykaas says: "It seems to us far more probable that these words of the Messianic passion-psalm were put into the mouth of Jesus by tradition than that he really uttered them. The sequel, too, throws great suspicion on the report; for the Jews were not allowed to approach the cross, and what did the Roman soldiers know about Elijah? Besides, if the Jews had really heard him cry "Eli!" or "Eloi!" they would hardly have mistaken the words of the twenty-second Psalm for a cry to the precursor of the Messianic kingdom—a mistake upon which their raillery is made to depend. We must, therefore, put aside these words, as in all probability unhistorical" (*Bible for Learners,* Vol. III, p. 454).

362

Did the thieves between whom he was crucified both revile him?

Matthew and Mark: They did. "And they that were crucified with him reviled him" (Mark xv, 32; Matt. xxvii, 44).

Luke: They did not; but one reviled him. "And one of the malefactors which were hanged railed on him. . . . But the other answering rebuked him, saying, Dost not thou fear God, seeing thou art in the same condemnation?" (xxiii, 39, 40.)

If these men were crucified with Jesus, as claimed, neither reviled him. Reason rejects the statement that a dying man, suffering unutterable agony, reviled a fellow sufferer.

363

What request did the penitent thief make of Jesus?

Luke: "And he said unto Jesus, Lord, remember me when thou comest into thy kingdom" (xxiii, 42).

Here the dying thief is represented as being familiar with a subject which the disciples themselves did not at this time comprehend.

364

What did Jesus say to the thief?

"Today shalt thou be with me in paradise" (Luke xxiii, 43).

Instead of going to the Christian Heaven above, they went to the Jewish-Pagan Sheol (Hell) below. Did Jesus recant on the cross? Did he renounce the Kingdom of God when God deserted him? Concerning this remarkable passage, *Smith's Bible Dictionary* says:

"The Rabbis in the time of our Savior taught there was a region of the world of the dead, of Sheol, in the heart of the earth. Gehenna was on one side, with its flames and torments; Paradise on the other, the intermediate home of the blessed. . . . It is significant, indeed, that the word 'paradise' nowhere occurs in the public teaching of our Lord, or in his intercourse with his disciples. Connected as it had been with the thoughts of a sensuous happiness, it was not the fittest nor the best word for those whom he was training to rise out of sensuous thoughts to the higher regions of the spiritual life. For them, accordingly, the Kingdom of Heaven, the Kingdom of God, are the words most dwelt on. With the thief dying on the cross the case was different. We can assume nothing in the robber-outlaw but the most rudimentary forms of the popular belief. The answer to his prayer gave him what he needed most, the assurance of immediate rest and peace."

The explanation of the apologist is as lame as the story of the Evangelist. Did Jesus go to Hell with the thief because the thief was unfit to go to Heaven with him? This apologist says that Jesus used these words—gave expression to a false doctrine—because the thief was incapable of comprehending the true doctrine. But this conflicts with the alleged words of the thief himself which show that he did comprehend the nature of the kingdom of Heaven. It was this, and not the peace of the grave, for which he prayed.

365

What were the centurion's words?

Luke: "Certainly this was a righteous man" (xxiii, 47).

Matthew: "Truly this was the Son of God" (xxvii, 54).

We have here the anomaly of a Roman officer—a Pagan—entertaining a Jewish doctrine of a Messiah, and accepting the Christian claim that Jesus was the Messiah. If this be true it is strange that he permitted his soldiers to insult and abuse Jesus.

366

After Jesus expired what did one of the soldiers do?

John: "One of the soldiers with a spear pierced his side" (xix, 34).

It is remarkable that the Synoptics, who pretend to relate every important incident connected with the crucifixion, make no mention of the spear thrust.

367

What is said to have issued from the wound?

John: "And forthwith came there out blood and water" (xix, 34).

According to a well known physiological fact, if Jesus was still alive or had but recently expired, not blood and water, but blood alone would have flowed from the wound. If he was dead, and it is stated that he was, then neither blood nor water would have flowed from it. When blood is drawn from a living body it becomes separated into two parts, a thick substance known as febrine, and a watery fluid known as serum. John was familiar with this fact and supposed that this also took place in a corpse, which is not the case.

Dr. Cabanes, a noted physician of Paris, writes as follows regarding the crucifixion of Jesus:

"It appears that crucifixion alone could not have produced the death of Jesus, and in reference to the wounds produced by the nails, these wounds being the result of crushing, the hemorrhage was small. A burning fever might possibly occur which would be manifested by an intense thirst, but the flow of blood could not be sufficient to cause death. Death in this case is preceded by a comatose condition which would be inconsistent with the cry uttered in a loud voice by Jesus shortly before his last breath. All the commentators of the gospels further agree that Jesus did not remain more than three to six hours on the cross, and death cannot be produced by an exposure of this duration to this mode of torture.

"The generally accepted version of the lance wound received by Jesus is that the blow was struck on the left side and that there flowed from the wound water mingled with blood. It has been correctly remarked that blood does not flow from a corpse, and therefore if blood followed the lance stroke, Jesus must have been alive; further, in order that the blow might have killed the dying man, it must have injured a vital organ. It must be observed that a lance directed upward and from right to left could not reach the right-hand cavities of the heart without first opening the peritoneal cavity, traversing the liver, the pericardium and perhaps the pleura. We must therefore ask how the few hundred grams of blood which a right ventricle could contain, could penetrate to the exterior of the body after such a great wound. Also with those who die slowly there is found a distended heart in which the blood has very rapidly coagulated, and it must follow that if a flood of the liquid appeared on the side of Jesus it could not have come from the heart. With regard to the vena cava, its situation is too far back to have allowed it to be touched by the lance. If the wound had been in the stomach a lesion of the digestive tube would have been disclosed by an ejection of blood mingled with alimentary matter, either from the mouth or the opening of the wound, or at least by a discharge of blood into the abdominal cavity. Had the liver been touched the symptoms of an internal hemorrhage would have been observed, as in the case of President Carnot, in whose case the blow of the poignard, directed downward, perforated the liver and the portal vein, inducing a state of coma, whereas Jesus, we have been told, cried out with a loud voice. We thus see that death was not due to the lance wound or to the torture of crucifixion, as so often stated."

368

Was Christ's suffering foretold by the prophets?

Peter: "But those things, which God before had showed by the mouth of all his prophets, that Christ should suffer, he hath so fulfilled" (Acts iii, 18).

God had not showed by the mouth of all his prophets, nor by the mouth of even one of his prophets, that Christ should suffer. The prophets know nothing of a suffering Messiah. There is not a text in the Old Testament referring to such a Messiah. The passages relating to suffering cited by the Evangelists and applied to Christ have no reference whatever to a Messiah. The *Encyclopedia Britannica* says: "That the Jews in the time of Christ believed in a suffering and atoning Messiah is, to say the least, unproved and highly improbable."

369

What marvelous events occurred at the time of the crucifixion?

Matthew: "There was darkness over all the land" (xxvii, 45). "The veil of the temple was rent in twain from the top to the bottom; and the earth did quake, and the rocks rent; and the graves were opened; and many bodies of the saints which slept arose" (51, 52).

Mark and Luke: "There was darkness over the whole land" (Mark xv, 33). "And the veil of the temple was rent in twain from the top to the bottom" (38).

Mark and Luke know nothing of two of the important events related by Matthew; John is ignorant of all of them. Had these events really happened, the naturalists and chroniclers of that age would have recorded them. As they make no mention of them, we know that they did not occur.

If we accept the claims of their followers, nearly all the gods and heroes of antiquity expired amid the convulsions of Nature. The soul of Romulus went out amid the battling of her elements; "the sun was darkened and the sky rained fire and ashes" when the Hindu Krishna left his saddened followers; "the earth shook, the rocks were rent, the graves opened, and in a storm which threatened the dissolution of the universe," Prometheus closed his earthly career; a pall of darkness settled over Egypt when her Osiris died; the death of Alexander was succeeded by six hours of preternatural gloom; and—

> "Ere the mighty Julius fell,
> The grave stood tenantless, and the sheeted dead
> Did squeak and gibber in the Roman streets."

370

How long did the darkness last?

Synoptics: From the sixth to the ninth hour (Matt. xxvii, 45; Mark xv, 33; Luke xxiii, 44).

According to Matthew and Luke this darkness lasted from the time that he was suspended upon the cross until he died. Yet his executioners are ignorant of it. Luke says: "His acquaintances, and the women that followed him from Galilee, stood afar off, beholding these things [the crucifixion]" (xxiii, 49), which they could not have done had this darkness really occurred.

If this darkness occurred, and began at the sixth hour, as stated by the Synoptics, then, according to John, the conclusion of the trial, the sentencing of Jesus, the preparations for his execution, and the journey to Golgotha, all took place during the darkness, a conclusion which the nature of the narrative utterly precludes.

Christian apologists have cited Phlegon who notices an eclipse which occurred about this time. But there is a variance of at least six years in regard to the time that Jesus was crucified. Besides an eclipse could not have occurred within two weeks of a Passover, on the occurrence of which he is declared to have been executed. Farrar says: "It could have been no darkness of any natural eclipse, for the Paschal moon was at the full" (*Life of Christ*, p. 505). Geikie says: "It is impossible to explain the origin of this darkness. The Passover moon was then at the full, so that it could not have been an eclipse. The earlier fathers, relying on a notice of an eclipse that seemed to coincide in time, though it really did not, fancied that the darkness was caused by it, but incorrectly" (*Life of Christ,* Vol. II, p. 624, Notes). "The celebrated passage of Phlegon," says Gibbon, "is now wisely abandoned" (*Rome,* Vol. I, p. 589, Note).

371

Was the veil of the temple rent, as our Gospel of Matthew declares?

The Gospel of Matthew, it is affirmed, originally appeared in Hebrew. St. Jerome, who had this original version, says: "In that Gospel which is written in Hebrew letters, we read, not that the veil of the temple was rent, but that a lintel (or beam) of a prodigious size fell down."

Commenting on this alleged prodigy, the rending of the veil, Strauss says: "Now the object of the divine Providence in effecting such a miracle could only have been this: to produce in the Jewish contemporaries of Jesus a deep impression of the importance of his death, and to furnish the first promulgators of the gospel with a fact to which they might appeal in support of their cause. But, as Schleiermacher has shown, nowhere else in the New Testament, either in the apostolic epistles or in Acts, or even in the Epistle to the Hebrews, in connection with the subject of which it could scarcely fail to be suggested, is this event mentioned: on the contrary, with the exception of this bare Synoptical notice, every trace of it is lost; which could scarcely have been the case if it had really formed a ground of apostolical argument. Thus the divine purpose in ordaining this miracle must have totally failed, or, since this is inconceivable, it cannot have been ordained for this object—in other words, since neither any other object of the miracle, nor yet a mode in which the event might happen naturally can be discovered, it cannot have happened at all" (*Leben Jesu,* p. 789).

372

Matthew declares that the dead arose on the day of the crucifixion. When did they come out of their graves?

Not until after Christ's resurrection, which did not occur until the following week. "And many bodies of the saints which slept arose, and came out of the graves after his resurrection" (Matt. xxvii, 52, 53).

"They were polite enough to sit in their open graves and wait for Christ to rise first."—Ingersoll.

373

From what source was Matthew's story regarding these marvelous events derived?

From Zechariah: "And his feet shall stand in that day upon the Mount of Olives, which is before Jerusalem on the East, and the Mount of Olives shall cleave in the midst thereof . . . and half of the mountain shall remove toward the North, and half of it toward the South. . . . Ye shall flee, like as ye fled from before the earthquake in the days of Uzziah King of Judah; and the Lord my God shall come, and all the saints with thee. And it shall come to pass in that day, that the light shall not be clear" (xiv, 4–6).

Concerning this Dr. Wise says: "God who comes, according to Zachariah, to fight for Jerusalem, will stand upon Mount Olivet. Therefore, Jesus, during his fight against Pharisees, Sadducees and priests, had to make his principal home on Mount Olivet. But he could not split the mountain, as Zachariah imagined God would, and move one part North and the other South; therefore, the curtain of the temple had to be torn in twain when Jesus died, although none has ever mentioned the fact. The curtain was there some thirty-five years after the death of Jesus; had it been torn, somebody must have noticed it. The earthquake mentioned by Zachariah, of course, was borrowed to embellish Calvary. . . . Because Zachariah states God coming to Jerusalem, 'And the Lord my God cometh, all the saints with thee,' therefore the saints and not the sinners had to resurrect and visit the city on that particular day. But in the fertile imagination of Zachariah, the day of that terrible combat must be dark. . . . This darkness was transported over to Calvary to embellish the scene. . . . So these miracles were not wrought, but the entire outer embellishment of Calvary is taken from Zachariah; not because it was believed this prophecy referred to Jesus, but simply because the evangelical writers were incompetent to invent original poetry" (*Martyrdom of Jesus,* p. 116).

374

What request did the Jews make of Pilate concerning Jesus and the malefactors?

John: They "besought Pilate that their legs might be broken" (xix, 31).

This punishment, known as crurifragium, was a distinct mode of execution and was never united with crucifixion. Crucifixion, we have seen, was not employed to punish theft. Neither was crurifragium. Yet we are asked to believe that both modes of execution, two of the cruelest forms of punishment, were combined to punish these offenders. The Synoptics do not mention this punishment.

375

When the soldiers broke the legs of the thieves, why did they spare those of Jesus?

John: "That the scripture should be fulfilled, A bone of him shall not be broken" (xix, 36).

This refers to Exodus xii, 46, and relates to the disposition to be made of the lamb used at the Passover. Nearly the entire chapter from which John quotes is devoted to this subject. Among other things it states that "They shall eat the flesh in that night, . . . his head with his legs, and with the purtenance thereof. And ye shall let nothing of it remain until the morning" (8–10). If a part of this prophecy was fulfilled, may not all of it have been fulfilled? And if all of it was fulfilled, will not this account for the empty sepulchre?

Regarding the failure of the soldiers to break the legs of Jesus, as ordered, *Supernatural Religion* says: "An order having been given to the Roman soldiers, in accordance with the request of the Jews, to break the legs of the crucified, we are asked to believe that they did not execute it in the case of Jesus. It is not reasonable to suppose, however, that Roman soldiers either were in the habit of disregarding their orders, or could have any motive for doing so in this case, and subjecting themselves to the punishment for disobedience inflicted by Roman military law. It is argued that they saw that Jesus was already dead, and, therefore, that it was not necessary to break his legs; but soldiers are not in the habit of thinking in this way; they are disciplined to obey" (p. 993).

376

What demand was made by the Jews on the evening of the crucifixion?

John: That their bodies be taken down from the cross (xix, 31).

John was evidently familiar with the Mosaic law (Deut. xxi, 22, 23) which, in cases of hanging, enjoined the burial of the body on the day of execution, but seemingly ignorant of the Roman law under which they were executed, which, in cases of crucifixion, prohibited burial, requiring the body to remain upon the cross until decayed, or birds and beasts had devoured it. The Jews esteemed it sinful to allow a criminal to "remain all night upon the tree;" but the Jewish law was inapplicable to the Roman mode of punishment which presupposed that the criminal would remain on the cross several days and nights before death ensued.

377

What additional reason was there for having the bodies taken down?

Mark: "Because it was the preparation, that is, the day before the Sabbath" (xv, 42).

The Sabbath began at sunset on the day that he is declared to have been crucified. The Jewish law would not permit his body, whether dead or alive, to be exposed on the Sabbath. Crucifixion, as we have seen, was a lingering death; several days usually elapsing before the victim expired. Now, is it reasonable to suppose that the Jews would demand, as claimed, a punishment lasting several days when they knew that he must be taken down from the cross in a few hours?

378

What did Pilate do when Joseph solicited the body of Jesus?

Mark: "Pilate marveled if he were already dead" (xv, 44).

Why should Pilate marvel if he were already dead when previous to this, according to John (xix, 31–33), he had, at the request of the Jews, ordered his soldiers to dispatch him if alive and take his body away?

379

Were the disciples present at the crucifixion?

John: They were, or one, at least (xix, 26).

According to the Synoptics, all were absent; all had forsaken their Master, all had fled. The Twelve Apostles at this time, unless Judas had already hung himself, as Matthew declares, numbered one traitor and eleven cowards.

380

What women followed Jesus and witnessed his execution?

Matthew and Mark: Women of Galilee (Matt. xxvii, 55; Mark xv, 40, 41).

Luke: "Daughters of Jerusalem," that is, women of Judea (xxiii, 28).

381

Where were Mary Magdalene and her companions during the crucifixion?

Matthew and Mark: "Looking on afar off" (Mark xv, 40; Matt. xxvii, 55, 56).

John: They "stood by the cross" (xix, 25).

382

Was Mary, the mother of Jesus, present?

John: She was (xix, 25).

Synoptics: She was not.

The Synoptics do not expressly state that she was absent, but if she was present, as John affirms, is it possible that they would ignore the fact when they mention "the strolling Magdalene" no less than seven times?

383

Who stood by the cross with the mother of Jesus?

John: "Now there stood by the cross of Jesus his mother, and his mother's sister, Mary, the wife of Cleophas" (xix, 25).

Mary must have been a very popular name to be given to two daughters of the same family. It is not probable that these sisters were both named Mary. John never mentions the name of Jesus' mother, and it is evident that he did not suppose her name was Mary. Were John the only Gospel, Christians would be ignorant of the Virgin's name. Mariolatry did not originate in the Johannine church.

384

To whom was entrusted the care of Jesus's mother?

John: "When Jesus therefore saw his mother, and the disciple standing by whom he loved [John], he saith unto his mother, Woman, behold thy son! Then saith he to the disciple, Behold thy mother! And from that hour that disciple took her unto his own house" (xix, 26, 27).

"The teacher who had been to him as a brother leaves to him a brother's duty. He is to be as a son to the mother who is left desolate."— *Bible Dictionary*.

Very touchingly expressed. But why was this duty imposed upon John when the Apostle James (the Less) was a brother of Jesus and a son of Mary? Was he a worthless ingrate, unable and unwilling to care for her? And what of Joses, and Juda, and Simon, and her daughters who remained at home? Had they turned their mother out of doors?

385

In whose sepulcher was the body of Jesus placed?

Matthew: Joseph "laid it in his own new tomb which he had hewn out in the rock" (xxvii, 60).

John: "Now in the place where he was crucified there was a garden; and in the garden a new sepulcher wherein was never man yet laid. There laid they Jesus therefore because of the Jew's preparation day; for the sepulcher was nigh at hand" (xix, 41, 42).

It is evident from John that the sepulcher did not belong to Joseph, but that it was one which happened to be convenient to the place of crucifixion; for, as Strauss justly argues: "The vicinity of the grave, when alleged as a motive, excludes the fact of possession."

386

Was his body embalmed when it was laid in the sepulcher?

John: It was. "He [Joseph] came therefore, and took the body of Jesus. And there came also Nicodemus, which at the first came to Jesus by night, and brought a mixture of myrrh and aloes, about an hundred pound weight. Then took they the body of Jesus, and wound it in linen clothes with the spices, as the manner of the Jews is to bury" (xix, 38–40).

Mark and Luke: It was not embalmed. "The women also, which came with him from Galilee, followed after, and beheld the sepulcher, and how his body was laid. And they returned, and prepared spices and ointments" (Luke xxiii, 55, 56); intending to embalm it "when the Sabbath was past" (Mark xvi, 1).

387

What is said in regard to wrapping the body of Jesus by Joseph?

Mark: "He bought fine linen, and took him down, and wrapped him in the linen" (xv, 46).

This statement is rejected by critics. A member of the Sanhedrim would not desecrate the Passover by making a purchase on it.

388

What was the amount of the material used in embalming Jesus?

John: A hundred pounds (xix, 39).

This was sufficient to embalm a dozen bodies. Yet after seeing his body literally buried in the material, the women, we are told, procured more.

389

When did the women procure materials for embalming Jesus?

Luke: "They returned, and prepared spices and ointments; and rested the Sabbath Day" (xxiii, 56).

Mark (New Ver.): "And when the Sabbath was past, Mary Magdalene and Mary the mother of James, and Salome, bought spices that they might come and anoint him" (xvi, 1).

According to Luke they prepared the spices before the Sabbath began, that is, before the end of the sixth day; according to Mark, they did not procure them until "the Sabbath was past," that is, not until the beginning of the first day.

390

When did they go to embalm the body?

Mark and Luke: "When the Sabbath was past, . . . the first day of the week" (Mark xvi, 1, 2; Luke xxiv, 1).

Is it reasonable to suppose that in that warm spring climate (Dr. Geikie speaks of the fierce heat that prevailed at the time), they would let a wounded body lie two days, until decomposition had commenced, and then attempt to embalm it?

391

When was the sepulcher closed?

All: When the body was placed in it (Matt. xxvii, 60; Mark xv, 46; Luke xxiii, 53, xxiv, 1, 2; John xix, 41, 42, xx, 1).

According to the Evangelists, the stone was rolled to the door of the sepulcher as soon as the body was deposited, and according to Mark and Luke, the women were troubled as to who should roll away the stone when they went to embalm the body.

In sepulture of this kind, the tomb was not closed until the third day, and when once closed it was not to be opened. This deviation from the customary mode is evidently for the purpose of establishing faith in the doctrine of the resurrection, by shutting off all means of escape or removal without supernatural aid. The Evangelists are particular to state that Joseph "rolled a great stone to the door."

In a single paragraph, *Scribner's Bible Dictionary* concedes no less than seven Synoptical errors regarding the trial, crucifixion and burial of Jesus: "The Synoptists make the Sanhedrim say beforehand that they will not arrest Jesus 'on the feast day,' and then actually arrest him on that day; that not only the guards, but one of the disciples carries arms, which on the feast day was not allowed; that the trial was also held on the feast day, which would be unlawful; that the feast day would not be called 'Preparation'; that the phrase 'coming from the field' (Mk. xv, 21) means properly 'coming from work'; that Joseph of Arimathea is represented as buying a linen cloth (Mk. xv, 46), and the women as preparing spices and ointments (Lk. xxiii, 56), all of which would be contrary to law and custom."

392

In what year was Jesus crucified?

Not one of the Evangelists knows. They agree that he was crucified during the time that Pontius Pilate was procurator of Judea, and Joseph Caiaphas was high priest of the Jews. But this, so far as Matthew, Mark and John are concerned, may have been any time from 26 to 36 A.D.

Luke, while he does not state the particular year, nor furnish data for determining it, is more definite. He says that Jesus began his ministry in "the fifteenth year of the reign of Tiberius Caesar," and his narrative clearly implies that he was crucified at the following Passover. Tiberius commenced his reign in August, 14 A.D. The fifteenth year of his reign, then, extended from August, 28 A.D., to August, 29 A.D. If Jesus began his ministry during the first months of this year, he might have been crucified as early as the spring of 29. But it is generally conceded that the time which this would allow for his ministry was far too brief, and that he could not have been crucified before 30 A.D.

The Christian Fathers who, for the most part, accepted the tradition of Luke and affirmed that his ministry lasted but one year, or less, held that the crucifixion occurred in 29 A.D.

Scribner's Bible Dictionary gives preference to 29 A.D. Cuthbert Hamilton Turner, M.A., Oxford, the New Testament chronologist of that work, after a lengthy review of the subject, says: "To sum up briefly, the separate results of five lines of enquiry harmonize with one another beyond expectation, so that each in turn supplies fresh security for the rest. The nativity in B.C. 7–6; the age of our Lord at the baptism, 30 years, more or less; the baptism in A.D. 26 (26–27); the duration of the ministry between two and three years; the crucifixion in A.D. 29."

This authority states that his ministry lasted two or three years. It was necessary to do this or reject John. By taking a year or more from John's ministry of Jesus and adding it to the one year ministry of the Synoptics—by assuming that the Synoptics omit to mention one or more Passovers, and that one of the Passovers mentioned by John was some other feast—it pretends to have reconciled the discrepancy regarding the length of Christ's ministry. But if his ministry lasted two or three years, as affirmed, he could not have been crucified in 29 A.D.

With orthodox commentators, a favorite method of reconciling Old Testament dates, as I have noted in a previous work, is to assume that a king, concerning the date of whose accession, or length of reign, a discrepancy appears, reigned in consort with his predecessor for a number of years sufficient to cover the discrepancy. This dishonest method of explanation—for it is a dishonest trick, intended to deceive the reader and hide from him an error—has been employed to reconcile Luke and John. By assuming that Tiberius divided the government with Augustus for two years preceding his accession to the throne, an assumption for which there is no credible authority, and that Luke accordingly reckons the fifteenth year from 12 A.D., instead of 14 A.D., when he really became emperor, it is possible to give Jesus a ministry of two or three years and still have him crucified in 29 A.D. But another irreconcilable difficulty remains. The Synoptics state that he was crucified on the Passover and on the day preceding the Sabbath, that is, on Friday. If so, he could not have been crucified in 29 A.D., for the Passover did not fall on Friday that year.

Dr. Farrar says it is "highly probable that the crucifixion took place at the passover of March, 30 A.D."

Justice Bradley of the United States Supreme Court, who made an exhaustive examination of all the evidence and arguments bearing on the question, decided in favor of 30 A.D. He says: "There were only three years from A.D. 27 to A.D. 36, inclusive, in which the 1st of Nisan, and consequently the 15th of Nisan, happened on Friday, and these were A.D. 27, 30 and 33, the last of which is very doubtful. But the crucifixion could not have happened before A.D. 28, and probably not later than A.D. 31. Therefore the year 30 is the only one which satisfies all the conditions of the problem. . . . Now, since in A.D. 30, the 1st of Nisan fell on Friday, the 24th of March, the 15th fell on Friday, the 7th of April, which was the day of the crucifixion."

Dr. Farrar and Justice Bradley are agreed in regard to the year of the crucifixion, but they are not agreed in regard to the calendar month in which it occurred. Dr. Farrar says it occurred in March; Justice Bradley says it occurred in April.

Justice Bradley says that 30 A.D. satisfies all the conditions. It does satisfy the conditions of the Synoptics, but it does not satisfy the conditions of John, as claimed. To satisfy the conditions of John it is necessary to adopt the untenable hypothesis of 12 A.D. as the date of Tiberius Caesar's accession. But whatever satisfies the conditions of John must necessarily conflict with those of the Synoptics.

Some Christian scholars place the crucifixion in 31 A.D., others in 32 A.D. But neither year can be harmonized with the Synoptics' statement that he was put to death on the Passover, or with John's that he suffered on the day of Preparation. Neither can they be harmonized with either the Synoptics or John in regard to the duration of his ministry.

It is probable that a majority of Christian scholars today believe that Jesus was crucified in 33. Renan accepted this date. He says. "According to the calculation we adopt, the death of Jesus happened in the year 33 of our era. It could not, at all events, be either before the year 29, the preaching of John and Jesus having commenced in the year 28, or after 35, since in the year 36, and probably before the Passover, Pilate and Kaiapha both lost their offices."

The adoption of 33 allows for the four years' ministry ascribed to Jesus by John, but it cannot be reconciled with the brief ministry ascribed to him by the Synoptics. As for Renan, who in the first edition of his *Jesus* accepted the authenticity of John, but subsequently rejected it and accepted only the Synoptics, he has no Evangelistic authority for 33.

The Dutch theologians, Kuenen, Oort and Hooykaas, and many other Rationalists, give 35 A.D. the preference. To accept this year, however, it is necessary to reject the Passover crucifixion, and to assign to Jesus a much longer ministry than even John assigns.

Of one hundred Christian authorities who attempt to name the year in which Christ was crucified, twenty-three say 29, eighteen 30, nine 31, seven 32, thirty-seven 33, and six 35 A.D.

Thus it will be seen that not a year that can be named can be harmonized with the accounts of the crucifixion given in the four gospels. The result is that there is as great a lack of agreement in regard to the time of Christ's death as there is in regard to the time of his birth. Christians do not know when he was born, they do not know when he died, they cannot prove that he lived.

393

On what day of the month was he crucified?

Synoptics: On the 15th of Nisan.

John: On the 14th of Nisan.

This discrepancy is conceded by *Scribner's Bible Dictionary*. It says:

"It is the Last Supper which the Synoptics appear to fix by identifying it with the Passover. They say expressly that on the morning of the 'first day of unleavened bread, when they sacrificed the passover' (Mk. xiv, 12), the disciples asked where the Passover was to be eaten. This would be on the morning of Nisan 14. In the evening, which from twilight onwards would belong to Nisan 15, would follow the Last Supper, and on the next afternoon (still, on the Jewish reckoning, Nisan 15) the crucifixion. St. John, on the other hand, by a number of clear indications (John xiii, 1, xviii, 28, xix, 14, 31) implies that the Last Supper was eaten before the time of the regular Passover, and that the Lord suffered on the afternoon of Nisan 14, about the time of the slaying of the Paschal lamb. We are thus left with a conflict of testimony."

394

On what day of the week was he crucified?

Synoptics: On Friday.

John: On Thursday.

The Synoptics agree that he was crucified on the day following the Preparation, that is, on the day of the Passover, and the day preceding the Sabbath. As the Jewish Sabbath fell on Saturday, he was, therefore, crucified on Friday.

John repeatedly declares that his trial and crucifixion occurred on "the preparation of the passover." If the Passover occurred on Friday, as the Synoptics state, he was crucified on the preceding day, or Thursday. It is claimed by some, though the claim is disputed, that the Synoptics are in error, that the Passover was never held on Friday.

395

On what day of the feast did the crucifixion occur?

Synoptics: On the Passover.

John: On the day of Preparation.

It is expressly stated in the Synoptics that he celebrated the Passover before his death. "Then came the day of unleavened bread, when the passover must be killed. And he sent Peter and John, saying, Go and prepare us the passover, that we may eat. . . . And they made ready the passover. And when the hour was come, he sat down, and the twelve apostles with him. And he said unto them, With desire I have desired to eat this passover with you before I suffer" (Luke xxii, 7–15; Matt. xxvi, 17–20; Mark xiv, 12–18).

The author of the Fourth Gospel declares that the Last Supper was not the Paschal meal, and that Jesus was crucified on the day preceding the Passover, that is, on the day of Preparation. He refers to the events connected with the Last Supper as having taken place "before the passover" (xiii, 1); after supper, when Jesus bade Judas do quickly what he proposed to do, he states that the disciples "thought because Judas had the bag, that Jesus had said unto him, Buy those things that we have need of against the feast" (xiii, 29); at the trial, he says, the Jews "themselves went not into the judgment hall, lest they might be defiled, but that they might eat the passover" (xviii, 28); when Pilate is about to deliver him up to be crucified, he even goes out of the way to repeat that "It was the preparation of the passover" (xix, 14).

This discrepancy is not, like many other Bible discrepancies, an unintentional error. It represents a conflict between two dogmas. The primitive church was rent with dissensions regarding this question, some contending that Christ suffered on the 14th Nisan, others that it was on the 15th. During the second century—the century in which our gospels appeared—this controversy was especially bitter.

According to John (i, 29, xix, 33, 36) Jesus was the Paschal Lamb, and as such, must be slain on the day of Preparation. The slaying of the lambs began at three o'clock in the afternoon, the hour at which Jesus is said to have expired. The Synoptics, on the other hand, in order to enable him to partake of the Paschal meal and institute the

Eucharist, which is a survival and perpetuation of the Passover, must prolong his existence until after this meal, and consequently his crucifixion cannot take place until the following day. It was impossible for him to be the Paschal Lamb and at the same time partake of the Paschal meal. This necessarily produced a schism. The Fourth Gospel was written in support of the one side, the Synoptics in support of the other.

It is declared by the most eminent fathers of the second century that the Apostle John, whom some of them had known, was accustomed to observe the Paschal meal. This is another argument against the Johannine authorship of the Fourth Gospel.

Referring to the Lord's Supper, as recorded in John, the *Bible for Learners* says: "It was not the Paschal meal. The Passover did not begin until the following evening; for he himself who was the true Paschal Lamb, and as such made an end of all sacrifices, must be put to death at the very day and hour ordained for the slaughter of the lamb—not twenty-four hours later as the Synoptic Gospels say" (Vol. III, p. 684).

Admitting the discrepancy, but without determining which is correct, *Smith's Bible Dictionary* says: "The crowning application of the Paschal rites to the truths of which they were the shadowy promises appears to be that which is afforded by the fact that our Lord's death occurred during the festival. According to the Divine purpose, the true Lamb of God was slain at nearly the same time as 'the Lord's Passover,' in obedience to the letter of the law."

It was not "according to the Divine purpose" that Jesus was slain at the Passover, but it was according to a human invention that he is declared to have been slain at this time. These attempts to connect the crucifixion with the Passover afford the strongest proof that it is a myth.

396

What led to the arrest and crucifixion of Jesus?

John: His miracle of raising Lazarus from the dead. On learning of it the Jewish council met, and "from that day forth they took counsel together for to put him to death" (xi, 47, 53).

This is more difficult to believe than the miracle itself. It is the most improbable statement ever penned—the one that does most violence to human reason. The cruelest savages on earth would not have slain nor even harmed a man who had proved himself the Conqueror and King of Death.

397

What did Christ say during his ministry concerning the cross?

"He that taketh not his cross, and followeth after me is not worthy of me" (Matthew x, 38; Luke xiv, 27).

"Whosoever will come after me, let him deny himself, and take up his cross, and follow me" (Mark viii, 34).

"If any man will come after me, let him deny himself, and take up his cross daily and follow me" (Luke ix, 23).

These utterances are alleged to have been made early in his ministry. Now, the cross as a Christian symbol is supposed to have been adopted after, and not until after, the crucifixion. Its introduction in the passages quoted suggests one of two things: either that the Synoptics put into the mouth of Jesus words that he never uttered, or that the cross, as a religious symbol, was used before the crucifixion, in which case its adoption by the church is no proof of the crucifixion.

398

The so-called historical books of the New Testament, the Four Gospels and the Acts of the Apostles, declare that Christ was crucified. Do the remaining books of the New Testament confirm it?

In the first four Pauline Epistles, known as the genuine Epistles of Paul, the verb crucify-crucified appears in ten different texts, as follows:

"Knowing this, that our old man is crucified with him, that the body of sin might be destroyed" (Romans vi, 6).

"Is Christ divided? Was Paul crucified for you?" (1 Corinthians, i, 13.)

"But we preach Christ crucified, unto the Jews a stumbling block, and unto the Greeks foolishness" (23).

"For I determined not to know any thing among you, save Jesus Christ, and him crucified" (ii, 2).

"For had they known it, they would not have crucified the Lord of glory" (8).

"For though he was crucified through weakness, yet he liveth by the power of God" (2 Corinthians xiii, 4).

"I am crucified with Christ" (Galatians ii, 20).

"O foolish Galatians, who hath bewitched you, that ye should not obey the truth, before whose eyes Jesus Christ hath been evidently set forth, crucified among you?" (iii, 1.)

"And they that are Christ's have crucified the flesh with the affections and lusts" (v, 24).

"But God forbid that I should glory, save in the cross of our Lord Jesus Christ, by whom the world is crucified unto me, and I unto the world" (vi, 14).

Webster defines this word as follows: "1. To nail to a cross; to put to death by nailing the hands and feet to a cross or gibbet, sometimes, anciently, by fastening a criminal to a tree with cords. 2. In scriptural language, to subdue; to mortify; to destroy the power or ruling influence of. 3. To reject and despise. 4. To vex or torment."

The first, only, denotes a physical crucifixion, which, it is claimed, Christ suffered. The word, as used by Paul, in most instances, clearly denotes a crucifying of the passions and carnal pleasures, and the exceptions, when taken in connection with Paul's well known teachings, and allowing for the probable corruption of the original text, do not confirm the Evangelistic accounts of the crucifixion. Besides this it is admitted that Paul did not witness the crucifixion, and that these Epistles, even if authentic, were not written until nearly thirty years after it is said to have occurred.

In the eighteen books which follow, the word crucify appears but twice—in Hebrews (vi, 6) and in Revelation (xi, 8). The word crucifixion does not appear once in the Bible.

Concerning the books we have been considering in this criticism, Paine writes as follows: "Whether the fourteen epistles ascribed to Paul were written by him or not, is a matter of indifference; they are either argumentative or dogmatical; and as the argument is defective and the dogmatical part is merely presumptive, it signifies not who wrote them. And the same may be said for the remaining parts of the Testament. It is not upon the Epistles, but upon what is called the Gospel, contained in the four books ascribed to Matthew, Mark, Luke, and John, and upon the pretended prophecies, that the theory of the church calling itself the Christian Church is founded. The Epistles are dependent upon those, and must follow their fate; for if the story of Jesus Christ be fabulous, all reasoning founded upon it as a supposed truth must fall with it" (*Age of Reason*).

399

How old was Jesus at the time of his death?

Luke: He was but little more than thirty years old.

John: He was nearly fifty. In a controversy with the Jews, during his ministry, he said: "Your father Abraham rejoiced to see my day: and he saw, and was glad. Then said the Jews unto him, Thou art not yet fifty years old, and hast thou seen Abraham?" (viii, 56, 57.) This implies that he was nearly fifty at this time.

Discussing the question of Jesus's age, St. Irenaeus, the most renowned of the early Christian Fathers, and the founder of the New Testament canon, who lived in the century immediately following Jesus, says:

"He [Christ] came to save all through means of himself—all I say, who through him are born again to God—infants and children, and boys, and youths, and old men. He therefore passed through every age; becoming an infant for infants, thus sanctifying infants; a child for children, thus sanctifying those who are of this age, being at the same time made to them an example of piety, righteousness and submission; a youth for youths, becoming an example to youths, and thus sanctifying them for the Lord. So likewise, he was an old man for old men, that he might be a perfect master for all; not merely as respects the setting forth of the truth, but also as regards age; sanctifying at the same time, the aged also, and becoming an example to them likewise. Then, at last, he came on to death itself, that he might be the first born from the dead, that in all things he might have the pre-eminence; the Prince of Life, existing before all, and going before all" (*Against Heresies,* Book iv, ch. xxii, sec. 4).

Commenting on the passage quoted from John, Irenaeus says: "But besides this, those very Jews who thus disputed with the Lord Jesus Christ, have most closely indicated the same thing. For when the Lord said to them, 'Your father Abraham rejoiced to see my day, and he saw it, and was glad'; they answered him, 'Thou art not yet fifty years old; and hast thou seen Abraham?' Now, such language is fittingly applied to one who has already passed the age of forty, without having yet reached his fiftieth year, yet is not far from this latter period. But to one who is only thirty years old, it would unquestionably be said, 'Thou art not yet forty years old.' For those who wished to convict him of falsehood, would certainly not extend the number of his years far beyond the age which they saw he had attained. . . . It is altogether unreasonable to suppose that they were mistaken by twenty years, when they wished to prove him younger than the times of Abraham. . . . He did not then want much of being fifty years old" (ibid., sec. 6).

Nor did Irenaeus depend upon the Fourth Gospel alone for his authority. He was the companion of the aged Polycarp, whom Christians claim to have been the companion of the Apostle John. Concerning the testimony of Polycarp and others, he writes: "Those who were conversant in Asia with John, the disciple of the Lord, [testify] that John conveyed to them that information. And he (John) remained among them up to the times of Tragan. Some of them, moreover, saw not only John, but the other apostles also, and heard the same account from them, and bear testimony to the statement" (ibid, sec. 5).

In regard to this testimony of the "divine Irenaeus," as he is called, Godfrey Higgins says: "The church has been guilty of the oversight of letting this passage from Irenaeus escape. One of the earliest, most respected, and most quoted of its ancient bishops, saints and martyrs, tells us in distinct words that Jesus was not crucified under Herod and Pontius Pilate, but that he lived to be turned fifty years of age. This he tells us on the authority of his master, St. Polycarp, also a martyr, who had it from St. John himself, and from all the old people of Asia" (*Anacalypsis*).

Of this testimony and its consequences, Judge Waite, in his *History of Christianity* (pp. 329, 330) says: "It must be remembered that Irenaeus had been a companion of Polycarp and others who had seen John, and that he was speaking of what had come to his personal knowledge from the elders in Asia. If, then, Irenaeus tells the truth, the evidence in favor of the fact is almost overwhelming. If, on the other hand, he would deliberately falsify in a matter of this importance what is his testimony worth as to the origin of the four gospels? Against this evidence, we have only the silence of the gospels. But if the silence of the Synoptics is consistent with a ministry of three or four years, why is not the further silence of all the gospels consistent with a ministry of twenty years?

"How would such a theory affect the received chronology concerning Christ? The date of the crucifixion at not later than A.D. 36, or when Christ was, by the received chronology, forty years old, is settled by the fact, that in that year, Pontius Pilate was removed from his government. . . . If, then, it be accepted as a historical fact that Christ was about fifty years old at his crucifixion, the date of his birth would have to be set back at least ten years."

Every line of these accounts of the trial and crucifixion of Christ bears the ineffaceable stamp of fiction. There was no Christ to crucify, and Jesus of Nazareth, if he existed, was not crucified as claimed.

For more than fifteen centuries an inoffensive, industrious and moral people have been persecuted, robbed and butchered by Christians, because their forefathers are said to have slain a mythical God.

Supposing that from the myth of Prometheus had sprung a popular religion, which, in its day, had, like the religions of Osiris, Bacchus, Krishna and Christ, overspread the earth. Then think of the devotees of this religion massacring the Hellenists because Zeus had crucified Prometheus! How long must our mythology, with all its attendant evils, rule and curse the world? How long must an innocent people suffer for an alleged crime that was never committed?

7

The Resurrection of Christ

400

How long did Jesus say he would remain in the grave?

"For as Jonas was three days and three nights in the whale's belly; so shall the Son of Man be three days and three nights in the heart of the earth" (Matthew xii, 40).

How long did he remain in the grave?

Synoptics: Being buried on Friday evening, and having risen on or before Sunday morning, he was in the grave, at the most, but two nights and one day.

401

What occurred on the morning of the resurrection?

Matthew: "There was a great earthquake" (xxviii, 2).

The other Evangelists know nothing of this earthquake. They not only omit it, but their accounts of the resurrection preclude the possibility of its occurrence.

402

Who were the first to visit the tomb on the morning of the resurrection?

John: "Mary Magdalene" (xx, 1).

Matthew: "Mary Magdalene and the other Mary" (xxviii, 1).

Mark: "Mary Magdalene, and Mary the mother of James, and Salome" (xvi, 1, 2).

Luke: "Mary Magdalene, and Joanna, and Mary the mother of James, and other women" (xxiv, 1-10).

403

Who was Salome?

"The wife of Zebedee, as appears from comparing Matt. xxvii, 56, with Mark xv, 40."—*Smith's Bible Dictionary.*

Matthew says that the women who witnessed the crucifixion were "Mary Magdalene, and Mary the Mother of James and Joses, and the mother of Zebedee's children." Mark says the women were "Mary Magdalene, and Mary the mother of James the less and of Joses, and Salome." This is a discrepancy that can be reconciled only by supposing that the mother of Zebedee's children (James and John) was Salome. But the Gospel of the Egyptians, older than either Matthew or Mark, and accepted by early Christians as authentic, states that Salome was a single woman.

404

At what time in the morning did the women visit the tomb?

Mark: "At the rising of the sun" (xvi, 2).

John: "When it was yet dark" (xx, 1).

If they came "at the rising of the sun," or "when the sun was risen" (New Ver.), it was not yet dark.

405

When does Matthew say they came?

"In the end of the Sabbath as it began to dawn toward the first day of the week" (xxviii, 1).

If they came "in the end of the Sabbath," and Jesus had already risen, then his resurrection took place, not on the first day of the week, as claimed, but on the seventh day. Matthew was a Jew; yet the author of this Gospel was seemingly ignorant of the Jewish method of computing time, according to which the Sabbath began and ended at sunset. He evidently supposed that the night preceding their visit to the tomb belonged to the seventh day, whereas it belonged to the first day.

406

Was the tomb open, or closed, when they came?

Luke: "They found the stone rolled away from the sepulchre" (xxiv, 2).

Matthew: The tomb was closed. The stone was not rolled from the door until after they came (xxviii, 1, 2).

This, in the opinion of most critics, is the meaning of Matthew's language.

407

Whom did they meet at the tomb?

Matthew: "The angel" (xxviii, 2-5).

Mark: "A young man" (xvi, 5).

Luke: "Two men" (xxiv, 4).

John: "Two angels" (xx, 12).

408

Were these men or angels in the sepulchre or outside of it?

Matthew: Outside of it (xxviii, 2).

Mark, Luke and John: Inside of it (Mark xvi, 5; Luke xxiv, 3, 4; John xx, 11, 12).

409·

Were they sitting or standing?

Luke: Standing (xxiv, 4).

Matthew, Mark and John: Sitting (Matt. xxviii, 2; Mark xvi, 1; John xx, 12).

410

What were the first words they spoke to the women?

Matthew and Mark: "Be not affrighted" (Mark xvi, 6; Matt. xxviii, 5).

Luke: "Why seek ye the living among the dead?" (xxiv, 5.)

John: "Woman, why weepest thou?" (xx, 13.)

411

Did Mary Magdalene observe the divine messengers when she first came to the tomb?

Synoptics: She did (Matt. xxviii, 1–5 ; Mark xvi, 1-5; Luke xxiv, 1–4).

John: She did not (xx, 1, 2, 11, 12).

412

Who became frightened at the messengers?

Matthew: "The keepers did shake, and became as dead men" (xxviii, 4).

Mark and Luke: "They [the women] were affrighted" (Mark xvi, 5; Luke xxiv, 5).

413

What did the women do when they became frightened?

Mark: "They went out quickly and fled" (xvi, 8).

Luke: "They bowed down their faces to the earth" (xxiv, 5).

414

Did the women see Jesus?

Matthew: They did. "As they went to tell his disciples, behold, Jesus met them" (xxviii, 9).

Luke: They did not see him (xxiv).

415

Did the women tell the disciples what they had seen?

Luke: They "returned from the sepulchre, and told all these things unto the eleven, and to all the rest" (xxiv, 9).

Mark: "Neither said they anything to any man; for they were afraid" (xvi, 8).

With these words the Gospel of Mark ends, the words that follow being an interpolation. In this appended passage Mary Magdalene is declared to have seen Jesus and informed them of it, but they "believed not."

416

How many disciples visited the tomb?
   Luke: But one, Peter (xxiv, 12).
   John: Two, Peter and John (xx, 3).

417

Who looked into the sepulchre and beheld the linen clothes?
   Luke: "Then arose Peter, and ran into the sepulchre; and stooping down, he beheld the linen clothes" (xxiv, 12).
   John: "So they ran both together: and the other disciple [John] did outrun Peter, and came first to the sepulchre. And he stooping down, and looking in, saw the linen clothes" (xx, 4, 5).

418

Did Peter enter into the sepulchre?
   John: He did. "Then cometh Simon Peter following him, and went into the sepulchre" (xx, 6).
   Luke: He did not. He looked into the sepulchre "and departed" (xxiv, 12).

419

State all of the appearances of Jesus mentioned by the Evangelists.

Matthew.
   1. To the two Marys (xxviii, 9).
   2. To the eleven in Galilee (17).

Mark.
1. To Mary Magdalene (xvi, 9).
2. To two of his disciples (12).
3. To the eleven at meat (14).

The appearances of Jesus mentioned in Mark are all in the apochryphal supplement. The Gospel of Mark proper does not record a single appearance of Jesus.

Luke.
1. To Cleopas and his companion (xxiv, 13-31).
2. To Simon (Peter) (34).
3. To the eleven and others (36).

John.
1. To Mary Magdalene (xx, 14-18).
2. To ten (?) disciples (19-24).
3. To the eleven (26-29).
4. To Peter, John and others (xxi).

The last chapter of this Gospel, which contains the account of his fourth appearance, and which ascribes the authorship of the Gospel to the "beloved disciple" (John), is a forgery.

No two of the Evangelists agree. No two of them are fully agreed in regard to a single appearance. Each not only omits the appearances mentioned by the others, but his narrative in nearly every instance excludes them. As Strauss says, "The designation of the locality in one excludes the appearances narrated by the rest; the determination of time in another leaves no space for the narratives of his fellow-evangelists; the enumeration of a third is given without any regard to the events reported by his predecessors; lastly, among several appearances recounted by various narrators, each claims to be the last, and yet has nothing in common with the others. Hence nothing but wilful blindness can prevent the perception that no one of the narrators knew and presupposed what another records."

Referring to the different accounts of the resurrection given by the

Evangelists, Dr. Westcott says: "They contain difficulties which it is impossible to explain with certainty" (*Introduction to Study of Gospels,* p. 329).

Dr. Farrar makes the following admission : "Any one who will attentively read side by side the narratives of these appearances on the first day of the resurrection, will see that they have only been preserved for us in general, interblended, and scattered notices, which, in strict exactness, render it impossible, without many arbitrary suppositions, to produce from them a certain narrative of the order of events. The lacunae, the compressions, the variations, the actual differences, the subjectivity of the narrators as affected by spiritual revelations, render all harmonies at the best uncertain" (*Life of Christ,* Vol. II, p. 432, note).

420

State the appearances mentioned by Paul.

1. "He was seen of Cephas."
2. "Then of the twelve."
3. "After that, he was seen of above five hundred brethren at once."
4. "After that he was seen of James."
5. "Then of all the apostles."
6. "And last of all he was seen of me also."

Paul says that his first appearance was to Peter.This contradicts all of the Evangelists. His next appearance, Paul declares, was to the twelve. But there were no twelve at this time; for Judas had deserted them and his successor had not been elected. Paul evidently knew nothing of the betrayal of Jesus by Judas. He says Jesus was seen by five hundred brethren at once. The Evangelists are all ignorant of this appearance, while the author of Acts states that there were but one hundred and twenty "brethren" in all, and even this number is considered too large by critics. He says that he appeared to James, an appearance of which the Evangelists know nothing. After this he states that he was seen of all the apostles. This is the only appearance mentioned by Paul which can be reconciled with any of the Evangelists, and this cannot be reconciled with all of them.

"Last of all He was seen of me also." Paul's belief in the resurrection was based solely upon Jesus's supposed appearance to him; for the other alleged appearances he had rejected. Not until he imagined that he had seen Jesus did he believe that the disciples had seen him, and the appearance of Jesus to him, which occurred several years after the resurrection and ascension, is represented as an occurrence of exactly the same character as his appearances to the disciples. Paul's vision was clearly a delusion, and if so the other appearances, measured by Paul's criterion, were delusions also. The Rev. John W. Chadwick truly says: "Paul's witness to the resurrection is the ruin of the argument."

421

To whom did Jesus first appear?

Matthew: To Mary Magdalene and the other Mary (xxviii, 1, 9).

Mark and John: To Mary Magdalene alone (Mark xvi, 9; John xx, 14-18).

Luke: To Cleopas and his companion (xxiv, 13-31).

Paul: To Cephas (Peter) (I Cor. xv, 5).

422

Where was Mary Magdalene when Jesus first appeared to her?

John: At the sepulchre (xx, 11-14).

Matthew: On her way home from the sepulchre (xxvii, 8,9).

423

Did Mary know Jesus when he first appeared to her?
>   Matthew: She did (xxviii, 9).
>   John: "She . . . knew not that it was Jesus" (xx, 14).

424

Was she permitted to touch him?
>   Matthew: "They [Mary Magdalene and her companion] came and
held him by the feet" (xxviii, 9).
>   John: "Jesus saith unto her, Touch me not" (xx, 17).

425

Where did he appear to his disciples?
>   Matthew: In Galilee.
>   Luke: In Jerusalem.

Matthew says that when Mary Magdalene and the other Mary visited the tomb an angel appeared to them and said: "Go quickly, and tell his disciples that he is risen from the dead; and, behold, he goeth before you into Galilee; there shall ye see him" (xxviii, 7). As they ran to convey this intelligence, Jesus himself met them and repeated the command: "Go tell my brethren that they go into Galilee, and there shall they see me" (10). "Then the eleven disciples went away into Galilee, into a mountain where Jesus had appointed them. And when they saw him they worshiped him" (16, 17).

Luke (xxiv, 13-35) states that on the day of the resurrection Jesus journeyed to Emmaus, a village some distance from Jerusalem, with Cleopas and his companion. They did not recognize him until after their arrival there, when they returned at once to Jerusalem and informed the disciples. "As they thus spake Jesus himself stood in the midst of them" (36). He conversed with them for a time, after which "he led them out as far as to Bethany" where he took his final leave of them and ascended to heaven (38-51). Instead of bidding them go to Galilee, a three days journey from Jerusalem, as Matthew states, his command was "Tarry ye in the city of Jerusalem, until ye be endued with power from on high," which, according to Acts (ii, 1-13), was not until the day of Pentecost, seven weeks later.

Matthew's narrative forbids the supposition of any meeting in Judea, while Luke's precludes the possibility of a meeting in Galilee.

Regarding this discrepancy Dean Alford says: "We must be content to walk by faith, and not by sight" (*Greek Testament,* p. 905).

426

How far from Jerusalem was Emmaus, where Jesus made his first appearance?

Luke: "Which was from Jerusalem about threescore furlongs" (xxiv, 13).

Threescore furlongs was seven and one-half Roman or about seven American miles. Emmaus of Judea was about twenty-five miles, or two hundred furlongs from Jerusalem. There was an Emmaus in Galilee, about seventy miles from Jerusalem. It is believed by some that the legend related to the latter place and was subsequently transferred by Luke to Judea.

427

How many disciples were present when he first appeared to them?

Matthew and Luke: Eleven (Matt. xxviii, 16, 17; Luke xxiv, 33-36).

John: But ten, Thomas being absent (xx, 19-24).

Paul: Twelve (I Cor. xv, 5).

428

What effect had his presence when he first appeared to them?

Luke: "They were terrified and affrighted" (xxiv, 36, 37).

John: "Then were the disciples glad, when they saw the Lord" (xx, 20).

429

How many of the disciples doubted the reality of his appearance?

Matthew: "Some doubted" (xxviii, 17).

John: But one doubted—Thomas (xx, 24, 25).

430

Were they all finally convinced of his resurrection?

John: They were.

Matthew: They were not.

431

When he appeared to them did they know that he must rise from the dead?

John: "For as yet they knew not that he must rise from the dead" (xx, 9).

This cannot be reconciled with the Synoptics, who state that during his ministry he had acquainted them with it. "From that time forth began Jesus to shew unto his disciples how that he must go unto Jerusalem, and suffer many things of the elders and chief priests and scribes, and be killed, and be raised again the third day" (Matthew xvi, 21 ; Mark viii, 31 ; Luke ix, 22).

432

Paul says that the last appearance of Jesus was to him. What did his companions do when they saw the light which attended the appearance?.
Acts: "The men which journeyed with him stood speechless" (ix, 7).
Paul: "We were all fallen to the earth" (Acts xxvi, 14).

433

Did Paul's companions see Jesus?
Acts: They did not. "The men which journeyed with him stood speechless, hearing a voice, but seeing no man" (ix, 7).
This shows that Jesus' alleged appearance to Paul was an imaginary and not a real appearance.

434

The author of Acts says that his companions heard a voice. Is this true?
Paul: "They that were with me . . . heard not the voice" (Acts xxii, 9).

435

Was Jesus seen by woman after his resurrection?
Matthew, Mark and John: He was.
Luke and Paul: He was not.
According to Luke and Paul his most faithful followers were not honored by a visit from their Lord, but were neglected and ignored. The resurrection was not for woman. Nowhere is sex prejudice more conspicuous than in the accounts of the resurrection written by Paul and the Pauline Evangelist. To ignore the testimony of Mary Magdalene is to ignore the testimony of the chief witness for the resurrection.

436

From where did Jesus rise?

All: From the dead. "He is risen from the dead" (Matt. xxviii, 7). "It behooved Christ to suffer, and to rise from the dead" (Luke xxiv, 46). "He was risen from the dead" (John xxi, 14).

According to the Evangelists Jesus rose, not from the grave—not from the place where the bodies of the dead were deposited—but from the lower world—from the realm of the dead—where the shades of the departed were supposed to repose. Regarding this Dr. Hooykaas says:

"Let us begin by considering what that word 'resurrection' really meant, whether applied to Jesus or to others. Later representations, down to our own times, have regarded it as equivalent to a rising from the grave; but the question is, what it meant in the faith and preaching of the Apostles, in the genuine original, primitive tradition that Jesus had risen. Now, 'resurrection' means elsewhere a return from the realm of shades to the human life on earth; and Jesus too had left the underworld, but not, in this case, to return at once to life upon the earth, but to be taken up provisionally into heaven. Originally the resurrection and ascension of Jesus were one. It was only later that the conception sprang up of his having paused upon earth, whether for a single day or for several weeks, on his journey from the abyss to the height.

"We may, therefore, safely assert that if the friends of Jesus had thought as we do of the lot of those that die, they would never have so much as dreamed of their Master's resurrection or ascension. For to the Christian belief of today it would be, so to speak, a matter of course that Jesus, like all good and noble souls—and indeed above all others—would go straight 'to a better world,' 'to heaven,' 'to God,' at the instant of his death; but in the conception of the Jews, including the Apostles, this was impossible. Heaven was the abode of the Lord and his angels only; and if an Enoch or an Elijah had been caught up there alive, to dwell there for a time, it was certain that all who died, without exception, ever, even the purest and most holy, must go down as shades into the realms of the dead in the bowels of the earth—and thence, of course, they would not issue excepting by 'rising again'.

And this is why we are never told that Jesus rose 'from death,' far less 'from the grave,' but always 'from the dead' " (*Bible for Learners*, Vol. III, p. 463).

437

Was he readily recognized by his friends?

Matthew, Luke and John: He was not.

Matthew says that when his disciples met him in Galilee, after having gone there for the express purpose of meeting him, "some doubted" (xxviii, 17). Luke says that two of his friends journeyed with him from Jerusalem to Emmaus, conversing with him on the way, and notwithstanding they had been informed of his resurrection, they did not recognize him until after they had reached the village. John says that when Mary Magdalene met him she "knew not that it was Jesus, . . . supposing him to be the gardener" (xx, 14, 15); and where he met his disciples at the Lake of Tiberius they "knew not that it was Jesus" (xxi, 4).

438

Did his appearances indicate a corporeal, or merely a spiritual existence?

The Evangelists declare that he was not only seen by his disciples and others, but that he conversed with them. Matthew says the two Marys held him by the feet, Luke says he invited the disciples to handle him, and John says that Thomas examined his wounds; while both Luke and John state that he partook of nourishment.

On the other hand, Luke says that while he sat at meat with Cleopas and his companion at Emmaus "He vanished out of their sight" (xxiv, 31). John says that while the disciples were assembled in a room in Jerusalem, "when the doors were shut," Jesus came "and stood in the midst" (xx, 19). Eight days later the appearance was repeated: "Then came Jesus, the doors being shut, and stood in the midst" (26). Mark says that after he appeared to Mary Magdalene "he appeared in another form" to two of his disciples (xvi, 12).

While the first named appearances can be reconciled with so-called spiritual manifestations, the latter cannot be reconciled with a corporeal existence.

In the preceding chapter we have shown that the alleged crucifixion of Jesus is unworthy of belief. If he was not crucified the story of his resurrection is, of course, a fiction. But conceding, for the sake of argument, that he was crucified; does this make his resurrection probable, or even possible? The crucifixion of a man is a possible occurrence; but the corporeal resurrection of a man who has suffered death is impossible. These reputed appearances of Jesus, if they have a historical foundation, were evidently mere subjective impressions or apparitions. Although he is declared to have remained on earth forty days, he made, at the most, but two or three brief visits to his disciples, appearing and disappearing like a phantom. Instead of abiding with them, teaching them the doctrines of his religion—of which they professed to be ignorant—and preparing them for their coming ministry he is represented as keeping in seclusion, or roaming aimlessly along the country highways, like some demented creature. Referring to his appearance to his disciples, Jerome says: "The apostles supposed him to be a spirit, or according to the Gospel which the Nazarenes receive [the Hebrew Gospel of Matthew] an incorporeal demon."

The possibility, and even prevalency, of apparitions similar to those related of Jesus are recognized by every student of psychology. Sir Benjamin Brodie, in his *Psychological Inquiries* (p. 78), says: "There are abundant proofs that impressions may be made in the brain by other causes simulating those which are made on it by external objects through the medium of the organs of sense, thus producing false perceptions, which may, in the first instance, and before we have had time to reflect on the subject, be mistaken for realities."

The appearance of Jesus to Mary Magdalene was not believed even by the disciples. If the disciples believed that Mary was deluded, is it unreasonable to believe that they were deluded also? Illusions are contagious and may affect many minds as well as one. Dr. Carpenter, one of the highest English authorities on mental science, says: "If not only a single individual, but several persons should be 'possessed' by one and the same idea or feeling, the same misinterpretation may be made by all of them; and in such a case the concurrence of their testimony does not add the least strength to it" (*Principles of Mental Physiology,* p. 208). In confirmation of this is cited the following from a work on *The Philosophy of Apparitions,* by Dr. Hibbert, F.R.S.E.: "A whole ship's company was thrown into the utmost consternation by the apparition of a cook who had died a few days before. He was distinctly seen walking ahead of the ship, with a peculiar gait by which he was distinguished when alive, through having one of his legs shorter than the other. On steering the ship towards the object, it was found to be a piece of floating wreck."

These supposed appearances of Jesus were, at the most, only apparitions, and "Apparitions," to quote Dr. Hibbert again, "are nothing more than morbid symptoms, which are indicative of an intense excitement of the renovated feelings of the mind" (*Philosophy of Apparitions,* p. 375).

Lord Amberley advocates a psychological explanation of the reputed appearances of Jesus from which I quote the following: "Whatever other qualities Jesus may have possessed or lacked, there can be no question that he had one—that of inspiring in others a strong attachment to himself. He had in his brief career surrounded himself with devoted disciples; and he was taken from their midst in the full bloom of his powers by a violent and early death. Now there are some who have been taught by the bitter experience of their lives how difficult, nay, how impossible it is to realize in imagination the fact that a beloved companion is in truth gone from them forever. . . . We fondly conceive that in some way the dead must still exist; and if so, can one, who was so tender before, listen to our cry of pain and refuse to come? Can one, who soothed us in the lesser troubles of our lives, look on while we are suffering the greatest agony of all and fail to comfort? It cannot be. Imagination declines to picture the long future that lies before us. We cannot understand that we shall never again listen to the tones of the familiar voice; never feel the touch of the gentle hand; never be encouraged by the warm embrace that tells us we are loved, or find a refuge from miserable thoughts and the vexations of the world in the affectionate and ever-open heart. All this is too hard for us. We long for a resurrection; we should believe in it if we could; we do believe in it in sleep, when our feelings are free to roam at pleasure, unrestrained by the chilling presence of the material world. In dreams the old life is repeated again and again. Sometimes the lost one is beside us as of old and we are quite untroubled by the thought of parting. Sometimes there is a strange and confusing consciousness that the great calamity has happened, or has been thought to happen, but that now we are again together, and that a new life has succeeded upon death. Granting only a strong emotion and a lively phantasy, we may comprehend at once how, in many lands, to many mourners, the images of their dreams may also become the visions of their waking hours" (*Analysis of Religious Belief*, pp. 275, 276).

Renan says: "For the historian, the life of Jesus finishes with his last sigh. But such was the impression he had left in the heart of his disciples, and of a few devoted women, that during some weeks more it was as if he were living and consoling them. Had his body been taken away or did enthusiasm, always credulous, create afterwards the group of narratives by which it was sought to establish faith in the resurrection? In the absence of opposing documents this can never be ascertained. Let us say, however, that the strong imagination of Mary Magdalene played an important part in the circumstance. Divine power of love! Sacred moments in which the passion of one possessed gave to the world a resuscitated God" (*Life of Jesus,* p. 296).

439

If Jesus appeared in a material body, was he naked, or clothed?

This is not a vital, but it is a pertinent question. It is stated that he appeared to Mary Magdalene immediately after the resurrection. Did he appear to her naked, or was he clothed? As she mistook him for the gardener, and as the gardener undoubtedly went clad, it may be presumed that Jesus was clad also. If so, where did he procure his clothes? His own garments were divided among the soldiers, and his grave clothes were left in the sepulchre. If it be assumed that he was taken from the tomb by his friends, as some critics believe, the difficulty vanishes.

440

What is said of the saints who arose on the day of the crucifixion?

Matthew: They "came out of the graves after the resurrection, and went into the holy city, and appeared unto many" (xxvii, 53).

Before Matthew's wholesale resurrection of the saints the resurrection of Jesus pales into insignificance. In the opinion of many supernaturalists Matthew has mixed too large a dose of the miraculous for even Christian credulity to swallow, and they would gladly omit this portion of it. Regarding this story Dr. Farrar says: "An earthquake shook the earth and split the rocks, and as it rolled away from their places the great stones which closed and covered the cavern sepulchres of the Jews, so it seemed to the imaginations of many to have disimprisoned the spirits of the dead, and to have filled the air with ghostly visitants, who after Christ had risen appeared to linger in the Holy City" (*Life of Christ*, Vol. II, p. 419) Dean Milman dismisses it in much the same way. Referring to the earthquake, he says: "The same convulsion would displace the stones which covered thc ancient tombs and lay open many of the innumerable rock-hewn sepulchres which perforated the hills on every side of the city, and expose the dead to public view. To the awe-struck and depressed minds of the followers of Jesus, no doubt, were confined these visionary appearances of the spirits of their deceased brethren" (*History of Christianity*, Vol. I, p. 336).

If the minds of the disciples were so greatly affected that they imagined they beheld the resurrected bodies of strangers whom they had never met and of whom they had probably never heard—for they were nearly a hunrdred miles from the graves of their own kindred—is it strange that they should imagine they saw the resurrected Master with whom they had daily associated for months and perhaps years? To charaterize these resurrected saints as "ghostly visitants" and "visionary appearances," and the resurrected Christ as a real being, is a distinction without a scintilla of evidence to support it. Both appearances, if they be historical, belong to the same class of mental phenomena; and are, indeed, the offspring of the same minds.

441

When did the resurrection take place?
 All: In the night.
 Who witnessed it?
 All: No one.
 The author of *Supernatural Religion* says: "The remarkable fact is, therefore, absolutely undeniable, that there was not, and that it is not even pretended that there was, a single eye-witness to the actual Resurrection. The empty grave, coupled with the supposed subsequent appearances of Jesus, is the only evidence of thc Resurrection" (p. 1004).

442

It is said that a guard was stationed at the tomb. Why was this done?
 Matthew: "The chief priests and Pharisees came together unto Pilate, saying, Sir, we remember that that deceiver said while he was yet alive, After three days I will rise again. Command, therefore, that the sepulchre be made sure until the third day, lest his disciples come by night, and steal him away, and say unto the people, He is risen from the dead" (xxvii, 62-64).
 Is it not strange that his enemies should he cognizant of this when his disciples "knew not the scripture, that he must rise again from the dead ?" (John xx, 9.)
 Regarding this the *Bible for Learners* says: "Was such a foolish report really circulated among the Jews? In any case this story, which is worked out elaborately in the Gospel of Nicodemus, is quite absurd. Is it likely that the enemies of Jesus would have heard a prophecy of his rising again when his very friends never dreamed of it for a moment, and when he had never once spoken of his 'resurrection' in public?" (Vol. III, p. 480.)

443

On what day did the Sanhedrim visit Pilate for the purpose of obtaining a guard?

Matthew: On the Sabbath (xxvii, 62).

Matthew, after describing the death and burial of Jesus, says: "Now the next day, that followed the day of the preparation, the chief priests and Pharisees came together unto Pilate." It is generally conceded by Christian commentators that by "the next day" Matthew refers to the Sabbath, for if Jesus was crucified and buried on Friday, no other day can be meant. To avoid the disagreeable consequences of such an admission a few have contended that by "the day of preparation" is meant the Preparation of the Passover. But this renders the passage unintelligible. By "preparation" Matthew means, not the Preparation of the Passover, but the preparation of the Sabbath. This is made clear by the other Synoptics. After relating the events of the crucifixion, Mark begins his account of the burial with these words: "And now when the even was come, because it was the preparation, that is, the day before the Sabbath" (xv, 42). Luke, after giving an account of the crucifixion and burial, says: "And that day was the preparation and the Sabbath drew on" (xxiii, 54).

It is claimed by the Evangelists that the Jewish priests of that period were such rigid observers of the Sabbath that they sought to put Jesus to death for simply healing the sick on that day. That the Sanhedrim desecrated the Sabbath, and especially the Passover Sabbath, by visiting and transacting business with a heathen ruler cannot be accepted as possible.

444

When was the guard placed at the tomb?

Matthew: *Not until the second night.*

It is argued that Jesus must have risen because a guard was placed at his tomb so that it was impossible for his disciples to "come by night, and steal him away." But had his body really been left in the tomb, as claimed, they would have taken it the first night had they desired it. The passage cited from Matthew in the preceding criticism declares that a guard was not requested of Pilate until the day following the crucifixion, so that the tomb was without a guard the first night. The sepulchre was not opened and examined when the guard was placed there on the following day. "So they went and made the sepulchre sure, sealing the stone, and setting a watch" (Matt. xxvii, 66). Had the seal been found unbroken at the end of three days it would not have proved that Jesus' body still remained in the tomb. It would merely have proved that the body had not been removed after the seal was placed on it.

It may be urged that Jesus had prophesied that he would not rise until the third day, and that an earlier disappearance of the body could not be harmonized with a strict fulfillment of the prophecy. But of this prophecy the disciples, we have seen, were ignorant.

445

What is said in regard to the opening of the tomb?

Matthew: "In the end of the Sabbath, as it began to dawn toward the first day of the week, came Mary Magdalene and the other Mary to see the sepulchre. And behold there was a great earthquake; for the angel of the Lord descended from heaven, and came and rolled back the stone from the door, and sat upon it. . . . And the angel answered and said unto the women, Fear not ye: for I know that ye seek Jesus, which was crucified. He is not here: for he is risen, as he said. Come, see the place where the Lord lay" (xxviii, 1–6).

Matthew's story of the guard was evidently inserted for the express purpose of establishing a belief in the resurrection by making it appear impossible for his friends to have removed the body from the sepulchre. Yet this story suggests, if it does not prove, the very thing that he attempts to prove impossible. The sepulchre was opened in the presence of witnesses—the guards and the women. Jesus did not emerge from it, nor did it contain his body. It was empty when opened. This renders probable, if not certain, one of two things: either his body was not deposited there, or it was removed before the watch was set.

Commenting on the empty tomb L. K. Washburn says: "If Jesus got out of the grave alive, he was put into it alive. If he was put into it dead, he was taken out dead. A depopulated sepulchre is not proof that its former tenant has moved to heaven. It is merely proof that somebody has stolen a dead body."

446

What did the guards do when they left the tomb?

Matthew: "Some of the watch came into the city, and showed unto the chief priests all the things that were done" (xxviii, 11).

To one acquainted with the discipline of the Roman army this story of the soldiers leaving their post thirty-six hours before the expiration of the watch assigned and going into the city and telling the Jews what had transpired is incredible.

447

What did the chief priests do?

Matthew: "They gave large sums of money unto the soldiers, saying, Say ye, His disciples came by night, and stole him away while we slept" (12, 13).

The penalty for sleeping while on duty was death, and no bribe could have induced them to declare that they were guilty of this offense even if the priests had promised to intercede for them. Again, had this transaction really occurred it would have been known only by the parties concerned in it, and when disclosure meant the direst punishment to both the bribe-givers and the bribe-takers, neither would have divulged the crime.

Strauss, criticising the alleged action of the Jewish priests, says: "Their conduct, where the guards returning from the grave apprised them of the resurrection of Jesus, is truly impossible. They believe the assertion of the soldiers that Jesus had arisen out of his grave in a miraculous manner. How could the council many of whose members were Sadducees, receive this as credible? Even the Pharisees in the Sanhedrim, though they held in theory the possibility of a resurrection, would not, with the mean opinion they entertained of Jesus, be inclined to believe in his resurrection, especially as the assertion in the mouth of the guards sounded just like a falsehood invented to screen a failure in duty. The real Sanhedrists, on hearing such an assertion from the soldiers would have replied with exasperation: You lie! you have slept and allowed him to be stolen; but you will have to pay dearly for this when it comes to be investigated by the procurator. But instead of this, the Sanhedrists in our gospel speak them fair, and entreat them thus; Tell a lie, say that you have slept and allowed him to be stolen; moreover they pay them richly for the falsehood, and promise to exculpate them to the procurator. This is evidently spoken entirely on the Christian presupposition of the reality of the resurrection of Jesus; a presupposition, however, which is quite incorrectly attributed to the Sanhedrim" (*Leben Jesu,* pp. 806, 807).

448

What is said of the resurrection by Peter?

"Him God raised up the third day, and showed him openly; not to all the people, but unto witnesses chosen before of God, even to us, who did eat and drink with him after he rose from the dead" (Acts x, 40, 41).

If God really wished to convince all the people, why did he not show him to all the people? It is said that more than two millions of Jews attended the Passover. Had he desired to prove to them that Jesus was the Christ he would have assembled this multitude at midday and in their presence raised his crucified and buried Son. Yet not a single human being witnessed the resurrection, and not a single disinterested witness is said to have seen him after his death. Like a thief he escapes from his prison in the night and avoids publicity. This story of the resurrection is clearly a priestly invention and the composer of the speech ascribed to Peter was conscious of the fact.

449

What did Paul teach regarding the resurrection of Christ?

"That Christ should suffer and that he should be the first that should rise from the dead" (Acts xxvi, 23).

If Christ was the first to rise from the dead what becomes of the miracles of Lazarus, of the widow of Nain's son, and of the daughter of Jairus? What becomes of Matthew's saints who rose from the dead on the day of the crucifixion, two days before Christ rose?

450

What did Paul teach regarding the resurrection of the dead in general?

"If the dead rise not, then is Christ not raised" (I Corinthians xv, 16).

"He that goeth down to the grave shall come up no more" (Job vii, 9).

451

When did the disciples receive the Holy Ghost?

John: "And when he had said this, he breathed on them, and saith unto them, Receive ye the Holy Ghost" (xx, 22).

This was on the evening of the resurrection. Forty days after this he said to them: "Ye shall be baptized with the Holy Ghost not many days hence" (Acts i, 5).

Acts: "And when the day of Pentecost was fully come . . . they were all filled with the Holy Ghost" (ii, 1–4).

This was seven weeks after the resurrection.

452

On what day of the week did it occur?

John: "The first day of the week" (xx, 19).

John, like the author of the first Gospel, is evidently ignorant of the Jewish method of reckoning time. He makes the evening (it was night) following the first day a part of that day instead of the next day to which it belonged.

453

Did Thomas receive the Holy Ghost?

John: He did not. He was absent when the disciples received it (xx, 19-25).

454

Who had Jesus said would send the Holy Ghost to his disciples?

"The Comforter which is the Holy Ghost whom the Father will send" (John xiv, 26).

"I [Jesus] will send him unto you" (xvi, 7).

455

What effect had the Holy Ghost upon them?

Acts: They "began to speak with other tongues, as the Spirit gave them utterance" (ii 4).

Concerning this "gift" Greg says: "Ignorance and folly too often became the arbiters of wisdom—and the ravings of delirium were listened to as the words of inspiration, and of God. If Jesus could have returned to earth thirty years after his death, and sat in the midst of an assembly of his followers, who were listening in hushed and wondering prostration of mind to a speaker in the 'unknown tongue,' how would he have wept over the humiliating and disappointing spectacle! how would he have grieved to think that the incoherent jargon of delirium or hysteria should be mistaken for the promptings of his Father's spirit!" (*Creed of Christendom*, p. 250.)

456

Who heard them speak in new tongues?

Acts: "Parthians, and Medes, and Elamites, and the dwellers in Mesopotamia, and in Judea, and Cappadocia, in Pontus, and Asia, Phrygia and Pamphylia, in Egypt, and in the parts of Libya about Cyrene, and strangers of Rome, Jews and proselytes, Cretes and Arabians" (ii, 9–11).

Did representatives of all these nations really assemble to hear the disciples, or was this merely an imaginary gathering of the writer? Evidently the latter.

457

To the charge of drunkenness what reply did Peter make?

"These are not drunken, as ye suppose, seeing it is but the third hour of the day" (Acts ii, 15).

A profane mind, unacquainted with Jewish customs, might infer from this that the disciples were not in the habit of becoming intoxicated before nine o'clock in the morning.

458

What inquiry did Paul make of John's disciples?

"Have ye received the Holy Ghost since ye believed ?"

What did they say in reply?

"We have not so much as heard whether there be any Holy Ghost" (Acts xix, 2).

This was many years after the death of Jesus. Either this colloquy is false, or the story of John the Baptist is false. If John was the forerunner of Christ, as claimed, his disciples became followers of Christ; and if they became followers of Christ, they were acquainted with the doctrine of the Holy Ghost—if it existed at this time.

459

When did Jesus' disciples begin to baptize?

Matthew and Mark: Not until after his resurrection (Matt. xxviii, 18, 19; Mark xvi, 15, 16).

John: At the beginning of his ministry. "After these things came Jesus and his disciples into the land of Judea; and there he tarried with them, and baptized" (iii, 22). "The Pharisees had heard that Jesus made and baptized more disciples than John. (Though Jesus himself baptized not, but his disciples.)" (iv, 1, 2)

460

What form of baptism is Jesus said to have prescribed for the use of his apostles?

"In the name of the Father, and of the Son, and of the Holy Ghost" (Matthew xxviii, 19).

The apostles did not baptize in the name of the Father, and of the Son, and of the Holy Ghost, but in the name of Christ alone.

"Then Peter said unto them, Repent, and be baptized every one of you in the name of Jesus Christ" (Acts ii, 38).

"They were baptized in the name of the Lord Jesus" (viii, 16).

"He commanded them to be baptized in the name of the Lord" (x, 48).

"They were baptized in the name of the Lord Jesus" (xix, 5).

Concerning this Greg says: "That this definite form of baptism proceeded from Jesus, is opposed by the fact that such an allocation of the Father, Son, and Spirit, does not elsewhere appear, except as a form of salutation in the epistles; while as a definite form of baptism it is nowhere met with throughout the New Testament. Moreover, it was not the form used, and could scarcely, therefore, have been the form commanded; for in the apostolic epistles, and even in the Acts, the form always is 'baptizing into Christ Jesus,' or, 'into the name of the Lord Jesus' " (*Creed of Christendom,* p. 191).

This ecclesiastical formula was not adopted by the church until late in the second century, and then, not for baptism, but for admission into the church. In regard to this the Rev. Dr. Hooykaas says: "Baptism into the name of God the Father, Jesus Christ the Son of God, and the Holy spirit, means baptism into the confession of or faith in these three, and is a short epitome of Christian doctrine of which Jesus certainly never dreamed; nay, it is obvious from all accounts that, even in the apostolic age, it was as yet quite unknown; and the still later age which drew up the words by no means intended them as a baptismal formula, but rather as a statement of the conditions of admission into the community. In making the utterance of these words, instead of the imposition of these conditions, the first act of admission into the community of Christ, the Church has confounded words with things" (*Bible for Learners,* Vol. III, pp. 472, 473).

461

What was his final command to the apostles?

"Go ye into all the world, and preach the gospel to every creature" (Mark xvi, 15).

This is utterly irreconcilable with Acts (xi, 1–18). Eight years after the death of Jesus, Peter is condemned for preaching to the Gentiles. "And the apostles and brethren that were in Judea heard that the Gentiles had also received the word of God. And when Peter was come to Jerusalem, they that were of the circumcision contended with him" (1, 2). How does he meet the accusation and justify his conduct? By reminding them that it was the express will of their Master? No; he tells them that while in a trance at Joppa he had a vision instructing him to carry the gospel to the Gentiles. "When they heard these things, they held their peace, and glorified God, saying, Then hath God also to the Gentiles granted repentance unto life" (18)

462

How long did Jesus remain on earth?

Luke: One day (xxiv).

John: At least ten days (xx, xxi).

Acts: He was "seen of them forty days" (i, 3).

The greatest discrepancy is between Luke and Acts, two books which it is claimed were written by the same author.

463

Where did the ascension take place?

Mark: In Jerusalem (xvi, 14, com. Luke xxiv, 33).

Luke: At Bethany (xxiv, 50, 51).

Acts: At Mount Olivet (i, 9-12).

464

Describe the ascension.

Luke: "And it came to pass while he blessed them he was parted from them and carried up into heaven" (xxiv, 51).

The ascension of Romulus doubtless suggested the story of the ascension of Jesus.

465

What occurred at the ascension?

Acts: "While they looked steadfastly toward heaven as he went up, behold, two men stood by them in white apparel; which also said, Ye men of Galilee, why stand ye gazing up into heaven? this same Jesus, which is taken up from you into heaven, shall so come in like manner as ye have seen him go into heaven" (i, 10, 11).

It is remarkable that the Evangelists who find space to record the sayings of lunatics and devils, leave not room to record the words of angels, or even note their presence.

466

For what purpose did Jesus ascend to heaven?

"I go to prepare a place for you" (John xiv, 2).

What was the need of this when the place had already been "prepared . . . from the foundation of the world" (Matthew xxv, 34)?

467

Did Jesus ascend bodily into heaven?

Luke: He ascended to heaven in a body of flesh and blood (xxiv, 36-43, 50, 51).

Paul: "But some man will say, How are the dead raised up and with what body do they come? Thou fool, that which thou sowest is not quickened except it die; and that which thou sowest thou sowest not that body that shall be" (I Corinthians xv, 35-37).

"It is sown a natural body; it is raised a spiritual body. There is a natural body, and there is a spiritual body" (44)

"Now this I say, brethren, that flesh and blood cannot inherit the Kingdom of God" (50).

The whole theology of Paul is opposed to the bodily resurrection and ascension of Jesus. The *Bible for Learners* says: "In speaking of the resurrection, he [Paul] does not mean the reanimation of the body of Jesus; and indeed he expressly excludes such a thought by ascribing to the Christ a glorified and spiritual body not made of flesh and blood. It is equally certain that he thinks of the Christ as having appeared from heaven; and his ranking the appearance to himself—unquestionably the product of his own fervid imagination—as parallel with those which preceded it [his appearances to the disciples] seems to indicate that they were all visions alike" (Vol. III, p. 467).

468

Do all the Evangelists record the ascension?

Matthew and John, both of whom are declared to have been apostles, and the only Evangelists who are supposed to have witnessed the ascension, know nothing of it. The last twelve verses of Mark, it is admitted, are spurious; while the words, "carried up into heaven," of Luke do not appear in the Sinaitic version, the oldest version of the New Testament extant. With this forged appendix to Mark and this interpolated passage in Luke eliminated, the Four Cospels contain no mention of the ascension.

469

Had any man ever ascended to heaven before Jesus?

Jesus: "No man hath ascended up to heaven, but he that came down from heaven, even the Son of man which is in heaven" (John iii, 13).

Then that story about Elijah is a fiction, is it?

In regard to the resurrection and ascension, Thomas Paine says: "As to the account given of his resurrection and ascension, it was the necessary counterpart of his birth. His historians having brought him into the world in a supernatural manner, were obliged to take him out again in the same manner, or the first part of the story must have fallen to the ground. The wretched contrivance with which this latter part is told exceeds every thing that went before it. The first part, that of the miraculous conception, was not a thing that admitted of publicity; and therefore the tellers of this part of the story had this advantage, that though they might not be credited, they could not be detected. . . . But the resurrection of a dead person from the grave, and his ascension through the air, is a thing very different as to the evidence it admits of, to the invisible conception of a child in the womb. The resurrection and ascension, supposing them to have taken place, admitted of public and ocular demonstration, like that of the ascension of a balloon, or the sun at noon-day, to all Jerusalem at least. A thing which everybody is required to believe, requires that the proof and evidence of it should be equal to all, and universal; and as the public visibility of this last related act was the only evidence that could give sanction to the former part, the whole of it falls to the ground, because that evidence never was given. . . . It is in vain to attempt to palliate or disguise this matter. The story, so far as relates to the supernatural part, has every mark of fraud and imposition stamped upon the face of it. Who were the authors of it is as impossible for us now to know, as it is for us to be assured that the books in which the account is related were written by the persons whose names they bear; the best surviving evidence we now have respecting this affair is the Jews. They are regularly descended from the people who lived in the times this resurrection and ascension is said to have happened, and they say, it is not true. It has long appeared to me a strange inconsistency to cite the Jews as a proof of the truth of the story. It is just the same as if a man were to say, I will prove the truth of what I have told you by producing the people who say it is false" (*Age of Reason,* pp. 10, 11).

"The story of Jesus Christ appearing after he was dead is the story of an apparition, such as timid imaginations can always create in vision, and credulity believe" (ibid., p. 161).

Supernatural Religion says: "The whole of the evidence for the Resurrection reduces itself to an undefined belief on the part of a few persons, in a notoriously superstitious age, that after Jesus had died and been buried they had seen him alive. These visions, it is admitted, occurred at a time of the most intense religious excitement, and under circumstances of wholly exceptional mental agitation and distress. The wildest alternations of fear, doubt, hope and indefinite expectation, added their effects to oriental imaginations already excited by indignation at the fate of their Master, and sorrow or despair at such a dissipation of their Messianic dreams. There was present every element of intellectual and moral disturbance. Now must we seriously ask again whether this bare and wholly unjustified belief can be accepted as satisfactory evidence for so astounding a miracle as the Resurrection? Can the belief of such men, in such an age, establish the reality of a phenomenon which is contradicted by universal experience? We have no evidence as to what actually occurred. We do not even know the facts upon which they based their inferences. We only know that they thought they had seen Jesus and that they, therefore, concluded that he had risen from the dead. It comes to us as bare belief from the Age of Miracles, unsupported by facts, uncorroborated by evidence, unaccompanied by proof of investigation, and unprovided with material for examination. What is such belief worth? We have no hesitation in saying that it is absolutely worth nothing" (pp. 1048, 1049).

The Rev. Dr. Phillip Schaff, one of the most eminent evangelical Christian scholars of this country, in his *History of the Christian Church,* makes this candid admission regarding the resurrection and ascension of Christ: "Truth compels us to admit that there are serious difficulties in harmonizing the accounts of the Evangelists, and in forming a consistent conception of Christ's resurrection body hovering as it were between heaven and earth, and a supernatural state, of a body clothed with flesh and blood and bearing the wound prints, and yet so spiritual as to appear and disappear through closed doors and to ascend visibly to heaven."

8

His Character and Teachings

470

Who was Jesus Christ?

    Mark: He was the son of man.

    Matthew and Luke: He was the Son of God.

    John: He was God himself.

    In the Four Gospels are presented three entirely different conceptions of the Christ. In Mark he is represented as the son of human parents— the Messiah—but simply a man. In Matthew and Luke we have the story of the miraculous conception—he is represented as the Son of God. In John he is declared to be God himself. "In the beginning was the Word [Christ], and the Word was with God, and the Word was God" (i, 1).

    According to Mark Christ is a man; according to Matthew and Luke, a demi-god; according to John, a God.

    Voltaire thus harmonizes these discordant conceptions: "The son of God is the same as the son of man; the son of man is the same as the son of God. God, the father, is the same as Christ, the son; Christ, the son, is the same as God, the father. This language may appear confused to unbelievers, but Christians will readily understand it."

This is quite as intelligible as the Christian Confession of Faith, Article II of which reads as follows: "The Son, which is the Word of the Father, begotten from everlasting of the Father, the very and eternal God, and of one substance with the Father, took man's nature in the womb of the blessed Virgin, of her substance: so that two whole and perfect Natures, that is to say, the Godhead and Manhood, were joined together in one Person, never to be divided, whereof is one Christ, very God and very Man."

"The theological Christ is the impossible union of the human and divine—man with the attributes of God, and God with the limitations and weaknesses of man."—Ingersoll.

471

Is God a visible Being?
Jacob: "I have seen God face to face" (Genesis xxxii, 30).
John: "No man hath seen God at any time" i, 18).

472

How many Gods are there?
Mark: One.
John: Three.
Mark teaches the doctrine of Unitarianism (Monotheism), or one God. John teaches, not the doctrine of Unitarianism or one God, nor yet the doctrine of Trinitarianism or three Gods in one, but the doctrine of Tritheism or three distinct Gods, separate and independent of each other.

473

Is the doctrine of the Trinity taught in the New Testament?
"For there are three that bear record in heaven, the Father, the

Word, and the Holy Ghost: and these three are one" (1 John v, 7).

This is the only passage in the New Testament which clearly teaches the doctrine of the Trinity, and this passage is admitted by all Christian scholars to be an interpolation.

When the modern version of the New Testament was first published by Erasmus it was criticised because it contained no text teaching the doctrine of the Trinity. Erasmus promised his critics that if a manuscript could be found containing such a text he would insert it. The manuscript was "found," and the text quoted appeared in a later edition. Concerning this interpolation Sir Isaac Newton, in a letter to a friend, which was afterward published by Bishop Horsley, says: "When the adversaries of Erasmus had got the Trinity into his edition, they threw by their manuscript as an old almanac out of date."

Alluding to the doctrine of the Trinity, Thomas Jefferson says: "It is too late in the day for men of sincerity to pretend they believe in the Platonic mysticism that three are one and one is three, and yet, that the one is not three, and the three not one. . . . But this constitutes the craft, the power, and profits of the priests. Sweep away their gossamer fabrics of fictitious religion, and they would catch no more flies" (*Jefferson's Works,* Vol. IV, p. 205, Randolph's ed.).

Again Jefferson says: "The hocus-pocus phantasy of a God, like another Cerberus, with one body and three heads, had its birth and growth in the blood of thousands and thousands of martyrs" (ibid., p. 360).

474

Was Christ the only begotten Son of God?

John: He was "the only begotten Son of God" (iii, 18).

"There were giants in the earth in those days; and also after that, when the sons of God came in unto the daughters of men, and they bare children unto them" (Genesis vi, 4).

475

By what agency and when was the Christ begotten?

Matthew and Luke: By the Holy Ghost at the time of his conception by the Virgin Mary.

According to Justin the Holy Ghost begat the Christ, not at the conception of Jesus, as claimed by these Evangelists, but at his baptism. At his baptism the voice from heaven said. "Thou art my son; this day have I begotten thee" (*Dialogues,* 88).

The correctness of Justin's statement is corroborated by Hebrews: "Christ glorified not himself to be made an high priest; but he that said unto him, Thou art my Son, today have I begotten thee" (v, 5). Christ's priesthood began at his baptism.

476

Of what gender is the Holy Ghost?

Matthew (Greek Ver.): Masculine gender.

Matthew (Hebrew Ver.): Feminine gender.

The Holy Ghost (Spirit), as was noted in a previous chapter, was with the Greeks of masculine gender, with the Jews of feminine gender. The Gospel According to the Hebrews, which, it is claimed, was the original Gospel of Matthew, represented Jesus as saying, "Just now my mother, the Holy Ghost, laid hold on me."

If the Holy Ghost was the mother of Jesus did he have two mothers? According to our Greek version of Matthew, as well as that of Luke, he had one mother and three reputed fathers—God, the Holy Ghost, and Joseph.

477

Christ, it is affirmed, was born of Mary. If so, what relation did she bear to him?

1. If he was born of Mary, she was his mother.

2. She "being with child by the Holy Ghost," and Father, Son and Holy Ghost being one, she bore to him the relation of wife.

3. God being the Father of all mankind, and God and Christ being one, she was his daughter.

4. She being the daughter of God, and Christ being the Son of God, she was therefore his sister.

Consequently Mary bore to him the relation of mother, wife, daughter and sister.

478

The greater portion of the Christian church affirms the perpetual virginity of Mary. It is claimed that Jesus was her only child and that the conception and birth of him did not destroy her virginity. Is this confirmed by the Evangelists?

It is not. Matthew and Mark say: "Is not his mother called Mary? and his brethren, James and Joses, and Simon, and Judas? and his sisters, are they not all with us?" (Matt. xiii, 55, 56; Mark vi, 3). Luke (viii, 19) and John (vii, 3) both declare that he had brothers.

To maintain this dogma it is affirmed that by "brethren and sisters" is meant cousins. Dr. Farrar, who in regard to this as in regard to most disputed points, assumes a non-committal or conciliatory attitude, concedes that "the natural supposition that, after the miraculous conception of our Lord, Joseph and Mary lived together in the married state, and that James, and Joses, and Judas, and Simon, with daughters, whose names are not recorded, were subsequently born to them," is "in accordance certainly with the prima facie evidence of the Gospels" (*Life of Christ,* p. 51).

479

Who did Mary say was the father of Jesus?

Luke: When he remained behind in Jerusalem, and they found him in the temple, "his mother said unto him, son, why hast thou thus dealt with us? behold thy father [Joseph] and I have sought thee sorrowing" (ii, 48).

To believe that a Jewish virgin was overshadowed by a spirit, and miraculously conceived and bore a child, requires more convincing proof than the dream of a credulous lover. We ought at least to have the testimony of the mother. But we have it not. She testifies that Joseph is his father.

480

What did Jesus's neighbors say regarding his paternity?

Matthew: They said, "Is not this the carpenter's [Joseph's] son?" (xiii, 55.)

Luke: "They said, Is not this Joseph's son?" (iv, 22.)

John: "They said, Is not this Jesus, the son of Joseph?" (vi, 42.)

The Rev. Dr. Crapsey, of the Episcopal church, in his work on *Religion and Politics* (p. 289), makes this significant admission regarding the divine origin of Jesus: "The fact of his miraculous birth was unknown to himself, unknown to his mother, and unknown to the whole Christian community of the first generations."

Thomas Jefferson, in a letter to John Adams, wrote: "The day will come when the mystical generation of Jesus, by the Supreme Being as his father, in the womb of a virgin, will be classed with the fable of the generation of Minerva in the brain of Jupiter" (*Jefferson's Works,* Vol. IV, p. 365, Randolph's ed.).

481

Who did Peter declare him to be?

"Jesus of Nazareth, a man approved of God" (Acts ii, 22).

Who did Paul declare hirm to be?

"There is one God, and one mediator between God and men, the man Christ Jesus" (1 Timothy ii, 5).

The Christ of Peter and Paul was not a God, but a man—a man upon whom had been bestowed divine gifts—but yet a man.

482

What testimony is ascribed to Paul?

"Great is the mystery of godliness: God was manifest in the flesh" (1 Timothy iii, 6).

This is a gross perversion of Scripture for the purpose of making Paul a witness to Christ's divinity. Regarding this text and the Trinitarian text inserted in 1 John, Sir Isaac Newton, in his letter previously quoted from, says:

"What the Latins have done in this text (1 John v, 7) the Greeks have done to Paul (1 Tim. iii, 16). They now read, 'Great is the mystery of godliness; God manifest in the flesh'; whereas all the churches for the first four or five hundred years, and the authors of all the ancient versions, Jerome as well as the rest, read, 'Great is the mystery of godliness, which was manifest in the flesh.' Our English version makes it yet a little stronger. It reads, 'Great is the mystery of godliness: God was manifest in the flesh.' "

In conclusion Newton says: "If the ancient churches, in debating and deciding the greatest mysteries of religion, knew nothing of these two texts, I understand not why we should be so fond of them now the debate is over."

483

Christ is declarerd by the Christian creed to be "the very and eternal God." God, it is claimed, is omnipotent. Was Christ omnipotent?

"The Son can do nothing of himself" (John v, 9).

"I can of mine own self do nothing" (30).

484

God is omniscient. Was Christ omniscient?

Referring to his second advent he says: "Of that day and hour knoweth no man, . . . neither the Son" (Mark xiii, 32).

485

God is omnipresent. Was Christ omnipresent?

"I am glad for your sakes that I was not there" (John xi, 15).

"Ye shall seek me, and shall not find me: and where I am, thither ye cannot come" (vii, 36).

"And now I am no more in the world" (xvii, 11).

486

God is self-existent. Was Christ self-existent?

"I live by the Father" (John vi, 57).

"He liveth by the power of God" (2 Corinthians xiii, 4).

487

Did Christ have a preexistence?

"Before Abraham was, I am" (John viii, 52).

According to the Synoptics his existence began with his life on earth.

488

Was he infinite in wisdom?

Luke: He "increased in wisdom" (ii, 52).

If he increased in wisdom his knowledge was limited, and limitation of knowledge is not an attribute of an infinite God.

489

Was he infinite in goodness?

"Why callest thou me good? There is none good but one, that is, God" (Mark x, 18).

490

Was he infinite in mercy?

"He that believeth not shall be damned" (Mark xvi, 16).

"Depart from me, ye cursed, into everlasting fire" (Matthew xxv, 41).

"Then began he to upbraid the cities wherein most of his mighty works were done, because they repented not: Woe unto thee, Chorazin! woe unto thee, Bethsaida! . . . It shall be more tolerable for Tyre and Sidon at the day of judgment, than for you. And thou, Capernaum, which art exalted unto heaven, shalt be brought down to hell" (Matthew xi, 20–23).

491

His resurrection is adduced as the chief argument in proof of his divinity. Did he raise himself from the dead?

Peter: He did not. God raised him. "Jesus Christ of Nazareth, . . . whom God raised from the dead" (Acts iv, 10).

If Christ, then, did not rise from the dead by his own volition, was his resurrection any proof of his divinity? No more than the resurrection of Lazarus was proof of Lazarus's divinity.

492

His miraculous conception is adduced as another proof of his divinity. Is this the only miraculous conception claimed in the Bible?

It is not. Isaac, Samson, Samuel and John the Baptist are all claimed to have been miraculously conceived (Genesis xviii, 10, 11; xxi, 1–3; Judges xiii, 2, 3, 24; 1 Samuel i, 9–11, 20; Luke i, 7–13).

493

His miracles, it is claimed, attest his divinity. Were he and his disciples the only ones who performed miracles?

These alleged miracles were performed before his time—the Old Testament abounds with them—and they have been performed since his time. They were performed by others in his own time—were performed by those who ignored and rejected him—were performed by the disciples of Satan himself (Matthew vii, 22; xii, 27; Mark ix, 38; xiii, 22; Luke ix, 49).

Supernatural Religion says: "The supposed miraculous evidence for the divine revelation, moreover, is without any special divine character, being avowedly common also to Satanic agency, but it is not original either in conception or details. Similar miracles to those which are supposed to attest it are reported long antecedent to the promulgation of Christianity, and continued to be performed for centuries after it. A stream of miraculous pretension, in fact, has flowed through all human history, deep and broad as it has passed through the darker ages, but dwindling down to a thread as it has entered days of enlightenment. The evidence was too hackneyed and commonplace to place any impression upon those before whom the Christian miracles are said to have been performed, and it altogether failed to convince the people to whom the revelation was primarily addressed. The selection of such evidence, for such a purpose, is much more characteristic of human weakness than of divine power" (p. 699).

Archbishop Trench says: "Side by side with the miracles which serve for the furthering of the kingdom of God runs another line of wonders, the counter-workings of him who is ever the ape of the Most High. . . . This fact that the kingdom of lies has its wonders no less than the kingdom of truth, is itself sufficient evidence that miracles cannot be appealed to absolutely and finally, in proof of the doctrine which the worker of them proclaims" (*Miracles of Our Lord,* p. 22).

The miracles of Christ, like the miracles of Satan, existed only in the minds of his credulous and deluded followers.

> Ye shall have miracles, aye, sound ones too,
> Seen, heard, attested, everything but true.
> —Thomas Moore.

494

Prophecy is appealed to in support of his divinity. It is claimed that the writers of the Old Testament predicted his coming. Do such predictions exist?

In his work on *The Bible,* as well as in a previous chapter of this work, the writer has shown that there is not a single passage in the Old Testament that, in the original text, refers in the remotest degree to Jesus Christ.

Greg shows that much of Old Testament history, like Deuteronomy, is presented in the form of anticipatory narrative. To the Christian argument that the Messianic predictions, at least, were written long anterior to the time of Christ, he replies: "This is true, and the argument would have all the force which is attributed to it, were the objectors able to lay their fingers on a single Old Testament prediction clearly referring to Jesus Christ, intended by the utterers of it to relate to him, prefiguring his character and career, and manifestly fulfilled in his appearance on earth. This they cannot do. Most of the passages usually adduced as complying with these conditions, referred, and were clearly intended to refer, to eminent individuals in Israelitish history; many are not prophecies at all; the Messiah, the anointed deliverer expected by the Jews, hoped for and called for by their poets and prophets, was of a character so different, and a career so opposite, to those of the meek, lowly, long-suffering Jesus, that the passages describing the one never could have been applied to the other, without a perversion of ingenuity, and a disloyal treatment of their obvious signification, which, if employed in any other field than that of theology, would have met with the prompt discredit and derision they deserve" (*Creed of Christendom,* pp. 135, 136).

495

His own prescience is cited in proof of his divinity. The destruction of the temple by the Romans, it is claimed, was a wonderful instance of the fulfillment of prophecy. But did his so-called prophecy have reference to this event?

No one can read this prophecy (Matthew xxiv, 1–3) and then honestly contend that it did. He clearly refers to his second coming and the end of the world when the temple, in common with all sublunary things, shall be destroyed. In the verse immediately following this prediction, his disciples say: "Tell us, when shall these things be? and what shall be the sign of thy coming, and of the end of the world?"

But even if this so-called prophecy had referred to this event it is rendered nugatory by the fact that the book containing it was not composed until a hundred years after the destruction of the temple.

496

When was Christ's second coming and the end of terrestrial things to take place?

"There be some standing here that shall not taste of death till they see the Son of man coming in his kingdom" (Matthew xvi, 28).

"This generation shall not pass away, till all be fulfilled" (Luke xxi, 32).

Seventy-five generations have passed, and still the world rolls on, unmoved by Christ's and Mother Shipton's prophecies.

497

Did the Apostles believe that the second coming of Christ and the end of the worid were at hand?

Peter: "The end of all things is at hand" (1 Peter iv, 7).

James: "The coming of the Lord draweth nigh" (James v, 8).

John: "Ye have heard that antichrist shall come, even now are there many antichrists: whereby we know that it is the last time" (1 John ii, 18).

Paul: "For the Lord himself shall descend from heaven with a shout, with the voice of the archangel, and with the trump of God: and the dead in Christ shall rise first; then we which are alive and remain shall be caught up together with them in the clouds to meet the Lord in the air" (1 Thessalonians iv, 16, 17).

Renan, ever ready to palliate or overlook the errors of his hero, frankly admits that the predictions concerning his second advent and the end of the world were a dismal failure. "It is evident, indeed," he says, "that such a doctrine, taken by itself in a literal manner, had no future. The world, in continuing to exist, caused it to crumble. One generation of man at the most was the limit of its endurance. The faith of the first Christian generation is intelligible, but the faith of the second generation is no longer so. After the death of John, or of the last survivor, whoever he might be, of the group which had seen the master, the word of Jesus was convicted of falsehood" (*Life of Jesus*, pp. 203, 204).

498

To what extent was the gospel to be preached before his second coming?

"Ye shall not have gone over the cities of Israel, till the Son of man be come" (Matthew x, 23).

"The gospel must first be published among all nations" (Mark xiii, 10).

499

Did Jesus claim to be the Christ or Messiah from the first?

John: He did. Early in his ministry "The woman [of Samaria] saith unto him, I know that Messias cometh, which is called Christ: when he is come, he will tell us all things. Jesus saith unto her, I that speak unto thee am he" (iv, 25, 26).

Synoptics: He did not announce his Messiahship until late in his ministry.

500

Who were the first to recognize his divinity?

Synoptics: Devils and unclean spirits (Matthew viii, 28, 29; Mark iii, 11, 12; Luke iv, 41).

501

What is said of Jesus in Hebrews?

"Jesus, who was made a little lower than the angels" (ii, 9).

"Being made so much better than the angels" (i, 4).

502

What did he say respecting his identity with God?

"My Father and I are one" (John x, 30).

"My Father is greater than I" (xiv, 28).

503

How did he attempt to establish his claims?

"It is also written in your law, that the testimony of two men is true. I am one that bear witness of myself, and the Father that sent me beareth witness of me" (John viii, 17, 18).

But if "I and my Father are one," how does that fulfill the law?

504

What did he say regarding the truthfulness of his testimony concerning himself?

"Though I bear record of myself, yet my record is true" (John viii, 14).

"If I bear witness of myself, my witness is not true" (v. 31).

505

Did Jesus's neighbors believe in his divinity?

Matthew: "When he was come into his own country," and to his own home, "He did not many mighty works there because of their unbelief" (xiii, 54, 58).

506

What opinion did his friends entertain of him?

Mark: "And when his friends heard of it [his work], they went out to lay hold on him; for they said, He is beside himself" (iii, 21).

507

Did even his brothers believe in him?

John: "Now the Jews' feast of tabernacles was at hand. His brethren therefore said unto him, Depart hence, and go into Judea, that thy disciples also may see the works that thou doest. For there is no man that doeth any thing in secret, and he himself seeketh to be known openly. If thou do these things, shew thyself to the world. For neither did his brethren believe in him" (vii, 2-5).

These three passages are fatal to the claim of Christ's divinity. If he was unable to convince his neighbors, his friends or even his own family of his divinity he was not divine. Much less was he the "very God," as claimed.

According to the Christian scheme, man by his disobedience fell— was lost. God desired to save him. Christ—God manifest in the flesh— came on earth for this purpose. What was required of man to secure salvation? Simply to believe that Jesus was the Christ. In order for him to believe this what was necessary? That Jesus should convince him that he was divine. If he was all-powerful, he could have done this; if he was all-just, he would have done this. Did he do this? His own race rejected him. Disbelief in Christ's divinity disproves his divinity.

508

The writings of the New Testament are adduced as the evidences of Christ's divinity and the divine character of Christianity. Do the writers of the New Testament claim to be inspired?

With the possible exception of the author of Revelation, they do not. Paul says, "All scripture is given by inspiration of God." But the "scripture" of Paul was the scripture of the Old Testament. His words have no reference whatever to the writings of the New which did not exist in his time.

If the New Testament is not inspired and infallible, what follows?

"If the New Testament is defective the church itself is in error, and must be given up as a deception."—Dr. Tischendorf.

"It is not a word too much to say that the New Testament abounds with errors."—Dean Alford.

509

What is said of the Apocryphal Gospels which appeared in the early ages of the church?

"Several histories of his [Christ's] life and doctrines, full of pious frauds and fabulous wonders, were composed by persons whose intentions perhaps were not bad, but whose writings discovered the greatest superstition and ignorance. Nor was this all; productions appeared which were imposed upon the world by fraudulent men, as the writings of the holy Apostles."—Mosheim.

Is the above less true of the books we are reviewing? Are not these writings "full of pious frauds and fabulous wonders"? Do not these writings display "the greatest superstition and ignorance"? Have not these writings been "imposed upon the world by fradulent men, as the writings of the holy (?) Apostles"?

If some of these apocryphal Gospels had been accepted as canonical, and the canonical Gospels had been rejected as apocryphal, these canonical Gospels would appear as untruthful and foolish to Christians as the apocryphal Gospels do.

510

Let us examine the religious teachings ascribed to Christ. For what purpose was his blood shed?

"This is my blood of the New Testament which is shed for many" (Mark xiv, 24).

"This cup is the New Testament in my blood, which is shed for you" (Luke xxii, 20).

"This is my blood of the New Testament which is shed for many FOR THE REMISSION OF SINS" (Matthew xxvi, 28).

The above is one of the most significant discrepancies in the Bible. The Atonement is the chief doctrine connected with Christ and orthodox Christianity. The text quoted from Matthew is the only text in the Four Gospels which clearly teaches this doctrine. "Two other texts (Matthew xx, 28; John i, 29) are adduced in support of it, but do not clearly teach it. Now Matthew has falsely ascribed to Jesus the revelation of the Atonement, or Mark and Luke have either ignorantly or intentionally omitted this greatest of Christian doctrines. They contain no mention of the Atonement as understood by orthodox Christians.

511

For whom did he say his blood was shed?

"This is my blood of the New Testament, which is shed for many [interpreted by the church to mean all mankind]" (Mark xiv, 24).

"This cup is the New Testament in my blood, which is shed for you [addressed to his disciples alone]" (Luke xxii, 20).

512

Was his blood really shed?

The crucifixion was not a bloody death, and aside from the self-confuted story of John about blood and water flowing from his corpse, the Evangelists do not state that a drop of blood was shed.

513

Christ, it is affirmed, was both God and man. Was it the human, or the divine part of him that suffered death?

If only the human, this sacrifice was not an exceptional one, for thousands have died for their fellow men. If the divine part was sacrificed, does God cease to exist?

514

His death is called an infinite sacrifice. If only the man died, can this be true?

The offering of a finite being, it must be admitted, would not constitute an infinite sacrifice.

515

If the God was crucified, does he suffer endless pain?

If not, then his suffering was not infinite, and the sacrifice in this case was not an infinite one.

516

If God died, but subsequently rose from the dead, was there not an interregnum when the universe was without a ruler?

If so, then it must he conceded that the existence of the universe is not dependent upon the existence of God.

517

Are all mankind to be saved by Christ?

"And I, if I be lifted up from the earth, will draw all men to me" (John xii, 32).

"Many be called but few chosen" (Matthew xx, 16).

518

What does Paul affirm concerning the Atonement?

"Christ died for our sins according to the scriptures" (1 Corinthians xv, 3).

By "scriptures" Paul means the Old Testament, and according to the scriptures of the Old Testament, "Every man shall be put to death for his own sins" (Deuteronomy xxiv, 16).

Like nearly all the doctrines ascribed to Christ, the atonement is in the highest degree unjust and absurd. Referring to this docirine, Lord Byron says: "The basis of your religion is injustice. The Son of God the pure, the immaculate, the innocent, is sacrificed for the guilty. This proves his heroism, but no more does away with man's sin than a school-boy's volunteering to be flogged for another would exculpate a dunce from negligence."

Greg justly charges Christians with "holding the strangely inconsistent doctrine that God is so just that he could not let sin go unpunished, yet so unjust that he could punish it in the person of the innocent." "It is for orthodox dialectics," he says, "to explain how divine justice can be impugned by pardoning the guilty, and yet vindicated by punishing the innocent!" (*Creed of Christendom,* pp. 338, 339.)

519

It is claimed that the sacrifice of Jesus was necessary for our salvation. Through whom was this sacrifice secured?

All: Judas Iscariot procurred it, and Pilate and the Jews offered it.

Are not Christians, then, in condemning these men, ungrateful to their greatest benefactors? A man is dangeronsly ill. The druggist provides a remedy, the physician administers it and saves his life. When restored does he show his gratitude by praising the drug and damning the doctor?

520

In permitting the crucifixion of Jesus, who committed the greater sin, Pilate or God?

John: "Jesus answered, Thou couldest have no power at all against me, except it were given thee from above: therefore he [God] that delivered me unto thee hath the greater sin" (xix, 11).

Hon. Allan L. McDermott, in his memorable speech in Congress, in 1906, protesting against the persecution of Jews by Christians, said: "If an omnipotent God orders anything done, the human instruments selected to carry out his orders cannot be charged with the acts commanded. The doctrine of repondeat superior applies. If what happened could have been prevented by the Romans or by the Jews, then the New Testament is worthless. Let us assume that the Jews crucified Christ. Could they have done otherwise? Were they greater than God? According to the Bible, the crucifixion was arranged for by the Father. Why blame the Jews or the Romans or any other mortals? They did not know what they were doing. The Roman soldiers did not believe that they were crucifying the son of God; they did not know they were crucifying God himself. Why blame the instruments? Why persecute the descendants? According to the Synoptic Gospels and according to John, the arrangements for the crucifixion—every detail—were made by Almighty God, and were known to Christ."

521

What was the character of his death?

Homicide. "Jesus of Nazareth, a man . . . ye have taken, and by wicked hands have crucified and slain" (Acts ii, 22, 23).

Regicide. "The Lord God shall give unto him the throne of his father David" (Luke i, 32). "This is the King of the Jews" (xxiii, 38). "There they crucified him" (33).

Deicide. "The Word [Christ] was God" (John i, 1). "I and my Father are one" (x, 30). "They crucified him" (xix, 18).

Suicide: "I [Christ] lay down my life, that I might take it again. No man taketh it from me, but I lay it down of myself" (John x, 17, 18).

522

What did Jesus teach respecting the resurrection of the dead and the doctrine of immortality?

"For the hour is coming in the which all that are in the graves shall hear his voice, and shall come forth" (John v. 28, 29).

"Search the scriptures; for in them ye think ye have eternal life" (39).

"As the cloud is consumed and vanisheth away, so he that goeth down to the grave shall come up no more."—Job (vii, 9).

"His breath goeth forth, he returneth to his earth; in that very day his thoughts perish."—Psalms (cxlvi, 4).

"For that which befalleth the sons of men befalleth beasts. . . . As one dieth, so dieth the other; yea, they have all one breath, so that man hath no preeminence over a beast."—Ecclesiastes (iii, 19).

523

His resurrection is accepted by Christians as a proof and type of man's resurrection and immortality. What was the nature of his resurrection?

According to all of the Evangelists it was merely a reanimation of his undecayed body. Other bodies supposedly dead have been revived, but neither these resuscitations nor the supposed reanimation of Jesus' corpse affords proof that bodies which ages ago crumbled into dust and whose particles subsequently entered into the composition of myriads of other bodies will be reunited into the original beings. And as Jesus almost immediately disappeared after his alleged resurrection and has never since been seen this resurrection did not evince his own immortality, much less that of mankind in general.

524

Did Christ descend into hell?

Peter: He did (Acts ii, 31; 1 Peter iii, 19).

Peter states that "his soul was not left in hell," which necessitates the assumption of his having gone there. He also declares that after his death he "went and preached unto the spirits in prison [hell]."

The Confession of Faith (Art. III) says: "As Christ died for us, and was buried; so also is it to be believed that he went down into hell."

For what purpose did Christ descend into hell and preach to its inhabitants? If it was to redeem them, his mission was fruitless; if it was not to redeem them, his mission was useless. Early Christian writers almost uniformly spelled the name of Christ, not "Christos" (the

Anointed), but "Chrestos." Chrestos was a Pagan name given to the judge of Hades or the lower world.

525

What is taught regarding justification by faith aud justification by works?

Paul: "A man is not justified by the works of the law, but by the faith of Jesus Christ, . . . for by the works of the law shall no flesh be justified" (Galatians ii, 16). "If righteousness come by the law then Christ is dead in vain" (21). "To him that worketh not, but believeth on him that justifieth the ungodly, his faith is counted for righteousness" (Romans iv, 5). "Therefore, we conclude that a man is justified by faith without the deeds of the law" (iii, 28).

James: "But wilt thou know, O vain man, that faith without works is dead?" (ii, 20). "Ye see then, how that by works a man is justified, and not by faith only" (24).

The church accepts the teachings of Paul and condemns or ignores the teachings of James. Martin Luther in his "Table Talk," thus defines the position of the Protestant church. "He that says the gospel requires works for salvation, I say flat and plain he is a liar." "Every doer of the law and every moral worker is accursed, for he walketh in the presumption of his own righteousness." "If men only believe enough in Christ they can commit adultery and murder a thousand times a day without periling their salvation." Luther rejected and denounced the book of James because it teaches the efficacy of good works.

The English *Confession of Faith* affirms the following: "That we are justified by Faith only, is a most wholesome doctrine, and very full of comfort" (Art. XI). "Works done before the grace of Christ, and the inspiration of the Spirit, are not pleasant to God, forasmuch as they spring not of faith in Jesus Christ. . . . Yea rather, for that they are not done as God hath willed and commanded them to be done, we doubt not but they have the nature of sin" (Art. XIII).

Morality! thou deadly bane,
Thy tens o' thousands thou hast slain!
Vain is his hope, whose stay and trust is
In moral mercy, truth and justice!
    No—stretch a point to catch a plack;
Abuse a brother to his back;

.   .   .   .

Be to the poor like onie whunstane,
And haud their noses to the grunstane;
Ply ev'ry art o' legal thieving:
No matter, stick to sound believing.
    Learn three-mile prayers, and half-mile graces,
Wi weel-spread loaves, and lang wry faces,
Grunt up a solemn, lengthen'd groan,
And damn a' parties but your own:
I'll warrant, then, ye're nae deceiver,
A steady, sturdy, staunch believer.
                          —Robert Burns.

526

What does Christ teach regarding salvation?

"Whosoever liveth and believeth in me shall never die" (John xi, 26).

"He that believeth on him is not condemned; but he that believeth not is condemned already" (iii, 18).

"He that believeth on the Son hath everlasting life: and he that believeth not on the Son shall not see life" (36).

A demand so preposterous could have been made only in support of claims that were realized to be untenable. Credulity was appealed to because convincing evidence could not be adduced. Claims which reason rejects are manifestly false, and it is only by a renunciation of reason that they can be accepted as true.

The absurdity of this requirement of Christ is thus exposed by the poet Shelley: "This is the pivot upon which all religions turn; they all assume that it is in our power to believe or not to believe: whereas the mind can only believe that which it thinks true. A human being can only be supposed accountable for those actions which are influenced by his will. But belief is utterly distinct from and unconnected with volition: it is the apprehension of the agreement or disagreement of the ideas that compose any proposition. Belief is a passion or involuntary operation of the mind, and, like other passions, its intensity is precisely proportionate to the degree of excitement. Volition is essential to merit or demerit. But the Christian religion attaches the highest possible degree of merit and demerit to that which is worthy of neither, and which is totally unconnected with the peculiar faculty of the mind whose presence is essential to their being" (*Notes to Queen Mab*).

527

Did Christ abrogate the Mosaic law?

"Till Heaven and earth pass, one jot or one tittle shall in no wise pass from the law" (Matthew v, 18).

"The law and the prophets were until John; since that time the Kingdom of God is preached" (Luke xvi, 16).

Paul: "The law was our schoolmaster to bring us unto Christ, that we might be justified by faith. But after that faith is come we are no longer under a schoolmaster" (Galatians iii, 24, 25). "But now we are delivered from the law" (Romans vii, 6).

"Christ certainly did come to destroy the law and the prophets."— Henry Ward Beecher.

528

What is taught regarding the forgiveness of sin?

"He [God] is faithful and just to forgive sins" (1 John i, 9).

"The Son of man hath power on earth to forgive sins" (Mark ii, 10).

"Today I offer you the pardon of the gospel—full pardon, free pardon. I do not care what your crime has been. Though you say you have committed a crime against God, against your own soul, against your fellow-man, against your family, against the day of judgment, against the cross of Christ—whatever your crime has been, here is pardon, full pardon, and the very moment you take that pardon your heavenly Father throws his arms about you and says: 'My son, I forgive you. It is all right. You are as much in my favor now as if you never had sinned.' "— Dr. Talmage.

This doctrine of forgiveness of sin is a premium on crime. "Forgive us our sins" means "Let us continue in our iniquity." It is one of the most pernicious of doctrines, and one of the most fruitful sources of immorality. It has been the chief cause of making Christian nations the most immoral of nations. In teaching this doctrine Christ committed a sin for which his death did not atone, and which can never be forgiven. There is no forgiveness of sin. Every cause has its effect; every sinner must suffer the consequences of his sins.

529

What is taught regarding future rewards and punishments?

"He that believeth and is baptized shall be saved; but he that believeth not shall be damned" (Mark xvi, 16).

These words, while appearing in the unauthentic appendix to Mark, yet express clearly the alleged teachings of Jesus. Above all they have formed the key note of orthodox Christianity in all ages of the church.

Between the lines of this passage the eye of the unfettered mind discerns in large capitals the word FRAUD. These words are the words of an impostor. Had Jesus been divine he would not have been compelled to resort to bribes and threats to secure the world's adherence. Had he even been a sincere man he would not have desired converts on such terms. These words are either the utterance of a false Messiah, conscious of his impotency, or the invention of priests who intended them to frighten the ignorant and credulous into an acceptance of their faith.

Concerning this teaching Col. Ingersoll says: "Redden your hands with human blood; blast by slander the fair fame of the innocent; strangle the smiling child upon its mother's knees; deceive, ruin, and desert the beautiful girl who loves and trusts you, and your case is not hopeless. For all this, and for all these, you may be forgiven. For all this, and for all these, that bankrupt court established by the gospel will give you a discharge; but deny the existence of these divine ghosts, of these gods, and the sweet and tearful face of Mercy becomes livid with eternal hate. Heaven's golden gates are shut, and you, with an infinite curse ringing in your ears, with the brand of infamy upon your brow, commence your endless wanderings in the lurid gloom of hell— an immortal vagrant, an eternal outcast, a deathless convict."

"A gloomy heaven above opening its jealous gates to the nineteen-thousandth part of the tithe of mankind! And below an inexorable Hell expanding its leviathan jaws for the vast residue of mortals! O doctrine comfortable and healing to weary wounded soul of man!"—Robert Burns.

530

Did he teach the doctrine of endless punishment?

"And these shall go away into everlasting punishment" (Matthew xxv, 46).

That is the most infamous passage in all literature. It is the language, not of an incarnate God but of an incarnate devil. The being who gave utterance to those words deserves not the worship, but the execration of mankind. The priests who preach this doctrine of eternal pain are fiends. There is misery enough in this world without adding to it the mental anguish of this monstrous lie.

Less than a hundred years ago, when Christ was yet believed to be divine, in nearly every pulpit, to frighten timid and confiding mothers, dimpled babes were consigned to the red flames of this eternal hell. Then came the preachers of humanity—the Ballous, the Channings, the Parkers and the Beechers—preachers with hearts and brains, who sought to humanize this heavenly demon, to make of him a decent man, and civilize his fiendish priests. To these men is due the debt of everlasting gratitude. With the return of every spring the emancipated of the race should build above their sacred dust a pyramid of flowers.

Not by the sects known as Universalists and Unitarians, small in numbers, though in the character of their adherents the greatest of the Christian sects, must we estimate the importance of the work of Ballou and Channing and other Liberal ministers. The influence of their teachings has permeated every Christian sect, and quickened every humane conscience. In the minds of all intelligent Christians, largely as the result of their labors, this heartless demon and this cruel dogma are dead. In their creeds they still survive. They are ashamed of the dogma; they abhor it. They should abhor its author, and banish both.

> What! I should call on that Infinite Love that
>   has served us so well?
> Infinite cruelty rather, that made everlasting hell,
> Made us, foreknew us, foredoom'd us, and does
>   what he will with his own;
> Better our dead brute mother who never has
>   heard us groan.
>   —Tennyson.

531

Is it possible to fall from grace?

Peter: "If after they have escaped the pollutions of the world through the knowledge of the Lord and Savior Jesus Christ, they are again entangled therein, and overcome, the latter end is worse with them than the beginning" (2 Peter ii, 20).

"My sheep hear my voice, and I know them, and they follow me: and I give unto them eternal life; and they shall never perish, neither shall any man pluck them out of my hand" (John x, 27, 28).

"There is no condemnation for them that believe and are baptized."—*Confession of Faith,* Art. IX.

532

Is baptism essential to salvation?

"He that believeth and is baptized shall be saved" (Mark xvi, 16).

"Except a man be born of the water and of the spirit, he cannot enter the Kingdom of God" (John iii, 5).

"Go ye, therefore, and teach all nations, baptising them" (Matthew xxviii, 19).

Was the penitent thief baptized?

Paul says: "I thank God that I baptized none of you, but Crispus and Gaius. . . . For Christ sent me not to baptize, but to preach the gospel" (1 Corinthians i, 14, 17).

533

What constitutes Christian baptism, immersion or sprinkling?

With millions of Bibles in circulation, the Christian does not know. If he affirms, as many scholars affirm, that immersion is the mode authorized by the Bible, then he must admit that the greater portion of Christendom has rejected this mode and adopted one not authorized by the Scriptures.

To whom is this rite to be administered, to both adults and infants, or to adults alone?

After eighteen centuries of controversy; after employing millions of priests to interpret the Scriptures; after Anabaptists and Pedobaptists have baptised their swords in each others' blood, the church is not prepared to answer.

534

Did Christ command his disciples to repeat and perpetuate the observance of the Eucharist?

Luke: He did. "This do in remembrance of me."

Matthew, Mark and John: He did not.

It is admitted by Dr. Westcott and others that the earlier versions of Luke did not contain the injunction quoted. Christ, then, according to the Four Gospels did not institute the Eucharist as a sacrament to be observed by his disciples and the church. Referring to the Twelve Apostles, the Rev. Dr. Minot J. Savage says: "They knew nothing about any sacraments; they had not been instituted" (*What is Christianity?*).

535

What did he teach in regard to the efficacy of prayer?

"All things whatsoever ye shall ask in prayer, believing, ye shall receive" (Matthew xxi, 22).

This is one of the cardinal doctrines of his religion. He is continually impressing upon the minds of his hearers the necessity and the efficacy of prayer. Referring to this doctrine, Greg says:

"This doctrine has in all ages been a stumbling block to the thoughtful. It is obviously irreconcilable with all that reason and revelation teach us of the divine nature; and the inconsistency has been felt by the ablest of the Scripture writers themselves. Various and desperate have been the expedients and suppositions resorted to, in order to reconcile the conception of an immutable, all-wise, all-foreseeing God, with that of a father who is turned from his course by the prayers of his creatures. But all such efforts are, and are felt to be, hopeless failures. They involve the assertion and negation of the same proposition in one breath. The problem remains still insoluble; and we must either be content to leave it so, or we must abandon one or other of the hostile premises.

"The religious man, who believes that all events, mental as well as physical, are pre-ordered and arranged according to the decrees of infinite wisdom, and the philosopher, who knows that, by the wise and eternal laws of the universe cause and effect are indissolubly chained together, and that one follows the other in inevitable succession—equally feel that this ordination—this chain—cannot be changed at the cry of man. To suppose that it can is to place the whole harmonious system of nature at the mercy of the weak reason and the selfish wishes of humanity. If the purposes of God were not wise, they would not be formed: if wise, they cannot be changed, for then they would become unwise. To suppose that an all-wise Being would alter his designs and modes of proceeding at the entreaty of an unknowing creature, is to believe that compassion would change his wisdom into foolishness. . . . If the universe is governed by fixed laws, or (which is the same proposition in different language), if all events are pre-ordained by the foreseeing wisdom of an infinite God, then the prayers of thousands of years and generations of martyrs and saints cannot change or modify one iota of our destiny. The proposition is unassailable by the subtlest logic. The weak, fond affections of humanity struggle in vain against the unwelcome conclusion" (*Creed of Christendom,* pp. 322, 323).

536

Where are we commanded to pray?
"When thou prayest enter into thy closet" (Matthew vi, 6).
How long ought we to continue in prayer?
"Men ought always to pray" (Luke xviii, 1).

537

Did Christ assume for himself the power of answering petitions?
"Whatsoever ye shall ask in my name that will I do" (John xiv, 13). But soon realizing that his capital was too small to conduct a business of such magnitude, he was compelled to announce that, "Whatsoever ye shall ask of the Father in my name, he may give it you" (xv, 16).

538

Does God know our wants?
"Your father knoweth what things ye have need of before ye ask him" (Matthew vi, 8).
Then what is the use of prayer? Is God a mischievous urchin taunting his hungry dog with a morsel of bread, and shouting, "Beg, Tray, beg!"?

539

What portion of their goods did he require the rich to give the poor to obtain salvation?
Rich Ruler, No. 1: "Good Master what shall I do to inherit eternal

life?" (Luke xviii, 18.)

Jesus: "Sell all that thou hast and distribute unto the poor" (22).

Rich Ruler, No. 2: "Lord, the half of my goods I give to the poor" (Luke xix, 8).

Jesus: "This day is salvation come to this house" (9).

540

What did he teach respecting the publicity of good works?

"Let your light so shine before men, that they may see your good works" (Matthew v, 16).

"Take heed that ye do not your righteousness before men to be seen of then," (vi, 1, New Ver.).

541

What original rules of table observance did he teach his disciples?

Matthew: To abstain from washing their hands before eating. "They wash not their hands when they eat bread" (xv, 2).

John: To wash their feet after eating. "He riseth from supper, and laid aside his garments; and took a towel and girded himself. After that he poured water into a basin, and began to wash the disciples' feet, and to wipe them with the towel wherewith he was girded" (xiii, 4, 5).

The proneness of Christ's followers to neglect his ordinances and precepts which require some sacrifice or effort to obey, and the readiness with which they observe those which do not, find a fitting illustration in the reception accorded these teachings. While the early Christians, many of them, accepted the first as a religious obligation not to be violated, the second was ignored. Writing of Christian monks and nuns, Lecky says: "The cleanliness of the body was regarded as a pollution of the soul, and the saints who were most admired had become one hideous mass of clotted filth. St. Athanasius relates with enthusiasm how St. Antony, the patriarch of monachism, had never, to extreme old age, been guilty of washing his feet. . . . St. Abraham the hermit, however, who lived for fifty years after his conversion, rigidly refused from that date to wash either his face or feet. . . . St. Euphraxia joined a convent of one hundred and thirty nuns, who never washed their feet, and who shuddered at the mention of a bath" (*European Morals,* Vol. II, pp. 109, 110).

542

What religious formula is to be found in the New Testament?

"In the name of Jesus."

"In the name of Jesus" the disciples cast out devils and performed other miracles; "In the name of Jesus" they baptised their converts; "In the name of Jesus" salvation was secured. This formula, with various modifications, is in general use in the church today. It betrays the heathen origin of Christianity. Referring to its use Prof. Meinhold of Bonn University says: "Name and person were at one time closely combined, and elementary religious ideas were connected with the words. He who knew the name of a divinity and could pronounce it was in this way able to secure a blessing. It was the use of the name of Jesus in the sacraments that made them effective, in the spirit of sorcery.

This idea came from the lowest type of religious thought, reflected in religious mysteries in the days of Jesus, and was embodied in the earliest Christianity."

543

What is taught respecting the use of oaths?

God: "Swear by my name" (Jeremiah xii, 16).

Christ: "Swear not at all" (Matthew v, 34).

544

What opposing rules of proselytism did Christ promulgate?

"He that is not with me is against me" (Luke xi, 23).

"He that is not against us is for us" (Luke ix, 50).

545

What is to befall him that hath nothing?

"Whosoever hath not, from him shall be taken away even that he hath" (Matthew xiii, 12).

Ex nihilo nihil fit.

546

What did he say would be the fate of those who took up the sword?

"They that take the sword shall perish with the sword" (Matthew xxvi, 52).

He evidently considered this commendable, for he immediately issued the following command to his disciples:

"He that hath no sword let him sell his garments and buy one" (Luke xxii, 36).

547

What did he say regarding the fear of death?

"Be not afraid of them that kill the body" (Luke xii, 4).

"After these things Jesus walked in Galilee: for he would not walk in Jewry, because the Jews sought to kill him" (John vii, 1).

548

What is to be the earthly reward of those that follow Christ?

"There is no man that hath left house, or brethren, or sisters, or father, or mother, or wife, or children, or lands, for my sake, and the gospel's, but he shall receive a hundred fold now in this time" (Mark x, 29, 30).

"Who is he that will harm you, if ye be followers of that which is good?" (1 Peter iii, 13.)

"For my yoke is easy, and my burden is light" (Matthew xi, 30).

"In the world ye shall have tribulation" (John xvi, 33).

"Ye shall be hated of all men for my name's sake" (Luke xxi, 17).

"Yea, and all that will live godly in Christ Jesus shall suffer persecution" (2 Tim. iii, 12).

"For whom the Lord loveth he chasteneth, and scourgeth every son whom he receiveth" (Hebrews xii, 6).

549

What promise did Christ make to Paul at the commencement of his ministry?

"I am with thee and no man shall set on thee to hurt thee" (Acts xviii, 10).

"Of the Jews five times received I forty stripes save one. Thrice was I beaten with rods, once was I stoned" (2 Corinthians xi, 24, 25).

550

How are Christ's true followers to be distinguished from those of the devil?

"Whosoever is born of God doth not commit sin" (1 John iii, 9).

"He that committeth sin is of the devil" (8).

Judged by this standard what is the comparative strength of these sovereigns' subjects?

"There is no man that sinneth not" (1 Kings viii, 46).

"There is not a just man upon earth" (Ecclesiastes vii, 20).

"There is none righteous, no, not one" (Romans iii, 10).

551

Great stress is placed upon the moral teachings of Jesus. What did he teach? Did he advocate industry and frugality?

"Lay not up for yourselves treasures upon earth" (Matthew vi, 19).

"Take no thought for your life what ye shall eat or what ye shall drink; nor yet for your body, what ye shall put on" (25).

"Take therefore no thought for the morrow" (34).

552

What were the early Christians?

Acts: They were Communists. "They had all things common. . . . For as many as were possessors of land or houses sold them, and brought the prices of the things that were sold, and laid them down at the apostles' feet; and distribution was made unto every man according as he had need" (iv, 32–35).

Most Christians condemn Communism; but was the Communism of nineteen hundred years ago better than the Communism of today? To condemn Communism is to condemn primitive Christianity. Yet, Christians profess to abhor the Communistic ideas of modern teachers, while they worship as a God the founder of this Communistic sect of Palestine.

553

What did he teach respecting poverty and wealth?

"Blessed be ye poor" (Luke vi, 20).

"Woe unto you that are rich" (24).

Poverty is a curse; wealth, honestly acquired and wisely used is a blessing. "The rich man's wealth is his strong city: the destruction of the poor is their poverty" (Proverbs x, 15).

554

In the parable of the Rich Man and Lazarus, what befell the representatives of vagrancy and respectability?

"The beggar died, and was carried by the angels into Abraham's bosom" (Luke xvi, 22).

"The rich man also died, . . . and in hell he lifted up his eyes" (22, 23).

> See the red flames around him twine
> Who did in gold and purple shine!
>
> While round the saint so poor below,
> Full rivers of salvation flow.
>
> Jesus, my Lord, let me appear
> The meanest of thy creatures here.

555

Why was Dives' request that his brothers be informed of their impending fate refused?

"They have Moses and the prophets; let them hear them" (Luke xvi, 29).

Moses and the prophets do not teach the doctrine of endless punishment, nor even that of a future existence, much less that the mere possession of wealth, acquired perhaps by honest industry, is a crime which can be expiated only by the sufferings of an endless hell.

Christ's Kingdom was a kingdom of vagrants and paupers. "A rich man shall hardly enter into the kingdom of heaven" (Matthew xix, 23). "It is easier for a camel to go through the eye of a needle, than for a rich man to enter the kingdom of God" (24).

556

While at the temple with his disciples what act did he commend?

Mark and Luke: That of the poor widow who threw two mites into the treasury (Mark xii, 43; Luke xxi, 3).

This widow's offering illustrates the characteristic generosity of the poor and the heartless greed of the church. This text has enabled a horde of indolent priests to prey upon widows and orphans; to filch the scanty earnings of the poor, and live like parasites upon the weak and sickly calves of humanity.

557

Did he practice the virtue of temperance?

"The Son of Man is come eating and drinking; and ye say, behold a gluttonous man and a winebibber" (Luke vii, 34).

558

What was his first miracle?

John: "There was a marriage in Cana of Galilee. . . . And both Jesus was called, and his disciples, to the marriage. And when they wanted wine, the mother of Jesus saith unto him, They have no wine. . . . And there were set there six water pots of stone, . . . containing two or three firkins apiece. Jesus saith unto them, Fill the water pots with water. And they filled them up to the brim" (ii, 1–7). This water he turned into wine.

Here is Christ supplying a party already "well drunk" with more than one hundred gallons of wine. As they were intoxicated when he performed the miracle, would it not have been better for them and better for the millions who have accepted him as a moral guide, if at the beginning of the feast he had turned the wine into water?

The morality taught by Jesus suffers in comparison with that taught by Mohammed. Mohammed prohibited the use of intoxicating drink, and the Mohammedans are a temperate people; Jesus sanctioned the use of intoxicating drink, and the Christian world abounds with drunkenness.

Referring to the miracle at Cana, Strauss says: "Not only, however, has the miracle been impeached in relation to possibility, but also in relation to utility and fitness. It has been urged both in ancient and modern times, that it was unworthy of Jesus that he should not only remain in the society of drunkards, but even further their intemperance by an exercise of his miraculous power" (*Leben Jesu,* p. 584).

559

Did he oppose slavery?

All: He did not.

"Slavery was incorporated into the civil institutions of Moses; it was recognized accordingly by Christ and his apostles."—Rev. Dr. Nathan Lord, President of Dartmouth College.

"At the time of the advent of Jesus Christ, slavery in its worst forms prevailed over the world. The Savior found it around him in Judea; the apostles met with it in Asia, Greece and Italy. How did they treat it? Not by denunciation of slave-holding as necessarily sinful."— Prof. Hodge of Princeton.

"I have no doubt if Jesus Christ were now on earth that he would, under certain circumstances, become a slaveholder."—Rev. Dr. Taylor of Yale.

Rousseau says: "Christ preaches only servitude and dependence. . . . True Christians are made to be slaves."

560

What did the apostles teach?

Peter: "Servants [slaves], be subjeet to your masters with all fear; not only to the good and gentle, but also to the froward" (1 Peter ii, 18).

Paul: "Let as many servants [slaves] as are under the yoke count their own masters worthy of all honor" (1 Timothy vi, 1). "Servants, be obedient to them that are your masters according to the flesh, with fear and trembling" (Ephesians vi, 5).

The Rev. Dr. Wilbur Fisk, president of Wesleyan University, says: "The New Testament enjoins obedience upon the slave as an obligation due to a present rightful authority."

561

Did he favor marriage?

Matthew: He advocated celibacy, and even self-mutilation as preferable to marriage (xix, 10–12).

Following this teaching of their Master, Christians, many of them, have condemned marriage. A Christian pope, Siricius, branded it as "a pollution of the flesh." St. Jerome taught that the duty of the saint was to "cut down by the axe of Virginity the wood of Marriage." Pascal says: "Marriage is the lowest and most dangerous condition of the Christian."

G. W. Foote of England says: "Jesus appears to have despised the union of the sexes, therefore marriage, and therefore the home. He taught that in Heaven, where all is perfect, there is neither marrying nor giving in marriage."

"Monks and nuns innumerable owe to this evil teaching their shriveled lives and withered hearts."—Mrs. Besant.

562

What did he encourage women to do?

Luke: To leave their husbands and homes, and follow and associate with him and his roving apostles—"Mary, called Magdalene, out of whom went seven devils, and Joanna the wife of Chuza, Herod's steward, and Susanna, and many others, which ministered unto him of their substance" (viii, 2, 3).

563

What did he say respecting children?

"Suffer little children to come unto me and forbid them not."

But it was only the children of Jews he welcomed. The afflicted child of a Gentile he spurned as a dog. When the woman of Canaan desired him to heal her daughter, he brutally replied: "It is not meet to take the children's bread and cast it to the dogs" (Matthew xv, 26). The soldiers who spit on Jesus in Pilate's hall did not do a meaner thing than Jesus did that day. And if he afterwards consented to cure the child it was not as an act of humanity to the sufferer, but as a reward for the mother's faith in him.

Concerning this brutal act of Jesus, Helen Gardener says: "Do you think that was kind? Do you think it was godlike? What would you think of a physician, if a woman came to him distressed and said, 'Doctor, come to my daughter; she is very ill. She has lost her reason, and she is all I have!' What would you think of the doctor who would not reply at all at first, and then, when she fell at his feet and worshiped him, answered that he did not spend his time doctoring dogs? Would you like him as a family physician? Do you think that, even if he were to cure the child then, he would have done a noble thing? Is it evidence of a perfect character to accompany a service with an insult? Do you think that a man who could offer such an indignity to a sorrowing mother has a perfect character, is an ideal God?"

564

He enjoined the observance of the commandment, "Honor thy father and thy mother." Did he respect it himself?

More striking examples of filial ingratitude are not to be found than are exhibited in the Gospel history of Jesus Christ. When visiting Jerusalem with his parents, he allows them to depart for home without him, thinking that he is with another part of the company; and when they return to search for him and find him, he manifests no concern for the trouble he has caused; when during his ministry his mother and brothers are announced, he receives them with a sneer; at the marriage feast, when his mother kindly speaks to him, he brutally exclaims, "Woman, what have I to to with thee?" Throughout the Four Gospels not one respectful word to that devoted mother is recorded. Even in his last hours, when the mental anguish of that mother must have equaled his own physical suffering, not one word of comfort or farewell greeting escapes from his lips; but the same studied disrespect that has characterized him all his life is exhibited here.

565

Did he not promote domestic strife?

"Suppose ye that I am come to give peace on earth? I tell you, Nay; but rather division: for from henceforth there shall be five in one house divided, three against two, and two against three. The father against the son, and the son against the father; the mother against the daughter, and the daughter against the mother; the mother-in-law against her daughter-in-law, and the daughter-in-law against her mother-in-law" (Luke xii, 51–53),

"Think not that I am come to send peace on earth: I came not to send peace, but a sword. For I am come to set a man at variance against his father, and the daughter against her mother, and the daughter-in-law against her mother-in-law" (Matthew x, 34, 35).

566

What did he require of his disciples?

"If any man come to me, and hate not his father, and mother, and wife, and children, and brethren and sisters, yea, and his own life also, he cannot be my disciple" (Luke xiv, 26).

It is scarcely possible in this age of enlightenment and unbelief to realize what sorrows and miseries these accursed teachings of Christ once caused. The eminent historian Lecky, in his *History of European Morals,* has attempted to describe some of their awful consequences.

From his pages I quote the following:

"To break by his ingratitude the heart of the mother who had borne him, to persuade the wife who adored him that it was her duty to separate from him forever, to abandon his children, uncared for and beggars, to the mercies of the world, was regarded by the true hermit as the most acceptable offering he could make to his God. His business was to save his own soul. The serenity of his devotion would be impaired by the discharge of the simplest duties to his family. Evagrius, when a hermit in the desert, received, after a long interval, letters from his father and mother. He could not bear that the equable tenor of his thought should be disturbed by the recollection of those who loved him, so he cast the letters unread into the fire. A man named Mutius, accompanied by his only child, a little boy of eight years old, abandoned his possessions and demanded admission into a monastery. The monks received him, but they proceeded to discipline his heart. 'He had already forgotten that he was rich; he must next be taught to forget that he was a father' His little child was separated from him clothed in rags, subjected to every form of gross and wanton hardship, beaten, spurned and ill-treated. Day after day the father was compelled to look upon his boy wasting away with sorrow, his once happy countenance forever stained with tears, distorted by sobs of anguish. But yet, says the admiring biographer, 'though he saw this day by day, such was his love for Christ, and for the virtue of obedience, that the father's heart was rigid and unmoved' (Vol. II, 125, 126).

"He [St. Simeon Stylites] had been passionately loved by his parents, and, if we may believe his eulogist and biographer, he began his saintly career by breaking the heart of his father, who died of grief at his flight. His mother, however, lingered on. Twenty-seven years after his disappearance, at a period when his austerities had made him famous, she heard for the first time where he was and hastened to visit him. But all her labor was in vain. No woman was admitted within the precincts of his dwelling, and he refused to permit her even to look upon his face. Her entreaties and tears were mingled with words of bitter and eloquent reproach. 'My son,' she is represented as having said 'why have you done this? I bore you in my womb, and you have wrung my soul with grief. I gave you milk from my breast, you have filled my eyes with tears. For the kisses I gave you, you have given me the anguish of a broken heart; for all that I have done and suffered for you, you have repaid me by the most cruel wrongs.' At last the saint sent a message to her to tell her that she would soon see him. Three days and three nights she had wept and entreated in vain, and now, exhausted with grief and age and privation, she sank feebly to the ground and breathed her last sigh before that inhospitable door. Then for the first time the saint, accompanied by his followers, came out. He shed some pious tears over the corpse of his murdered mother, and offered up a prayer consigning her soul to heaven" (ibid., 130).

567

Did he not indulge in vituperation and abuse?
"Ye fools and blind" (Matthew xxiii, 17).
"Woe unto you, scribes and Pharisees, hypocrites" (14).
"All that ever came before me are thieves and robbers" (John x, 8).
"Ye serpents, ye generation of vipers, how can ye escape the damnation of hell?" (Matthew xxiii, 33.)
Regarding these abusive epithets of Christ, Prof. Newman says: "The Jewish nation may well complain that they have been cruelly slandered by the gospels. The invectives have been burnt into the heart of Christendom, so that the innocent Jews, children of the dispersion, have felt in millennial misery—yes, and to this day feel—the deadly sting of these fierce aud haughty utterances" (*Jesus Christ,* p. 25).

568

Relate his treatment of the Pharisee who invited him to dine with him.
Luke: "And as he spake, a certain Pharisee besought him to dine with him; and he went in, and sat down to meat. And when the Pharisee saw it, he marveled that he had not first washed before dinner. And the Lord said unto him, now do ye Pharisees make clean the outside of the cup and the platter; but your inward part is full of ravening

and wickedness, Ye fools . . . hypocrites!" (xi, 37–44.)

Was such insolence of manners on the part of Jesus calculated to promote the interest of the cause he professed to hold so dear at heart? Supposing a Freethinker were to receive an invitation to dine with a Christian friend and were to repay the hospitality of his host with rudeness and abuse, interrupting the ceremony of "grace" with an oath or a sneer, and showering upon the head of his friend such epithets as "hypocrite" and "fool." Would such insolent behavior have a tendency to gain for him ,he world's esteem or aid the cause he represents? And are we to approve in a God conduct that we regard as detestable in a man? It may be urged that God is not subject to the rules of human conduct. Grant it; but is it necessary for him in order to exhibit his divine character to assume the manners of a brute?

569

Do the Pharisees deserve the sweeping condemnation heaped upon them by Christ and his followers?

In marked contrast to the diatribes of Jesus is the testimony of Josephus: "Now, for the Pharisees, they live meanly [plainly] and despise delicacies in diet, and they follow the conduct of reason; and what that prescribes to them as good for them, they do; and they think they ought earnestly to strive to observe reason's dictates for practice. . . . The cities give great attestations to them on account of their entire virtuous conduct, both in the actions of their lives, and their discourses also" (*Antiquities,* Book xviii, chap. i, sec. 3).

Paul, the Christian, when arraigned before Agrippa, believed that no loftier testimonial to his character could be adduced than the fact that he had been a Pharisee (Acts xxvi, 4, 5).

570

What is said in regard to his purging the temple?

John: "And the Jews' Passover was at hand, and Jesus went up to Jerusalem, and found in the temple those that sold oxen and sheep and doves, and the changers of money sitting: and when he had made a scourge of small cords, he drove them all out of the temple, and the sheep, and the oxen; and poured out the changers' money, and overthrew the tables" (ii, 13–15).

No currency but the Jewish was accepted in the temple while doves, lambs, and other animals were required for offerings. These persons performed the very necessary office of supplying the Jews with offerings and exchanging Jewish coins for the Roman money then in general circulation. What right he had to interfere with the lawful business of these men, and especially in the manner in which he did, it is difficult to understand.

571

Describe the cursing of the fig tree.

Matthew: "Now in the morning as he returned into the city, he hungered. And when he saw a fig tree in the way, he came to it, and found nothing thereon, but leaves only, and said unto it, let no fruit grow on thee henceforward for ever. And presently the fig tree withered away" (xxi, 18, 19).

Jesus cursed a living tree and it died; Mohammed blessed a dead tree and it lived. The alleged conduct of Jesus on many occasions, notably his harsh treatment of his mother, his abuse of the Pharisees, his purging the temple and his cursing the fig tree, is not the conduct of a rational being, but rather that of a madman. If these stories be historical they would indicate that he was not wholly responsible for his words and acts. Dr. Jules Soury, of the University of France, believes that he was the victim of an incurable mental disorder. In a work on morbid psychology, entitled *Studies on Jesus and The Gospels,* Dr. Soury cites a long array of seemingly indisputable facts in support of his theory. From his preface to the work, I quote the following:

"Jesus the God, gone down in his glory, like a star sunk beneath the horizon but still shedding a few faint rays on the world, threw a halo round the brow of Jesus the Prophet. In the dull glow of that twilight, in the melancholy but charming hour when everything seemed wrapped in vague, ethereal tints, Jesus appeared to Strauss and Renan such as he had shown himself to his first disciples, the Master par-excellence, a man truly divine. Then came the night; and as darkness descended on those flickering gospel beginnings there remained nought to be descried through the obscurity of dubious history, but dimly looming, the portentous outline of the gibbet and its victim.

"In the present work Jesus makes his appearance, perhaps for the first time, as a sufferer from a grave malady, the course of which we have attempted to trace.

"The nervous, or cerebral disorder, at first congestive and then inflammatory, under which he labored, was not only deep-seated and dangerous—it was incurable. Among us at the present time that affection may be seen daily making kings, millionaires, popes, prophets, saints, and even divinities of poor fellows who have lost their balance; it has produced more than one Messiah.

"If we be right in the interpretation of data which has been followed in the study of morbid psychology, Jesus, at the time of his death, was in a somewhat advanced stage of this disorder. He was, to all appearance, cut off opportunely; the gibbet saved him from actual madness.

"The diagnosis which we have ventured to draw is based on three sets of facts which are attested by the most ancient and trustworthy of the witnesses of his career.

"1. Religious excitement, then general in Palestine, drove Jesus to the wilderness, where he lived some time the life of a recluse, as those who considered themselves to have the prophetic mission often did. Carried away with the idea that he was divinely inspired to proclaim the coming of the Messiah he left his own people and his native place, and, attended by a following of fishermen and others of the same class, went about among the towns and villages of Galilee announcing the speedy approach of the Kingdom of Heaven.

"2. After having proclaimed the coming of the Messiah, like other contemporary Jewish prophets, Jesus gradually came to look upon himself as the Messiah, the Christ. He allowed himself to be called the Son of David, the Son of God, and had among his followers one, if not more, of those fanatical Sicarii, so graphically described by Josephus, who were waiting for the deliverance of Israel from the yoke of Rome. Progressive obliteration of the consciousness of his personal identity marks the interval between the somewhat vague revelation which he made to his disciples at the foot of Mount Hermon and the day when, before Caiaphas and before Pilate, he openly declared that he was the Messiah, and by that token the King of the Jews.

"3. The cursing of the fig tree whereon there were no figs, because 'the time of figs was not yet,' the violent conduct toward the dealers and changers at the temple, were manifestly foolish acts. Jesus had come to believe that everything was permitted him, that all things belonged to him, that nothing was too hard for him to do. For a long time he had given evident signs of perversion of the natural affections, especially with respect to his mother and brethren. To the fits of anger against the priests and religious ministers of his nation, to the ambitious extravagance of his words and acts, to the wild dream of his Messianic grandeur, there rapidly supervened a characteristic depression of the mental faculties and strength, a giving way of the intellectual and muscular flowers.

"Each of those periods in the career of Jesus corresponds to a certain pathological state of his nervous system.

"By reacting on the heart, the religious excitement he labored under and the attendant functional exacerbations had the immediate effect of accelerating the circulation, unduly dilating the blood vessels, and producing cerebral congestion.

"Chronic congestion of the brain, subjectively considered, is always attended in the initial stage with great increase of the moral consciousness, extraordinary activity of the imagination, often leading to hallucinations, and later on with absurdly exaggerated, frequently delirious ideas of power and greatness. That stage is also usually characterized by irritability and fits of passion.

"Objectively considered what is observable is hypertrophy of the cellules and nerve-tubes, excessive cerebral plethora and vascularity due to the great efflux of blood and superabundant nutrition of the encephalon. Inflammation of the meningeal covering, and of the brain itself, is, sooner or later, a further result of the chronic congestion. The vessels, turgid and loaded with blood, permit the transudation of the blood globules; the circulation becomes impeded, then arrested, with the result of depriving the cortical cerebral substance of arterial blood, which is its life; the histological elements undergo alteration, degenerate, become softened, and as the disorganization proceeds are finally reduced to inert detritus.

"The brain may remain capable more or less well of performing its functions when deprived to a large extent of its necessary food, but not so when the cerebral cellules are disorganized. Dementia consequently is the rational sequel of the congestive stage. To the destruction of the cortical substance supervenes partial or total loss of consciousness, according to the extent of the lesion. Such portions of the encephalon as continue capable of performing any duty being in a state of hyperaemia, there is often delirium more or less intense up to the last.

"The process of the disorder is irregular; remissions occur during which the reasoning faculties seem to be recovered. But whether the duration extends only to a few months or to several years, the increasing weakness of the patient, the intellectual and muscular decay, the cachetic state into which he falls, the lesions of other organs performing essential functions which ensue, bring life to a close, and frequently without suffering.

"This is how Jesus would have ended had he been spared the violent death of the cross."

Nearly all the religious founders have been affected to a greater or less extent, with insanity. Genius itself is closely allied to insanity—is indeed, in many cases, a form of insanity. Moreau de Tours in his *La Psychologie Morbide* (p. 234) says: "The mental disposition which causes a man to be distinguished from his fellows by the originality of his mind and conceptions, by his eccentricity, and the energy of his affective faculties, or by the transcendence of his intelligence, take their rise in the very same organic conditions which are the source of the various mental perturbations whereof insanity and idiocy are the most complete expressions." Buddha, Mohammed, and probably Jesus, united with certain strong mental and moral characteristics, a form of insanity which manifested itself in a sort of religious madness—a madness that was contagious and which has attacked and afflicted the greater portion of the human race.

572

Did he not teach the doctrine of demoniacal possession and exorcism?

Synoptics: He did.

After alluding to the prevalency of superstition among the Jews of this period, Renan says: "Jesus on this point differed in no respect from his companions. He believed in the devil, whom he regarded as a kind of evil genius, and he imagined, like all the world, that nervous maladies were produced by demons who possessed the patient and agitated him" (*Life of Jesus,* p. 59). Dr. Geikie says: "The New Testament leaves us in no doubt of the belief, on the part of Jesus and the Evangelists, in the reality of these demoniacal possessions" (*Life of Christ,* Vol. II, p. 573).

Demonology was born of ignorance and superstition. In this debasing superstition Jesus believed. It was a part of his religion, and has remained a part of Christianity; for while the more intelligent of his professed disciples have outgrown this superstition they have to the same extent outgrown Christianity. The more ignorant, the more depraved, and, at the same time, the more devout of his followers, still accept it.

Regarding this superstition, the author of *Supernatural Religion* says: "The diseases referred to by the gospels, and by the Jews of that time, to the action of devils, exist now, but they are known to proceed from purely physical causes. The same superstition and medical ignorance would enunciate the same diagnosis at the present day. The superstition and ignorance, however, have passed away, and, with them, the demoniacal theory. In that day the theory was as baseless as in this. It is obvious that, with the necessary abandonment of the theory of 'possession' and demoniacal origin of disease, the largest class of miracles recorded in the gospels is at once exploded. The asserted cause of the diseases of this class, said to have been miraculously healed, must be recognized to be a mere vulgar superstition" (p. 159).

Prof. Huxley, in one of his essays, discussing the Gadarene miracle, says: "When such a story as that about the Gadarene swine is placed before us, the importance of the decision, whether it be accepted or rejected, cannot be overestimated. If the demonological part of it is to be accepted, the authority of Jesus is unmistakably pledged to the demonological system current in Judea in the first century. The belief in devils who possess men and can be transferred from men to pigs becomes as much a part of Christian dogma as any article of the creeds."

573

What became of the swine into which Jesus ordered the devils to go?

Matthew. "And behold, the whole herd of swine ran violently down a steep place into the sea, and perished in the waters" (viii, 32).

It may be pertinent to inquire what these inoffensive animals had done that they should merit such cruelty, or what their owner had done that his property should be thus wantonly destroyed.

In his narrative of this miracle Fleetwood says: "The spectators beheld, at a distance, the torments these poor creatures suffered; with what amazing rapidity they ran to the confines of the lake, leaped from the precipices into the sea, and perished in the waters" (*Life of Christ*, p. 121).

In striking contrast to the religion of Buddha, the religion of Christ has made its adherents cruel and unmerciful. To this Christian writer the torture and destruction of these domestic animals is no more than the burning of a field of stubble. In this miracle he sees only a manifestation of love and kindness on the part of his Savior. Referring to the request of the inhabitants that he depart from their country, he says: "The stupid request of the Gadarenes was complied with by the blessed Jesus, who, entering the ship, returned to the country from whence he came, leaving them a valuable pledge of his love, and us a noble pattern of perseverance in well-doing, even when our kindnesses are condemned or requited with injuries" (ibid., p. 122).

574

What did Jesus say to the strange Samaritan woman whom he met at the well?

"Thou hast had five husbands; and he whom thou now hast is not thy husband" (John iv, 18).

"Christ here makes himself a wandering gypsy, or Bohemian fortune teller, and I much wonder that our gypsies do not account themselves the genuine disciples of Jesus, being endowed with like gifts, and exercising no worse arts than he himself practiced."—Woolston.

575

Was he not an egotist and given to vulgar boasting?

Speaking of himself he said: "Behold a greater than Solomon is here" (Matthew xii, 41, 42).

576

Did he not practice dissimulation?

John: "And Jesus lifted up his eyes, and said, Father, I thank thee that thou hast heard me. And I know that thou hearest me always, but because of the people which stand by I said it" (xi, 41, 42).

Luke: After his resurrection when he intended to stop at Emmaus with his companions, "He made as though he would have gone further" (xxiv, 28).

577

After performing one of his miraculous cures, what charge did he make to those who witnessed it?

Mark: "He charged them that they should tell no man: but the more he charged them, so much the more a great deal they published it" (vii, 36).

Did he desire them to disregard his commands? If he did, he was a hypocrite; if he did not, he was an impotent—in either case a fallible man instead of an omnipotent God.

578

On the approach of the Passover what did he say to his brethren?

"Go ye up unto this feast; I go not up yet unto this feast" (John vii, 8).

The correct reading of the last clause is, "I go not up unto the feast." The American revisers, to their credit, urged the adoption of this reading; but the Oxford revisers retained the error. In uttering these words, Jesus, if omniscient, uttered an untruth; for John says: "But when his brethren were gone up, then went he also up unto the feast, not openly, but as it were in secret" (10).

579

Why did he teach in parables?

"That seeing they may see, and not perceive; and hearing they may hear, and not understand; lest at any time they should be converted, and their sins should be forgiven them" (Mark iv, 12).

He deceived the people that he might have the pleasure of seeing them damned.

580

What immoral lesson is inculcated in the Parable of the Steward?

He commends as wise and prudent the action of the steward, who, to provide for his future welfare, causes his master's creditors to defraud him. "There was a certain rich man, which had a steward; and the same was accused unto him that he had wasted his goods. And he called him, and said unto him, How is it that I hear this of thee? give an account of thy stewardship; for thou mayest be no longer steward. Then the steward said within himself, What shall I do? for my lord taketh away from me the stewardship: I cannot dig; to beg I am ashamed. I am resolved what to do, that, when I am put out of the stewardship, they may receive me into their houses. So he called every one of his lord's debtors unto him, and said unto the first, How much owest thou unto my lord? And he said, An hundred measures of oil. And he said unto him, Take thy bill and sit down quickly, and write fifty. Then said he unto another, And how much owest thou? And he said, An hundred measures of wheat. And he said unto him, Take thy bill and write fourscore. And the lord commended the unjust steward, because he had done wisely; for the children of this world are in their generation wiser than the children of light. And I say unto you, Make to yourselves friends of the mammon of unrighteousness; that, when ye fail, they may receive you into everlasting habitations" (Luke xvi, 1–9).

581

In the parable of the Laborers what unjust doctrine is taught?

The assignment of equal rewards for unequal burdens. He justifies the dishonest bargaining of the householder who received twelve hours of labor for a penny, when he paid the same amount for one (Matthew xx, 1–16).

Regarding the parables of Jesus, W. P. Ball, an English writer, says:

"With one single exception, the parables attributed to Jesus are thoroughly religious and decidedly inferior in their moral tone, besides possessing minor faults. The God who is to be the object of our adoration and imitation is depicted to us as a judge who will grant vengeance in answer to incessant prayer, as a father who loves and honors the favorite prodigal and neglects the faithful and obedient worker, as an employer who pays no more for a life-time than for the nominal service of a death-bed repentance, as an unreasonable master who reaps where he has not sown and punishes men because he made them defective and gave them no instructions, as a harsh despot who delivers disobedient servants to tormentors and massacres those who object to his rule, as a judge who is merciful to harlots and relentless towards unbelievers, as a petulant king who drives beggars and outcasts into the heaven which is ignored by the wise and worthy, as a ruler of the universe who freely permits his enemy the devil to sow evil and then punishes his victims, as a God who plunges men in the flames of hell and calmly philosophizes over the reward of the blest who from Abraham's bosom behold the sight and are not permitted to bestow even so much as a drop of cold water to cool the parched tongues of their fellow-creatures amidst hopeless and unending agonies, in comparison with which all earthly sufferings are but momentary dreams."

582

What did he teach regarding submission to theft and robbery?

"Of him that taketh away thy goods ask them not again" (Luke vi, 30).

583

Why was the woman taken in adultery released without punishment?

John: Because those having her in custody were not without sin themselves (viii, 3–11).

The adoption of this principle would require the liberation of every criminal, because all men are fallible. If man cannot punish crime because not free from sin himself, is it just in God, the author of all sin, to punish man for his sins?

584

Whom did he pronounce blessed?

"Blessed are the poor in spirit" (Matthew v, 3),

"Is poverty of spirit a blessing? Surely not. Manliness of spirit, honesty of spirit, fulness of rightful purpose, these are virtues; but poverty of spirit is a crime."—Bradlaugh.

585

Did he teach resistance to wrong?

"Unto him that smiteth thee on the one cheek offer also the other" (Luke vi, 29).

"He who courts oppression shares the crime." Lord Amberley, referring to this teaching of Jesus, says: "A doctrine more convenient for the purposes of tyrants and malefactors of every description it would be difficult to invent" (*Analysis of Religious Belief*, p. 355).

586

He taught his hearers to return good for evil. Did he do this himself?

"I pray for them [his followers], I pray not for the world" (John xvii, 9).

"Whosoever shall deny me before men, him will I also deny before my Father" (Matthew x, 33).

587

The Golden Rule has been ascribed to Christ. Was he its author?

Five hundred years before the time of Christ Confucius taught "What you do not like when done to yourself do not to others." Centuries before the Christian era Pittacus, Thales, Sextus, Isocrates and Aristotle taught the same.

588

What maxim does Paul attribute to Jesus?

"Remember the words of the Lord Jesus, how he said, It is more blessed to give than to receive" (Acts xx, 35).

These are not "the words of the Lord Jesus," but of the Pagan Epicurus, a man whose character Christians have for centuries defamed.

Concerning the teachings of Jesus, Col. Thomas W. Higginson says: "When they tell me that Jesus taught a gospel of love, I say I believe it. Plato taught a gospel of love before him, and you deny it. If they say, Jesus taught that it is better to bear an injury than to retaliate, I say, yes, but so did Aristotle before Jesus was born. I will accept it as the statement of Jesus if you will admit that Aristotle said it too. I am willing that any man should come before us and say, Jesus taught that you must love your enemies, it is written in the Bible; but, if he will open the old manuscript of Diogenes Laertus, he may there read in texts that have never been disputed, that the Greek philosophers, half a dozen of them, said the same before Jesus was born."

Buckle says: "That the system of morals propounded in the New Testament contained no maxim which had not been previously enunciated, and that some of the most beautiful passages in the apostolic writings are quotations from Pagan authors, is well known to every scholar. . . . To assert that Christianity communicated to man moral truths previously unknown, argues on the part of the asserted either gross ignorance or wilful fraud" (*History of Civilization,* Vol. I, p. 129).

John Stuart Mill says: "It can do truth no service to blind the fact, known to all who have the most ordinary acquaintance with literary history, that a large portion of the noblest and most valuable moral teaching has been the work not only of men who did not know, but of men who knew and rejected the Christian faith" (*Liberty*).

589

We are told that Christ manifested "a strong and enduring courage which never shrank or quailed before any danger however formidable." Is this true?

It is not. When he heard that John was imprisoned, he retreated to the Sea of Galilee (Matthew iv, 12, 13); when John was beheaded, he took a ship and retired to a desert (xiv, 13); in going from Galilee to Judea, he went beyond the Jordan to avoid the Samaritans; when his brethren went up to Jerusalem he refused to accompany them for fear of the Jews (John vii, 8, 9); when the Jews took up stones to stone him he "hid himself" (viii, 59); when the Pharisees took council against him he fled (Matthew xii, 14, 16); at Gethsemane, in the agonies of fear, he prayed that the cup might pass from him; at Calvary, he frantically exclaimed, "My God, my God, why hast thou forsaken me!"

Commenting on this dying exclamation of Christ, Dr. Conway says: "That cry could never be wrung from the lips of a man who saw in his own death a prearranged plan for the world's salvation, and his own return to divine glory temporarily renounced for transient misery on earth. The fictitious theology of a thousand years shrivels beneath the awful anguish of that cry."

590

What was the character of Christ's male ancestors?

Assuming Matthew's genalogy to be correct, nearly all of those whose histories are recorded in the Old Testament were guilty of infamous crimes or gross immoralities. Abraham married his sister and seduced her handmaid; Jacob, after committing bigamy, seduced two of his house-maids; Judah committed incest with his daughter-in-law; David was a polygamist, an adulterer, a robber and a murderer; Solomon had a thousand wives and concubines; Rehoboam Abijam, Joram, Ahaziah, Jotham, Ahaz, Manasseh, Amon and Jehoiachin, are all represented as monsters of iniquity; while others are declared to have been too vile to even name in his genealogy.

591

What female ancestors are named in his genealogy?

Matthew: Thamar, Rachab, Ruth and Bathsheba.

Regarding these women the Rev. Dr. Alexander Walker says: "It is remarkable that in the genealogy of Christ, only four women have been named: Thamar who seduced the father of her late husband; Rachab, a common prostitute; Ruth, who, instead of marrying one of her cousins, went to bed with another of them; and Bathsheba, an adulteress, who espoused David, the murderer of her first husband" (*Woman,* p. 330).

Matthew Henry, a noted Christian commentator, says: "There are four women, and but four, named in this genealogy, . . . Rachab, a Canaanitess, and a harlot besides, and Ruth, the Moabitess. . . . The other two were adulteresses, Tamar and Bathsheba" (*Commentary,* Vol. V).

592

Who was his favorite female attendant?

Luke: "Mary called Magdalene, out of whom went seven devils" (viii, 2).

Referring to this woman, Dr. Farrar says: "This exorcism is not elsewhere alluded to, and it would be perfectly in accordance with the genius of Hebrew phraseology if the expression had been applied to her in consequence of a passionate nature and an abandoned life. The Talmudists have much to say respecting her—her wealth, her extreme beauty, her braided locks, her shameless profligacy, her husband Pappus, and her paramour, Pandera" (*Life of Christ,* p. 162).

In a chapter on "Sanctified Prostitution," Dr. Soury writes: "The Jewess is full of naive immodesty, her lip red with desire, her eye moist and singularly luminous in the shade. Yearning with voluptuousness, superb in her triumphs, or merely feline and caressing, she is ever the 'insatiable,' the woman 'with seven devils' of whom the scripture speaks, a kind of burning furnace in which the blond Teuton melts like wax. So far as in her lay, the Syrian woman, with her supple and nervous arms, drew into the tomb the last exhausted sons of Greece and Rome. But who can describe the grace and the soft languor of these daughters of Syria, their large black eyes, the warm bistre tints of their skin? All the poets of the decadence, Catullus, Tibullus, Propercius, have sung this wondrous being. With soft and humble voice, languid and as though crushed by some hidden ill, dragging her limbs over the tiles of a gynaecium, she might have been regarded as a stupid slave. Often, her gaze lost in long reveries, she seemed dead, save that her bosom began to swell, her eye lighted up, her breath quickened, her cheeks became covered with crimson. The reverie becoming a reality by a matchless power of invovation and desire, such is the sacred disease which, thanks to Mary Magdalene, gave birth to Christianity" (*Religion of Israel,* pp. 70, 71).

593

Who were his apostles?

"A dozen knaves, as ignorant as owls and as poor as church mice."—Voltaire.

"Palestine was one of the most backward of countries; the Galileans were the most ignorant of the inhabitants of Palestine; and the disciples might be counted among the most simple people of Galilee."—Renan.

"His followers were 'unlearned and ignorant men,' chosen from the humblest of the people."—Farrar.

594

What power is Christ said to have bestowed on Peter?

"And I will give unto thee the keys of the kingdom of heaven: and whatsoever thou shalt bind on earth shall be bound in heaven: and whatsoever thou shalt loose on earth shall be loosed in heaven" (Matthew xvi, 19).

On this remarkable bestowal of power, which has exerted such a mighty influence in the government of the church, but of which Mark, Luke and John know nothing, Greg comments as follows: "Not only do we know Peter's utter unfitness to be the depositary of such a fearful power, from his impetuosity and instability of character, and Christ's thorough perception of this unfitness, but we find immediately after it is said to have been conferred upon him, his Lord addresses him indignantly by the epithet of Satan, and rebukes him for his presumption and unspirituality; and shortly afterwards this very man thrice denied his master. Can any one maintain it to be conceivable that Jesus should have conferred the awful power of deciding the salvation or damnation of his fellow-men upon one so frail, so faulty, and so fallible? Does any one believe that he did?" (*Creed of Christendom,* p. 189).

595

When Peter discovered that Jesus was the Christ what did he do?

Mark: "And Peter took him [Christ] and began to rebuke him" (viii, 32).

What did Jesus do in turn?

Mark: "He rebuked Peter, saying, Get thee behind me Satan" (33).

What a spectacle! The incarnate God of the universe and his vicegerent on earth indulging in a petty quarrel!

596

Give an account of Peter's denial of his Master.

Matthew: "Now when Peter sat without in the palace: and a damsel came unto him saying, Thou also wast with Jesus of Galilee. But he denied before them all, saying, I know not what thou sayest. And when he was gone out into the porch, another maid saw him, and said unto them that were there, This fellow was also with Jesus of Nazareth. And again he denied with an oath, I do not know the man. And after a while came up to him they that stood by, and said to Peter, Surely thou also art one of them; for thy speech betrayeth thee. Then began he to curse and to swear, saying, I know not the man" (xxvi, 69-74).

597

What did Peter say to Jesus in regard to compensation for his services?

"Behold, we have forsaken all, and followed thee; what shall we have therefore?" (Matthew xix, 27).

What request was made by James and John?

Mark: "They said unto him, Grant unto us that we may sit, one on thy right hand, and the other on thy left hand, in thy glory" (x, 37).

This shows that self-aggrandisement inspired the actions of his followers then as it does today.

598

What is said of John in the Gospel of John?

"There was leaning on Jesus' bosom one of his disciples whom he loved" (xiii, 23).

"The disciple standing by whom he [Jesus] loved" (xix, 26).

"The other disciple whom Jesus loved" (xx, 2).

"Then Peter, turning about, seeth the disciple whom Jesus loved following; which also leaned on his breast at supper. . . . This is the disciple which testifieth of these things, and wrote these things" (xxi, 20, 24).

If the Apostle John wrote this Gospel, as claimed by Christians and as declared in the Gospel, he was a vulgar egotist.

599

What is said regarding the conduct of his Apostles on the evening preceding the crucifixion?

Luke: "And there was also a strife among them, which of them should be accounted the greatest" (xxii, 24).

This was immediately after he had announced his speedy betrayal and death and when his disciples, if sincere, must have manifested the deepest sadness and humility. If the Evangelist is not a base calumniator the Apostles were a set of heartless knaves.

600

When the Jews came to arrest Jesus what did the disciples do?

Matthew: "Then all the disciples forsook him, and fled" (xxvi, 56).

Mark: "And they all forsook him, and fled" (xiv, 50).

Justin says: "All his friends [the Apostles] stood aloof from him, having denied him" (*Apology,* i, 50).

One scarcely knows which to detest the more, the treachery of Judas in betraying his Master, or the imbecility and cowardice of the other apostles who took no measures to prevent it and who forsook him in the hour of danger.

601

What became of the Twelve Apostles?

The New Testament, a portion of which is admitted to have been written as late as the latter part of the first century and nearly all of which was really written in the second century, is silent regarding them. Christian martyrology records their fates as follows:

St. Peter was crucified, at his own request head downward, and buried in the Vatican at Rome.

St. Andrew, after having been scourged seven times upon his naked body, was crucified by the proconsul of Achaia.

St. James was beheaded by Herod Antipas in Palestine.

St. John was "thrown into a cauldron of boiling oil" by Domitian, but God "delivered him."

St. Philip was scourged and crucified or hanged by the magistrates of Hierapolis.

St. Bartholomew was put to death by a Roman governor in Armenia.

St. Matthew suffered martyrdom at Naddabar in Ethiopia.

St. Thomas was shot to death with arrows by the Brahmans in India.

St. James the Less was thrown from the pinnacle of the temple at Jerusalem and dispatched with a club where he fell.

St. Simon was "crucified and buried" in Britain.

St. Jude was "cruelly put to death" by the Magi of Persia.

St. Matthias, the successor of Judas Iscariot, if Christian tradition is to be credited, was put to death three times, crucified, stoned, and beheaded.

Nothing can be more incredible than these so-called traditions regarding the martyrdom of the Twelve Apostles, the most of them occurring in an empire where all religious sects enjoyed as perfect religious freedom as the different sects do in America today. Whatever opinion may be entertained respecting the existence of Jesus, the Twelve Apostles belong to the realm of mythology, and their alleged martyrdoms are pure inventions. Had these men really existed Christian history at least would contain some reliable notice of them, yet all the stories relating to them, like the story of Peter at Rome, and John at Ephesus, are self-evident fictions. In the significant words of the eminent Dutch theologians, Dr. Kuenen, Dr. Oort and Dr. Hooykaas, "All the Apostles disappear without a trace."

602

What are Paul's teachings regarding woman and marriage?

"It is good for a man not to touch a woman" (1 Corinthians vii, 1).

"I say therefore to the unmarried and widows, It is good for them if they abide even as I. But if they cannot contain, let them marry; for it is better to marry than to burn" (8, 9).

"Art thou loose from a wife? seek not a wife" (27).

"He that is unmarried careth for the things that belong to the Lord, how he may please the Lord; but he that is married careth for the things that are of the world, how he may please his wife. There is difference also between a wife and a virgin. The unmarried woman careth for the things of the Lord, that she may be holy in body and spirit; but she that is married careth for the things of the world, how she may please her husband" (32–34).

"So then he that giveth her in marriage doeth well; but he that giveth not in marriage doeth better" (38).

"This coarse and insulting way of regarding women, as though they existed merely to be the safety-valves of men's passions, and that the best men were above the temptation of loving them, has been the source of unnumbered evils."—Annie Besant.

"Wives, submit yourselves to your own husbands" (Colossians iii, 18).

"As the church is subject unto Christ so let the wives be to their own husbands in everything" (Ephesians v, 24).

"Let your women keep silence in the churches, for it is not permitted unto them to speak, but they are commanded to be under obedience, as also saith the law. And if they will learn anything, let them ask their husbands at home; for it is a shame for a woman to speak in the church" (1 Corinthians xiv, 34, 35).

"Let women learn in silence with all subjection" (1 Timothy ii, 11).

"That she [woman] does not crouch today where St. Paul tried to bind her, she owes to the men who are grand and brave enough to ignore St. Paul, and rise superior to his God."—Helen Gardener.

603

Did Paul encourage learning?

"The wisdom of this world is foolishness with God" (1 Corinthians iii, 19).

"Knowledge puffeth up" (viii, 1).

"If any man be ignorant let him be ignorant" (xiv, 38).

"Beware lest any man spoil you through philosophy" (Colossians ii, 8).

"The clergy, with a few honorable exceptions, have in all modern countries been the avowed enemies of the diffusion of knowledge, the danger of which to their own profession they, by a certain instinct, seem always to have perceived."—Buckle.

"We know the clerical party; it is an old party. This it is which has found for the truth those two marvelous supporters, ignorance and error. This it is which forbids to science and genius the going beyond the Missal and which wishes to cloister thought in dogmas. Every step which the intelligence of Europe has taken has been in spite of it. Its history is written in the history of human progress, but it is written on the back of the leaf. It is opposed to it all. This it is which caused

Prinelli to be scourged for having said that the stars would not fall. This it is which put Campanella seven times to torture for saying that the number of worlds was infinite and for having caught a glimpse of the secret of creation. This it is which persecuted Harvey for having proved the circulation of the blood. In the name of Jesus it shut up Galileo. In the name of St. Paul it imprisoned Christopher Columbus. To discover a law of the heavens was an impiety, to find a world was a heresy. This it is which anathematized Pascal in the name of religion, Montaigne in the name of morality, Moliere in the name of both morality and religion. There is not a poet, not an author, not a thinker, not a philosopher, that you accept. All that has been written, found, dreamed, deduced, inspired, imagined, invented by genius, the treasures of civilization, the venerable inheritance of generations, you reject."—Victor Hugo.

"There is in every village a lighted torch, the schoolmaster; and a mouth to blow it out, the parson."—ibid.

604

What admissions are made by Paul regarding his want of candor and honesty?

"Being crafty, I caught you with guile" (2 Corinthians xii, 16).

"Unto the Jews I became as a Jew, that I might gain the Jews" (1 Corinthians ix, 20).

"I am made all things to all men" (22).

"For if the truth of God hath more abounded through my lie unto his glory, why yet am I also judged as a sinner?" (Romans iii, 7.)

"I robbed other churches, taking wages of them, to do your service" (2 Corinthians xi, 8).

605

What is said of the persecutions of Paul?

"And Saul, yet breathing out threatenings and slaughter against the disciples of the Lord, went unto the high priest, and desired of him letters to Damascus to the synagogues, that if he fouud any of this way, whether they were men or women he might bring them bound unto Jerusalem" (Acts ix, 1, 2).

This was Paul the Jew.

"But there be some that trouble you, and would pervert the gospel of Christ. . . . If any man preach any other gospel than that ye have received, let him be accursed" (Galatians i, 7, 9).

"I would they were even cut off which trouble you" (v, 12).

This was Paul the Christian. The leopard changed his name but did not change his spots.

The alleged cause of Paul's sudden conversion and the transference of his hatred from Christianity to Judaism may well be questioned. The story of the apparition will not account for it. A genuine change of belief is not usually effected suddenly. Men sometimes change their religion for gain or revenge. It has been charged that Paul twice changed his, the first time for the hope of gain, the second from a desire for revenge. The Ebionites, one of the earliest of the Christian sects, claimed that Paul was originally a Gentile, that becoming infatuated with the daughter of the high priest he became a convert to Judaism for the purpose of winning her for a wife, but being rejected, he renounced the Jewish faith and became a vehement opponent of the law, the Sabbath, and circumcision (*Epiphanius Against Heresies,* chapter xxx, sec. 16).

606

What was Christ's final command to his disciples?

"Love one another" (John xiii, 34).

Christian writers prate about brotherly love, and yet from the very beginning the church of Christ has been filled with dissensions. Christ himself quarreled with his apostles. Paul opposed the teachings of James (Galatians ii, 16–21); James condemned the teachings of Paul (ii, 20). Paul proclaimed himself the divinely appointed apostle to the Gentiles. "The gospel of the uncircumcision was committed unto me" (Galatians ii, 7). Peter contended that the mission had been assigned to him: "And when there had been much disputing, Peter rose up, and said unto them, Men and brethren, ye know how that a good while ago God made choice among us, that the Gentiles by my mouth should hear the word of the gospel" (Acts xv, 7).

Paul declared Peter to be a dissembler. "But when Peter was come to Antioch, I withstood him face to face, because he was to be blamed. For before that certain came from James, he did eat with Gentiles; but when they were come, he withdrew and separated himself, fearing them which were of the circumcision. And the other Jews dissembled likewise with him" (Galatians ii, 11–13).

John denounced Paul as a liar. "Thou hast tried them which say they are apostles, and are not, and hast found them liars" (Revelation ii, 2).

From these seeds of dissension death has reaped a bloody harvest. Dr. Talmage says: "A red line runs through church history for nearly nineteen hundred years—a line of blood; not by hundreds, but millions we count the slain."

Lord Byron says, "I am no Platonist; I am nothing at all. But I would sooner be a Paulician, Manichean, Spinozist, Gentile, Pyrrhonian, Zoroastrian, than one of the seventy-two villainous sects who are tearing each other to pieces for the love of the Lord and hatred of each other."

607

Quote Paul's characterization of Christians.

"Not many wise . . . not many noble are called" (1 Corinthians i, 26).

"Base things of the world, and things which are despised, hath God chosen" (28).

"We are made as the filth of the world, and are the offscouring of all things" (iv, 13).

"We are fools for Christ's sake" (10).

608

What did Christ say respecting the intellectual character of his converts?

"I thank thee, O Father, Lord of heaven and earth, because thou hast hid these things from the wise and prudent, and hast revealed them unto babes" (Matthew xi, 25; Luke x, 21).

Commenting on this expression of thanks, Celsus, who lived at the time the Four Gospels made their appearance, says: "This is one of their [the Christians'] rules. Let no man that is learned, wise, or prudent come among us: but if they be unlearned, or a child, or an idiot, let him freely come. So they openly declare that none but the ignorant, and those devoid of understanding, slaves, women, and children, are fit disciples for the God they worship."

Concerning the Christian teachers of that age Celsus writes as follows: "You may see weavers, tailors, fullers, and the most illiterate of rustic fellows, who dare not speak a word before wise men, when they can get a company of children and silly women together, set up to teach strange paradoxes among them."

609

Whom did Christ declare to be among the first to enter the Kingdom of Heaven?

Harlots and thieves.

"The harlots go into the Kingdom of God before you" (Matthew xxi, 43).

"Today shalt thou [the thief] be with me in paradise" (Luke xxiii, 43).

610

What promise did he make to his followers?

"In my Father's house are many mansions. . . . I go to prepare a place for you. And if I go and prepare a place for you, I will come again, and receive you unto myself" (John xiv, 2, 3).

"Christians believe themselves to be the aristocracy of heaven upon earth, they are admitted to the spiritual court, while millions of men in foreign lands have never been presented. They bow their knees and say they are 'miserable sinners,' and their hearts rankle with abominable pride. Poor infatuated fools! Their servility is real and their insolence is real but their king is a phantom and their palace is a dream."— Winwood Reade.

The Christ is a myth. The Holy Ghost Priestcraft overshadowed the harlot Superstition; this Christ was born; and the Joseph of humanity, beguiled by the Gabriel of credulity, was induced to support the family. But the soldiers of Reason have crucified the illegitimate impostor; he is dead; and the ignorant disciples and hysterical women who still linger about the cross should take his body down and bury it.

9

The Christ a Myth

The conceptions regarding the nature and character of Christ, and the value of the Christian Scriptures as historical evidence, are many, chief of which are the following:

1. Orthodox Christians believe that Christ is a historical character, supernatural and divine; and that the New Testament narratives, which purport to give a record of his life and teachings, contain nothing but infallible truth.

2. Conservative Rationalists, like Renan, and the Unitarians, believe that Jesus of Nazareth is a historical character and that these narratives, eliminating the supernatural elements, which they regard as myths, give a fairly authentic account of his life.

3. Many radical Freethinkers believe that Christ is a myth, of which Jesus of Nazareth is the basis, but that these narratives are so legendary and contradictory as to be almost if not wholly, unworthy of credit.

4. Other Freethinkers believe that Jesus Christ is a pure myth—that he never had an existence, except as a Messianic idea, or an imaginary solar deity.

The first of these conceptions must be rejected because the existence of such a being is impossible, and because the Bible narratives which support it are incredible. The second cannot be accepted because, outside of these incredible narratives, there is no evidence to confirm it. One of the two last is the only true and rational conception of the Christ.

Jesus Christ is a myth. But what do we understand by the term myth? Falsehood, fable, and myth, are usually considered synonymous terms. But a falsehood, a fable, and a myth, while they may all be fictions and equally untrue, are not the same. A falsehood is the expression of an untruth intended to deceive. A fable is an avowed or implied fiction usually intended to instruct or entertain. A myth is a falsehood, a fable, or an erroneous opinion, which eventually becomes an established belief. While a falsehood and a fable are intentional and immediate expressions of fiction, a myth is, in most cases, an unconscious and gradual development of one.

Myths are of three kinds: Historical, Philosophical, and Poetical.

A Historical myth according to Strauss, and to some extent I follow his language, is a real event colored by the light of antiquity, which confounded the human and divine, the natural and the supernattiral. The event may be but slightly colored and the narrative essentially true, or it may be distorted and numberless legends attached until but a small residuum of truth remains and the narrative is essentially false. A large portion of ancient history, including the Biblical narratives, is historical myth. The earliest records of all nations and of all religions are more or less mythical. "Nothing great has been established," says Renan, "which does not rest on a legend. The only culprit in such cases is the humanity which is willing to be deceived."

A Philosophical myth is an idea clothed in the caress of historical narrative. When a mere idea is personified and presented in the form of a man or a god it is called a pure myth. Many of the gods and heroes of antiquity are pure myths. John Fiske refers to a myth as "a piece of unscientific philosophizing," and this is a fairly good definition of the philosopitical myth.

A Poetical myth is a blending of the historical and philosophical, embellished by the creations of the imagination. The poems of Homer and Hesiod, which were the religious text books of the ancient Creeks, and the poetical writings of the Bible, which helped to form and foster the Semitic faiths of Judaism, Christianity, and Mohammedanism, belong to this class.

It is often difficult, if not impossible, to distinguish a historical from a philosophical myth. Hence the non-agreement of Freethinkers in regard to the nature of the Christ myth. Is Christ a historical or a philosophical myth? Does an analysis of his alleged history disclose the deification of a man, or merely the personification of an idea?

The following hypothesis, written by Mrs. Besant, of England, is, to a considerable extent, an epitome of the views of Strauss, who, in his masterly "Leben Jesu," adopts the historical myth:

"The mythic theory accepts an historical groundwork for many of the stories about Jesus, but it does not seek to explain the miraculous by attenuating it into the natural. . . . It attributes the incredible portions of the history to the Messianic theories current among the Jews. The Messiah would do this and that; Jesus was the Messiah; therefore, Jesus did this and that—such, argue the supporters of the mythical theory, was the method in which the mythus was developed. . . . Thus, Jesus is descended from David, because the Messiah was to come of David's lineage; his birth is announced by an angelic visitant, because the birth of the Messiah must not be less honored than that of Isaac or of Samson; he is born of a virgin, because God says of the Messiah, 'this day have I begotten thee,' implying the direct paternity of God, and because the prophecy in Is. vii, 14, was applied to the Messiah by the later Jews; born at Bethlehem, because there the Messiah was to be born (Micah v, 2); announced to shepherds, because Moses was visited among the flocks, and David taken from the sheepfolds at Bethlehem; heralded by a star, because a star should arise out of Jacob (Num. xxiv, 17), and 'the Gentiles shall come to thy light' (Is. lx, 3); worshiped by Magi, because the star was seen by Balaam, the magus, and astrologers would be those who would most notice a star; presented with gifts by these Eastern sages, because kings of Arabia and Saba shall offer gifts (Ps. lxxii, 10); saved from the destruction of the infants by a jealous king, because Moses, one of the great types of the Messiah, was so saved; flying into Egypt and thence returning, because Israel, again a type of the Messiah, so fled and returned, and 'out of Egypt have I called my son' (Hos. xi, 1); at twelve years of age found in the temple, because the duties of the law devolved on the Jewish boy at that age, and where should the Messiah then be found save in his Father's temple? recognized at his baptism, by a divine voice, to fulfil Is. xlii, 1; hovered over by a dove, because the brooding spirit (Gen. i, 2) was regarded as dove-like, and the spirit was to be especially poured on the Messiah (Is. xlii, 1); tempted by the devil to test him because God tested his greatest servants, and would surely test the Messiah; fasting forty days in the wilderness, because the types of the Messiah—Moses and Elijah—thus fasted in the desert; healing all manner of disease, because Messiah was to heal (Is. xxxv, 5–6); preaching, because Messiah was to preach (Is. lxi, 1–2); crucified, because the hands and feet of Messiah were to be pierced (Ps. xxii, 16); mocked, because Messiah was to be mocked (Ib. 6–8); his garments divided, because thus it was spoken of Messiah (Ib. 18); silent before his judges, because Messiah was not to open his mouth (Is. liii, 7); buried by the rich, because Messiah was thus to find his grave (Ib. 9); rising again, because Messiah could not be left in hell (Ps. xvi, 10); sitting at God's right hand, because there Messiah was to sit as king (Ps. cx, 1). Thus the form of the Messiah was cast, and all that had to be done was to pour in the human metal; those who alleged that the Messiah had come in the person of Jesus of Nazareth, adapted his story to the story of the Messiah, pouring the history of Jesus into the mould already made for the Messiah, and thus the mythus was transformed into a history."

The foregoing theory, with various modifications, is accepted by a majority of Freethinkers at the present time.

The hypothesis that Christ is a philosophical myth, based, like the preceding one, upon the Messianic idea, is thus presented by T. B. Wakeman:

"Never was there an example of a word becoming a believed person, under this law of materialization, more plainly and evolutionally than the 'Messiah' and 'Son of Man' of the Hebrew prophecies. . . . The Christ, 'Jesus,' was no man, for the reason that he was prophesied and visioned into this world and life to do a work that it would be utterly absurd to suppose a man could ever do. The Romans had killed, and could easily kill, every man who had tried to resist their oppression. Now the God Yahweh by his 'eternally begotten son,' spiritized as the 'Son of Man,' that is the 'Soul of the State,' as Shakespeare makes Ulysses say it, must, in order to be of any avail appear with supernatural powers. He was the personified people, Israel; he had been crucified alive, in their subjection and massacre even to the death and Hades.

But by supernatural power he, the Israel, would rise again and bring the final judgment backed by the infinite power of the nation's Father, Yahweh. It was only a Spirit-God who could do this—nothing less could be originated, or thought of, or provided, for such a superhuman purpose. A person, a man, a reformer, a weak edition of Socrates, or Savonarola or Bruno! How absurd! The human heart in its despair by its imagination, brought a God into the world to do a God's work. 'No man,' said Napoleon; 'nor a God,' says Science, except the idea. Such it was that finally united the millions of Asia, Africa, Europe, and America, in a dream so intoxicating that it dares not to be awakened though the dawn of Science is here."

Mr. Wakeman argues that the silence of history for one hundred years after the alleged appearance of Christ can be explained only upon this hypothesis of an ideal Christ. To this the advocate of the historical mythus may, I think, very properly reply: History, for the most part, takes cognizance only of noted men and important events; and while this silence precludes the existence of the supernatural Christ of Christians, and even that of the human Jesus of Renan, it does not necessarily preclude the existence of an obscure religious teacher and an insignificant sect which subsequently, by a chain of fortuitous circumstances, became the mightiest among the religions of the world.

Again, this hypothesis presupposes a considerable degree of intellectuality on the part of those who evolved this ideal Christ, while tradition represents the founders of the Christian religion as grossly ignorant. Had this Christ originally sprung from the Hellenistic Jews of intellectual Alexandria instead of from the Jewish dregs of illiterate Galilee, Mr Wakeman's theory would appeal with surprising force. Still it must be admitted that some of the earliest Christian sects denied the material existence of Christ.

Another philosophical hypothesis, the astronomical, which regards Christ as a solar myth, is advanced by Volney.

"These mythological traditions recounted that, 'in the beginning, a woman and a man had, by their fall, introduced into the world sin and misery.'

"By this was denoted the astronomical fact that the celestial virgin and the herdsman (Bootes), by setting heliacally at the autumnal equinox, delivered the world to the wintry constellations, and seemed, on falling below the horizon, to introduce into the world the genius of evil (Ahrimanes), represented by the constellation of the serpent.

"These traditions related that the woman had decoyed and seduced the man.

"And, in fact, the virgin setting first seems to draw the herdsman after her.

"That the woman tempted him by offering him fruit fair to the sight, and good to eat, which gave the knowledge of good and evil.

"And, in fact, the virgin holds in her hand a branch of fruit which she seems to offer to the herdsman; and the branch, emblem of autumn, placed in the picture of Mithra between winter and summer seems to open the door and give knowledge, the key to good and evil.

"That this couple had been driven from the celestial garden, and that a cherub with a flaming sword had been placed at the gate to guard it.

"And, in fact, when the virgin and the herdsman fall beneath the western horizon, Perseus rises on the other side; and this genius, with a sword in his hand, seems to drive them from the summer heaven, the garden and dominion of fruits and flowers.

"That of the virgin should be born, spring up, an offspring, a child, who should bruise the head of the serpent, and deliver the world from sin.

"This denotes the sun, which at the moment of the winter solstice, precisely when the Persian magi drew the horoscope of the new year, was placed on the bosom of the virgin, rising heliacally in the eastern horizon. On this account he was figured in their astrological pictures under the form of a child suckled by a chaste virgin, and became afterward, at the vernal equinox, the ram, or lamb, triumphant over the constellation of the serpent, which disappeared from the skies.

"That, in his infancy, the restorer of divine and celestial nature would live abased, humble, obscure and indigent.

"And this, because the winter sun is abased below the horizon and that this first period of his four ages or seasons is a time of obscurity, scarcity, fasting and want.

"That being put to death by the wicked, he had risen gloriously that he had reascended from hell to heaven, where he would reign forever.

"This is a sketch of the life of the sun, who, finishing his career at the winter solstice, when Typhon and the rebel angels gain the dominion, seems to be put to death by them; but who soon after is born again, and rises into the vault of heaven, where he reigns."

Count Volney's portraiture of the second member of the Christian godhead is, for the most part, accurate. Numerous other analogies between him and the ancient sun gods might be named.

It is the belief of many, however, that these solar attributes of Christ are later accretions borrowed by the Roman Catholic church from the pagan religions which it supplanted.

While all Freethinkers are agreed that the Christ of the New Testament is a myth they are not, as we have seen, and perhaps never will be, fully agreed as to the nature of this myth. Some believe that he is a historical myth; others that he is a pure myth. Some believe that Jesus, a real person, was the germ of this Christ whom subsequent generations gradually evolved; others contend that the man Jesus, as well as the Christ, is wholly a creation of the human imagination. After carefully weighing the evidence and arguments in support of each hypothesis the writer, while refraining from expressing a dogmatic affirmation regarding either, is compelled to accept the former as the more probable.

10

Sources of the Christ Myth—
Ancient Religions

Christ and the religion he is said to have founded are composite products, made up, to a great extent, of the attributes, the doctrines, and the customs of the gods and the religions which preceded them and existed around them. The Christian believes that Christ is coexistent with his father, Jehovah—that he has existed from the foundations of the world. This is in a measure true. The years that have elapsed since his alleged incarnation are few compared with the years of his gestation in the intellectual womb of humanity.

To understand the origin and nature of Christ and Christianity it is necessary to know something of the religious systems and doctrines from which they were evolved. The following, some in a large and others in but a small degree, contributed to mold this supposed divine incarnation and inspire this supposed revelation: Nature or Sex Worship. Solar Worship. Astral Worship. Worship of the Elements and Forces of Nature. Worship of Animals and Plants. Fetichism. Polytheism. Monotheism. The Mediatorial Idea. The Messianic Idea. The Logos. The Perfect Man.

Nature or Sex Worship

The deification and worship of the procreative organs and the generative principles of life is one of the oldest and one of the most universal of religions. It has been called the foundation of all religions. In some nations the worship of the male energy, Phallic worship, predominated; in others the worship of the female energy, Yoni worship, prevailed. But in all both elements were recognized. Mrs. Besant says: "Womanhood has been worshiped in all ages of the world, and maternity has been deified by all creeds: from the savage who bowed before the female symbol of motherhood, to the philosophic Comtist who adores woman 'in the past, the present, and the future,' as mother, wife, and daughter, the worship of the female element in nature has run side by side with that of the male; the worship is one and the same in all religions, and runs in an unbroken thread from the barbarous ages to the present time."

Among the life generating gods may be named Vishnu, Osiris, Zeus, Priapus, Adonis, Bacchus, Saturn, Apollo, Baal, Moloch, and Jehovah. Among the receptive life producing goddesses were Isis, Rhea, Ceres, Venus, Istar, Astarte, Aschera, Devaki, Eve, and Mary. Where the worship of the female element largely prevailed the Virgin and Child was a favorite deity. Isis and Hortrs, Rhea and Quirinus, Leto and Apollo, Devaki and Krishna, Mary and Christ, all had their inception in the sex worship of primitive man.

The symbol of Phallic worship, the cross, has become the emblem of Christianity. I quote again from our English authoress: "We find the cross in India, Egypt, Tibet, Japan, always as the sign of life-giving power; it was worn as an amulet by girls and women, and seems to have been specially worn by the women attached to the temples [sacred prostitutes], as a symhol of what was, to them, a religious calling. The cross is, in fact, nothing but the refined phallus, and in the Christian religion is a significant emblem of its pagan origin; it was adored, carved in temples, and worn as a sacred emblem by sun and nature worshipers, long before there were any Christians to adore, carve, and wear it. The crowd kneeling before the cross in Roman Catholic and in High Anglican churches is a simple reproduction of the crowd who knelt before it in the temples of ancient days, and the girls who wear it amongst ourselves are—in the most innocent unconsciousness of its real significance—exactly copying the Indian and Egyptian women of an elder time."

The *American Cyclopedia* says: "The crux ansata, so common on Egyptian monuments, symbolizes the union of the active and passive principles of nature. In the Etruscan tombs have been found crosses of four phalli."

Regarding this subject, McClintock and Strong's *Cyclopeclia of Biblical, Theological and Ecclesiastical Literature,* a standard orthodox Christian authority, says: "The sign of the cross is found as a holy symbol among several ancient nations. . . . Sometimes it is the phallus" (Art. "Cross"). The same authority says that the Tau or sign of life (one form of the Phallic cross) "was adopted by some of the early Christians in lieu of the cross . . . Christian inscriptions at the great oasis are headed by this symbol; it has been found on Christian monuments at Rome" (Art. "Egypt").

Dr. Thomas Inman, of England, one of the foremost authorities on ancient symbolism, says: "It has been reserved for Christian art to crowd our churches with the emblems of Bel and Astarte, Baalim and Ashtoreth, linga and yoni, and to elevate the phallus to the position of the supreme deity" (*Ancient Pagan and Modern Christian Symbolism,* p. 16).

Describing the chasuble, worn by Christian priests, Dr. Inman says: "Its form is that of the vesica piscis, one of the most common emblems of the yoni. It is adorned by the Triad. When worn by the priest, he forms the male element, and with the chasuble completes the sacred four. When worshiping the ancient goddesses, whom Mary has displaced, the officiating ministers clothed themselves in feminine attire. Hence the rise of the chemise, etc. Even the tonsured head, adopted from the priests of the Egyptian Isis, represents 'l'anneau'; so that on head, shoulders, breast and body, we may see on Christian priests the relics of the worship of Venus, and the adoration of woman! How horrible all this would sound if, instead of using veiled language, we had employed vulgar words. The idea of a man adorning himself, woven ministering before God and the people, with the effigies of those parts which nature as well as civilization teaches us to conceal, would be simply disgusting, but when all is said to be mysterious and connected with hidden signification, almost everybody tolerates and many eulogize or admire it!" (ibid., p. 104).

Westropp and Wake, in their *Ancient Symbol Worship,* state that Judaism and Christianity have been largely derived from Phallic worship. Westropp says: "Circumcision was in its inception a purely Phallic ordinance." Our Christian marriage ceremonies, he says, are relics of this worship. Wake says: "In the recognition of God as the universal father, the great Parent of mankind, there is a development of the fundamental idea of Phallism. In the position assigned to Mary as the mother of God the paramount principle of the primitive belief is again predominant. The nimbus, the aureole, the cross, the fish, and even the spires of churches, are symbols retained from the old Phallic worship."

Dr. Alexander Wilder says: "There is not a fast or festival, procession or sacrament, social custom or religious symbol, existing at the present day which has not been taken bodily from Phallism, or from some successive system of Paganism."

Aschera, the voluptuous goddess of fertility, was a Hebrew goddess and was worshiped, along with Jehovah, in the temple itself at Jerusalem. Jules Soury, of France, in his *Religion of Israel* (p. 68), says: "Under the kings of Judah and Israel, the symbol of Aschera [the phallus] became an object of general piety which was found in every house. Thus in the provinces of France, we still find gigantic crosses on the high roads, on the crossways of the woods which serve as resting places at the Fete Dieu, while, under the porches of churches, vendors of religious toys still sell little Christs in wood or metal for a few half-pence. The rich women of Israel, the bourgeoises of Jerusalem, wore the symbols of Aschera in gold and silver, a sort of medals of the Virgin of the time, which were at once jewels and objects of devotion." Dulaure, another French author, tells us that the worship of Priapus, the god of procreation, under the name of St. Fontin, with rites of the most indelicate character, prevailed in the Catholic church in several provinces of France and Italy up to the middle of the eighteenth century, or later.

The sex worship of the Semitic tribes of Western Asia had its origin, it is believed, in India, where, under the name of Sakti worship, it prevails today, three-fourth of the Hindoos, it is claimed, belonging to this sect. The worship is thus described by the *Encyclopedia Britan-*

nica's chief authority on the subject, Prof. H. H. Wilson: "The ceremonies are mostly gone through in a mixed society, the Sakti being personified by a naked female, to whom meat and wine are offered and then distributed amongst the company. These eat and drink alternately with gesticulations and mantras—and when the religious part of the business is over, the males and females rush together and indulge in a wild orgy."

The foregoing is almost an exact description of the Agapae, or Love Feasts, as they were observed for a time in the early Christian church.

Associated with the worship of Aschera and other goddesses of this character was what is known as sacred prostitution. Thousands of women, the fairest and best lured of their race, and also men (sodomites), prostituted themselves for the support of their religion. John Clark Ridpath, in his *History of the World*, dwells upon this institution. It was practiced for centuries among the Hebrews, constituting a part of the temple worship, the Jewish kings, with the exception of a few, like Hezekiah and Josiah, sanctioning it. Solomon's temple was largely a Pagan temple. Before it stood two Phallic pillars, while its doors were ornamented with symbols of Phallic and Solar worship. Solomon worshiped, in addition to other Pagan deities, Astarte (Ashtoreth), the Sidonian Aschera (1 Kings, xi, 5, 7). The pietistic writers of the Bible condemn it, but in spite of a few spasmodic efforts to suppress the worship, it continued to flourish until long after the Captivity. From Soury's account of the sanctified prostitution of Israel I quote the following: "The tents of the sacred prostitutes were generally erected on the 'high places,' where sacrifices were offered, beside the tablet of Baal or Iahveh [Jehovah] and the symhol of Aschera (Isaiah lvii, 7, et seq.; Ezekiel xxiii, 14; Hosea iv, 17). These tents were woven and ornamented with figures by the priestesses of Aschera. Robed in splendid garments, their tresses dripping with perfumes, their cheeks painted with vermilion, their eyes lilack-circled with antimony their eyelashes lengthened with a compound of gums, musk and ebony, the priestesses awaited the worshipers of the goddess within these tents (Numbers xxv, 8) on spacious beds (Isaiah lvii, 8); they fixed their own price and conditions, and poured the money into the treasury of the temple" (*Religion of Israel*, p. 71). After describing the temple of Zarpanit, which was furnished with cells for the use of the Babylonian women, Dr.

Soury says: "Cells of the same kind, serving the same purpose, existed at Jerusalem in the very temple of Jehovah, wherein Aschera had her symbol and was adored" (ibid., 72). "Prostitutes," says this writer, "were of both sexes. The men were called kedeschim, the women kedeschoth— that is 'holy, vowed, consecrated.' Deuteronomy bears witness that both the one and the other brought the hire of their prostitution into the treasury of the temple of Jehovah. This paid in part the expenses of worship at Jerusalem" (ibid., 73).

"If then, in Hebrew law and practice," says Dr. Inman, "we find such a strong infusion of the sexual element, we cannot be surprised if it should be found elsewhere, and gradually influence Christianity" (*Ancient Symbolism*). "The worship of God the Father has repeatedly clashed with that of God the Mother, and the votaries of each respectively have worn badges characteristic of the sex of their deity. . . . Our sexual sections are as well marked as those in ancient Jerusalem, which swore by Jehovah and Ashtoreth respectively" (ibid.).

It is well known that religious prostitution has been practiced in some form by Christ's devotees from the earliest ages of the church down to the present time. Writing of the middle ages Lecky, the historian of European morals, says: "We may not lay much stress on such isolated instances of depravity as that of Pope John XXII, who was condemned, among many other crimes, for incest and adultery; or the abbot-elect of St. Augustine, at Canterbury, who in 1171 was found, on investigation, to have seventeen illegitimate children in a single village; or an abbot of St. Pelayo, in Spain, who in 1130 was proved to have kept no less than seventy concubines; or Henry III, bishop of Liege, who was deposed in 1274 for having sixty-five illegitimate children; but it is impossible to resist the evidence of a long chain of Councils and ecclesiastical writers, who conspire in depicting far greater evils than simple concubinage. . . . The writers of the middle ages are full of accounts of nunneries that were like brothels, of the vast multitude of infanticides within their walls, and of that inveterate prevalence of incest among the clergy, which rendered it necessary again and again to issue the most stringent enactments that priests should not be permitted to live with their mothers or sisters" (*History of European Morals,* Vol. II, p. 331).

For centuries the worship of the Virgin Mary, the Christian goddess of reproduction and motherhood, was supreme; the worship of God and Christ being subordinated to it. During these centuries, Hallam tells us, chastity was almost unknown. In every land, every class ignored the seventh commandment, because it was taught and believed that all offenses of this character were condoned by the Virgin. Hallam cites numerous instances of her alleged interventions in behalf of those who indulged in illegitimate practices. The following is one: "In one tale the Virgin takes the shape of a nun, who had eloped from the convent, and performs her duties ten years, till, tired of a libertine life, she returns unsuspected. This was in consideration of her having never omitted to say an Ave as she passed the Virgin's image" (*Middle Ages,* p. 604).

Christian chivalry, so much lauded in our day, was simply a form of sex worship. Hallam characterizes it as unbridled libertinism. The writings of that age, like those of Boccaccio, he says, indicate "a general dissoluteness in the intercourse of the sexes. . . . The violation of marriage vows passes in them for an incontestable privilege of the brave and the fair" (ibid., p. 666).

Holy pilgrimages to the shrines of saints were usually pilgrimages to the shrine of Venus. "Some of the modes of atonement which the church most approved, were particularly hostile to public morals. None was so usual as pilgrimage; whether to Jerusalem or Rome, which were the great objects of devotion, or to the shrine of some national saint, a James of Compostella, a David, or a Thomas Becket. This licensed vagrancy was naturally productive of dissoluteness, especially among the women. Our English ladies, in their zeal to obtain the spiritual treasures of Rome, are said to have relaxed the necessary caution about one that was in their own custody" (ibid., p. 607).

The prelates of the church, being equally culpable, winked at the licentiousness of the lower orders of the clergy. "In every country," says Hallam, "the secular and parochial clergy kept women in their houses, upon more or less acknowledged terms of intercourse, by a connivance of their ecclesiastical superiors" (ibid., p. 353). "A writer of respectable authority asserts that the clergy frequently obtained a bishop's license to cohabit with a mate" (ibid., p. 354).

Another form of "sanctified" sexual indulgence, and which received the sanction of the church, was what is known as Marquette. Concerning this custom Mrs. Matilda Joslyn Gage, in her *Woman, Church and State,* says: "The law known as Marchetta, or Marquette, compelled newly-married women to a most dishonorable servitude. They were regarded as the rightful prey of the Feudal Lord from one to three days after their marriage, and from this custom the eldest son of the serf was held as the son of the Lord. . . . Marquette was claimed by the Lord's Spiritual, as well as by the Lord's Temporal. The Church, indeed, was the bulwark of this base feudal claim." This is affirmed by the French historian, Michelet. He says: "The lords spiritual (clergy) had this right no less than the lords temporal. The parson, being a lord, expressly claimed the first fruits of the bride" (*La Sorcerie,* p. 62).

The brazen lewdness of medieval Christianity has been driven into privacy. But it still exists, and it is still religious. The Italian patriot, Garibaldi, bears this testimony: "In Rome, in 1849, I myself visited every convent. I was present at all the investigations. Without a single exception we found instruments of torture, and a cellar with the bodies of infant children." Referring to the priests connected with certain convents, Dr. Inman says: "Their practice was to instruct their victims that whatever was said or done must be accompanied by a pious sentence. Thus, 'I love you dearly' was a profane expression; but 'I desire your company in the name of Jesus,' and 'I embrace in you the Holy Virgin,' was orthodox."

Protestant readers, generally, will accept this testimony as true of Catholic countries. But have Protestant countries a purer record? Lecky, classed as a Protestant historian, says: "The two countries which are most thoroughly pervaded by Protestant theology are probably Scotland and Sweden; and if we measure their morality by the common though somewhat defective test that is furnished by the number of illegitimate births, the first is well known to be considerably below the average morality of European nations, while the second, in this as in general criminality, has been pronounced by a very able and impartial Protestant witness, who has had the fullest means of judging, to be very far below every other Christian nation" (*European Morals,* Vol. I, p. 391).

The religion of Christ as it exists today is not only in its external forms, but in its very essence, largely a survival of the nature worship of old. That it is closely allied to it is admitted by Christian ministers themselves. The Rev. Frederick Robertson says: "The devotional feelings are often singularly allied to the animal nature. They conduct the unconscious victim of feelings that appear divine, into a state of life, at which the world stands aghast; fanaticism is always united with either excessive lewdness or desperate asceticism," (Essays). The Rev. S. Baring-Gould, in *Freaks of Fanaticism,* says: "The religious passion verges so closely on the sexual passion that a slight additional pressure given to it bursts the partition, and both are confused in a frenzy of religious debauch." The Rev. J. H. Noyes says: "Religious love is a very near neighbor to sex love, and they always get mixed in the intimacies and social excitement of [religious] revivals."

Solar Worship

Scarcely less prevalent than sex worship was the worship of the sun. While sex worship was confined chiefly to the generation of human life, sun worship comprehended the generation of all life. The sun was recognized as the generative power of the universe. He overshadows the receptive earth from whom all life is born. I quote from M. Soury: "Amid all these forces, the mightiest is, without contradiction, the sun, the fire of heaven, father of earthly fire, unique and supreme cause of motion and life on our planet. There is no need or reason to understand that the very life, and as it were the blood of our celestial father flows in the veins of the Earth, our mother. In the time of love, when the luminous heaven embraces her, from her fertilized womb springs forth a world. It is she who quivers on the plains where the soft moist air waves gently on the grasses; it is she who climbs in the bush, who soars in the oak, who fills the solitude with the joyous twitter of birds beneath the cloudlet, or from the leaf-lined nests; it is she who in seas and in rurrning waters, or mountains and in woods, couples the gorgeous male with the ardent female, throbs in every bosom, loves in every life. But all this terrestrial life, all this warmth and all this light are but effluents from the sun." (*Religion of Israel,* pp. 3, 4.)

Prof. Tyndall says: "We are no longer in a poetical but in a purely mechanical sense, the children of the sun." "The sun," said Napoleon Bonaparte, "gives all things life and fertility. It is the true God of the earth."

John Newton, M.R.C.S., of England, says: "The glorious sun, that 'god of this world' the source of life and light to our earth, was early adored, and an effigy thereof used as a symbol. Mankind watched with rapture its rays gain strength daily in the Spring until the golden, glories of Midsummer had arrived, when the earth was bathed during the longest days in his beams, which ripened the fruits that his returning course had started into life. When the sun once more began its course downwards to the winter solstice, his votaries sorrowed, for he seemed to sicken and grow paler at the advent of December, when his rays scarcely reached the earth, and all nature, benumbed and cold, sunk into a death-like sleep. Hence feasts and fasts were instituted to mark the commencement of the various phases of the solar year, which have continued from the earliest known period, under various names, to our own times" (*The Assyrian Grove*).

The most prominent deities in the pantheons of the gods were solar deities. Among these were Osiris, Vishnu, Mithra, Apollo, Hercules, Adonis, Bacchus, and Baal. In the worship of some of these gods sex and solar worship were united.

The early Israelites were mostly sun worshipers. And even in later times, the sun god, Baal, divided with Jehovah the worship of the Jews. Saul, Jonathan, and David named their children in honor of this god. "Saul begat Jonathan, . . . and Esh-baal. And the son of Jonathan was Merib-baal" (1 Chron. viii, 33, 34). David named his last son, save one, Beeliada, "Baal Knows" (1 Chron. xiv, 7). Solomon's worship included not merely the worship of Jehovah, but that of Baal and other gods. His temple was filled with Pagan ornaments and emblems pertaining to solar worship. Regarding this the Rev. Dr. Oort of Holland says: "Solomon's temple had much in common with heathen edifices, and slight modifications might have made it a suitable temple for Baal. This need not surprise us, for the ancient religion of the Israelitish tribes was itself a form of Nature-worship just as much as the religions of the Canaanites, Phenicians, Philistines, and other surrounding peoples were. Most of the Israelites certainly saw no harm in these ornaments, since they were not aware of any very great difference between the character of Yahweh [Jehovah] and that of Baal, Astarte, or Moloch" (*Bible for Learners,* Vol. II, p. 88). Long after the time of Solomon the horses and chariots of the Sun were kept in the temple (2 Kings xxiii, 11). Many of the stories concerning Moses, Joshua, Jonah, and other Bible characters are solar myths. Samson was a sun god. Dr. Oort says: "Sun-worship was by no means unknown to the Israelites. . . . The myths that were circulated among these people show that they were zealous worshipers of the sun. These myths are still preserved, but, as in all other cases, they are so much altered as to be hardly recognizable. The writer who has preserved them for us lived at a time when the worship of the sun had long ago died out. He transforms the sun god into an Israelite hero [Samson]" (ibid., I, p. 414). St. Augustine believed that Samson and the sun god Hercules were one.

Charles Francois Dupuis, in his *Origin of Worship,* one of the most elaborate and remarkable works on mythology ever penned, shows that nearly all the religions of the world, including Christianity, were derived largely from solar worship. All the solar deities, he says, have a common history. This history, summarized, is substantially as follows: "The god is born about December 25th, without sexual intercourse, for the sun, entering the winter solstice, emerges in the sign of Virgo, the heavenly Virgin. His mother remains ever-virgin, since the rays of the sun, passing through the zodiacal sign, leave it intact. His infancy is begirt with dangers, because the new-born Sun is feeble in the midst of the winter's fogs and mists, which threaten to devour him; his life is one of toil and peril, culminating at the spring equinox in a final struggle with the powers of darkness. At that period the day and night are equal, and both fight for the mastery. Though the night veil the urn and he seems dead; though he has descended out of sight, below the earth, yet he rises again triumphant, and he rises in the sign of the Lamb, and is thus the Lamb of God, carrying away the darkness and death of the winter months. Henceforth he triumphs, growing ever stronger and more brilliant. He ascends into the zenith, and there he glows, on the right hand of God, himself God, the very substance of the Father, the brightness of his glory, and the express image of his person, upholding all things by his lifegiving power."

Dr G. W. Brown, author of *Researches in Oriental History,* says: "Strange as it may seem whilst Mithras and Osiris, Dionysos and Bacchus, Apollo and Serapis, with many others [including Christ] in name, all masculine sun gods, and all interblended, a knowledge of one is generally a knowledge of the whole, wherever located or worshiped."

If Christ was not originally a solar god he wears today the livery of one. His mother, the Virgin, was the mother of the solar gods; his birthday, Christmas, is the birthday of all the gods of the sun; his Twelve Apostles correspond to the twelve signs of the Zodiac; according to the Gospels, at his crucifixion the sun was eclipsed, he expired toward sunset, and rose again with the sun; the day appointed for his worship, the Lord's day, is the dies solis, Sunday, of the sun worshipers; while the principal feasts observed in memory of him were once observed in honor of their goals. "Every detail of the Sun myth," says the noted astronomer, Richard A. Proctor, "is worked into the record of the Galilean teacher."

The cross we have seen was a symbol of Phallic worship. The cross, and especially the crucifix, was also an emblem of solar worship. It was carved or painted on, or within, a circle representing the horizon, the head and feet and the outstretched arms of the sacrificial offering or crucified Redeemer pointing toward the four quarters of the horizon. The Lord's Supper, observed in memory of Christ, was observed in memory of Mithra, Bacchus, and other solar gods. The nimbus, or aureola, surrounding the head of Jesus in his portraits represents the rays of the sun. It was thus that the ancient adorers of the sun adorned the effigies of their god. There still exists a pillar erected by the sun worshipers of Carthage. On this pillar is carved the sun god, Baal, with a nimbus encircling his head.

The Christian doctrine of the resurrection had its origin in sun worship. As the sun, the Father, rose from the dead, so it was believed that his earthly children would also rise from the dead. "The daily disappearance and the subsequent rise of the sun," says Newton, "appeared to many of the ancients as a true resurrection; thus, while the east came to be regarded as the source of iight and warmth, happiness and glory, the west was associated with darkness and chill, decay and death. This led to the custom of burying the dead so as to face the east when they rose again, and of building temples and shrines with an opening toward the east. To effect this, Vitruvius, two thousand years ago, gave precise rules, which are still followed by Christian architects."

Max Mueller in his *Origin of Religion* (pp. 200, 201), says: "People wonder why so much of the old mythology, the daily talk, of the Aryans was solar: what else could it have been? The names of the sun are endless and so are his stories; but who he was, whence he came and whither he went, remained a mystery from beginning to end. . . . Man looked up to the sun, yearning for the response of a soul, and though that response never came, though his senses recoiled, dazzled and blinded by an effulgence which he could not support, yet he never doubted that the invisible was there, and that, where his senses failed him, where he could neither grasp nor comprehend, he might still shut his eyes and trust, fall down and worship."

This worship of old survives in the worship of today. A knowledge of the location, the limits and the nature of the sun has gradually convinced the world that this is not God's dwelling place; but somewhere in the infinite expanse of the blue beyond they fancy he has his throne. To this imaginary being is rendered the same adoration that was rendered to him by primitive man—the adoration of childish ignorance.

Astral Worship

The worship of the planets and stars was probably a later development than sex and solar worship. It flourished for a time in nearly every part of the world, and left its impress on the religions that succeeded it.

In Chaldea, one of the principal sources of Judaism and Christianity, the worship of the stars prevailed. I quote from Dr. Ridpath: "In their aspirations for communion with the higher powers, the yearning of the ancient Chaldeans turned upwards to the planets and the stars. The horizon of the Babylonian plain was uniform and boundless. It was the heaven above rather than the earth beneath, which exhibited variety and life. The Zodiac was ever new with its brilliant evolutions. Through the clear atmosphere the tracks of the shining orbs could be traced in every phase and transposition. With each dawn of morning light, with each recurrence of the evening twilight, a new panorama spread before the reverent imagination of the dreamer, and he saw in the moving spheres not only the abode but the manifested glory of his gods" (*History of the World,* Vol. 1, p. 138).

"Until today, in the high light of civilization, the idea of some kind of domination of the stars over the affairs of human life has hardly released its hold on the minds of men; and the language of the old Chaldean ritual of signs has still a familiar sound in the ears of the credulous" (ibid., p. 140).

After alluding to the ancient Vedic religion, which recognized in the stars the souls of our departed ancestors, Prof. John Fiske says: "The Christianised German peasant, fifty centuries later, tells his children that the stars are angels' eyes, and the English cottager impresses it on the youthful mind that it is wicked to point to the stars, though why he cannot tell" (*Myths and Myth Makers,* p. 76).

In the Zodiac the Sun had twelve palaces. Each palace had a star for a god, and each was subject to the Sun. Each day of the week was governed by a planet, and each hour of the day had its controlling star. Many scholars, including Jefferson, have held that Christ and his twelve Apostles relate to the zodiac and were derived from this stellar worship. The seven days of the week are still dedicated to the old planetary gods, and, with a few modifications, bear their names.

Chambers' Encyclopedia says: "The Jews, as well as the early Christians, had no special names for the single days, but counted their number from the previous Sabbath, beginning with Sunday, as the first after the Sabbath, and ending with Friday, as the sixth after the previous, or eve (Ereb) of the next Sabbath. After a very short time, however, young Christianity, which in the same manner had endeavored to count from the feria secunda, or second day after Sunday, to the Septima (or Saturday), had to fall back again upon the old heathen names" (Art. "Week").

The planetary gods Nardouk (Jupiter), Adar (Saturn), Istar (Venus), Nergal (Mars), and Nebo (Mercury),* were all worshiped by the ancient Israelites. Istar was called "Queen of the Stars." Moloch, the rival of Jehovah, who shared for centuries the worship of the Hebrews, had

---

*Scholars have now decided that the Babylonian names of Jupiter, Saturn, and Mercury should be written Marduk, Adad, and Nabu, respectively—ed.

his blazing star, the emblem of his implacable cruelty. The worship of Astarte, daughter of the moon, and "Queen of Heaven," whose emblem was a star, was introduced by Solomon himself (1 Kings xi, 5; 2 Kings xxiii, 13). For more than three hundred years she had her temple in Jerusalem. And even today devout Jews address orizons to the new moon, a relic of the worship of Astarte. The rosary is a survival of astral worship. It was once a symbol of the stars.

The author of *Supernatural Religion* says: "The belief that sun, moon and stars were living entities possessed of souls was generally held by the Jews at the beginning of our era."

The same belief was entertained by the Christian Fathers. Origen says: "As the stars move with so much order and method that under no circumstances whatever do their course seem to be disturbed, is it not the extreme of absurdity to suppose that so much order, so much observance of discipline and method could be demanded from or fulfilled by irrational beings?"

Out of astral worship grew the so-called science of astrology. Of this *Chambers' Encyclopedia* says: "Astrology is one of the most ancient forms of superstition, and is found prevailing among the nations of the east at the very dawn of history. The Jews became much addicted to it after the Captivity."

One of the so-called Messianic prophecies of the Old Testament reads: "There shall come a star out of Jacob" (Num. xxiv, 17). "Note when Jesus was born in Bethlehem of Judea in the days of Herod the King, behold, there came wise men from the east to Jerusalem, saying, Where is he that is born king of the Jews? For we have seen his star in the east, . . . and, lo, the star, which they saw in the east, went before them, till it came and stood over where the young child was" (Matt. ii, 1, 2, 9). This marvelous event at the advent of the Christian Messiah was a complete "fulfillment" of what had been predicted centuries before concerning the appearance of the expected Persian Messiah, the original of the expected Messiah of the Jews.

Graves says that the language of Matthew clearly betrays the astrological origin of his story. "The practice of calculating nativities by the stars was in vogue in the era and country of Christ's birth, and had been for a long time previously in various countries. 'We have seen his star in the east, and have come to worship him.' Now mark, here, it was not the star, nor a star, but 'his star'; thus disclosing its unmistakable astrological features" (*Sixteen Crucified Saviors*, p. 53).

After referring to the prevalency of astrology at the beginning of, and anterior to, the Christian era, Strauss says: "When such ideas were afloat, it was easy to imagine that the birth of the Messiah must be announced by a star, especially as, according to the common interpretation of Balaam's prophecy, a star was there made the symbol of the Messiah. It is certain that the Jewish mind effected this combination; for it is a rabbinical idea that at the time of the Messiah's birth a star will appear in the east and remain for a long time visible. . . . In the time of Jesus it was the general belief that stars were always the forerunners of great events."

Jesus in the Apocalypse declares himself to be "the bright and morning star" (xxii, 16). He "had in his right hand seven stars" (i, 16). "The seven stars are the angels of the seven churches" (20). His second coming will be heralded by "signs in the sun, and in the moon, and in the stars" (Luke xxi, 25).

The star of the Magi which pointed so unerringly to the cradle of Christ points not less unerringly to one of the sources from which Christ came.

Worship of the Elements and Forces of Nature

The elements and forces of nature, Volney believes, inspired the first ideas of God and religion:

"Man, reflecting on his condition, began to perceive that he was subjected to forces superior to his own, and independent of his will. The sun enlightened and warmed him, fire burned him, thunder terrified him; the wind beat upon him, and water drowned him."

"Considering the action of the elements on him, he conceived the idea of weakness and subjection on his part, and of power and domination on theirs; and this idea of power was the primitive and fundamental type of every idea of the Divinity."

"The action of these natural existences excited in him sensations of pleasure and pain, of good or evil; and by a natural elect of his organization he conceived for them love or aversion; he desired or dreaded their presence; and fear or hope gave rise to the first idea of religion."

From this elemental worship Indra, Agni, Zeus, Odin, Jehovah and other gods were evolved. Jehovah was originally a god of the atmosphere. He manifested himself in the tempest; he unchained the waves of the sea; the wind has his breath; the thunder was his voice, the lightning his messenger. He filled the air with frost; he precipitated the hail; he blanketed the earth with snow; he deluged the land with rain; he congealed the water of the stream, and parched the verdure of the field.

Fire worship overspread Asia, and Jehovah, like Moloch, became a god of fire. "There went up a smoke out of his nostrils, and fire out of his mouth devoured; coals were kindled by it" (2 Sam. xxii, 9). He appeared to Abram as "a smoking furnace and a burning lamp" (Gen. xv, 17). He revealed himself to Moses in the burning bush. "The bush burned with fire, but the bush was not consumed" (Ex. iii, 2). When David called to him "he answered him from heaven by fire" (1 Ch. xxi, 26). To the fleeing Israelites he was a "pillar of fire" (Ex. xiv, 24). "The Lord descended upon" Sinai "in fire" (xix, 18). When he appeared upon Horeb "the mountain burned with fire unto the midst of heaven" (Deut. iv. 11), "and the Lord spake out of the midst of the fire" (12). "The cloud of the Lord was upon the tabernacle by day, and fire was on it by night" (Ex. xl, 38). On the Jewish altar for centuries the sacred fire was kept burning. When Aaron, Gideon, Solomon and Elijah made offerings to Jehovah "there came a fire out from before the Lord, and consumed" the offerings (Lev. ix, 24; Jud. vi, 21; 2 Ch. vii, 1; 1 K. xviii, 38). Elijah was translated in "a chariot of fire" (2 K. ii, 11). Elisha was surrounded by "horses and chariots of fire" (vi, 17). With fire he consumed his enemies. "The Lord rained upon Sodom and Gomorrah brimstone and fire" (Gen. xix, 24), When Nadab and Abihu "offered strange fire before the Lord" (Lev. x, 1), "there went out fire from before the Lord and devoured them" (2). When the Israelites displeased him at Taberah, "the fire of the Lord burnt among them and consumed them" (Num. xi, 1). When the hosts of Satan encompassed the Christian saints, "fire came down from God out of heaven and devoured them" (Rev. xx, 9).

"It is now a matter of demonstration," says M. Soury, "that at the time of the Exodus from Egypt, in the desert, and even in the time of Judges, light and fire were not to the Israelites mere symbols of the deity, but were the deity himself."

Christ inherited the fiery nature of his Father. He baptized his disciples with fire. "He shall baptize you with the Holy Ghost, and with fire" (Matt. iii, 11). "And there appeared unto them cloven tongues like as of fire, and it sat upon each of them" (Acts ii, 3). He consigned his enemies to everlasting punishment in the unquenchable fires of hell. "The Son of man shall send forth his angels, and they shall gather out of his kingdom all things that offend, and them which do iniquity; and shall cast them into a furnace of fire" (Matt. xiii, 41, 42). "Depart from me, ye cursed, into everlasting fire" (xxv, 41). "To be cast into hell fire: where their worm dieth not, and the fire is not quenched. For every one shall be salted with fire" (Mark ix, 47–49). His disciples were imbued with the same spirit and belief. "And they (the Samaritans) did not receive him. . . . And when his disciples James and John saw this, they said, Lord, wilt thou that we command fire to come down from heaven and consume them?" (Luke ix, 53, 54.)

Some vestiges of ancient fire worship have been transmitted to our time. John Newton says: "A sacred fire, at first miraculously kindled, and subsequently kept up by the sedulous care of priests and priestesses, formed an important part of the religion of Judea, Babylonia, Persia, Greece and Rome, and the superstition lingers amongst us still. So late as the advent of the Reformation, a sacred fire was kept ever burning on a shrine at Kildare, in Ireland, and attended by virgins of high rank, called 'inghean au dagha,' or daughters of fire. Every year is the ceremony repeated at Jerusalem of the miraculous kindling of the Holy Fire at the reputed sepulchre, and men and women crowd to light tapers at the sacred flame" (*The Assyrian Grove*).

Worship of Animals and Plants

In the infancy of the world animals were deified and adored, and trees and plants were regarded as sentient beings and received the homage of man.

Nearly every animal has been an object of worship. This worship flourished for ages in Egypt and India. In Egypt the worship of the bull (Apis) was associated with that of Osiris (Serapis). The cow is still worshiped in India. Serpent worship has existed in every part of the world.

Remnants of animal worship survived in Judaism and Christianity. Satan was a serpent; Jehovah, like Osiris, was worshiped as a bull; Christ was the lamb of God, and the Holy Ghost appeared in the form of a dove.

Closely allied to this worship, and to some extent a part of it, is the doctrine of the transmigration of souls. Some of the Jews believed in this. So did many of the early Christians, including Origen.

The leek, the lotus, and other plants were held as sacred or divine. The rose was the divine flower of Greece. Its petals had been dyed with the blood of her favorite goddess. In many nations the lily was the sacred emblem of virginity. Christians still attach a sort of sacredness to it.

"The groves were God's first temples," says Bryant. The groves, too, were among man's first gods. Volumes have been written on the ancient worship of trees. Not only the Druids of Britain, but the Greeks, and the Semitic races of Asia were worshipers of trees. The giant oaks and the symmetrical evergreens were gods. The rustling of the aspen and the moaning of the pines were the audible whisperings of Divinity which the prophets interpreted.

"The worship of trees," says Soury, "only disappeared in Syria at a very late date. . . . The largest and tallest trees, and the evergreen ones, were adored as gods. A great many Semitic myths were connected with the vegetable world. Thus the pomegranate, famous for the richness of its fruit, was sacred to Adonis and Aphrodite. The almond, which, while nature seems inanimate, comes forth first from winter's sleep, the amygdalis, the 'great mother,' gave birth to a crowd of Semitic legends" (*Religion of Israel*, pp. 66, 67).

The tree, like the serpent, was an emblem of immortality. The Garden of Eden had its Tree of Life. Newton says: " 'I am come that they might have Life, and that they might have it abundantly' (John x, 10). Life is the reward which has been promised under every system, including that of the founder of Christianity. A Tree of Life stood in the midst of that Paradise which is described in the book of Genesis;

. . . and in a second Paradise, which is promised to the blessed by the author of the book of Revelation, a tree of life shall stand once more 'for the healing of the nations.' "

There still exist in Palestine venerable trees which receive not merely the reverence, but the worship of Mussulmans and Christians. Some of these trees they believe possess divine curative powers. Travelers have observed them covered with strips of cloth or strings, which are tied to the twigs. This is done to induce the spirit of the tree to heal or drive away disease.

Sex worship, as we have seen, bequeathed some of its doctrines and rites to nearly every religion that has existed since its time. It became associated with tree worship. The Bible abounds with "sacred groves." In Palestine hundreds of them were consecrated to Aschera, the favorite goddess of the ancient Jews. These groves were devoted to sacred prostitution. In some of them the worship of Baal and Aschera were combined; in others that of Jehovah and Aschera. "These sanctuaries of Aschera," says M. Soury, "were charming spots, shady groves of green trees, often watered by running streams, mysterious retreats where all was silence save the cooing of the doves sacred to the goddess. The symbol of Aschera, a simple pillar, or the trunk of a tree, perhaps with its leaves and branches, was the emblem of generative power." The spots once occupied by these groves are still deemed holy ground. Many of them are marked by Mohammedan mosques and Christian chapels.

The sacred groves of Palestine where devout and voluptuous Jews mingled the worship of Jehovah and Aschera live, too, in the Protestant camp meetings of our western world, where, in shady bowers, Christians worship fervently at the altar of Christ, and then, not infrequently, meet clandestinely and pay their vows to Aschera.

The palm tree, and where the palm did not grow, the pine, both symbols of the phallus, were worshiped. Newton says: "Palm-branches have been used in all ages as emblems of life, peace, and victory. They were strewn before Christ. Palm-Sunday, the feast of palms, is still kept. Even within the present [19th] century, on this festival, in many towns of France, women and children carried in procession at the end of their palm-branches a phallus made of bread, which they called, undisguisedly, 'la pine,' whence the festival was called 'La Fete des Pinnes.' The 'pine' having been blest by the priest, the women carefully preserved it during the following year as an amulet" (*The Assyrian Grove*).

Fetichism

Closely related to the foregoing worship is fetichism, the worship of idols and images. This is popularly supposed to be the religion only of savages and barbarians; but it also prevails to some extent among people who are considered civilized and enlightened.

While it was opposed by some of the kings, priests, and prophets, idolatry flourished among the Jews from the earliest ages down almost to the Christian era. Abraham's father, Terah, was an idolater (Josh. xxv, 2). Jacob's wives were daughters of an idolater. Rachel stole and hid her father's images (Gen. xxxi, 30–34). Jacob's family were, for a time at least, idolaters. "Then Jacob said unto his household, and all that were with him, Put away the strange gods that art among you. . . . And they gave unto Jacob all the strange gods that were in their hands, . . . and Jacob laid them under the oak which was by Shechem" (Gen. xxxv, 2–4). The kingdoms of Israel and Judah were steeped in idolatry. Israel "set them up images" and "served idols" (2 Kings, xvii, 10, 11), and "did offer sweet savor to their idols" (Ezek. vi, 13). Judah was "full of idols" (Is. ii, 8).

The fetichism of Christ's ancestors reappeared in the image worship of his devotees. The Christians of the middle ages, Dr. Draper says, "were immersed in fetichism." "The worship of images, of fragments of the cross, or bones, nails and other relics, a true fetich worship, was cultivated" (*Conflict,* p. 49). "A chip of the true cross, some iron filings from the chain of St. Peter, a tooth or bone of a martyr, were held in adoration; the world was full of the stupendous miracles which these relics had performed. But especially were painted or graven images of holy personages supposed to be endowed with such powers. They had become objects of actual worship" (*Intellectual Development of Europe,* Vol. I, p. 414).

Concerning the fetichism of the church, *Chambers' Encyclopedia* says: "It was usual not only to keep lights and burn incense before the images, to kiss them reverently; and to kneel down and pray before them, but some went so far as to make the images serve as godfathers and godmothers in baptism and even to mingle the dust of the coloring matter scraped from the images with the Eucharist elements in the Holy Communion. . . . In many foreign churches, especially in Italy, in southern Germany, and in France [at the present time], are to be found images which are popularly reputed as especially sacred, and to which, or to prayers offered before which, miraculous effects are ascribed."

Bishop Newton, of England, admits and deplores the existence of Christian fetichism. He says: "The consecrating and bowing down to images; the attributing of miraculous powers and virtues to idols; the setting up of little oratories, altars and statues in the streets and highways and on the tops of mountains; the carrying of images and relics in pompous procession, . . . all these are equally parts of pagan and popish superstition."

Greek, Lutheran, and Anglican churches are not free from fetichism, and even the Evangelical churches of this country make a fetich of a book.

Polytheism

Polytheism, the doctrine of a plurality of gods, has prevailed in every part of the world. The most interesting pantheons of the gods were those of India, Egypt, Greece, and Rome. The Hebrews, who were polytheists, borrowed their gods from Assyria and Babylonia. The pantheon of these nations comprised twelve principal gods and nearly a thousand minor deities. The chief of these gods was El. His consort was Elath. The Hebrews worshiped El under the name of El Shaddai and various other names. Elohim of the Bible, translated God, denotes the plural and included El and the minor gods who surrounded him. Yahweh, Iahveh, Jehovah, etc., as he is variously called—for Jews and Christians cannot spell and do not even know the name of their principal deity—is a god of Assyro-Babylonian origin. In addition to their national god, Jehovah, many of the Jews worshiped Baal, Moloch, and Tammous, male deities, and Astarte, Aschera, and Istar, female deities.

That the writers of the Bible recognized a plurality of gods—were polytheists—is proved by the following: "And the Lord God said, Behold, the man is become as one of us" (Gen. iii, 22). "Who is like unto thee, O Lord, among the gods?" (Ex. xv, 11.) "Among the gods, there is none like unto thee, O Lord" (Ps. lxxxvi, 8). "The Lord is a great God, and a great king above all gods" (Ps. xcv, 3). "Thou shalt not revile the gods" (Ex. xxii, 28).

Monotheism, the doctrine of one god, is not merely the worship of one god, but the belief in the existence of one god only. Many were monotheistic in worship—worshiped one god, their national deity—while at the same time they were polytheistic in belief—believed in the existence of many gods. The Jews who worshiped Jehovah have been called monotheists. And yet, for a thousand years, they believed in the existence of Kemosh, Baal, Moloch, Tammouz, and other deities. They believed that Jehovah was their national god and that they owed allegiance to him; just as the subjects of an earthly king profess their loyalty to him without denying the existence of other kings.

While Christians profess monotheism they are really polytheists—worship three gods—Father (Jehovah), Son (Christ), and Holy Ghost; and recognize a god of Evil, Satan. To these must also be added a female deity, the Virgin Mary, who is to the devout Catholic as much of a divinity as Isis and Venus were to ancient polytheists. The canonization and adoration of the saints, too, are analogous to the worship of the inferior deities of ancient times.

After recounting what he believes to be the salutary influences exerted by the medieval conception of the Virgin, Lecky says: "But the price, and perhaps the necessary price, of this was the exaltation of the Virgin as an omnipresent deity of infinite power as well as infinite condescension. The legends represented her as performing every kind of prodigy. . . . The painters depicted her invested with the divine aureole, judging men on equal terms with her Son, or even retaining her ascendancy over him in heaven. In the devotions of the people she was addressed in terms identical with those employed to the Almighty. A reverence similar in kind but less in degree was soon bestowed upon the other saints, who speedily assumed the position of the minor deities of paganism" (*History of Rationalism,* Vol. I, pp. 226, 227).

Regarding the deification and worship of saints Hallam says: "Every cathedral or monastery had its tutelar saint, and every saint his legend, fabricated in order to enrich the churches under his protection, by exaggerating his virtues, his miracles, and consequently his power of serving those who paid liberally for his patronage. Many of those saints were imaginary persons; sometimes a blundered inscription added a name to the calendar; and sometimes, it is said, a heathen god was surprised at the company to which he was introduced, and the rites with which he was honored" (*Middle Ages,* p. 603).

The church historian Mosheim admits and deplores the truth of this: "It is, at the same time, as undoubtedly certain, as it is extravagant and monstrous, that the worship of the martyrs was modeled, by degrees, according to the religious services that were said to the goals before the coming of Christ" (*Ecclesiastical History,* p. 98).

Bishop Newton says: "The very same temples, the very same images, which were once consecrated to Jupiter and the other demons [gods], are now consecrated to the Virgin Mary and the other saints."

Milman says that at an early period "Christianity began to approach to a polytheistic forms or at least to permit what it is difficult to call by any other name than polytheistic, habits and feelings of devotion" (*History of Christianity,* Vol. III, p. 424).

Monotheism

Monotheism, as previously stated, is the doctrine of one god only. It has gradually displaced, to a great extent, the fetichism and polytheism of earlier times.

Comte's law of human development is as follows:
1. Theological, or fictitious,
2. Metaphysical, or abstract,
3. Scientific, or positive.

"In the Theological state, the human mind, seeking the essential nature of things, the first and final causes (the origin and purpose) of all effects—in short Absolute knowledge—supposes all phenomena to be produced by the immediate action of supernatural beings.

"In the Metaphysical state, which is only a modification of the first, the mind supposes, instead of supernatural beings, abstract forms, veritable entities (that is, personified abstractions) inherent in all things, and capable of producing all phenomena.

"In the final, the Positive state, the mind has given over the vain search after Absolute notions, the origin and destination of the universe, and the causes of phenomena, and applies itself to the study of their laws—that is, their invariable relations of succession and resemblance" (*Positive Philosophy*, pp. 26, 27).

The lowest state of human development is the theological. Here the masses of mankind still repose. Only the scholars and thinkers have advanced beyond this and many of these have only reached the second or metaphysical state. The highest point in the theological state is monotheism.

To Judaism Christians ascribe the glory of having been the first religion to teach a pure monotheism. But monotheism existed long before the Jews attained to it. Zoroaster and his earliest followers were monotheists, dualism being a later development of the Persian theology. The adoption of monotheism by the Jews, which occurred only at a very late period in their history, was not, however, the result of a divine revelation, or even of an intellectual superiority, for the Jews were immeasurably inferior intellectually to the Greeks and Romans, to the Hindus and Egyptians, and to the Assyrians and Babylonians, who are supposed to have retained a belief in polytheism. This monotheism of the Jews has chiefly the result of a religious intolerance never before equaled and never since surpassed, except in the history of Christianity and Mohammedanism, the daughters of Judaism. Jehovistic priests and kings tolerated no rivals of their god and made death the penalty for disloyalty to him. The Jewish nation became monotheistic for the same reason that Spain, in the clutches of the Inquisition, became entirely Christian.

Jesus of Nazareth and his disciples, if they existed, were probably monotheists, believed that Jehovah was the only God, and neither believed nor claimed that Jesus was other than the son of man. As generations passed the man became obscured, his deeds were magnified until at length he was accepted as the Son of God, and a God himself. The deification of Jesus, then, together with the apotheosis of other mortals, cannot be regarded as an evolution from Jewish monotheism to a higher plane, but rather as a relapse from monotheism to polytheism.

The Mediatorial Idea

This idea had its origin chiefly in the worship of the elements and forces of nature by primitive man. He believed that these elements and forces were intelligent beings. He realized that in their presence he was in a measure helpless. He therefore sought to win their favor and appease their wrath. He made offerings to them; he prayed to them; he worshiped them. But other men, more wise, more cunning, and more fortunate, appeared to have greater influence with these deities. He employed them to intercede for him; and thus the priesthood was established. The priest was the first mediator.

More complex religions systems were in time evolved, and in some of them mediatorial gods appeared. The mediatorial idea was prominent in the Persian system. Mithra was the Persian mediator. The worship of Mithra was carried to Rome and the Romans became acquainted with the mediatorial idea. In an exposition of Philo's philosophy, Mrs. Evans says: "The most exalted spirits are able to raise themselves to the pure essence and find peace and joy which earthly conditions cannot disturb; but weaker natures need a helper in a Being, who, coming from above, can dwell below and lift their souls to God. The majority of mankind, in their passage along the slippery path of life, are sure to fall, and would perish if it were not for a mediator between themselves and God. . . . The power of the Caesars, culminating in Augustus, enabled them to claim divine honors from the people, already disposed to see in them chosen agents of celestial sovereignty. Rome, according to the expression of Valerius Maximus, recognized in the Caesars the mediators between heaven and earth. And that was before Christianity introduced its anointed mediator" (*The Christ Myth,* pp. 90, 92).

The God of the Jews, to quote the words of Jefferson, was "cruel, vindictive, capricious and unjust." He had cursed his creation; he had drowned a world; he had imposed the sentence of death—spiritual as well as physical—upon his children. To placate this monster, to induce him to remit this sentence, the priests were powerless. Millions of animals, and even human beings, had been sacrificed to him in vain. At length his "only begotten son," Jesus Christ, offered himself as a sacrifice to atone for the sins of the world. The sacrifice was accepted, and a reconciliation was elected between God and man. Thus Christ became the great mediator of Christianity. "There is one God, and one mediator between God and men, the man Christ Jesus" (1 Tim. ii, 5). "He is the mediator of the new testament" (Heb. ix, 15). From Persia and from Rome this mediatorial God has come.

The Messianic Idea

The desire for a deliverer naturally arises in the minds of a people who are in subjection and bondage. This desire was the germ of the Messianic idea. While there are traces of this idea in the earlier writings of the Hebrews, it reached its highest development during and immediately following the Captivity, and again in the Maccabean age.

The Messiah of Judaism and the Messiah, or Christ, of Christianity, were derived from the Persian theology, the adherents of each system modifying the doctrine to suit their respective notions. In its article on Zoroaster, *Chambers' Encyclopedia* says: "There is an important element to be noticed, viz., the Messiah, or Sosiosh, from whom the Jewish and Christian notions of a Messiah are held by many to have been derived. . . . Even a superficial glance at this sketch will show our readers what very close parallels between Jewish and Christian notions on the one hand, and the Zoroastrian on the other, are to be drawn."

Christians cite numerous passages from the writings of the Old Testament, which they claim foretold the advent of Jesus. Not one of these passages, as originally penned, refers in the remotest degree to him, though many of them do refer to the office he is said to have filled. The Jews hoped for a deliverer, for a national leader who would reestablish the kingdom of Israel, and restore to it the glory of David's reign. They were loyal to the house of David and believed that this deliverer would be a descendant, a son, of David. Pietists, too, in the fervor of their religious enthusiasm dreamed of universal conversion to the Jehovistic theocracy. In the writings of their prophets and poets these hopes and dreams found expression. "I have made a covenant with my chosen, I have sworn unto David, my servant, thy seed will I establish forever, and build up thy throne to all generations" (Ps. xxxix, 3, 4). "And the kingdom and dominion, and the greatness of the kingdom under the whole heaven, shall be given to the people of the saints of the most High, whose kingdom is an everlasting kingdom, and all dominions shall serve and obey him" (Dan. vii, 27).

While the Messianic idea was originally a Persian idea, the materials used in the formation of the Christian Messiah were drawn largely from the Jewish Scriptures. There are passages in the Old Testament, as we have seen, which predict the coming of a Messiah. These furnished a portion of the materials out of which this Messianic deity, Christ, was formed. There are many more which have no reference whatever to a Messiah, which have been made to serve as Messianic prophecies. The Old Testament, as we have it, is alleged to be a Jewish work. It is, rather, a Christian work. It is a Christian version of ancient Jewish writings, every book of which has been more or less Christianized. Much of it is scarcely recognizable to a Jewish scholar. This is especially true of so-called Messianic prophecies.

The Christian Messiah was, on the one hand, modeled, to a considerable extent, after the Jewish ideal, while the Jewish materials, on the other hand, were freely altered to fit the new conception. Referring to the work of the Evangelists, M. Renan says: "Sometimes they reasoned thus: 'The Messiah ought to do such a thing; now Jesus is the Messiah, therefore Jesus has done such a thing.' At other times, by an inverse process, it was said: 'Such a thing has happened to Jesus; now Jesus is the Messiah; therefore such a thing was to happen to the Messiah.' " (*Jesus,* p. 27).

That the so-called Messianic prophecies of the Jewish Scriptures were the immediate source of the Christ is apparent. That he was, however, merely a borrowed idea and not a historical realization of these prophecies is equally apparent. The Jews were expecting a Messiah. Had Jesus realized these expectations they would have accepted him. But he did not realize them. These prophecies were not fulfilled in him. He was not a son of David; he did not deliver his race from bondage; he did not become a king; the important events that were to attend and follow Messiah's advent form no part even of his alleged history. His rejection by the Jews proves him to be either a false Messiah, or an imaginary being—a historical myth or a pure myth—in either case a myth.

The Jewish argument against Jesus as the Messiah is unanswerable. "We do not find in the present comparatively imperfect stage of human progress the realization of that blessed condition of mankind which the propiret Isaiah associates with the era when Messiah is to appear. And as our Hebrew Scriptures speak of one Messianic advent only, and not of two advents; and as the inspired Book does not preach Messiah's kingdom as a matter of faith, but distinctly identifies it with matters of fact which are to be made evident to the senses, we cling to the plain inference to be drawn from the text of the Bible, and we deny that Messiah has yet appeared, and upon the following grounds: First, because of the three distinctive facts which the inspired seer of Judah inseparably connects with the advent of the Messiah, vis., (1) the cessation of war and the uninterrupted reign of peace, (2) the prevalence of a perfect concord of opinion on all matters bearing upon the worship of the one and only God, and (3) the ingathering of the remnant of Judah and of the dispersed ten tribes of Israel—not one has, up to the present time, been accomplished. Second, we dissent from the proposition that Jesus of Nazareth is the Messiah announced by the prophets, because the church which he founded, and which his successors developed, has offered, during a succession of centuries, most singular contrast to what is described by the Hebrew scriptures as the immediate consequence of Messiah's advent, and of his glorious kingdom. The prophet Isaiah declares that when the Messiah appears, peace, love, and union will be permanently established; and every candid man must admit that the world has not realized the accomplishment of this prophecy. Again, in the days of Messiah, all men, as Scripture saith, 'are to serve God with one accord'; and yet it is very certain that since the appearance of him whom Christians believe to be Messiah, mankind has been split into more hostile divisions on the ground of religious belief, and more antagonistic sects have sprung up, than in any historic age before Christianity was preached."

With orthodox Jews the belief in a Messiah is a deep rooted conviction. For 2500 years there has been displayed in front of the synagogue this sign: "Wanted—a Messiah." During this time many, including Jesus, Bar-Cocheba, Moses of Candia, and Sabatai Zevi, have applied for the place, but all applicants have been rejected, and the Messianic predictions of the Jewish prophets are yet to be fulfilled. So, too, are those of the Persian prophet. In the meantime the followers of Jesus—turning from the Jews to the Gentiles—have from this borrowed idea evolved a deity who divides with Brahma, Buddha, and Allah, the worship of the world.

The Logos (Word)

The exaltation and deification of Jesus is thus described by the Dutch theologian, Dr. Hooykaas. "When Jesus was gone, those who had known him personally insensibly surrounded him with a glory that shone at last with a more than human splendor. The spiritual blessings which flowed in ever rich measure from his person and his gospel compelled the Christians to exalt him ever more and more. The title of Son of God, which his followers had given him as the future Messiah, was elastic and ambiguous enough to lend itself very readily to this process. The idea of his being the Messiah now no longer sufficed; he was something other and something far more than the Jewisn Messiah. The philosophy and theology of the day were laid under contribution; and nothing could so well indicate his significance for all humanity and his unapproachable exaltation as the idea that he was the Word" (*Bible for Learners,* Vol. III, pp. 670, 671).

The doctrine of the Logos, or Word: as an emanation or essence of divine wisdom is very old. It is found in the ancient religions of Egypt and India. It was recognized in the Persian theology, and was incorporated into the Jewish theology by the Babylonian exiles. It constitutes an important element in the Platonic philosophy. It received its highest development and exposition in the writings of the Jewish philosopher Philo, a contemporary of Jesus.

Concerning the Logos, Dean Milman, in his *History of Christianity,* says: "This Being was more or less distinctly impersonated, according to the more popular or more philosophic, the more material or the more abstract, notions of the age of the people. This was the doctrine from the Ganges, or even the shores of the Yellow Sea, to the Ilissus: it was the fundamental principle of the Indian religion and the Indian philosophy; it was the basis of Zoroastrianism; it was pure Platonism; it was the Platonic Judaism of the Alexandrian school." Another English clergyman, Mr. Lake, says: "We can trace its [the Word's] birthpiace in the philosophic speculations of the ancient world; we can note its gradual development and growth; we can see it in its early youth passing (through Philo and others), from Grecian philosophy into the current of Jewish thought" (*Philo, Plato, and Paul,* p. 71).

The presentation of Jesus as an incarnation of the Logos belongs to the second century and is prominent in the Fourth Gospel. The ideas are chiefly those of Plato and Philo. Plato's trinity was Thought, Word and Deed. The Word occupies the second place in the Platonic trinity as it does in the Christian trinity. That the author of the gospel of John, written more than a century after the time of Philo, borrowed largely from that philosopher, is shown by the following parallels drawn from their writings:

Philo.—"The Logos is the Son of God" (*De Profugis*).
John.—"This [the Word] is the Son of God" (i, 34).
Philo.—"The Logos is considered the same as God" (*De Somniis*).
John.—"The Word was God" (i, 1).
Philo.—"He [the Logos] was before all things" (*De Leg. Allegor.*).
John.—"The same [the Word] was in the beginning with God" (i, 2).
Philo.—"The Logos is the agent by whom the world was made" (*De Leg. Allegor.*).
John.—"All things were made by him [the Word]" (i, 3).
Philo.—"The Logos is the light of the world" (*De Somniis*).
John.—"The Word was the true light" (i, 9).
Philo.—"The Logos only can see God" (*De Confus. Ling.*).
John.—"No man hath seen God. . . . He [the Word] hath declared him" (i, 18).

The Perfect Man

The New Testament contains at least five different mythical types or conceptions of Jesus Christ: 1. The Messiah of the synoptics, omitting the opening chapters of Matthew and Luke. 2. The Son of God, or demi-god, introduced in these opening chapters. 3. The incarnate Logos or God of John. 4. The Christ of Paul. 5. Eliminating these more or less supernatural types, there remains in these writings, in addition to the purely natural and purely human Jesus of Nazareth, a type known as the Ideal or Perfect Man. This type is not only mythical, but, in the stricter sense, supernatural and superhuman; for the perfect man must always remain an ideal rather than a real type of man.

The last type is believed by many to represent the primal stage in the deification of Jesus. This conception of Jesus has been held by many Rationalistic Christians, and by some conservative Rationalists in all ages. This, too, forms a part of the dualistic conception of Christ entertained by orthodox Christians, a conception which supposes him to have combined in his incarnation both a human and a divine element which made him both man and God. The portrayal of the vicarious suffering and death of this man has been one of the most powerful agents in the propagation of Christianity.

The molders of primitive Christianity were greatly influenced by various philosophical speculations—by the teachings of Pythagoras and Plato among the earlier, and by the writings of Philo and Seneca among the later philosophers. To Philo, we have seen, they were indebted largely for the Logos; to Seneca they were indebted chiefly for the Ideal or Perfect Man. The following extracts are from *The Christ Myth* of Mrs. Evans:

"Seneca advises the cherishing of a hope that victory in the form of a wise man will finally appear, because humanity requires that the exemplification of perfection should be visible."

"Seneca's conception of perfect humanity was a combination of the wise man of the Platonists and Stoics and the gentle sufferer who endures insult and sorrow."

"The Logos of Philo was too ethereal to answer all the demands of feeble humanity. The Godman must live and suffer and die among and for the people in order to make the sacrifice complete."

"Philo endowed the Logos of Heraclitus with the authority of a priestly mediator, who, floating between earth and heaven, brings God and man together; Seneca places this mediator as a suffering man among men. Philo, from his Jewish standpoint, made the Logos the priestly intercessor; Seneca, from the standpoint of his Stoical society, believed in the possibility of a perfect man as savior and guide of weaker men."

Cognizant of the striking resemblance between some of the writings of the New Testament and the writings of the Stoics, particularly of Seneca, modern Christian apologists affect to believe that this philosopher was acquainted with the history and the gospel of Christ. But the Stoical philosophy propounded by Seneca had been forming ever since the time of Zeno, three centuries before the time of Christ. Seneca himself was born before the Christian era, and no part of the New Testament was in existence when he wrote. Relative to this contention Lecky writes: "It is admitted that the greatest moralists of the Roman empire either never mentioned Christianity, or mentioned it with contempt. . . . The Jews, with whom the Christians were then identified, he (Seneca) emphatically describes as 'an accursed race.' " (*European Morals,* Vol. 1 pp. 340, 342). During the second and third centuries Christian scholars ransacked pagan literature for recognitions of Christ and Christianity. Regarding this, Lecky says: "At the time, when the passion for discovering these connections was most extravagant, the notion of Seneca and his followers being inspired by the Christians was unknown" (ibid., p. 346). Gibbon says: "The new sect [Christians] is totally unnoticed by Seneca" (*Rome,* Vol. I, 587, note).

Out of all these various religious systems and doctrines—out of sex worship and sun worship—out of the worship of the stars and the worship of the elements—out of the worship of animals and the worship of idols—out of Polytheism and Monotheism—out of the Mediatorial and Messianic ideas—out of the Logos and the Ideal Man of the philosophers—this Christ has come.

11

Sources of the Christ Myth—
Pagan Divinities

In the preceding chapter I have noticed some of the typical religious systems and beliefs from which Christ and Christianity were to a great extent derived. I shall next notice more particularly some of the so-called divine beings—some of the gods, and some of the mortals endowed with supernatural gifts, belonging to these systems. I shall show that there were many sons of gods besides Jehovah's "only begotten Son"; that each of them possessed some attribute possessed by him; that all of them lived or existed in the minds of men centuries before his time; and that many of them were prototypes of him, and furnished in a large degree the ideas which suggested him, or which are associated with him and his religion. My list will comprise the following, all of whom were believed by their worshipers or followers to be of divine descent: Krishna, Buddha, Confucius, Laou-tse, Zoroaster, Mithra, Sosiosh, Adonis, Osiris, Horus, Zeus, Apollo, Perseus, Hercules, Dionysos, Prometheus, Esculapius, Plato, Pythagoras, Bacchus, Saturn, Quirinus, Odin, Thor, and Baldur.

Krishna

Krishna was the eighth Avatar or incarnation of the god Vishnu, one of the Hindoo Trinity. In this incarnation Vishnu, it is said, "appeared in all the fullness of his power and glory." His mother was Devaki. He is believed to be a historical character, but his real history, like that of Jesus, is almost entirely obscured by myths. He lived from 900 to 1,200 years before the Christian era. The story of his life is to be found in the "Bhagavat," one of the "Puranas," while his religious teachings are given in the "Bhagavad-Gita," a poem belonging to the "Mahabarata."

The points of resemblance between Krishna and Christ that have been printed would fill a volume. Some of these are apocryphal, and not confirmed by the canonical scriptures of India. The limits of this chapter preclude an extended list even of the undoubtedly genuine. I shall confine myself chiefly to a presentation of the most important ones relating to their births. These, according to the Christian translator of the "Bhagavat Purana," Rev. Thomas Maurice, are as follows:

1. Both were miraculously conceived.
2. Both were divine incarnations.
3. Both were of royal descent.
4. Devatas or angels sang songs of praise at the birth of each.
5. Both were visited by neighboring shepherds.
6. In both cases the reigning monarch, fearing that he would be supplanted in his kingdom by the divine child, sought to destroy him.
7. Both were saved by friends who fled with them in the night to distant countries.
8. Foiled in their attempts to discover the babes both kings issued decrees that all the infants should be put to death.

Writing of Krishna in the eighteenth century, Sir William Jones says: "In the Sanscrit dictionary, compiled more than two thousand years ago, we have the whole history of the incarnate deity, born of a virgin, and miraculously escaping in infancy from the reigning tyrant of his country" (*Asiatic Researches,* Vol. I, p. 273).

The subsequent careers of these deities are analogous in many respects. Their missions were the same—the salvation of mankind. Both performed miracles—healed the sick and raised the dead. Both died for man by man. There is a tradition, though not to be found in the Hindoo scriptures, that Krishna, like Christ, was crucified.

Various incidents recorded in the life of Christ were doubtless suggested by similar incidents in the life of Krishna. He washed the feet of his disciples because Krishna had washed the feet of the Brahmins. He taught his disciples the possibility of removing a mountain, because Krishna, to protect his worshipers from the wrath of Indra, raised Mount Goverdhen above them. His parents in their flight with him, as related in the Gospel of the Infancy, stopped at a place called Maturea. Krishna was born at Mathura.

The earliest followers of each were from the lower classes of society, those of Krishna being herdsmen and milkmaids. Christ's most ardent worshipers have from the first been women: "Chrishna," to quote the authority last mentioned, "continues to this hour the darling god of the women of India."

McClintock and Strong's *Cyclopedia* notes the following events in the history of Krishna which correspond with those related of Christ: "That he was miraculously born at midnight of a human mother and saluted by a chorus of Devatas [angels]; that he was cradled among cowherds, during which period of life he was persecuted by the giant Kansa, and saved by his mother's flight; the miracles with which his life abounds, among which were the raising of the dead and the cleansing of the leprous" (Art. "Krishna").

The celebrated missionary and traveler, Pere Huc, who made a journey of several thousand miles through China and Tibet, says. "If we addressed a Mogul or Tibetan this question, Who is Krishna? the reply was instantly 'The savior of men.'" "All that converting the Hindoos to Christianity does for them," says Robert Cheyne, "is to change the object of their worship from Krishna to Christ." Of Krishna's gospel, the "Bhagavad-Gita," *Appleton's Cyclopedia* says, "Its correspondence with the New Testament is indeed striking."

The parallels between Krishna and Christ to be found in the Hindoo scriptures and the Christian Gospels are too numerous and too exact to be accidental. The legends of the one were borrowed from the other. It is admitted by Christian scholars that Krishna lived many centuries before Christ. To admit the priority of the Krishna legends is to deny, to this extent, the originality of the Gospels. To break the force of the logical conclusion to be drawn from this some argue that while Krishna himself antedated Christ, the legends concerning him are of later origin and borrowed from the Evangelists. Regarding this contention Judge Waite, in his *History of the Christian Religion,* says: "Here then, we have the older religion and the older god. This, in the absence of any evidence on the other side, ought to settle the question. To assume without evidence that the older religion has been interpolated from the later, and that the legends of the older hero have been made to conform to the history of a later character, is worse than illogical—it is absurd."

Sir William Jones, one of the best Christian authorities on Sanscrit literature, and the translator of the "Bhagavad-Gita," says: "That the name of Krishna, and the general outline of his history were long anterior to the birth of our Savior, and probably to the time of Homer [950 B.C.], we know very certainly" (*Asiatic Researches,* Vol. I. p. 254).

Buddha

The ninth incarnation of Vishnu was Buddha. The word Buddha, like the word Christ, is not a name, but a title. It means "the enlightened one." The name of this religious founder was Siddhartha Gautama. He was born about 643 B.C., and died 563 B.C. His mother, Mahamaya, was a virgin. Dean Milman, in his *History of Christianity,* says: "Buddha, according to a tradition known in the West, was born of a virgin" (Vol. I, p. 99, note). Devaki, Mary and Mahamaya, all gave birth to their children among strangers. Krishna was born in a prison, Christ in a stable, and Buddha in a garden. *Werner's Encyclopedia,* in its article on Buddha, speaks of "the marvelous stories which gathered round the belief in his voluntary incarnation, the miracles at his birth, the prophecies of the aged saint at his formal presentation to his father, and how nature altered her course to keep a shadow over his cradle, whilst the sages from afar came and worshiped him."

The "Tripitaka," the principal Bible of the Buddhists, containing the history and teachings of Buddha, is a collection of books written in the centuries immediately following Buddha. The canon was finally determined at the Council of Pataliputra, held under the auspices of the Emperor Asoka the Great, 244 B.C., more than 600 years before the Christian canon was established, The "Lalita Vistara," the sacred book of the Northern Buddhists, was written long before the Christian era.

Buddha was "about 30 years old" when he began his ministry. He fasted "seven times seven nights and days." He had a "band of disciples" who accompanied him. He traveled from place to place and "preached to large multitudes." Bishop Bigandet calls his first sermon the "Sermon on the Mount." At his Renunciation "he forsook father and mother, wife and child." His mission was "to establish the kingdom of righteousness." "Buddha," says Max Mueller, "promised salvation to all; and he commanded his disciples to preach his doctrine in all places and to all men." "Self-conquest and universal charity" are the fundamental principles of his religion. He enjoined humanity, and commanded his followers to conceal their charities. "Return good for evil"; "overcome anger with love"; "love your enemies," were some of his precepts.

Buddha formulated the following commandments. "Not to kill; not to steal; not to lie; not to commit adultery; not to use strong drink." Christ said. "Thou knowest the commandments, do not commit adultery; do not kill; do not steal; do not bear false witness; honor thy father and thy mother" (Luke xviii, 20). Christ ignored the Decalogue of Moses and, like Buddha, presented a pentade which, with the exception of one commandment, is the same as that of Buddha.

Prof. Seydel, of the University of Leipsig, points out fifty analogies between Christianity and Buddhism. Dr. Schleiden calls attention to over one hundred. Baron Hiarden-Hickey says: "Countless analogies exist between the Buddhistic and Christian legends—analogies so striking that they forcibly prove to an impartial mind that a common origin must necessarily be given to the teachings of Sakay-Muni and those of Jesus."

Concerning the biographical accounts of the two religious teachers Harden-Hickey says: "One account must necessarily be a copy of the other, and since the Buddhist biographer, living long before the birth of Christ, could not have borrowed from the Christian one, the plain inference is that the early creed-mongers of Alexandria were guilty of an act of plagiarism." The following are some of the parallels presented by this writer:

Both have genealogies tracing their descent from ancestral kings.

Both were born of virgin mothers.

The conception of each was announced by a divine messenger.

The hymns uttered at the two annunciations resemble each other.

Both were visited by wise men who brought them gifts.

Both were presented in the temple.

The aged Simeon of the one account corresponds to the aged Asita of the other.

As "the child (Jesus) grew and waxed strong in spirit," so "the child (Sakay-Muni) waxed and increased in strength."

Both in childhood discoursed before teachers.

Both fasted in the wilderness.

Both were tempted.

Angels or devatas ministered to each.

Buddha bathed in the Narajana, and Christ was baptized in the Jordan.

The mission of each was proclaimed by a voice from Heaven. Both performed miracles. Both sent out disciples to propagate their faiths.

In calling their disciples the command of each was, "Follow me."

Buddha preached on the Holy Hill, and Christ delivered his sermon on the Mount.

The phraseology of the sermons of Buddha and the sermon ascribed to Christ is, in many instances, the same.

Both Buddha and Christ compare themselves to husbandmen sowing seed.

The story of the prodigal son is found in both Scriptures.

The account of the man born blind is common to both.

In both the mustard seed is used as a simile for littleness.

Christ speaks of "a foolish, man, which built his house upon the sand"; Buddha says, "Perishable is the city built of sand."

Both speak of "the rain which falls on the just and on the unjust."

The story of the ruler, Nicodemus, who came to Jesus by night, has its parallel in the story of the rich man who came to Buddha by night.

A converted courtesan, Magdalena, followed Jesus, and a converted courtesan, Ambapali, followed Buddha.

There is a legend of a traitor connected with each.

Both made triumphal entries, Christ into Jerusalem, and Buddha into Rajagriba.

Both proclaimed kingdoms not of this world.

The eternal life promised by Christ corresponds to the eternal peace, Nirvana, promised by Buddha.

Both religions recognize a trinity.

"Catholic and Protestant missionaries," to quote Max Mueller again, "vie with each other in their praises of Buddha." Bishop Bigandet, one of the leading Christian writers on Buddha, says: "In reading the particulars of the life of Buddha it is impossible not to feel reminded of many circumstances relating to our Savior's life as sketched by the evangelists. It may be said in favor of Buddhism that no philosophic-religious system has ever upheld to an equal degree the notions of a savior and deliverer, and the necessity of his mission for procuring the salvation of man." St. Hilaire says: "He [Buddha] requires humility, disregard of worldly wealth, patience and resignation in adversity, love to enemies . . . non-resistance to evil, confession of sins and conversion." The bishop of Ramatha says: "There are many moral precepts equally commanded and enforced in common by both creeds. It will not be rash to assert that most of the moral truths prescribed in the gospel are to be met with in the Buddhistic scriptures." Writing of Buddhisim Mrs. Spier, in her *Life in Ancient India,* says: "Before God planted Christianity upon earth, he took a branch from the luxuriant tree, and threw it down to India."

The external forms of Christianity, especially of Catholic Christianity, are modeled in a large degree after those of Buddhism. Of Northern Buddhism (Lamaism) the *Encyclopedia Britannica* says: "Lamaisnu with its shaven priests, its bells and rosaries, its images and holy water, its popes and bishops, its abbots and monks of many grades, its processions and feast days, its confessional and purgatory, and its worship of the double Virgin, so strongly resembles Romanism that the first Catholic missionaries thought it must be an imitation by the devil of the religion of Christ." The central object in every Buddhist temple is an image of Buddha. The central object in every Catholic church is an image of Christ. Holy relics and the veneration of saints are prominent in both.

Buddha commanded his disciples to preach his gospel to all men. Christ commanded his disciples to do the same. In obedience to these commands the world was filled with missionaries, and largely as the result of this the adherents of these religious systems outnumber those of all others combined. Christian tradition says that Thomas visited India. Some believe that it was in this way that the early Christians became acquainted with the history and teachings of Krishna and Buddha. This may be true, but so far as the Buddhistic element in Christianity is concerned it is quite as reasonable to suppose that Buddhist missionaries had previously carried their religion to Alexandria and Rome, where the molders of the Christian creed obtained their knowledge of it. "That remarkable missionary movement, beginning 300 B.C.," says Max Mueller, "sent forth a succession of devoted men who spent their lives in spreading the faith of Buddha over all parts of Asia." Harden-Hickey says: "It is not doubted at the present day that Indian religious ideas, and indeed more particularly those of Buddhism, reached and were even propagated as far as Egypt, Asia Minor, and Palestine, long before the Christian era."

Connected with the triumphs of these religious faiths there is a historical analogy deserving mention. Three centuries after the time of Buddha, Asoka the Great, emperor of India, became a convert to the Buddhist faith, made it the state religion of the empire, and did more than any other man to secure its supremacy in the East. Three centuries after Christ, Constantine the Great, emperor of Rome, became a convert to the Christian faith, made it the state religion of his empire, and won for it the supremacy of the West.

Remuset says: "Buddhism has been called the Christianity of the East." It would be more appropriate to call Christianity the Buddhism of the West. Buddha, and not Christ, was "The Light of Asia." At this torch Christians lighted their taper and called it "The Light of the World."

Confucius

This great Chinese sage and religious founder was born 551 B.C. His followers believed him to be divine. His birth was attended by prodigies. Magi and angels visited him, while celestial music filled the air.

His disciples invented a genealogy for him, giving him a princely descent from Hoang-ti, a Chinese monarch, just as the Christian Evangelists at a later period invented genealogies for Christ, giving him a princely pedigree from David. Concerning his deification the *International Encyclopedia* says: "By the irony of fate he was deified after his death, and, like Buddha, Confucius, who had little belief in the supernatural, became a divinity."

As Boulger states, "His name and his teachings were perpetuated by a band of devoted disciples, and the book which contained the moral and philosophical axioms of Confucius passed into the classical literature of the country and stood in the place of a Bible for the Chinese" (*History of China*, p. 16).

Of all the great religious systems which have appeared since the dawn of history Buddhism and Confucianism, as originally presented, from a rational standpoint, stand pre-eminent. In both the supernatural is almost entirely absent. Both are godless religions, and both have been, for the most part, bloodless religions. The adherents of both have practiced in the highest degree what the adherents of their great rival have only professed: "On earth peace, good will toward men." Both systems, like primitive Christianity, have been corrupted; but the system of Confucius has suffered less than that of Buddha. The religious, or rather ethical, system taught by Confucius, is the religion of the intellectual aristocracy of China, and, to a great extent, the religion of the most enlightened everywhere.

Christian scholars have been surprised to find in the writings of Confucius some of the best teachings attributed to Christ. The Golden Rule has been ascribed to the Christian founder. And yet this rule is the very essence of Confucianism and was borrowed from it. In a presentation of the teachings of the Chinese sage, Rev. James Legge of Oxford University, the highest European authority on China and Confucius, says: "Foremost among these we must rank his distinct enunciation of the Golden Rule, deduced by him from his study of man's mental condition. Several times he gave that rule in express words: 'What you do not like when done to yourself do not to others.' "

To retain for Christ a portion of the credit due Confucius, Christians assert that the Chinese moralist merely taught the negative form of this rule, the abstaining from doing to others what we dislike to have them do to us, while Christ taught the positive form, the doing to others what we desire them to do to us. Regarding this Mr. Legge says: "It has been said that he only gave the rule in a negative form; but he understood it also in its positive and most comprehensive form, and deplored on one occasion at least, that he had not himself always attained to taking the initiative in doing to others as he would have them do to him."

Another analogy may be noticed. The religion of Confucius enjoins absolute obedience to national rulers. "This, too, is a prominent tenet of the Christian religion. As the result of this, Confucianism became and has remained the state religion of China, while Christianity became and has remained the state religion of Europe

Laou-tsze

Laou-tsze, the other great religious founder of China, was born 604 B.C. His entry into the world and his exit from it were attended by miracles. Like Christ he was miraculously conceived; like Christ he ascended bodily into heaven. He was believed to be an incarnation of an astral god.

His gospel, the "Tao Teh King," was written by him. "Tao" means "the Way." Christ was called "the Way." Man, according to this gospel, is both a material and a spiritual being. By the renunciation of riches and worldly enjoyments the soul attains to immortality. The most divine of mortals are, like Enoch and Elijah, translated to heaven without suffering death. Laou-tsze taught that men to be righteous must become "as little children." Christ said: "Except ye be converted and become as little children, ye shall not enter into the kingdom of heaven" (Matt. xviii. 3).

The more ignorant followers of Laou-tsze, like the more ignorant followers of Christ, believe that many diseases are caused by evil spirits, and their priests, like Christ, practice exorcism to expel them. Like the Catholics, they have monasteries and convents.

Of Laou-tsze's writings Prof. Montuci, the Italian philologist, says: "Many things about a triune God are so clearly expressed that no one who has read this book can doubt that the mystery of the Holy Trinity was revealed to the Chinese five centuries before the coming of Christ."

There is one element in Christianity which was not borrowed from Paganism—religious intolerance. Referring to Buddhism, Confucianism, and Taouism, a writer on China says: "Between the followers of the three national religions there is not only a total absence of persecution and bitter feeling, but a very great indifference as to which of them a man may belong. . . . Among the politer classes, when strangers meet, the question is asked: 'To what sublime religion do you belong,' and each one pronounces a eulogium, not on his own religion, but on that professed by the others, and concludes with the oft-repeated formula: 'Religions are many; reason is one; we are all brothers.' "

Zoroaster

The Persian prophet Zoroaster lived and wrote at least 1200 years before the Christian era. From his teachings some of the most important doctrines of Christianity, as well as of Judaism, were derived.

According to the Persian theology the universe is ruled by two great powers, Ormuzd (God) and Ahrimanes (Satan). The one represents light, the other darkness; the one is good, the other evil. Between these two powers there is perpetual war. The center of battle is man, each striving for his soul. God created man with a free will to choose between good and evil. Those who choose the good are rewarded with everlasting life in heaven; those who choose the evil are punished with endless misery in hell; while those in whom the good and evil are balanced pass into an intermediate state (purgatory), to remain until the last judgment.

To save mankind God sent a savior in the person of Zoroaster with a divine revelation, the "Zend Avesta." Like Christ, Zoroaster was of supernatural origin and endowed with superhuman powers. Like Christ, he believed that Satan would be dethroned and cast into hell; like Christ he believed that the end of the world and the kingdom of God were at hand; like Christ, he taught his followers to worship God; like Christ he declared that God heard and answered prayer; like Christ he was tempted by Satan; like Christ he performed miracles; like Christ he was slain by those whom he had come to save.

McClintock and Strong's *Cyclopedia* gives a summary of the principal doctrines of Zoroaster among which are the following:

"The principal duty of man in this life is to obey the word and commandments of God.

"Those who obey the word of God will be free from all defects and immortal.

"God exercises his rule in the world through the works prompted by the Divine Spirit, who is working in man and nature.

"Men should pray to God and worship him. He hears the prayers of the good.

"All men live solely through the bounty of God.

"The soul of the pure will hereafter enjoy everlasting life; that of the wicked will have to undergo everlasting punishment" (Art. "Zoroaster").

Devils and angels are of Persian origin. Dr. Kalisch, the eminent Jewish scholar, says: "When the Jews, ever open to foreign influence in matters of faith, lived under Persian rule, they imbibed, among many other religious views of their masters, their doctrines of angels and spirits, which, in the region of the Eurphrates and Tigris, were most luxuriantly developed" (*Leviticus,* Part II, p. 287). "The belief in spirits and demons was not a concession made by educated men to the prejudices of the masses, but a concession which all—the educated as well as the uneducated—made to Pagan polytheism" (ibid.).

Strauss says: "It is in the Maccabean Daniel and in the Apocryphal Tobit that this doctrine of angels, in the most precise form, first appears; and it is evidently a product of the influence of the Zend religion of the Persian or the Jewish mind. We have the testimony of the Jews themselves that they brought the names of the angels with them from Babylon" (*Leben Jesu,* p. 78).

Baptism, communion, and even confirmation, are rites that were performed in Persia a thousand years before the advent of Christ. Dr. Hyde, in his *Religion of the Ancient Persians,* says: "They do not use circumcision for their children, but only baptism or washing for the inward purification of the soul. . . . After such washing, or baptism, the priest imposes on the child the name given by his parents. Afterwards, in the fifteenth year of his age, when he begins to put on the tunic, the sudra, and the girdle, that he may enter upon religion, and is engaged in the articles of belief, the priest bestows upon him confirmation."

The following, from the *Britannica,* was written by England's leading authority on Zoroaster, Professor Gildner. "Like John the Baptist and the Apostles of Jesus, Zoroaster also believed that the fullness of time was near, that the kingdom of heaven was at hand. Through the whole of the Gathas (the Psalms of Zoroaster) runs the pious hope that the end of the present world is not far off. He himself hopes along with his followers to live to see the decisive turn of things, the dawn of the new and better aeon. Ormuzd will summon together all his powers for a final struggle and break the power of evil forever; by his help the faithful will achieve the victory over their detested enemies, the daeva worshipers, and render them powerless. Thereupon Ortmuzd will hold a judicium universale upon all mankind and judge strictly according to justice, punish the wicked, and assign to the good the hoped-for reward. Satan will be cast, along with all those who have been delivered over to him to suffer the pains of hell, into the abyss, where he will thenceforward lie powerless. Forthwith begins the one undivided kingdom of God in heaven and on earth."

Substitute "Christ" for "Zoroaster," "God" for "Ormuzd," and "Gospels" for "Gathas," in the above, and we have almost an exact exposition of the teachings of Christ. And Zoroaster taught at least 1200 years before Christ taught, and wrote his "Gathas" more than 1300 years before the Gospels were written. The writings of Zoroaster were the principal source of the most important theological doctrines ascribed to Christ, as the Buddhistic writings were of his ethical teachings.

Mithra(s)

This god was the offspring of the Sun, and, next to Ormuzd and Ahrimanes, held the highest rank among the gods of ancient Persia. He was represented as a beautiful youth. He is the Mediator. From the Rev. J. W. Lake I quote the following: "Mithras is spiritual light contending with spiritual darkness, and through his labors the kingdom of darkness shall be lit with heaven's own light; the Eternal will receive all things back into his favor, the world will be redeemed to God. The impure are to be purified, and the evil made good, through the mediation of Mithras, the reconciler of Ormuzd and Ahriman. Mithras is the Good, his name is Love. In relation to the Eternal he is the source of grace, in relation to man he is the life-giver and mediator" (*Plato, Philo, and Paul,* p. 15).

The *International Encyclopedia* says: "Mithras seems to have owed his prominence to the belief that he was the source of life, and could also redeem the souls of the dead into the better world. . . . The ceremonies included a sort of baptism to remove sins, anointing, and a sacred meal of bread and water, while a consecrated wine, believed to possess wonderful power, played a prominent part."

Concerning Mithra *Chambers' Encyolopedia* says: "The most important of his many festivals was his birthday, celebrated on the 25th of December, the day subsequently fixed—against all evidence—as the birthday of Christ. The worship of Mithras early found its way into Rome, and the mysteries of Mithras, which fell in the spring equinox, were famous even among the many Roman festivals. The ceremonies observed in the initiation to these mysteries—symbolical of the struggle between Ahriman and Ormuzd (the Good and the Evil)—were of the most extraordinary and to a certain degree even dangerous character. Baptism and the partaking of a mystical liquid, consisting of flour and water, to be drunk with the utterance of sacred formulas, were among the inauguration acts."

In the catacombs at Rome was preserved a relic of the old Mithraic worship. It was a picture of the infant Mithra seated in the lap of his virgin mother, while on their knees before him were Persian Magi adoring him and offering gifts.

Prof. Franz Cumont, of the University of Ghent, writes as follows concerning the religion of Mithra and the religion of Christ: "The sectaries of the Persian god, like the Christians', purified themselves by baptism, received by a species of confirmation the power necessary to combat the spirit of evil; and expected from a Lord's supper salvation of body and soul. Like the latter, they also held Sunday sacred, and celebrated the birth of the Sun on the 25th of December. . . . They both preached a categorical system of ethics, regarded asceticism as meritorious and counted among their principal virtues abstinence and continence, renunciation and self-control. Their conceptions of the world and of the destiny of man were similar. They both admitted the existence of a Heaven inhabited by beatified ones, situated in the upper regions, and of a Hell, peopled by demons, situated in the bowels of the earth. They both placed a flood at the beginning of history; they both assigned as the source of their condition, a primitive revelation; they both, finally, believed in the immortality of the soul, in a last judgment, and in a resurrection of the dead, consequent upon a final conflagration of the universe" (*The Mysteries of Mithras*, pp. 190, 191).

The Rev. Charles Biggs, D.D., says: "The disciples of Mithra formed an organized church, with a developed hierarchy. They possessed the ideas of Mediation, Atonement, and a Savior, who is human and yet divine, and not only the idea, but a doctrine of the future life. They had a Eucharist, and a Baptism, and other curious analogies might be pointed out between their system and the church of Christ (*The Christian Platonists*, p. 240).

I quote again from McClintock and Strong: "In modern times Christian writers have been induced to look favorably upon the assertion that some of our ecclesiastical usages (e.g., the institution of the Christmas festival) originated in the cultus of Mithraism. Some writers who refuse to accept the Christian religion as of supernatural origin, have even gone so far as to institute a close comparison with the founder of Christianity; and Dupuis and others, going even beyond this, have not hesitated to pronounce the Gospel simply a branch of Mithraism" (Art. "Mithra").

The Christian Father Manes, founder of the heretical sect known as Manicheans, believed that Christ and Mithra were one. His teaching, according to Mosheim, was as follows: "Christ is that glorious intelligence which the Persians called Mithras. . . . His residence is in the sun" (*Ecclesiastical History*, 3rd century, Part 2, ch. 5).

The Mithraic worship at one time covered a large portion of the ancient world. It flourished as late as the second century, but finally went down before its young and invincible rival which appropriated, to a great extent, its doctrines, rites and customs.

Sosiosh

The Messianic idea, as we have seen, came from Persia. The expected Messiah of the Jews and the Christ of Christians are of Persian origin. Sosiosh, the Messiah of the Persians, is the son of Zoroaster, "begotten in a supernatural way." He constitutes a part of the Persian Trinity. He exists, as yet, only in a spiritual form. His incarnation and advent on earth, are yet to be. When he comes he will bring with him a new revelation. He will awaken the dead and preside at the last judgment. Zoroaster, it is claimed, predicted his coming declaring that he would be born of a virgin, and that a star would indicate the place of his birth. "As soon, therefore," said Zoroaster, "as you shall behold the star, follow it whithersoever it shall lead you and adore that mysterious child, offering your gifts to him with profound humility." "And, lo, the star, which they saw in the east, went before them till it came and stood over where the young child was. And when they were come into the house, they saw the young child with Mary, his mother, and fell down, and worshiped him; and when they had opened their treasures, they presented unto him gifts" (Matthew ii, 9, 11).

Adonis

From Babylonia, including Accadia, Chaldea, and Assyria, much of Christianity was come. Christ himself was descended from the Babylonian pantheon; his father, Jehovah, being originally a Babylonian god. Adonis, Tammouz, Tamzi, or Du-zi, as he was variously called, was a Babylonian deity whose worship gradually spread over Syria, Phoenicia and Greece. He was one of the most ancient of the sons of gods. His origin may be traced to that fertile, and perhaps earliest, source of gods and religions, Accadia. His worship was a combination of sun worship and sex worship. He was the god of light, and life, and love. Associated with his worship in Babylonia and Syria was the worship of Istar; and in Phoenicia and Greece the worship of Venus.

Under the name of Tammouz, Adonis was worshiped by the Jews. At the very gates of the temple, Ezekiel tells us, "There sat women weeping for Tammouz" ("Adonis" in Catholic ver.) (viii, 14). In the Bible he is frequently referred to as "the only son." One of the months of the Hebrew calendar was named in honor of him. The abstaining from the use of pork by the Jews had its origin in the legend of the slaying of Adonis by the wild boar. And the eating of fish on Friday by Christians is doubtless due to the fact that Friday was consecrated to Venus by her Asiatic worshipers and fish was eaten in her honor.

In a citation of Babylonian and Biblical analogies, the *Encyclopedia Britannica* says: "The resemblance is still more striking when we examine the Babylonian mythology. The sacred tree of Babylonia, with its guardian cherubs—a word, by the way, which seems of Accadian origin—as well as the flaming sword or thunderbolt of fifty pounds and seven heads, recall Biblical analogies, while the Noachian deluge differs but slightly from the Chaldean one. Indeed, the Jehovistic version of the flood story in Genesis agrees not only in details, but even in phraseology with that which forms the eleventh lay of the great Babylonian epic. The hero of the latter is Tam-zi or Tammuz, 'the sun of life,' the son of Ubaratutu, 'the glow of sunset,' and denotes the revivifying luminary of day, who sails upon his 'ark' behind the clouds of winter to reappear when the rainy season is past. He is called Sisuthrus by Berosus, that is, Susru 'the founder,' a synonym of Na 'the sky.' The mountain on which his ark rested was placed in Nisir, southwest of Lake Urumiyeh. Its peak, whereon the first altar was built after the deluge, was the legendary model after which the zigurats or towers of the Babylonian temples were erected. Besides the account of the flood, fragments have been met with of stories resembling those of the tower of Babel or Babylon, of the creation, of the fall, and of the sacrifice of Isaac—the latter, by the way, forming the first lay of the great epic. The sixth lay we possess in full. It describes the descent of Istar into Hades in pursuit of her dead husband Du-zi, 'the off-spring,' the Babylonian Adonis. Du-zi is but another form of Tam-zi and denotes the sun when obscured by night and winter."

Concerning the two lays of this Babylonian or Assyrian epic which pertain to Adonis, Dr. Soury says: "The two important episodes of this epic hitherto discovered, 'The Deluge,' and 'The Descent of Istar into Hell,' yield the best commentary on the biblical stories of the deluge and hell (sheol). We have henceforth the epigraphic proof, confirming the valuable testimony of Berosus, that these legends—like those of the creation, of the Tower of Babel, etc.—did not originate in Palestine, but were carried thither by the Hebrews with the civilization and worship of the people of the valley of the Tigris and Euphrates, amid whom they had sojourned for centuries. . . . The Babylonian deluge is also a chastisement from the deity; it is the consequence of man's corruption (Assyrian poem, line 22). The details of the building of the Babylonian ark (line 24), into which are introduced the various pairs of male and female animals (line 80), of the shutting of the doors of the ark (line 89), of the duration, increase and decrease of the flood (lines 123–129), of the sending out of a dove, a swallow and a raven (lines 140–144), etc., leave no doubt as to the origin of the legend of Genesis" (*Religion of Israel,* p. 10).

The noted Assyriologist, George Smith, of the British Museum, who discovered the tablets containing these fragments of the Babylonian epic, says that the original text of these legends cannot be later than the 17th century B.C., and may be much earlier, thus antedating the oldest books of the Bible nearly 1,000 years. From these and other Babylonian and Persian legends the most of the Old Testament legends were borrowed. This fact disproves the existence of the orthodox Christ. If the accounts of the creation, the fall of man, and the Noachian deluge, as given in the Bible, are not authentic, but merely borrowed fables, then there remains no foundation for an atoning Savior.

Describing the worship of Adonis, *Chambers' Encyclopedia* says: "His festivals were partly the expressions of joy, partly of mourning. In the latter the women gave themselves up to the most unmitigated grief over the 'lost Adonis.' . . . This period was followed by a succession of festive and joyful days, in honor of the resurrection of Adonis." These festivals correspond to the Good Friday and Easter of Christians, commemorating the death and resurrection of Christ.

The most ardent worshipers of Adonis were women. No other character, real or imaginary, has so stirred the passions and the emotions of woman as this beautiful young lover of Venus. His tragic death bathed with immortal sadness the hearts of his devotees, and from the remotest ages down to a very late period moved to tears the daughters of men who adored him. Writing of Bethlehem at the close of the fourth century, St. Jerome says: "The lover of Venus is mourned in the grotto where Christ wailed as an infant." Along with the "Holy Sepulchre" of Christ, there still exists the "Tomb of Adonis" where "the women of the ancient mysteries, in the intoxication of a voluptuous grief, came to cover with tears and kisses the cenotaph of the beautiful youth." "Even at the present time," says Renan, "the Syrian hymns sung in honor of the Virgin are a kind of tearful sigh, a strange sob.

Moved by the same passions and the same emotious that thrilled the hearts of the female worshipers of Adonis, it is the women of Christendom, who, more than any other cause, keep alive the memory and the religion of Christ. Thus writes a Carmelite nun describing the passionate adoration of her Christian sisters:

"One day they have raised their eyes to an adorable face. A horrible diadem of interlaced branches binds the august forehead; rubies of blood roll slowly upon the livid pallor of the cheeks; the mouth has forgotten how to smile. It is a man of sorrows. They have looked upon him and found him more beautiful, more noble, more loyal than any spouse. They have felt a stronger heart-beat in his divine breast; they have understood that death no more dare touch his emaciated figure, and that his conjugal fidelity is eternal.

"Captivated, ravished, enamoured, enraptured, they have loved him. Rendered insensible by love, they have trampled cruelly upon the broken hearts of fathers and desolate mothers; they have listened, tearless, to the woeful beseechings of those who desire them for companions; they have followed to Carmel the unique lover, the immortal husband."

The ancient adoration of Adonis survives in this modern adoration of Jesus. We see here the same strange commingling of superstition and fanaticism, of love and sorrow, of ecstasy and agony, of chastity and lust. The religion is the same; the worship is the same. The divine lovers only have been changed. The beautiful Pagan has been supplanted by the Ideal Man.

Writing of the Protestant women of his day, Thomas Jefferson says: "In our Richmond there is much fanaticism, but chiefly among the women. They have their night meetings and praying parties, where, attended by their priests, . . . they pour forth their love to Jesus in terms as amatory and carnal as their modesty would permit to a mere earthly lover" (*Jefferson's Works,* Vol. IV, p. 358, Randolph's ed.).

Osiris

One of the most ancient and one of the most renowned of all the gods was Osiris, the Savior of Egypt. He was the son of Seb (earth) and Nu (heaven). He appears in the hieroglyphics of Egypt as early as 3427 B.C. Two thousand years before Christ his worship was universal in Egypt, and during the succeeding centuries spread over much of Asia and Europe, including Greece and Rome. Its priests looked confidently forward to the time when all men would be brought to Osiris, just as Christian priests today look forward to the time when all men will be brought to Christ.

Osiris was slain by Typhon (Satan), but rose again and became the ruler of the dead. He presides at the judgment of the departed where the good are rewarded with everlasting life, and the wicked are destroyed. The Osirian Bible is called the "Book of the Dead."

Christians are indebted to this religion largely for their views concerning immortality and a bodily resurrection. They believe that through the death and resurrection of Christ they have inherited eternal life, that when their earthly career is ended they will live again in him. Regarding the Egyptians' belief, the *International Encyclopedia* says: "Just as Osiris died and lived again, so the spiritual personality of the deceased lived again and was merged in Osiris." Of Osiris the Rev. Dr. Charles Gillett, of Union Theological Seminary, says: "The belief in him and in the immortality which he symbolized was the deepest in Egyptian religious thought." Sir John Gardner Wilkinson, one of the most eminent Egyptologists, says: "The peculiar character of Osiris, his coming upon earth for the benefit of mankind, with the titles of 'Manifester of Good' and 'Revealer of Truth'; his being put to death by the malice of the Evil One; his burial and resurrection, and his becoming the judge of the dead are the most interesting features of the Egyptian religion." John Stuart Glennie, another English writer, notes the following analogies between the religion of Osiris and the religion of Christ: "In ancient Osirianism, as in modern Christianism, we find the worship of a divine mother and child. In ancient Osirianism as in modern Christianism, there is a doctrine of atonement. In ancient Osirianism, as in modern Christianism, we find the vision of a last judgment, and resurrection of the body. And finally, in ancient Osirianism, as in modern Christianism, the sanctions of morality are a lake of fire and torturing demons on the one hand, and on the other, eternal life in the presence of God" (*Christ and Osiris,* p. 14).

Referring to Osiris, McClintock and Strong's *Cyclopedia* says: "He was regarded as the personification of moral good. He is related to have been on earth instructing mankind in useful arts; to have been slain by his adversary Typhon by whom he was cut in pieces; to have been bewailed by his wife and sister Isis; to have been embalmed; to have risen again, and to have become the judge of the dead, among whom the righteous were called by his name and received his form— a wonderful fore-feeling of the Gospel narrative" (Art. "Egypt").

Isis, the sister and wife of Osiris, was the greatest of female divinities. Her worship was coexistent and coextensive with that of her divine brother and husband. We have the following picture of her in the Apocalypse: "And there appeared a great wonder in heaven; a woman clothed with the sun, and the moon under her feet, and upon her head a crown of twelve stars" (Revelation xii, 1). The worship of Isis existed in Rome and Alexandria during the formative period of Christianity and Christians borrowed much from it.

Horus

This popular Egyptian god was the son of Osiris and Isis. Osiris and Horus were both solar deities. Osiris was the setting sun, Horus the rising sun. Christ, it is claimed, existed before his incarnation; and Horus, it was claimed, existed even before the incarnation of his father. Christ when an infant was carried into Egypt to escape the wrath of Herod; Horus when an infant was carried out of Egypt to escape the wrath of Typhon. To avenge the death of his father he afterward vanquished Typhon. He was the last of the gods who reigned in Egypt. Festivals and movable feasts similar to those celebrated in honor of Christ were held in his honor.

In India and Egypt, ages before the appearance of Christianity, the doctrine of the Trinity prevailed. Brahma, Vishnu, and Siva constituted the principal trinity of India, while the most important Trinity of Egypt was Osiris, Isis, and Horus. Even the Christian doctrine of a Trinity in Unity, an absurdity which Christianity alone is supposed to have taught, was an Egyptian doctrine. Samuel Sharp, in his *Egyptian Mythology* (p. 14), says: "We have a hieroglyphical inscription in the British Museum as early as the reign of Sevechus of the eighth century before the Christian era, showing that the doctrine of Trinity in Unity already formed part of their religion and that . . . the three goals only made one person."

Dr. Draper says: "For thirty centuries the Egyptians had been familiar with the conception of a triune God. There was hardly a city of any note without its particular triads. Here it was Amum, Maut, and Khonso; there Osiris, Isis, and Horus" (*Intellectual Development*, Vol. I, p. 191).

Dr. Inman affirms the Egyptian origin of the Christian trinity: "The Christian trinity is of Egyptian origin, and is as sureiy a pagan doctrine as the belief in heaven and hell, the existence of a devil, of archangels, angels, spirits and saints, martyrs and virgins, intercessors in heaven, gods and demigods, and other forms of faith which deface the greater part of modern religions" (*Ancient Pagan and Modern Christian Symbolism*, p. 13).

There are two myths connected with Horus analogous to stories found in the Old Testament, and which were old when these stories were written. The hiding of Horus in a marsh by his mother undoubtedly suggested the myth of the hiding of Moses in a marsh by his mother. When Horus died Isis implored Ra, the sun, to restore him to life. Ra stopped his ship in mid-heaven and sent down Thoth, the moon, to bring him back to life. The stopping of the sun and moon by Isis recalls the myth of the stopping of the sun and moon by Joshua.

The deification and worship of the Virgin had its origin in the worship of Isis, and the adoration of the Virgin and Child is but the adoration of Isis and Horus transferred to Mary and Jesus. Describing the Paganization of Christianity Dr. Draper says: "Views of the Trinity, in accordance with Egyptian tradition, were established. Not only was the adoration of Isis under a new name restored, but even her image standing on the crescent moon reappeared. The well-known effigy of that goddess, with the infant Horus in her arms, has descended to our days in the beautiful artistic creations of the Madonna and Child" (*Conflict*, p. 48).

That the Virgin Mary of the Roman Catholic church was borrowed from Egypt is shown by the fact that in the earlier representations of her, she was, like Isis, veiled. Concerning this Draper, in his *Intellectual Development* (Vol. I, p. 361), says: "Of the Virgin Mary, destined in later times to furnish so many beautiful types of female loveliness, the earliest representations are veiled. The Egyptian sculptors had thus depicted Isis; the first form of the Virgin and child was the counterpart of his and Horus."

Dr. G. W. Brown, author of *Researches in Oriental History,* writes: "Mural illustrations of this mother and child are not confined to Egypt, but are scattered all over Asia Minor, and are numerous in Italy, while many temples and shrines are yet found which were erected to their memory. Matthew ii, 15, claims to be a quotation from one of the prophets: '*Out of Egypt have I called my son.*' "

Writing of the ancient Gnostics, C. W. King, a noted English author, says: "To this period belongs a beautiful sard in my collection, representing Serapis, . . . whilst before him stands Isis, holding in one hand the sistrum, in the other a wheatsheaf, with the legend: 'Immaculate is our lady Isis,' the very term applied afterwards to that personage who succeeded to her form, her symbols, rites, and ceremonies" (*Gnostics and Their Remains*, p. 71).

Regarding the transferrence of the attributes of Isis to Mary, Newton, in his *Assyrian Grove and Other Emblems,* says: "When Mary, the mother of Jesus, took the place in Christendom of 'the great goddess,' the dogmas which propounded her immaculate conception and perpetual virginity followed as a matter of course."

"The 'Black Virgins,' " says King, "so highly reverenced in certain French cathedrals during the middle ages, proved, when critically examined, basalt figures of Isis."

Mrs. Besant believes that Christianity was derived chiefly from Egypt:

"It grew out of Egypt; its gospels came from thence [Alexandria]; its ceremonies were learned there; its Virgin is Isis; its Christ Osiris and Horus."

Of the antiquity of Egypt's religion, and the mutability of the gods, that brilliant young Englishman, Winwood Reade, thus writes: "Buried cities are beneath our feet; the ground on which we tread is the pavement of a tomb. See the pyramids towering to the sky, with men, like insects, crawling round their base; and the Sphinx, couched in vast repose, with a ruined temple between its paws. Since those great monuments were raised the very heavens have been changed. When the architects of Egypt began their work, there was another polar star in the northern sky, and the southern cross shone upon the Baltic shores. How glorious are the memories of those ancient men, whose names are forgotten, for they lived and labored in the distant and unwritten past. Too great to be known, they sit on the height of centuries and look down on fame. . . . The men are dead, and the gods are dead. Naught but their memories remain. Where now is Osiris, who came down upon earth out of love for man, who was killed by the malice of the evil one, who rose again from the grave and became the judge of the dead? Where now is Isis the mother, with the child Horus in her lap? They are dead; they are gone to the land of the shades. To-morrow, Jehovah, you and your son shall be with them."

Zeus

Zeus, Jove, or Jupiter, as he is variously called, was the greatest of the sons of gods and held the highest place in the pantheons of Greece and Rome. He was the son of the god Kronos and the goddess Rhea.

The gods of Greece, while mostly pure myths, were yet intensely human. In these gods human vices sank to the lowest depths and human virtues rose to the loftiest heights. Zeus was one of the most puerile, one of the most sublime, one of the most depraved and one of the most beneficent of deities. In the words of Andrew Lang, "He is the sum of the religious thought of Hellas, found in the numberless ages between savagery and complete civilization."

Zeus, like Christ, assumed the form of man. The life of the infant Pagan deity, like that of the infant Christian deity, was imperiled. Kronos tried to destroy him, but he was secreted in a cave and saved. There was a widely accepted tradition among primitive Christians, before the myth of the shepherd's manger gained credence, that Christ was cradled in a cave. Concerning these myths, Strauss says: "The myths of the ancient world more generally ascribed divine apparitions to countrymen and shepherds; the sons of the gods, and of great men were frequently brought up among shepherds. In the same spirit of the ancient legend is the apocryphal invention that Jesus was born in a cave, and we are at once reminded of the cave of Jupiter (Zeus) and the other gods" (*Leben Jesu,* p. 154).

This god, like Jehovah, became the ruler of heaven and earth. Like Jehovah he became dissatisfied with the human race, and with the aid of Pandora, who brought death into the world, tried to destroy it that he might create a new race.

Seneca refers to Zeus as "the guardian and ruler of the universe, the soul and spirit, the lord and master of this mundane sphere . . . from whom all things proceed, by whose spirit we live." Lecky says: "The language in which the first Greek dramatists asserted the supreme authority and universal providence of Zeus was so emphatic that the Christian fathers commonly attributed it either to direct inspiration or to a knowledge of the Jewish writings" (*European Morals,* Vol. I, p. 161).

One of the daughters of Zeus was Persephone, Life. Her mother was Demeter, the earth. Hades seized Persephone and carried her to his regions in the lower world where she became his wife. Then Earth became disconsolate and could not be consoled. To assuage the grief of the sorrowing mother Hades agreed to give her back to earth for half the year. While Life dwells with her mother, Earth, we have summer, and flowers, and fruits, and joy. When Life returns to her husband, Hades, winter and desolation return to Earth. Of this goddess Ridpath says: "Persephone is close to Eve. Eve means Life, and should have been so rendered, and would have been but for the blundering of the English translators" (*History of the World,* Vol. II, p. 501).

The realm of Hades was called by his name. The term was borrowed by the writers of the New Testament but has been translated "hell."

Christians took possession of Hades' kingdom; but Hades was dethroned to make room for the Oriental Satan, and the sad yet peaceful abode of departed spirits was transformed into a lake of fire, the habitation of the damned.

The inhabitants of Crete, who believed in the incarnation and death of Zeus, guarded for centuries with zealous care what they alleged to be the tomb of their god.

Apollo

This god, one of the principal solar deities, was the son of Zeus. His mother was Leto. Like Mary, Leto had no hospitable palace for her accouchement, and brought her child forth on the barren isle of Delos, where female divinities ministered to them. The isle was illuminated by a flood of light, the prototype of a later scene where "the glory of the Lord shone round about" the shepherds in the field at Bethlehem; while sacred swans, like the celestial visitants of Luke, made joyous gyrations in the air above them.

Apollo was the best beloved god of Greece, and was represented as one of the most perfect types of manly beauty. Like Christ he led on earth a lowly life, following for a time the humble avocation of a herdsman. Like Christ he came to reveal the will of his father. He chose for his disciples a crew of sailors or fishermen. These, like the disciples of Christ, were endowed with miraculous powers. Apollo was regarded as a savior. He rescued the people from the deadly python, which was desolating the land. Numerous festivals, similar to those held in honor of Christ, were held in honor of Apollo.

In its article on this god McClintock and Strong's *Cyclopedia* says: "Towards the later period of the supremacy of paganism in the Roman Empire, Apollo, as the deity of the sun, had assumed the chief place in heathen worship. As indicating that Christ was the true 'light of the world,' the 'Sun of righteousness'—the most favorite figure used in speaking of the Savior in the early centuries—this very figure of Apollo was often introduced as indicating Christ."

Leto, the mother of Apollo, was believed to be, like Mary, the mother of Christ, a mortal raised to divinity. Her worship, like that of Mary, was widespread and lasted for centuries.

Perseus

The Virgin myth, the Holy Ghost myth, and the Herodian myth all have their prototypes in Perseus. Long before his birth, it was prophesied that he would be born of the virgin Danae, and that he would supplant Acrisius in his kingdom. To prevent this Acrisius confined Danae in a tower. Here she was overshadowed by Zeus in "a shower of gold" and Perseus was born. To destroy him Acrisius placed him with his mother in a chest and cast them into the sea. They drifted to an island and the child was saved. He grew to manhood, performed many wonderful works, vanquished his enemy and ascended the throne.

Hercules

This god was the son of Zeus and the virgin Alcmeni. His mother, like the mother of Jesus, retained her virginity after the birth of her child. The Greek babe, like the Jewish babe, had an enemy. Hera attempted to destroy the former, just as Herod afterward attempted to destroy the latter. Like Christ he died a death of agony. When his labors were finished, he closed his earthly career by mounting a funeral pyre from which, surrounded by a dark cloud, amid thunder and lightning, he ascended to heaven.

The Tyrian Hercules was worshiped by the Jews, and Jason, the Jewish high-priest, sent a religious embassy with an offering of 300 drachms of silver to this god.

Prof. Meinhold, of the University of Bonn, says: "The transfiguration and ascension of Christ may be compared to the heathen apotheosis of such heroes as Hercules, while the story of the descent into Hades is modeled after such narratives as those describing the visit of Hercules and Theseus to the lower world."

Max Mueller pronounces Hercules a solar god. His twelve labors, like the twelve apostles of Christ, correspond to the twelve signs of the Zodiac. Christians have admitted the resemblance of this god to Christ. Parkhurst's *Hebrew Lexicon* says: "The labors of Hercules seem to have had a still higher view and to have been originally designed as emblematical memorials of what the real son of God and savior of the world was to do and suffer for our sakes."

The Rev. Heinrich Rower says: "We are all acquainted with the fact that in their mythological legends the Greeks and the Romans and other nations of antiquity speak of certain persons as the sons of the gods. An example of this is Hercules, the Greek hero who is the son of Jupiter and an earthly mother. . . . All those men who performed greater deeds than those which human beings usually do are regarded by antiquity as of divine origin. This Greek and heathen notion has been applied to the New Testament and churchly conception of the person of Jesus. We must remember that at the time when Christianity sprang into evidence, Greek culture and Greek religion spread over the whole world. It is accordingly nothing remarkable that the Christians took from the heathens the highest religious conceptions that they possessed, and transferred them to Jesus. They accordingly called him the son of God, and declared that he had been supernaturally born of a virgin. This is the Greek and heathen influence which has determined the character of the account given by Matthew and Luke concerning the birth of Jesus."

Dionysos

Zagreus was the son of Zeus. He was slain by the Titans, buried at the foot of Mount Parnassus, and rose from the dead as Dionysos. He was the god of fruit and wine. Like those of Christ his most devoted followers were women. He is the beloved son and occupies a throne at the right hand of his father, Zeus. His empty tomb at Delphi was long preserved by his devotees as proof of his death, and resurrection.

The stories of the resurrection of Adonis in Phoenicia, of Osiris in Egypt and of Dionysos in Greece were old when Christ was born, and paved the way for the origin and acceptance of the story of his resurrection.

Justin Martyr recognized the analogies between Christianity and Paganism. Addressing the Pagans, he writes: "When we say that the Word, who is the first born of God, was produced without sexual union, and that he, Jesus Christ, our teacher, was crucified and died, and rose again, and ascended into heaven; we propound nothing different from what you believe regarding those whom you esteem sons of Jupiter (Zeus)" (*First Apology,* ch. xxi).

Festivals, called Lenaea and the Greater Dionysia, corresponding in a measure to the Christmas and Easter of Christians, were celebrated in honor of this god. Prof. Gulick, professor of Greek in Harvard University, describing these festivals, says: "In the winter came various celebrations in honor of Dionysos, god of nature and the vine, the object of which was to wake the sleeping spirit of generation and render him propitious for the coming of spring and the sowing of crops. . . . The wine-casks were opened, and all, even slaves, were allowed perfect holiday and liberty to drink in honor of the god. The last day of the festival was a sort of All Souls' Day, being devoted to the gods of the underworld and the spirits of the dead" (*Life of the Ancient Greeks,* pp. 274, 275). "The Great Dionysia," says Prof. Gulick, "held in the spring, was the occasion of display and magnificence" (ibid., p. 113).

So-called Christian burial is identical with Greek burial. Ancient Greek sepulture is thus described by Ridpath: "To the dead were due the sacred rites of sepulture. . . . When a Greek fell into his last slumber, the friends immediately composed the body. . . . The corpse was clad in white and laid upon a bier. Flowers were brought by the mourning friends, who put on badges of sorrow. . . . Cemeteries were arranged outside the city walls. . . . Over each [grave] was raised a mound of earth, and on this were planted ivy and roses. . . . Over the grave was erected a memorial stone or monument, and on this was an inscription giving the name of the dead, an effigy perhaps of his person, a word of praise for his virtues, and an epigram composed for his memory" (*History of the World,* Vol. II, p. 497).

Prometheus

The Titan god, Prometheus, was the son of Iapetus and Asia. He is one of the most sublime creations of the human imagination. When Zeus, like Jehovah, became enraged at mankind and sought to destroy it, Prometheus, like Christ, came on earth to intercede and suffer for the race. Hurried to Tartarus by the thunderbolts of Zeus he came again to endure, if need be, eternal agony for man.

For centuries Greeks and Romans believed the story of this vicarious god to be historical. Grote, the historian, says: "So long and so firmly did this belief continue, that the Roman general Pompey, when in command of an army in Kolchis, made with his companion, the literary Greek Theophanes, a special march to view the spot in Caucasus where Prometheus had been transfixed" (*Greek Mythology,* pp. 92, 93).

Referring to the Greeks and their great tragedy, "Prometheus Bound," A. L. Rawson says: "Its hero was their friend, benefactor, creator, and savior, whose wrongs were incurred in their behalf, and whose sorrows were endured for their salvation. He was wounded for their transgressions, and bruised for their iniquities; the chastisement of their peace was upon him, and by his stripes they were healed" (Isaiah iv, 5), (*Evolution of Israel's God,* p. 30). Alluding to this subject, Dr. Westbrook writes: "The New Testament description of the crucifixion and the attending circumstances, even to the earthquake and darkness, was thus anticipated by five centuries" (*Bible: Whence and What?*).

The dying Christ shares with the dying Prometheus the sympathies of men. But how trivial the crucifixion, how light the suffering, and how weak the courage of the Christian god appear compared with the cruel crucifixion, the infinite suffering, and the deathless courage of the immortal Pagan. Transfixed to the rock on Caucasus, the Golgotha of Greek mythology, with the devouring eagle feeding forever on his vitals, there falls from his lips no murmur of pain, no Sabachthani of despair. What lofty heroism, what enduring patience, what unselfish love, this tragic story has inspired!

To suffer woes which hope thinks infinite;
To forgive wrongs darker than death or night;
   To defy power which seems omnipotent;
To love and bear; to hope till hope creates
From its own wreck the thing it contemplates;
   Neither to change, to falter, nor repent;
This, like thy glory, Titan, is to be
Good, great, and joyous, beautiful and free.
                          —Shelley.

Esculapius

Esculapius was the illegitimate son of the nymph Coronis, by Apollo. The mother, at the instigation of Apollo, was slain by Diana; but the child was spared. He became noted for his wonderful curative powers. He healed all diseases, and even restored the dead to life. He was called "The Good Physician." He was struck by a thunderbolt and ascended to heaven. The Greeks worshiped him.

    The miraculous cures ascribed to Christ, many of them, doubtless, had their origin in the legends of Esculapius. Justin Martyr says: "In that we say he [Christ] made whole the lame, the paralytic, and those born blind, we seem to say what is very similar to the deeds said to have been done by Esculapius" (*First Apology,* ch. xxi).

Plato

One of the most gifted of mortals was Plato. His followers believed him to be of divine descent. Concerning his parentage, Dr. Draper says: "Antiquity was often delighted to cast a halo of mythical glory around its illustrious names. The immortal works of this great philosopher seemed to entitle him to more than mortal honors. A legend into the authenticity of which we will abstain from inquiring, asserted that his mother, Perictione, a pure virgin, suffered an immaculate conception through the influence of Apollo. The god declared to Ariston, to whom she was about to be married, the parentage of the child" (*Intellectual Development,* Vol. I, p. 151).

Concerning this myth, McClintock and Strong's *Cyclopedia* says: "Legend, which is traced back to Spensipus, the nephew of Plato, ascribed the paternity of Plato to the god Apollo; and, in the form in which the story is told by Olympiodorus, closely imitates the record in regard to the nativity of Christ" (Art. "Plato").

Immaculate conceptions were common in Greece. "The furtive pregnancy of young women, often by a god," says Grote, "is one of the most frequently recurring incidents in the legendary narratives of the country." The Christian story of the miraculous conception has not even the merit of originality. With the Platonic legend before him, all that the Evangelist had to do was to substitute Jehovah for Apollo, Joseph for Ariston, Mary for Perictione, and Jesus for Plato.

The philosophy of Plato is a strange compound of profound wisdom concerning the known and of vague speculations respecting the unknown. The latter form no inconsiderable portion of the religion ascribed to Christ. The Christian religion is supposed to be of Semitic origin; but its doctrines are, many of them, the work of Greek theologians; its incarnate God bears a Greek name, and its early literature was mostly Greek. Draper recognizes three primitive modifications of Christianity: 1. Judaic Christianity; 2. Gnostic Christianity; 3. Platonic Christianity. Platonic Christianity, he says, endured and is essentially the Christianity of today.

The following are some of the principles of Plato's philosophy:

There is but one God, and we ought to love and serve him.

The Word formed the world and rendered it visible.

A knowledge of the Word will make us happy.

The soul is immortal, and the dead will rise again.

There will be a final judgment; the righteous will be rewarded, and the wicked punished.

The design argument, the chief argument relied upon by Christians to prove the divine origin of the universe, is a Platonic argument.

In a letter to the author twenty-five years ago, James Parton wrote: "Read carefully over the dialogue, Phaedo. You will see what you will see: the whole Christian system and the entire dream of the contemplative monk."

Phaedo deals chiefly with the soul—its nature and destiny. The following quotations are from the translation of Henry Cary, M.A., of Oxford:

Death is defined by Plato as "the separation of the soul from the body."

"Can the soul, which is invisible, and which goes to another place like itself, excellent, pure, and invisible, and therefore truly called the invisible world, to the presence of a good and wise God, (whither if God will, any soul also must shortly go), can this soul of ours, I ask, being such and of such a nature, when separated from the body, be immediately dispersed and destroyed, as most men assert? Far from it."

"If that which is immortal is imperishable, it is impossible for the soul to perish, when death approaches it."

"When, therefore, death approaches a man, the mortal part of him, as it appears, dies, but the immortal part departs safe and uncorrupted, having withdrawn itself from death."

After death, Plato says, the souls are concluded to a place where they "receive sentence and then proceed to Hades."

If the soul "arrives at the place where the others are, impure, . . . every one shuns it, and will neither be its fellow traveler or guide, but it wanders about oppressed with every kind of helplessness. . . . But the soul which has passed through life with purity and moderation, having obtained the gods for its fellow travelers and guides, settles each in the place suited to it."

"If the soul is immortal, it requires our care not only for the present time, which we call life, but for all time; and the danger would now appear to be dreadful, if one should neglect it. For if death were a deliverance from everything, it would be a great gain for the wicked, when they die, to be delivered at the same time from the body, and from their vices together with the soul; but now, since it appears to be immortal, it can have no other refuge from evils, nor safety, except by becoming as good and wise as possible."

Christ, it is claimed, "brought immortality to light." Yet Phaedo was written nearly four centuries before Christ came.

McClintock and Strong's *Cyclopedia* concedes Plato's "near approximation to the doctrines of Christianity—some of which," it says, "he announces almost in the language of the Apostles." Continuing, this authority says: "We know no more terrible and sublime picture than the passage in which he depicts the dead presenting themselves for judgment in the other world, scarred and blotched and branded with the ineradicable marks of their earthly sins. Yet this is but one of many analogous passages. This approximation to revealed truth is among the most insoluble problems bequeathed to us by antiquity. . . . We offer no solution of the enigma, which awaits its Oedipus. We only note the existence of the riddle" (Plato).

Prof. Gunkel, of Berlin, says: " 'Christianity is a syncretistic religion. It is providential that it passed safely over from the Orient into the Greek world. It imbibed both influences, and acquired many features that were foreign to the original gospel.' "

Pythagoras

This religio-philosophical teacher lived in the sixth century B.C., the century in which flourished Buddha, Laou-tsze, and Confucius, three of the world's greatest religious founders. Greece was his native, and Italy his adopted, country. His history is largely obscured by myths. He was claimed to be, like Plato, the son of Apollo. He was said to have performed miracles and to have been endowed with the gift of prophecy. He traveled in Egypt and India, and his system contains some elements of the Egyptian and Buddhist religions.

There was a small Jewish sect, known as the Essenes, which adopted to a large extent the teachings of Pythagoras. Jesus is believed to have belonged to this sect. There is an Essene element in the New Testament which is especially prominent in the teachings ascribed to Christ. Josephus, in his "Wars of the Jews," describes at length the doctrines and customs of this sect. From Josephus and the New Testament I cite a few of the parallels between the religion of the Essenes and the religion of Christ.

"These men are despisers of riches" (*Wars,* B. II, ch. viii, sec. 3).

"A rich man shall hardly enter into the kingdom of heaven" (Matt. xix, 23).

"It is a law among them, that those who come to them must let what they have be common to the whole order" (ibid.).

"Neither said any of them that aught of the things which he possessed was his own; but they had all things common" (Acts. iv, 32).

"They carry nothing at all with them when they travel into remote parts" (Sec. 4).

"Provide neither gold, nor silver, nor brass in your purses, nor scrip for your journey" (Matt. x, 9, 10).

"Every one of them gives what he hath to him that wanteth it" (ibid.).

"Give to him that asketh thee" (Matt. v, 42.)

"A priest says grace before meat" (Sec. 5).

"And he took bread, and gave thanks" (Luke xxii, 19).

"They . . . are the ministers of peace" (Sec. 6).

"Blessed are the peacemakers" (Matt. v, 9).

"Whatsoever they say also is firmer than an oath; but swearing is avoided by them" (Sec. 6).

"But I say unto you, Swear not at all; . . . but let your communication be, yea, yea; nay, nay" (Matt. v, 34, 37).

Closely allied to the Essenes and the primitive Christians is another Pythagorian sect, known as the Therapeuts of Egypt. Regarding this sect, four different theories are held: 1. That they were a Jewish sect. 2. That they were a Jewish Christian sect. 3. That they were Pagans, many of whose teachings were incorporated into the Christian creed. 4. That they are a myth, that the *De Vita Contemplativa* of Philo, which contains the only account of them, is a Christian forgery, written for the purpose of extolling the monastic life, the celibacy, and the asceticism of the church.

Bacchus

Bacchus was a Roman god, or rather a Roman modification of the Greek god, Dionysos. He was the god of wine. He cultivated the vine, made wine, and encouraged its use. His worship extended over nearly the whole of the ancient world. It consisted largely of protracted festivals, where wine flowed freely, and joyous and noisy ceremonies were indulged in.

This god and his worship have survived in Christ and Christianity. Christ was called a "winebibber" (Luke vii, 34); he made wine—his first miracle was the conversion of water into wine (John ii, 1–10); he blessed the winecup, and commanded his disciples to drink in remembrance of him (Luke xxii, 17), just as the devotees of Bacchus drank in remembrance of their god. Christianity, more than all other religions combined, was contributed to keep alive the Bacchanalian feasts and revelries.

"Bacchus," says Volney, "in the history of his whole life, and even of his death, brings to mind the history of the god of Christians" (*Ruins,* p. 169). The cabalistic names of Bacchus and Jesus, Volney says, were the same.

United with the worship of Bacchus, and similar to it, was the worship of the goddess Ceres (Demeter). Her rites were known as the Eleusinian mysteries. Cakes were eaten in her honor. And thus in the bread of Ceres and the wine of Bacchus we have the bread and wine of the Christian Eucharist. "It is well known," says Dr. Westbrook, "that the Athenians celebrated the allegorical giving of the flesh to eat of Ceres, the goddess of corn, and in like manner the giving his blood to drink by Bacchus, the god of wine." This worship, like the Mithraic worship, which also included the communion, had its origin in the East, and was one of the first, as well as one of the last, of the religions of ancient Greece and Rome.

Another rite connected with the mysteries was the use of holy water. Lempriere, in his *Classical Dictionary,* describing the Eleusinian mysteries as they existed in Greece centuries before the Christian era, says: "As the candidates for initiation entered the temple, they purified themselves by washing their hands in holy water."

The mysteries comprehended the origin of life, and nature worship was included in the ceremonies. At the festivals women carried the phallus in their processions. Regarding the worship of Bacchus and Ceres at Rome, *Chambers' Encyclopedia* says: "These rites degenerated, and came to be celebrated with a licentiousness that threatened the destruction of morality and of society itself. They were made the occasion of the most unnatural excesses. At first, only women took part in these mysterious Bacchic rites, but latterly men also were admitted."

The Roman government suppressed the later Bacchanalian and Eleusinian feasts, together with the Christian Agapae, because of their debaucheries, obscenities, and supposed infant sacrifices. Meredith, in *The Prophet of Nazareth* (pp. 225-231), institutes an examination to ascertain "how far the Eleusinian and Bacchanalian feasts resembled the Christian Agapae." His conclusion is that the facts "show clearly that the Christian Agapae were of pagan origin—were identically the same as the pagan feasts." Gibbon says: "The language of that great historian [Tacitus, in his allusion to Christians] is almost similar to the style employed by Livy, when he relates the introduction and the suppression of the rites of Bacchus" (*Rome,* Vol. I, p. 579).

Referring to the Agapae, Dr. Cave says it was commonly charged that Christians "exercised lust and filthiness under a pretense of religion, promiscuously calling themselves brothers and sisters, that by the help of so sacred a name their common adulteries might become incestuous" (*Primitive Christianity,* Part II, chap. v). Describing the Carpocratians, an early Christian sect, Dr. Cave says: "Both men and women used to meet at supper (which was called their love-feast), when after they had loaded themselves with a plentiful meal, to prevent all shame, if they had any remaining, they put out the lights, and then promiscuously mixed in filthiness with one another" (ibid.).

The *International Cyclopedia* says: "With the increase of wealth and the decay of religious earnestness and purity in the Christian church, the Agapae became occasions of great riotousness and debaucheries."

The Agapae, with their excesses eliminated, survive in the love-feasts of modern Christians. Webster defines "love-feast" as "a religious festival, held quarterly by the Methodists, in imitation of the Agapae of the early Christians."

That these mysteries of Bacchus and Ceres were adopted by the early Christians is largely admitted by the great church historian himself. Writing of the second century, Moshein, says: "The profound respect paid to the Greek and Roman mysteries, and the extraordinary sanctity that was attributed to them, was a further circumstance that induced the Christians to give their religion a mystic air, in order to put it upon an equal foot, in point of dignity, with that of the Pagans. For this purpose they gave the name of 'mysteries' to the institutions of the gospel, and decorated particularly the holy Sacrament with that solemn title. They used in that sacred institution, as also in that of baptism, several of the terms employed in the heathen mysteries and proceeded so far at length, as even to adopt some of the rites and ceremonies of which these renowned mysteries consisted." (*Ecclesiastical History,* p. 56.)

England's highest authority on early Christian history, Dean Milman, says: "Christianity disdained that its God and its Redeemer should be less magnificently honored than the demons (gods) of Paganism. In the service it delighted to breathe, as it were, a sublimer sense into the common appellations of the Pagan worship, whether from the ordinary ceremonial or the more secret mysteries. The church became a temple; the table of the communion an altar; the celebration of the Eucharist, the appalling, or unbloody sacrifice. . . . The incense, the garlands, the lamps, all were gradually adopted by zealous rivalry, or seized as the lawful spoils of vanquished Paganism and consecrated to the service of Christ.

"The church rivaled the old heathen mysteries in expanding by slow degrees its higher privileges. . . . Its preparatory ceremonial of abstinence, personal purity, ablution, secrecy, closely resembled that of the Pagan mysteries (perhaps each may have contributed to the other)" (*History of Christianity,* Vol. III, pp. 312, 313).

Smith's *Dictionary of Antiquities* says: "The mysteries occupied a place among the ancients analogous to that of the holy sacraments in the Christian church." The *Encyclopedia Britannica* makes the same statement.

James Anthony Froude, in a letter to Prof. Johnson, of England, says: "I have long been convinced that the Christian Eurcharist is but a continuation of the Eleusinian mysteries. St. Paul, in using the word *teleiois,* almost confirms this."

Saturn

One of the oldest and most renowned of the European gods was Saturn, whose name was given by the ancients to one of the planets and to one of the days of the week. He was worshiped by the inhabitants of Italy more than a thousand years before Christ came, and centuries before Rome took her place among the nations of the earth. His temples were located in various parts of Italy, the latest and the principal one being at Rome. His chief festival, and the greatest of all the Roman festivals was the Saturnalia celebrated at the time of the winter solstice. This festival survives in the Christian festival of Christmas.

The following description of the Saturnalia is from the pen of Ridpath: "The most elaborate of all the celebrations of Rome was that of Saturn, held at the winter solstice, and afterwards extended so as to include the twenty-fifth of December. . . . The festival was called the Saturnalia. Labor ceased, public business was at an end, the courts were closed, the schools had holiday. Tables, laden with bounties, were spread on every hand, and at these all classes for the nonce sat down together. The master and the slave for the day were equals. It was a time of gift-giving and innocent abandonment. In the public shops every variety of the present, from the simplest to the most costly, could be found. Fathers, mothers, kinspeople, friends, all hurried thither to purchase, according to their fancy, what things soever seemed most tasteful and appropriate as presents" (*History of the World,* Vol. III, p. 97).

Concerning this festival the *Encyclopedia Britannica* says: "All classes exchanged gifts, the commonest being wax tapers and clay dolls. These dolls were especially given to children, and the makers of them held a regular fair at this time." One of the principal rites, the *Britannica* says, was the burning of many candles. "The modern Italian carnival," says *Chambers' Encyclopedia,* "would seem to be only the old pagan Saturnalia baptized into Christianity."

Quirinus

Nearly every reader is familiar with the story of the founding of Rome. Rhea Silvia, a vestal virgin, bears twins by the god Mars. As they are heirs to the throne which Amulius has usurped, he attempts to destroy them by drowning. They are miraculously preserved and finally rescued by a shepherd. One of them, Romulus, becomes the founder and king of Rome. After a reign of 37 years he is translated by his father, and eventually becomes the tutelary god of the Romans, under the name of Quirinus. The following account of his translation is from *Chambers' Encyclopedia*: "While he was standing near the 'Goat's Pool' in the Campus Martius, reviewing his militia, the sun was eclipsed, and a dark storm swept over the plain snd hills. When it had passed, the people looked round for their king, but he was gone. His father, Mars, had carried him up to heaven (like the prophet Elijah) in a chariot of fire. Some time after he reappeared in a glorified form to Proculus Julius, announced the future greatness of the Roman people, and told him that henceforth he would watch over them as their guardian god, under the name of Quirinus" (Art. "Romulus").

Next to the Saturnalia, the most important religious festival of Pagan Rome was the Quirinalia, which celebrated the ascension of Quirinus. It corresponds to Ascension Day, one of the principal religious festivals of the Christian church, which celebrates the ascension of Christ.

The supernatural darkness of the Roman myth, it is believed, suggested the supernatural darkness of the crucifixion myth. The reappearance of Quirinus in a glorified form is also believed by some to have suggested the transfiguration.

Odin

Odin, the All-Father, held the highest rank in the Northern pantheon. He was the son of Boer and Bestla. Freya was his queen. His religion prevailed among the Scandinavians and among the Goths, the Saxons, and other ancient German tribes. Some believe that he was an ancient hero who with a horde of Goths or Scythians conquered the North a thousand years or more before the Christian era. The prevailing opinion, however, is that the Norse mythology had its birth in Asia—in India, Persia, or Accadia—and was carried by the Aryans to northern Europe, where it underwent many modifications.

This mythology recognized as existing in the beginning, two worlds— one the warm South, the other the icy North. The entrance to the South- land was guarded by a flaming sword. Between heat and cold, as between good and evil, there was perpetual strife. From heat Ymir (Chaos), the father of giants, was evolved. Odin and his brothers slew Ymir and from his body created the earth, his flesh forming the land, his blood the sea. Out of two trees Odin made man and woman, and breathed into them the breath, of life. For the abode of man a fruitful garden was planted in the center of the earth and called Midgard. Beneath the earth, dwells Hel, the goddess of the dead.

Loki is the god of evil. He will be chained for a time and then released. A bloody war will follow. On one side, led by Loki, will fight the hosts of Hel; on the other Odin and his followers. Loki will triumph, for a while, mankind will be destroyed, and heaven and earth will be consumed by fire. But Odin will be victorious in the end. He will create a new heaven and a new earth. He will be the ruler of all things, and will dwell in heaven, where the best and bravest of his followers are to be received after death.

The Norse, the Persian, and the Christian doctrines, regarding the destruction of the world by fire, all had a common origin.

Thor

Thor was the son of Odin and the virgin Earth. He was called the first born son of God. His worship was more widespread than that of any other Northern god. In the temple at Upsala he occupied the same place in the Scandinavian Trinity that Christ does in the Christian Trinity. Like Christ he died for man and was worshiped as a Savior. Midgard had a serpent, more formidable if not more wily than that of Eden, which threatened to destroy the human race. Thor attacked and slew the monster, but was himself killed by the venom which was exhaled from it. The slaying of the serpent of Midgard by Thor, the slaying of the python by the Greek god, and the bruising of the head of the serpent of Hebrew mythology by Christ, are analogous myths.

Thor dwells in a mansion in the clouds. The thunder we hear in the sky is the noise of his chariot wheels, and the flashes of lightning are from his hammer which he dashes against the mountains. The *Britannica* says: "Some of the monks of a later period endeavored to persuade the Northmen that in Thor their forefathers had worshiped Christ, the strong and mighty Savior of the oppressed, and that his mallet was the rude form of the cross." "The sign of the hammer," says *Chambers,* "was analogous to that of the cross among Christians."

Baldur

One of the purest, one of the gentlest, and one of the best beloved of all the gods was Baldur, the beautiful son of Odin and Freya. In him were combined all things good and noble. The envious gods, inspired by Loki, shot their arrows at him in vain until the blind god Hoder pierced his body with an arrow of mistletoe and he passed into the power of Hel, the pallid goddess of death. Sometime—when the old order of things has passed away—in another and better world, where envy, and hatred, and war are unknown, Baldur will live again.

"The death of Baldur," says Prof. Rasmus B. Anderson, the highest authority on Norse mythology, "forms the turning point in the great drama. . . . While he lived the power of the asas (gods) was secure, but when Baldur, at the instigation of Loki, was slain, the fall of creation could not be prevented."

Writing of Norse mythology, Andrew Lang says: "There is, almost undoubtedly, a touch of Christian dawn on the figure and myth of the pure and beloved and ill-fated god Baldur, and his descent into hell." Odin, and Thor, and Baldur, and their divine companions are worshiped no longer; but their religion has left a deep impress on the religion that supplanted it. The Christianity of Scandinavia, of northern Germany, of England, and of America, the whole of Protestant Christianity, in short, and to some extent Catholicism itself, has been modified by this strange and fascinating faith. Regarding this subject *Chambers' Encyclopedia* says: "So deep-rooted was the adhesion to the faith of Odin in the North, that the early Christian teachers, unable to eradicate the old ideas, were driven to the expedient of trying to give them a coloring of Christianity."

The selection of December 25th as the date of the Nativity was doubtless suggested by the Mithraic or some other solar worship of the East, but the Protestant Christmas came from the North. The mistletoe with which Baldur was slain reappears in this festival. The fire wheel, a remnant of the old Norse sun worship, existed among German Christians until the nineteenth century. The burning of the Yule log still survives. In some provinces of Germany the festival is still called by its Pagan name.

Rev. Samuel M. Jackson, D.D., LL.D., Professor of Church History, New York University, says: "The Romans had, like other Pagan nations, a nature festival, called by them Saturnalia, and the Northern peoples had Yule; both celebrated the turn of the year from the death of winter to the life of spring—the winter solstice. As this was an auspicious change the festival was a very joyous one. . . . The giving of presents and the burning of candles characterized it. Among the Northern people the lighting of a huge log in the houses of the great and with appropriate ceremonies was a feature. The Roman church finding this festival deeply intrenched in popular esteemm, wisely adopted it" (*Universal Cyclopedia*).

The festival of Easter belongs to this religion. It was observed in honor of the Saxon goddess Eastre, or Ostara, the goddess of Spring. It celebrated, not the resurrection of Christ, but the resurrection of Spring and flowers. It still retains the name of this goddess. Nearly every festival of the church—and the Catholic and English churches have many— are of Pagan origin. Every day of the week bears a Pagan name— four of them the names of Scandinavian gods—Tuesday the name of Tiu (Tyr), Wednesday the name of Woden (Odin), Thursday the name of Thor, and Friday that of Freya. Even the Christian "hell" was derived from "Hel," the name of the Norse goddess of the lower world.

12

Sources of the Christ Myth—Conclusion

In each of these divinities we find some element or lineament of Christ. And all of them existed, either as myths or mortals, long anterior to his time. Plato, the latest of them to appear, was born in the fifth century B.C. These Pagan divinities and deified sages, together with the religious systems and doctrines previously noticed, were the sources from which Christ and Christianity were, for the most part, derived.

The following religious elements and ideas, nearly all of which Christians believe to have been divinely revealed, and to belong exclusively to their religion, are of Pagan origin:

Son of God
Messiah
Mediator
The Word
The Ideal Man
Annunciation
Immaculate conception
Divine incarnation
Genealogies showing royal descent
Virgin mother
Angelic visitants
Celestial music
Visit of shepherd

Visit of Magi
Star of Magi
Slaughter of innocents
Temptation
Transfiguration
Crucified Redeemer
Supernatural darkness
Resurrection
Ascension
Descent into Hell
Second advent
Unity of God
Trinity in Unity
Holy Ghost (Spirit)
Devil
Angels
Immortality of the soul
Last judgment
Future rewards and punishments
Heaven, Hell, and Purgatory
Fatherhood of God
Brotherhood of man
Freedom of the will
Fall of man
Vicarious atonement
Kingdom of God
Binding of Satan
Miracles
Prophecies
Obsession
Exorcism
The priesthood
Pope and bishops
Monks and nuns
Worship of Virgin
Adoration of Virgin and Child

Worship of saints
Worship of relics
Image worship
Inspired Scriptures
The cross as a religious symbol
Crucifix
Rosary
Holy water
Lord's Day (Sunday)
Christmas
Easter
Baptism
Eucharist
Washing of feet
Anointing
Confirmation
Masses for the dead
Fasting
Prayer
Auricular confession
Penance
Absolution
Celibacy
Poverty
Asceticism
Tithes
Community of goods
Golden Rule and other precepts

The Old Testament consists largely of borrowed myths. Nearly everything in Genesis, and much of the so-called history which follows, are but a recital of Assyrian, Babylonian, Chaldean and other legends. Dr. Draper says: "From such Assyrian sources, the legends of the creation of the earth and heaven, the garden of Eden, the making of man from clay, and of woman from one of his ribs, the temptation by the serpent, the naming of animals, the cherubim and flaming sword, the Deluge and the ark, the drying up of the waters by the wind, the building of the Tower of Babel, and the confusion of tongues, were obtained by Ezra" (*Conflict*, p. 223).

The ten antediluvian patriarchs, Adam, Seth, Enos, Cainan, Mahalaleel, Jared, Enoch, Methuselah, Lamech, and Noah, whom Luke presents as the first ten progenitors of Christ, are now known to have been a dynasty of Babylonian kings. Abram, Isaac, Jacob, and Judah, whom both Matthew and Luke declare to have been ancestors of Christ, and whom Matthew places at the head of his genealogy, were not persons at all, but merely tribes of people. In regard to this Rev. Dr. Oort, professor of Oriental languages at Amsterdam, says: "They do not signify men, so much as groups of nations or single tribes. Abram, for instance, represents a great part of the Terachites; Lot, the Moabites and Ammonites, whose ancestor he is called; Ishmael, certain tribes of Arabia; Isaac, Israel and Edom together; Jacob, Israel alone; while his twelve sons stand for the twelve tribes of Israel. . . . Here and there the writers of the old legend themselves point out, as it were, that the patriarchs whom they bring upon the scene as men are personifications of tribes" (*Bible for Learners,* Vol. I, pp. 100–102). Moses, the reputed founder of Judaism and archetype of Christ, doubtless existed; but nearly all the Bible stories concerning him are myths. David and Solomon, from whose house Christ is said to have been descended, are historical characters; but the accounts respecting the greatness of their kingdom and the splendor of their reigns are fabulous.

Christ and Christianity are partly creations and partly evolutions. While the elements composing them were mostly derived from preexisting and contemporary beliefs, they were not formed as a novelist creates a hero and a convention frames a constitution. Their growth was gradual. Jesus, if he existed, was a Jew, and his religion, with a few innovations, was Judaism. With his death, probably, his apotheosis began. During the first century the transformation was slow; but during the succeeding centuries rapid. The Judaic elements of his religion were, in time, nearly all eliminated, and the Pagan elements, one by one, were incorporated into the new faith.

Regarding the establishment of this religion Lecky says: "Christianity had become the central intellectual power of the world, but it triumphed not so much by superseding rival faiths as by absorbing and transforming them. Old systems, old rites, old images were grafted into the new belief, retaining much of their ancient character but assuming new names and a new complexion" (*Rationalism,* Vol. I. p. 223).

Its origin is thus traced by Mrs. Besant: "From the later Jews comes the Unity of God; from India and Egypt the Trinity in Unity; from India and Egypt the crucified Redeemer; from India, Egypt, Greece, and Rome, the virgin mother and the divine son; from Egypt its priests and its ritual; from the Essenes and the Therapeuts its asceticism; from Persia, India, and Egypt, its sacraments; from Persia and Babylonia its angels and devils; from Alexandria the blending into one of many lines of thought." (*Freethinkers' Text Book,* p. 392.)

Concerning this, Judge Strange, another English writer, says: "The Jewish Scriptures and the traditionary teachings of their doctors, the Essenes and Therapeuts, the Greek philosophers, the Neo-Platonism of Alexandria and the Buddhism of the East, gave ample supplies for the composition of the doctrinal portion of the new faith; the divinely procreated personages of the Grecian and Roman pantheons, the tales of the Egyptian Osiris, and of the Indian Rama, Krishna, and Buddha, furnished the materials for the image of the new Savior of mankind." (*Portraiture and Mission of Jesus,* p. 27.)

Dr. G. W. Brown, previously quoted, says: "The Eclectics formed the nucleus into which were merged all the various religions of the Orient. Mithra, of the Zoroastrians; Krishna and Buddha, of the Brahmans; Osiris, of the Egyptians, and Bacchus, of the Greeks and Romans, all disappeared and were lost in the new God Jesus, each of the predecessors contributing to the conglomerate religion known as Christian, Buddha and probably Bacchus contributing the most."

Dr. John W. Draper, recognized on both sides of the Atlantic as one of the most erudite, one of the most philosophic, and one of the most impartial of historians, in the following paragraphs tells the story of the rise and triumph of this everchanging faith:

"In a political sense, Christianity is the bequest of the Roman Empire to the world.

"Not only as a token of the conquest she had made, but also as a gratification to her pride, the conquering republic brought the gods of the vanquished peoples to Rome. With disdainful toleration, she permitted the worship of them all. That paramount authority exercised by each divinity in his original seat disappeared at once in the crowd of gods and goddesses among whom he had been brought. Already, as we have seen, through geographical discoveries and philosophical criticism, faith in the religion of the old days had been profoundly shaken. It was, by this policy of Rome, brought to an end.

"In one of the Eastern provinces, Syria, some persons in very humble life had associated themselves together for benevolent and religious purposes. The doctrines they held were in harmony with that sentiment of universal brotherhood arising from the coalescence of the conquered kingdoms. They were doctrines inculcated by Jesus.

"From this germ was developed a new, and as the events proved, all-powerful society—the Church; new, for nothing of the kind had existed in antiquity; powerful, for the local churches, at first isolated, soon began to confederate for their common interest. Through this organization Christianity achieved all her political triumphs.

"After the abdication of Diocletian (A.D., 305), Constantine, one of the competitors for the purple, perceiving the advantages that would accrue to him from such a policy, put himself forth as the head of the Christian party. This gave him, in every part of the empire, men and women ready to encounter fire and sword in his behalf; it gave him unwavering adherents in every legion of the armies. In a decisive battle, near the Milvian bridge, victory crowned his schemes. The death of Maximian, and subsequently that of Licinius, removed all obstacles. He ascended the throne of the Caesars—the first Christian emperor.

"Place, profit, power—these were in view of whoever now joined the conquering sect. Crowds of worldly persons, who cared nothing about its religious ideas, became its warmest supporters. Pagans at heart, their influence was soon manifested in the paganization of Christianity that forthwith ensued.

"As years passed on, the faith described by Tertullian was transmuted into one more fashionable and more debased. It was incorporated with the old Greek mythology. Olympus was restored, but the divinities passed under other names. The more powerful provinces insisted on the adoption of their time-honored conceptions. Views of the Trinity, in accordance with Egyptian traditions, were established.

"Heathen rites were adopted, a pompous and splendid ritual, gorgeous robes, mitres, tiaras, wax-tapers, processional services, lustrations, gold and silver vases, were introduced. The Roman lituus, the chief ensign of the augurs, became the crozier. Churches were built over the tombs of martyrs, and consecrated with rites borrowed from the ancient laws of the Roman pontiffs. Festivals and commemorations of martyrs multiplied with the numberless fictitious discoveries of their remains. Fasting became the grand means of repelling the devil and appeasing God; celibacy the greatest of the virtues. Pilgrimages were made to Palestine and the tombs of the martyrs. Quantities of dust and earth were brought from the Holy Land and sold at enormous prices, as antidotes against devils. The virtues of consecrated water were upheld. Images and relics were introduced into the churches, and worshiped after the fashion of the heathen gods. . . . The apotheosis of the old Roman times was replaced by canonization; tutelary saints succeeded to local mythological divinities.

"As centuries passed, the paganization became more and more complete.

"The maxim holds good in the social as well as the mechanical world, that, when two bodies strike, the form of both is changed. Paganism was modified by Christianity. Christianity by Paganism" (*Conflict*, pp. 34–52).

While affirming the divine origin of Christianity, the church historian Mosheim admits its early paganisation. He says: "The rites and institutions, by which the Greeks, Romans, and other nations had formerly testified their religious veneration for fictitious deities, were now adopted, with some slight alterations, by Christian bishops, and employed in the service of the true God. . . . Hence it happened that in these times the religion of the Greeks and Romans differed very little in its external appearance from that of the Christians. They had both a most pompous and splendid ritual. Gorgeous robes, mitres, tiaras, wax-tapers, croziers, processions, lustrations, images, gold and silver vases, and many such circumstances of pageantry, were equally to be seen in the heathen temples and the Christian churches" (*Ecclesiastical History*, p. 105).

The Rev. Dr. R. Heber Newton, in an article which appeared in the *North American Review,* says: "There is, in fact, as we now see, nothing in the externals of the Christian church which is not a survival from the churches of paganism. . . . The sacramental use of water and bread and wine, the very sign of the cross—all are ancient human institutions, rites and symbols. Scratch a Christian and you come upon a Pagan. Christianity is a rebaptized paganism." "Christendom," says Dr. Lyman Abbott, "is only an imperfectly Christianized paganism."

The creeds of old are dead or dying, and the celestial kings, who seemed so real to their worshipers, are mostly crownless phantoms now. Buddha, Laoutsze, and Confucius, the wise men of the East, command the reverence of nearly half the world, and the Persian prophet has a few followers; but from these faiths the supernatural is vanishing. Millions yet believe that Krishna, the Christ of India, is the son of God; but this faith, too, is waning. The intellectual offspring of Plato's brilliant brain survive, but all that remains of his divine father is a mutilated effigy. The genial Sun still warms and lights the earth, but centuries have flown since Mithra, his beloved, received the adoration of mankind. The fire still glows upon the hearth, but the great Titan who brought it down from Heaven lives only in a poet's dream. The crimson nectar of the vine moves men to mirth and madness now as when the swan of Teos sang its praise, but Bacchus and the ancient mysteries are dead. Above storm-wrapped Olympus, as of old, is heard the thunder's awful peal, but it is not the voice of Zeus. The voice of this, the mightiest of all the gods, is hushed forever. The populous and ever-growing empire of the dead still flourishes, but in its solemn court Osiris no longer sits as judge. The mother, as of yore, presses to her loving heart her dimpled babe and fondly gazes into its azure eyes to woo its artless smile; but Egypt's star-crowned virgin and her royal child, who once received the homage of a world, are now but mythic dust. Manly beauty thrills our daughters' hearts with love's strange ecstasy, and the feigned suffering of the dying hero on the mimic stage moistens their eyes with tears; but Adonis sleeps in his Phoenician tomb, his slumbers undisturbed by woman's sobs. The purple flower, substance of his clear self, which Venus carried in her bosom, withered long ago. When, at eve, the summer shower bathes with its cooling drops the verdure of the fields, across the sun-kissed cloud which veils the Orient sky may still be seen the gorgeous bridge of Bifrost; but over its majestic arch the dauntless Odin rides no more.

The fair humanities of old religions,
The flower, the beauty, and the majesty,
That had their haunts in dale, or piny mountain,
Or forest by slow stream or pebbly spring,
Or chasms and watery depths; all these have vanished;
They live no longer in the faith of reason.

—Schiller

What has been the fate of the Pagan gods will be the fate of the Christian deity. Christianity, which supplanted the ancient faiths, will, in turn, be supplanted by other religions. On two continents already the cross has gone down before the crescent. The belief in Christ as a divine being is passing away. The creeds, as of old, affirm his divinity, but in the minds of his more enlightened followers the divine elements are disappearing. What was formerly believed to be supernatural is now known to be natural. What were once living verities are now clear formalities. Slowly and painfully, but surely and clearly, men are becoming convinced that there are no divine beings and no supernatural religions—that all the gods, including Christ, are myths, and all the religions, including Christianity, human productions. In the words of Jules Soury, "Time, which condenses nebulae, lights up suns, brings life and thought upon planets theretofore steeped in death, and gives back ephemeral worlds to dissolution and the fertile chaos of the everlasting universe—time knows nought of gods nor of the dim and fallacious hopes of ignorant mortals."

With these sublime pictures—a retrospect and a prophecy—from the gallery of the great master, I close this long-drawn subject:

"When India is supreme, Brahma sits upon the world's throne. When the sceptre passes to Egypt, Isis and Osiris receive the homage of mankind. Greece, with her fierce valor, sweeps to empire, and Zeus puts on the purple of authority. The earth trembles with the tread of Rome's intrepid sons, and Jove grasps with mailed hand the thunderbolts of Heaven. Rome falls, and Christians, from her territory, with the red sword of war, carve out the ruling nations of the world, and now Christ sits upon the old throne. Who will be his successor?"

"I look again. The popes and priests are gone. The altars and the thrones have mingled with the dust. The aristocracy of land and cloud have perished from the earth and air. The gods are dead. A new religion sheds its glory on mankind. And as I look Life lengthens, Joy deepens, Love intensifies, Fear dies—Liberty at last is God, and Heaven is here."

Index

Abbott, Dr. Lyman, on the paganization of Christianity, 417

Abiathar, eating shew bread in the days of, 118

"Abilene, Tetrarch of," 92

Aceldama, 166

Acts, not authentic, 39, 40

Adonis, 384–88; and Jesus, 387

Adultery, woman taken in, 128

Aenon near to Salim, a geographical error, 117

Agapae, debaucheries of, 403

Alford, Dean, on conflicting accounts of Matthew and Luke regarding the first appearance of Jesus to his disciples, 232; on errors of N.T., 272

Amberly, Lord, on submission to wrong, 311; supposed appearances of Jesus explained by, 239–40; on the bribing of Judas, 164–65

Ambrose, on passage in Josephus, 21

American Cyclopedia, on Phallic worship, 336

Ancestors of Christ, female, 314

Anderson, Prof. Rasmus B., on Baldur, 408

Andrew, when called, 98

Animals and plants, worship of, 351–54

Annas and Caiaphas, 91–92

Annunciation, the, 70–71

Anointing of Jesus, the, discrepancies concerning, 150–51

Apollo, 391–93

Apollonius, teachings of analogous to teachings of Christ, 15–16

Apostle, favorite, 101

Apostles, chief, 95–96; character and fate of, 315–20; their denunciation of each other, 323–24

Apostolic Fathers, gospels unknown to, 36–37

Appleton's Cyclopedia, on correspondence of Krishna's gospel with N.T., 369

Archelaus, 45–46, 73

421

Arnold, Matthew, on miracles, 16

Ascension of Jesus, 252–56

Aschera, worship of by Jews, 337

Assyrian and Babylonian legends, 383–84, 412–13

Astral worship, 346–49

Astrology, belief of Jews and early Christians in, 348–49

Atonement, the, 273–76

Augustine, St., on omissions in Matthew's genealogy, 54

Augustus Caesar, the decree of, 73–74

Babylonian and Assyrian legends, 383–84, 412–13

Bacchus, 401–404

Baldur, 408–409

Ball, W. P., on parables, 310–11

Baptism, form of prescribed, 250–51; essential to salvation, 284; modes of, 285

Barachias, 149

Baring-Gould, Rev. S., on forgery in Josephus, 24–25; on Gospel of Marcion as the basis of Luke's Gospel, 38; on close relation of religious and sexual passions, 342

Barrabas, release of 185

Bartimeus, the blind, Mrs. Evans on, 137

Baur, the Four Gospels pronounced spurious by, 39; on Colossians and Philippians, 42; miracle at Nain similar to one performed by Apollonius, 115

Beatitudes, common to Matthew and Luke, 107–108

Beecher, on abrogation of Mosaic law by Christ, 281

Berosis, on Babylonian legends, 383

Besant, Mrs. Annie, the Christ a historical myth, 329–30; on sex worship, 335; Egyptian origin of Christianity affirmed by, 389–90; on sources of Christianity, 414

Bethany, where located, 87

Bethlehem, birth of Jesus at, must be given up, 50; prophecy concerning, 50–51

Bethsaida, location of, 100

Bible for Learners, declares Acts purposely inaccurate, 39–40; on First John, 40; why December 25th was fixed as date of Jesus' birth, 48; on place of Jesus' birth, 50; on manger legend, 75; on Mark's geography, 130; on Paul's views of resurrection, 253

Bigandet, Bishop, on religion of Buddha, 371

Boulger, writings of Confucius, the Chinese Bible, 375

Bradley, Justice, on date of crucifixion, 231–14

Briggs, Rev. Charles, analogies between Mithra and Christ, 381

Brodie, Sir Benjamin, on apparitions, 238

Brown, Dr. G. W., on solar gods, 345; Virgin and child of Egyptian origin, 389; sources of the Christ myth, 414

Buckle, moral teachings of N.T. not original, 313; on the clergy and learning, 321

Buddha, 370–74; commandments of, 371

Buddhist missionaries, 374

Burns, Robert, on morality, 280

Byron, Lord, on atonement, 276; on Christian hatred, 324

Cabanes, Dr., on cause of Jesus' death, 199–200

Caiaphas, prophecy of concerning Jesus, 171

Calvary, 190

Carmelite nun, on adoration of Jesus, 385

Carlyle, Thomas, would bid Christ depart, 7

Carpenter, Dr., on contagious character of illusions, 238–39

Catholic epistles, the seven, not authentic, 40

Cave, Dr., on debaucheries of Christian Agapae, 403

Celsus, on ignorance of early Christians, 325

Centurion's servant, healing of, 112

Cephas, meaning of, 97

Ceres, worship of, 402

Chadwick, Rev. John W., on Paul's witness to resurrection, 231

Chalmers, Dr., on forgery in Josephus, 25

Chambers' Encyclopedia, on pagan origin of names of days, 347; on fetichism in the church, 354–55; on Mithraic worship, 380; on worship of Adonis, 384; on worship of Bacchus and Ceres, 402–403; on adoption of Saturnalia by

Christians, 405; on an ascension of Quirinus, 406

Cheyne, Prof. T.K., on Isaiah ix, 6, 68

Cheyne, Robert, on Krishna and Christ, 369

Chivalry, Christian, a form of sex worship, 340

Christ, wrongs inspired by name of, 7; the meaning of the term, 9; the, an impossible character, 11; his alleged miracles, 11–14; no mention of by Jewish and Pagan writers for a hundred years after his time, 18–19; the, attributes of, 263–65; by whom raised from the dead, 265; miracles of not proof of his divinity, 265–67; second advent of, 268–69; religious teachings of, 273–92; nature of his death, 277; descent of into hell, 278–79; on necessity of belief, 280–81; on forgiveness of sin, 281–82; the, moral teachings of, 292–313; on poverty and riches, 292–94; intemperance encouraged by, 294; his brutal treatment of woman of Canaan, 297; he promotes domestic strife and family hatred, 298–300; his abuse of Pharisees, 300–301; his belief in demoniacal possession, 306–307; guilty of dissimulation, 308, 309; immoral lessons inculcated in his parables, 309–11; submission to theft and robbery enjoined by, 311; his want of courage, 313–14; character of his male ancestors, 314; his female ancestors, 314–15; on intellectual character of his followers, 325; the, different conceptions of, 257–58, 327; paternity of, 260–62; his rules of table observance, 288–89; minor teachings of, 289–91; solar attributes of, 345; the, teachings of derived from fire worship, 351; the, different types of in N.T., 365; *see also* Jesus.

Christian doctrines, list of derived from Paganism, 410–13

Christianity, decadence of, 418

Christians, characterization of by Paul, 324

Christmas, Pagan origin of, 409

Chronology, Christian, 45–46

Clarke, Dr. Adam, on Nativity, 48

Clergy, licentiousness of, 339, 340–41

Compte, on laws of human development, 357–58

Commandments, the two great, by whom stated, 145–46; prescribed by Jesus, 139

Communism of early Chrisitians, 292

Confession of Faith, the Godhead, 258; on futility of good works, 279

Confucius, 374–76

Conway, M. D., on dying exclamation of Christ, 314

Crapsey, Rev. Algernon S., on miraculous birth of Jesus, 262

Cross, Christ's allusions to during ministry, 218; an emblem of sex worship, 335–36; an emblem of sun worship, 345

Crucifixion, not a Jewish punishment, 177; Kitto on death by, 194; source of Matthew's story concerning marvelous events attending that of Christ's, 204–205; women at, 207–209; opinions of Christian scholars regarding date of, 212–14; discrepancy between Synoptics and John regarding day of, 215–17; alleged cause of, 217–18; references to in other books of N.T., 218–20

Crurifragium, 205

Cumont, Prof. Franz, on analogies between relgions of Mithra and Christ, 380–81

Cyrenius, 45–46, 74–75; claim that he was twice governor of Syria untenable, 4–6

Darkness, the supernatural, 202–203

Davidson, Dr. Samuel, Gospels unknown to Papias, 37; author of Matthew unknown, 37; author of Mark unknown, 38; Johannine authorship rejected by, 39

Dead, raising the, no instance of related by an Evangelist which is confirmed by another Evangelist, 139–41

Demoniacal possession, 306–307

Demons, expulsion of, 114

Devils and swine, 113–14

De Wette, on Peter's speech, 165

Dionysius, Bishop, on Revelation, 41

Dionysos, 394–95

Disciples, concerning presence of at crucifixion, 207; character and fate of, 316–20

Doctrine, Christian, derived from Paganism, 410–13

Dodwell, Dr., Gospels not mentioned by Apostolic Fathers, 36

Draper, Dr. John W., on Christian fetichism, 354; on a triune God, 388; Virgin and child the counterpart of Isis and Horus, 388–89; concerning divinity of Plato, 397; on primitive modifications of Christianity, 398; on Assyrian origin of O.T. legends, 412–13; on the paganization of Christianity, 414–16

Dupuis, Charles François, on derivation of other religions from solar worship, 344

Easter, origin of, 409

Edinburgh Review, on Revelation, 41

Egypt, sojourn in, 78; prophecy concerning, 80–81

Elements and forces of nature, worship of, 349–51

Eleusinian mysteries, 402–404; their identity with Christian Agapae, 403–404

Emerson, on necessity of getting rid of Christ, 7

Emmaus, where located, 233

Encyclopedia Biblica, regarding existence of Nazareth, 50; on gradual formation of Synoptics, 38; a suffering Messiah unknown to Jews, 201; on Lamaism and Romanism, 373; on Babylonian and Biblical analogies, 383; on Saturnalia, 405; on analogies between Thor and Christ, 408

Endless punishment, doctrine of, 283–84

Esculapius, 397

Eucharist, 285

Eusebius, on passage in Josephus, 22; on genealogies, 64

Evans, Elizabeth M., story of blind Bartimeus of Buddhistic origin, 137; on manner of putting Jesus to death, 177–78; on Mediator, 359; on Seneca and Philo, 365–66

Farrar, Dr., on Christianity and miracles, 14; passage in Josephus declared a forgery by, 25; on dearth of evidence concerning Christ, 35; date of Jesus' birth unknown, 49; concedes as probable Justin Martyr's statement that Jesus was born in a cave, 75; on silence of Josephus, 79; on difficulties concerning chronology of miracles, 105; concerning coin in fish's mouth, 135; identifies Luke's "sinful woman" with the Magdalene, 150; on last words of Jesus, 194; on supernatural darkness, 202; on date of crucifixion, 213; on discrepancies in the Gospels regarding appearances of Jesus, 230; on resurrection of saints, 241; concerning Mary Magdalene, 315

Faustus, Bishop, on anonymous character of Gospels, 39

Feeding of five thousand, the, 124–25

Fetichism, 354–55

Fig-tree, the, cursing of, 148–49, 302

Fishes, miraculous draught of, 105–106

Fiske, Prof. John, on relics of astral worship, 347

Fleetwood, on destruction of swine, 307

Foote, G. W., on Jesus and marriage, 296

Forgiveness of sin, 281–82

Froude, James Anthony, identity of Christian Eucharist and Eleusinian mysteries affirmed by, 404

Future rewards and punishments, 282–83

Gadarenes, country of, 114

Gage, Mrs. Matilda Joslyn, on Marquette, 341

Galilee not a province of Syria, 73; prophets of, 127–28

Gardener, Helen, on Christ's treatment of woman of Canaan, 297; on Paul, 321

Garibaldi, testimony of, concerning Italian convents, 341

Geikie, Dr., concerning date of Nativity, 48; on genealogies, 63; regarding inn at Bethlehem, 76; on age of Jesus when he began his ministry, 85; on location of Bethany, 123; Jesus and John the Baptist unknown to each other previous to baptism, 88; admissions of regarding alleged trial before Sanhedrim, 176–77; last words of Jesus, 194; on supernatural darkness, 202–203

Genealogies of Jesus, 51–66

Genealogy, from Abraham to Jesus; disagreement of Luke's with O.T., 52; from Abraham to David, 52–53; from David to the Captivity, 53–55; from the Captivity to Christ, 55–56

Generations, average age of, 56–57

Gergesenes, country of, 114

Gethsemane, agony of, 157

Gibbon, on prodigies attending the crucifixion, 32–33; on December 25th as date of the Nativity, 48; on passage in Phlegon, 203; Christians unnoticed by Seneca, 366; on language of Tacitus and Livy, 403

Gildner, Prof., on religion of Zoroaster, 379

Giles, Rev. Dr., on forgery in Josephus, 24; Gospels not mentioned by Justin Martyr, 36; on the word "legion," 113

Gillett, Rev. Dr. Charles, on Osiris, 386

Glennie, John Stuart, analogies between Osirianism and Christianity, 386–87

Gods, planetary, 347–48; the passing of, 417–19

Golden Rule, 108; borrowed from Pagans, 312; Confucius and the 375–76

Golgotha, 190

Gospels, the, existence of unknown to other writers of N.T., 36; late appearance of, 35–39; their want of credibility, 44; value of as historical evidence, 327

Graves, story of Magi of astrological origin, 348–49

Great Feast, the parable of, 142–43

Greg, W. R., on speaking in new tongues, 248; on baptism, 250; on genealogies, 63; on prayer, 286–87; on bestowal of power on Peter, 316–17; on Messianic prophecies, 267–68; on atonement, 276

Gregorie, Rev. John, translation of Kadish by, 110

Grote, on belief of Greeks and Romans in Prometheus as a historical character, 396

Groves, sacred, 253

Guard at tomb, concerning, 242–46

Gulick, Prof., on Dionysian festivals, 395

Gunkel, Prof., on Greek modifications of Christianity, 400

Hades, discourse concerning, 27, 391–92

Hallam, Henry, on licentiousness of Christians during middle ages, 340; on worship of saints, 357

Harden-Hickey, Baron, analogies between Christ and Buddha, 371

Hardwicke, Dr., on origin of the Lord's Prayer, 110

Hartmann, Dr. Edward von, on folly of reverencing Jesus, 9

Hell, of Pagan origin, 391–92, 409

Henry, Matthew, on Christ's female ancestors, 315

Hercules, 393–94; worship of by Jews, 393

Herod, the Great, in what year of his reign was Jesus born? 47; his massacre of babes, 78–80

Herod Antipas, his remarks concerning words of Jesus, 122; trial of Jesus before, 180–81

Herodias, 123–24

Hibbert, Dr., on apparitions, 239

Higgins, Godfrey, on testimony of Irenaeus, 221

Higginson, Col. T. W., on non-originality of Jesus' teachings, 313

High Priest, office of held by whom? 170

Hilaire, St., on Buddha's teachings, 373

Hitchcock, Rev. Dr., on date of Chronicles, 58

Hodge, Prof., on sanction of slavery by Christ, 295

Holy Ghost, the, gender of, 71, 260; when disciples received, 247–48; effect of on the disciples, 248; disciples of John the Baptist and, 249

Holy water, use of by Greeks, 402

Hooykaas, Rev. Dr., on passage in Josephus, 25–26; on Pauline Epistles, 41–42; concerning Gabriel's prediction, 72; on the census, 74–75; on Levi and Matthew, 98; pronounces story of beheading John the Baptist a fiction, 123; on last words of Jesus, 196–97; on resurrection of Jesus from the dead, 236; on baptismal formula, 251; on deification of Jesus, 363

Horus, 387–90; the hiding of Moses and the stopping of the sun and moon borrowed from, 388

Huc, Pere, on Krishna, 369

Hug, Dr., on Zacharias, son of Barachias, 149

Hugo, Victor, on the clergy and learning, 321–32

Hume, argument of against miracles, 14–15

Huxley, Prof., on demonology, 306–307

Hyde, Dr., on religion of Persians, 378–79

Immortality, teachings of Bible concerning, 277–78; Christ's resurrection no proof of, 278

Ingersoll, Robert G., on miracles, 16–17; on forgiveness of sin, 282–83; a retrospect and a prophecy, 418–19

Inman, Dr. Thomas, on modern Christian symbolism, 336, 337; on practices of priests in convents, 341; affirms Egyptian origin of Christian trinity, 388

Inscription, the, on the Cross, 190

Intemperance encouraged, 294

International Encyclopedia, on deification of Buddha and Confucius, 375; on Mithra, 380; debaucheries of Christian Agapae, 403

Irenaeus, all of the Gospels first mentioned by, 37; on duration of Jesus' ministry, 158–59; on age of Jesus at death, 220–22, 158–59

Isis, 388; and Mary, 388–90

Israelites, idolatry of, 354; polytheism of, 355–56

Istar, descent of into Hell, 383–84

Jackson, Rev. Samuel, Pagan origin of Christmas affirmed by, 409

James, not mentioned by John, 101–102; on justification by works, 279

James and John, the calling of, 97–98; request of, or concerning, 141

James the Less and Joses, parents of, 99

Jairus, daugher of, 119

Jechonias, who was his father? when was he begotten? 59–60; curse pronounced against, 61

Jefferson, Thomas, on the Trinity, 259; on miraculous conception, 262; believed Christ and his Twelve Apostles to be derived from stellar worship, 347; on carnal affection of women for Jesus, 385–86

Jehovah, a god of the atmosphere, 350; a god of fire, 350–51

Jerome, on marriage, 296; on Adonis and Christ, 385

Jesus of Nazareth, his existence possible, 9, 11, 18; conflicting statements regarding the date of his birth, 45–50; various opinions of Christian scholars regarding time he was born, 45–47; place of birth, 49–50; genealogies of, 51–66; from which of David's sons was he descended? 62; the naming of, 70; residence of his parents prior to his birth, 81–82; mediums of communication concerning, 84; age at beginning of his ministry, 85; age of when John the Baptist began his ministry, 87–88; had J. B. been cast into prison when he began his ministry?, 94–95; charge of concerning Samaritans, 102; had he a home? 103; did he perform many miracles at the beginning of his ministry? 104–105; discrepancies regarding events at beginning of his ministry, 109–13; refers to John the Baptist's advent as an event long past, on "a prophet not without honor," etc., 121; the carpenter—the carpenter's son, 122; number baptized by his disciples, 124; reason of for going into a mountain, 125–26; walking on the sea, 127; his Messiahship, when revealed to his disciples, 130–31; his route to last Passover, 136; healing of blind Bartimeus, 137; on divorce, 138; his lamentation on Jerusalem, 149–50; number of visits to Jerusalem, 157; to what country was ministry chiefly confined? 157–58; length of ministry, 158–59; teachings ascribed to, not authentic, 159–60; announcement of his betrayal, 161–62; manner of disclosing his betrayer, 162; arrest of, 166–68; preliminary examination of, 168–69; trial of before Sanhedrim, 171; charge of blasphemy, 172; words of regarding temple of his body, 173–74; mistreatment of during trials, 178, 184, 187; trial of before Herod, 180–81; trial of before Pilate, 182–83; scourging of, 184; the mocking of, 186–87; the crucifixion of, 187–208; by whom crucified, 187–88; casting lost for the garments of, 192–93; last words of, 194–97; reasons for removing body of from cross, 206–

207; burial of, 209; embalming of, 209–11; age of, at time of death, 220–22; how long did he remain in the grave? 223; discrepancies regarding visits to tomb of, 223–28; appearances of mentioned by Evangelists, 228–30; appearances of mentioned by Paul, 230–31; doubts of disciples concerning resurrection of, 234; nature of his appearances, 237–40; final command of to disciples, 251; number of days remained on earth after resurrection, 252; prophecy of concerning destruction of temple, 268; filial ingratitude of, 297–98; when did he announce his Messiahship? 270; opinions of neighbors, friends, and brothers concerning divinity of, 271–72; *see also* Christ.

John, egotism of, 318

John, the Gospel of, internal evidence against authenticity of, 38–39; baptism of Jesus not mentioned by, 90

John the Baptist, who was he? 86; the advent of fulfilled what prophecy? 86; prediction concerning, 86; was he acquainted with Jesus prior to his baptism? 88; his testimony concerning Jesus, 89; number baptized by, 90; is he a historical character? 90–91; reason for beheading, 122–23

Jones, Sir William, on Krishna, 368, 370

Joseph, who was his father? 62; not

subject to taxation, 73; on substitution of for "father" in A. V., 82

Josephus, F., knew nothing of Christ, 19–20; passage in relating to Christ a forgery, 20–27; arguments against genuineness of passage in, 21–26; passage rejected by Christian Fathers, 22; clause containing name of Christ in passage relating to James an interpolation, 26–27; concerning Herod, Archelaus and Cyrenius, 45–46; on high priests, 91–92; concerning an alleged prophet, 173–74; his tribute to Pharisees, 301; on teachings of Essenes, 400–401

Josiah, successor of, 59–60; relation to Jechonias, 60

Judas, apostles bearing the name of, 100; his betrayal of Jesus, 162–63; what he did with the money, 163–64; fate of, 165–66

Judea, coasts of beyond Jordan, 135–36

Justus of Tiberius, no mention of Christ by, 20

Kadish, the, Lord's Prayer borrowed from, 110

Kalisch, Dr., devils and angels of Persian origin, 378

Keim, Theodor, on passage in Josephus, 25

King, C. W., on Isis and Mary, 389

Kitto, on death by crucifixion, 194

Krishna, 368–70; parallels between Krishna and Christ, 368–70

Kuenin, Dr., on Pauline Epistles, 42

Lake, Rev. J. W., on Logos, 364; on Mithra, 379–80

Lang, Andrew, on Baldur, 408

Laou-Tsze, 376–77

Lardner, Dr., his arguments against genuineness of passage in Josephus, 22–23, 24

Last Supper, day of occurrence, 153–54

Lazarus, the raising of, 139–41; rich man and, 293

Lebbeus, 100

Lecky, W. E. H., on filthiness of early Christians, 288–89; on Christian asceticism, 299–300; on Zeus, 391; on absorption of rival faiths by Christianity, 413–14; on sexual depravity of Christians during middle ages, 339; Scotland and Sweden, 341; on polytheism of medieval Christians, 356; on Seneca and Christianity, 366

Legge, Rev. James, on Confucius and the Golden Rule, 376

Lempriere, on use of holy water by Greeks, 402

Lepers, cleansing of, 136–37

Leto, 392–93

Levirate Marriage, 64

Logos (word), the, 363–64; the idea ancient and widespread, 363

Lord, Rev. Dr. Nathan, on slavery, 295

Lord's Prayer, origin of, 109–10

Luke, his statement concerning annual visits of Jesus to Jerusalem conflicts with Matthew, 83

Luther, James, Jude, Hebrews, and Revelation rejected by, 40, 41;

justification by works denounced by, 279

Macherus, location of, 123
Magi, the star of, 77
Manes, on identity of Mithra and Christ, 381
Mansel, Dean, on Christianity and miracles, 14
Marquette, Mrs. Gage on, 341
Marriage, teachings of Christ regarding, 296; teachings of Paul regarding, 320–21
Martyr, Justin, Gospels unknown to 36; declares that the Magi were from Arabia, 77; Jesus Christ and sons of Jupiter, 395; on similarity of the cures of Christ and Esculapius, 397
Mary, lineage of, 65–66; hymn of, borrowed from Samuel, 72; relationship of to Christ, 260–61; on perpetual virginity of, 261
Mary Magdalene, visit of to tomb, 224; appearance of Jesus to, 231
Massacre of innocents, 78–80
Matthew, a Roman Catholic Gospel, 37; was James the Less a brother of?, 99
Maurice, Rev. Thomas, on births of Krishna and Christ, 368
McClintock and Strong's *Cyclopedia,* on Phallic Worship, 336; on analogous events in the histories of Krishna and Christ, 369; on doctrines of Zoroaster, 378; on Christianity and Mithraism, 381; on Osiris, 387; on Apollo, 392; on

Christ and Plato, 398, 399–400
McDermott, Hon. Allan L., on injustice of holding Jews responsible for death of Christ, 276–77
McNaught, Rev. Dr., on genealogies, 63
Mediatorial idea, the, 359–60; of Persian and Roman origin, 359
Meinhold, Prof., on religious formulas, 289; on Hercules and Christ, 393
Meredith, E. P., on identity of Christian Agapae with Bacchanalian and Eleusinian feasts, 403
Messiah, the, must be a son of David, 51, 64; Jewish argument against Jesus as, 362–63
Messianic idea, the, 360–63; of Persian origin, 360–61
Messianic prophecies, Isaich vii, 14; Genesis, xlix, 10; Isaiah ix, 6; Jeremiah xxiii, 5, 6; Daniel ix, 25; 67–70; two kinds of, 70, 360–61
Michelet, on first fruits of bride claimed by parson, 341
Mill, John Stuart, best moral teachings not of Christian origin, 313
Milman, Dean, on passage in Josephus, 25; on resurrection of saints, 241; on polytheistic forms of Christianity, 357; on Logos, 363–64; Pagan mysteries adopted by the church, 404
Miracles of Christ, 12–13; impossibility of, 14; arguments of Hume against, 14–15
Mithra, 379–81; picture of, 380
Monotheism, 357–59; Jewish, 358

Montuci, Prof., on revelation of Trinity in Laou-Tsze's writings, 376

Mosaic law, on abrogation of, 281

Mosheim, on Apocryphal Gospels, 273; polytheism of church admitted by, 357; on adoption of heathen mysteries by early Christians, 403–404; early paganization of Christianity conceded by, 416

Mueller, Max, on sun worship, 346; on Buddha, 371, 373, 374

Mustard seed, the, 141–42

Myth, meaning of, 328; different kinds of, 328; various hypotheses regarding nature of Christ, 328–33; sources of Christ, 334–419

Nain, widow of, raising from the dead the son of, 115

Napoleon Bonaparte, declares the sun to be the true God, 343

Nature-worship, 349–51

Nazarene and Nazarite, 81

Nazareth, texts affirming as the place of Jesus' birth, 49–50

Neander, on motive of Judas for betraying Jesus, 164–65

Newman, Prof. F. W., on the healing of the blind man and the raising of Lazarus, 140; on Zacharias, son of Barachias, 149; on Christ's abuse of Jews, 300

Newton, Bishop, on Christian fetichism, 335; on worship of Virgin and saints, 357

Newton, Sir Isaac, on the Trinity, 259; on corruptions of text, 263

Newton, John, on relics of sun-worship, 343, 345–46; on vestiges of ancient fire-worship, 351; on the palm as a Phallic symbol, 353–54; on transference of dogmas of immaculate conception and perpetual virginity from Isis to Mary, 389

Newton, Rev. Dr. R. Heber, on the paganization of Christianity, 416–17

Norse Mythology, 407; survivals of in Christianity, 408–409

Noyes, Rev. J. H., sexual irregularities fostered by religious revivals, 342

Oaths, respecting, 289

Odin, 406–407

Oort, Rev. Dr., on sun-worship among early Israelites, 344; Abram, Isaac, etc., names of tribes, 413

Origen, believed stars to be rational beings, 348

Osiris, 386–87

Ozias, relation of to Joram, 59

Pagan Writers, no mention of Christ by, 20

Paganism, list of Christian ideas and doctrines derived from, 410–12

Paine, Thomas, on Epistles, 219–220; on resurrection and ascension, 254–55

Papias, not acquainted with Four Gospels, 36

Parkhurst's *Hebrew Lexicon*, Hercules a prototype of Christ, 394

Parton, James, Platonic origin of Christian system affirmed by, 398

Pascal, on marriage, 296

Paschal Meal, description of, 154–55

Patriarchs, antediluvian, a dynasty of Babylonian kings, 413

Paul, the miraculous conception and miracles of Christ unknown to, 43; the doctrine of a material resurrection denied by, 43; discordant statements concerning appearance of Jesus to, 235; Christ the first to rise from dead affirmed by, 247; on nature of Christ, 262; on justification by faith, 279; on woman and marriage, 320–22; his condemnation of learning, 321–22; persecutions of, 322–23; his characterization of Christians, 324

Pauline Epistles, all but four of spurious, 41–42

Perfect Man, the, 365–66

Perseus, 393

Peter, the calling of, 95–96; son of whom, 97; attempt of to walk on the water, 127; his discovery of Jesus' Messiahship, 131; coin in fish's mouth, 134–35; speech of before disciples, 165; his denial of Jesus, 178–80, 317; concerning witnesses to Christ's resurrection, 246; on nature of Christ, 262

Phallic Worship; *see* Sex Worship.

Philo, no mention of Christ by, 19; the mocking of Jesus borrowed from, 186–87; and John, parallels drawn from concerning Logos, 364

Phlegon, concerning eclipse, 202

Photius, passage in Josephus rejected by, 22

Pilate, Pontius, trial of Jesus before, 182–83

Pilgrimages, Holy, dissoluteness attending, 340

Plato, 547–551; his immaculate conception, 397–98; his philosophy, 398–99; on the immortality of the soul, 398–400

Pliny the Younger, letter of, 30; arguments against genuineness of letter, 30–32

Polytheism, 355–57

Potter's Field, prophecy concerning purchase of, 164–65

Poverty and Riches, 292–93

Prayer, efficacy of, 286–87

Proctor, Richard A., sun myths connected with Jesus, 345

Prometheus, 396–97

Prostitution, sacred, 338–40

Publicans and Sinners, dining with, 117–18

Punishment, endless, doctrine of, 283–84

Pythagoras, 400–401; parallels between teachings of and Christ, 401

Quirinalia, its correspondence to Ascension Day, 406

Quirinus, 406; his ascension, 406

Ramatha, Bishop of, on Buddhist and Christian scriptures, 373

Rawson, A. L., on Prometheus, 396

Reade, Winwood, on Christians, 326; on antiquity of Egypt's religion, 390

Religious Formula, "In the name of Jesus," 289

Renan, his *Life of Jesus,* 7–8; on miracles, 15; Mark oldest of Gospels affirmed by, 38; on date of crucifixion, 214; on alleged appearances of Jesus, 240; on second advent, 269; on belief of Jesus in demoniacal possession, 306; on Messiahship of Jesus, 361

Resurrection, the; *see* Jesus.

Resurrection of Saints, 241

Revelation, canonicity of questioned by Christian scholars, 41

Rich Man and Lazarus, parable of, 293

Ridpath, John Clarke, on astral worship, 346–47; on Persephone and Eve, 539; on Greek sepulture, 395; on Saturnalia, 405

Robertson, Rev. Frederick, on fanaticism and lewdness, 342

Rousseau, on Christ and slavery, 295

Rower, Rev. Heinrich, affirms Greek origin of Matthew's and Luke's stories concerning birth of Jesus, 394

Sala, relation of to Arphaxad, 59

Salathial, son of whom? 61

Sanday, Rev. Wm., on the feeding of 4,000, 129; on the hour of crucifixion, 192

Sanhedrim, trial and treatment of Jesus before, 171–78

Saturn, 405

Saturnalia, identity of with festival of Christmas, 405

Savage, Dr. M. J., on sacraments, 285

Schaff, Rev. Dr. Philip, on resurrection, 256

Schleiermacher, Dr., declares Luke to be a mere compilation, 37–38; on conflicting accounts of events following the birth of Jesus, 78

Scott, Thomas, on corruption of text of John xviii, 24; 169

Scribner's Bible Dictionary, on discrepancy between Synoptics and John regarding Last Supper, 153–54; on conflicting statements of Mark and John regarding anointment, 152–54; on double mention of the cup, 156; on errors of Synoptics concerning crucifixion, 211; concerning day of crucifixion, 212

Seneca, his writings chief source of the Ideal or Perfect Man, 365–66; on Zeus, 391

Sermon on the Mount, where delivered, 106–107

Seventy, the, 102

Sex-Worship, 335–42; gods and goddesses connected with, 335

Sharp, Samuel, Trinity in Unity, 388

Shelley, on accountability for belief, 280–81; on Christ, 2; on Prometheus, 397

Shepherds, the 76

"Siloam," meaning of, 128

Simeon, prediction of, 82

Simon, the Cyrenian, 188–89

Slavery Sanctioned, 295

Smith, George, on antiquity of Babylonian legend, 384

Smith, Prof. Goldwin, on flight of Jesus, 7

Smith, Prof. Robertson, on Synoptics, 38

Smith's Bible Dictionary, attempt of to reconcile genealogies, 63; on lineage of Mary, 65; on parentage of James the Less and Joses, 99; concerning Christ's promise to penitent thief, 198

Smith's Dictionary of Antiquities, ancient mysteries analogous to Christian sacraments, 404

Solar-Worship, 342–46; prevailed among Israelites, 343–44

Somerset, Duke of, on heavenly voices, 152

Sosiosh, 382

Soury, Dr. Jules on Renan's *Life of Jesus,* 8, on date of First Peter, 40; he pronounces Jesus a victim of insanity, 302–305; on Mary Magdelene, 315–16; on Jewish worship of Aschera, 337; on sacred prostitution, 338–39; on the sun as the father of life, 342; on Biblical and Babylonian legends, 383–84; on deluge legend, 383–84; on the fallaciousness of religious beliefs, 418

South, Dr., on Revelation, 41

Staves, command respecting, 120

Strauss, his Life of Jesus, 7–8; Mark latest of Synoptics affirmed by, 38; on Messianic requirements, 64; on Annunciation, 70–71; raising of Lazarus, 139–40; different versions of the anointment, 152; on trial of Jesus before Herod, 181; on rending of veil of the temple, 203; on bribing the soldiers, 245–46; on conflicting statements of Evangelists regarding appearances of Jesus, 229; astrology associated with birth of Messiah, 349; angels of Persian origin, 378

Suetonius, 32

Sun Gods, list of, 343

Sun-Worship, doctrine of the resurrection derived from, 345

Supernatural Religion, on miraculous evidence, 351; no trace of Gospels for a century and a half after the death of Jesus, 39; declares Paul's vision a hallucination, 42; on Last Supper, 153; on discrepancy regarding length of ministry, 158; on Jesus' examination before Annas, 170; on failure of soldiers to break legs of Jesus, 205–206; on resurrection, 242, 255–56; on demoniacal possession, 306

Sychar, no city of this name, 117

Symbolism, Christian, Inman on, 336–37

Synoptics, evidences of common origin of, 115

Syria, governors of, 46

Tacitus, passage in Annals of, 28; arguments against genuineness of passage, 28–30

Talents, the, parable of, 144–45

Talmage, Dr., on forgiveness of sin, 281–82

Tammouz. *See* Adonis.

Tao Teh King, gospel of Laou-Tsze, 376

Taxing, the, 73–75

Taylor, Rev. Dr., on slavery, 295

Temple, the, time required to build, 106; the, purging of, 148, 301–302

Temptation, the, 93–94

Thaddeus, 100

Theophilus, first Christian writer to mention any one of Four Gospels, 37

Therapeuts, different theories regarding, 401

Thieves, the two, 193, 197–98

Thor, 407–408

Tischendorf, Dr., on consequences of N.T. errors, 272

Transfiguration, the, discrepancies concerning, 131–34; the story borrowed from Exodus, 133–34

Trees, worship of, 351–54

Trench, Archbishop, concerning coin in fish's mouth, 135; on miracles of Satan, 266–67

Tribute, nature of demanded of Jesus, 134–35

Trinity, the, origin of, 388–89; on the, 258–59

Tripitaka, Bible of Buddhists, 370–71

Triumphal entry, the, discrepancies concerning, 146–48

Turner, Cuthbert, Hamilton, on date of crucifixion, 212

Twelve Apostles, names of, 95; character of, 316–19; fate of, 319–20

Tyndall, Prof., declares us to be children of the sun, 342–43

Veil of Temple, rending of, 203

Virgin, offenses against chastity condoned by, 340

Virgin and Child, derived from Isis and Horus, 388–89

Voice from Heaven, 89, 152

Volney, Count, the Christ a solar myth, 331–33, on worship of elements, 349–50; on identity of Jesus and Bacchus, 402

Voltaire, on the Godhead, 257

Waite, C. B., on parallels between Mark and the other Synoptics, 38; on testimony of Irenaeus, 222; on Krishna and Christ, 369–70

Wakeman, T. B., the Christ a philosophical myth, 330–31

Walker, Dr. Alexander, on Christ's female ancestors, 314–15

Washburn, L. K., on empty tomb, 245

Webster, on modern love feasts as imitations of the ancient Agapae, 403

Wilkinson, Sir John Gardner, on Osiris, 386

Werner's Encyclopedia, on miracles attending birth of Buddha, 370

Westbrook, R. B., on N.T. story of crucifixion as borrowed from Greek tragedy of "Prometheus Bound," 396; concerning origin of Eucharist, 402

Westcott, Dr., on Christianity and miracles, 14; on the Synoptics, 38; contrast between Synoptics and John 159–60; on discrepancies regarding appearances of Jesus, 230

Westropp and Wake, on derivation of Christianity from ancient Phallic worship, 337

Whiston, Dr., concerning death of

James, 27; on letter of Pliny, 32

Wicked Husbandman, the parable of, 144

Wilder, Dr. Alexander, modern religious customs borrowed from Phallism, 337

Wilson, Prof. H. H., on Sakti-worship, 338

Wise, Dr. Isaac, on Paschal Meal, 155; on false witnesses, 172–73; on story of marvelous events at crucifixion, 204–205

Woolston, on Jesus as a fortune teller, 308

Writers, list of ancient Jewish and Pagan, 18–19

Zabulon and Naphthali, 103–104

Zacharias, punishment of for his doubt, 87

Zacharias, son of Barachias, 149

Zeus, 390–92; cave of Jesus and, 391; analogies between Jehovah and, 391; tomb of, 392

Zoroaster, 377–79; analogies between his teachings and those of Christ, 377; prediction of concerning Sosiosh, 382